'That Damn'd Thing Called Honour'

'That Damn'd Thing Called Honour'
Duelling in Ireland
1570–1860

JAMES KELLY

CORK UNIVERSITY PRESS

First published in 1995 by
Cork University Press
University College
Cork
Ireland

British Library Cataloguing in Publication Data
A CIP catalogue record for this book is available from the British Library.

ISBN 1 85918 039 6 hardback
1 85918 043 4 paperback

Typeset by Seton Music Graphics, Bantry, Co. Cork
Printed by ColourBooks, Baldoyle, Dublin

Contents

Tables

Acknowledgements

Duelling was practised in Ireland for nearly three centuries. Acquiring information on affairs of honour over this period has involved a trawl of archival and printed primary material over a longer time-frame than I have previously explored. I may, in consequence, have overlooked important sources; there would have been more but for the sage counsel and generous help of friends and colleagues. I wish particularly to thank Dr Raymond Gillespie, without whose help the account of duelling in the seventeenth century presented here would have been visibly poorer. Dr Desmond McCabe was generous with material on early nineteenth-century Mayo. Dr Toby Barnard, Dr Kevin Whelan, Dr Christopher Woods, Mr John McHugh, Mr Eugene Coyle, Dr Bill Vaughan, Professor Tom Bartlett, Mr John Bergin, Mr Peter MacDonagh, Ms Brenda Clifford and Mr Eamonn Ó Ciardha drew my attention to sources or incidents I might otherwise have neglected. Dr Pauric Travers and Dr Patrick O'Donoghue, C.M. continue to provide a supportive working environment. I offer them all sincere and grateful thanks.

I wish also to thank the custodians and owners of the manuscripts consulted in the British Library, Keele University Library, East Sussex Record Office, the Friendly Brothers of St Patrick (particularly Mr Derek Hill), Hampshire Record Office, the Henry Huntington Library, the Library of Congress, Limerick Archives Office, the National Archives, the National Library of Ireland, the National Library of Scotland, Northumberland Record Office, the Public Record Office, London, the Public Record Office of Northern Ireland, the Royal Irish Academy, Sheffield City Library, Trinity College, Dublin, the Beinecke, Sterling and Lewis Walpole Libraries of Yale University, and the Warwickshire Record Office. Mr John Hunt and Dr A. P. W. Malcomson graciously allowed me to consult manuscripts in their possession.

Last but not least, a modish unit cost analysis would probably conclude that Judith Brady and Eva Kelly offered more distraction than help, but they have lived with duelling nearly as long as I have; for this and for many other reasons it is appropriate that I dedicate this book to them.

Abbreviations

B.L., Add. MS	British Library, Additional Manuscript
C.H.O.P.	*Calendar of Home Office Papers 1760–72*
C.S.P.D.	*Calendar of State Papers, Domestic*
C.S.P.I.	*Calendar of State Papers, Ireland*
D.C.	*Dublin Chronicle*
D.E.P.	*Dublin Evening Post*
D.N.B.	*Dictionary of National Biography*
F.D.J.	*Faulkner's Dublin Journal*
F.J.	*Freeman's Journal*
F.L.J.	*Finn's Leinster Journal*
H.J.	*Hibernian Journal*
H.M.C.	Historical Manuscripts Commission
I.H.S.	*Irish Historical Studies*
J.C.H.A.S.	*Journal of the Cork Historical and Archaeological Society*
N.A.	National Archives
N.L.I.	National Library of Ireland
N.L.S.	National Library of Scotland
P.C.	Privy Council
P.O.	*Pue's Occurrences*
P.R.O.	Public Record Office
P.R.O.N.I.	Public Record Office of Northern Ireland
Q.U.B.	Queen's University Belfast
R.I.A.	Royal Irish Academy
T.C.D.	Trinity College, Dublin
U.C.D.	University College, Dublin
V.E.P.	*Volunteer Evening Post*
V.J.(C.)	*Volunteer Journal (Cork)*
V.J.(D.)	*Volunteer Journal (Dublin)*

Introduction

Ireland was known internationally in the early nineteenth century as 'the land of [the] duel', Joseph Hamilton maintained in 1829.[1] As an arch-critic of duelling and the code of honour to which it appealed for legitimation, Hamilton is not an impartial witness, but in this instance he was simply articulating what he and many others were convinced was the truth. Hamilton's portrayal of Ireland as a duellist's Elysium was reinforced by Sir Jonah Barrington — who remains the best-known contemporary chronicler of the duelling phenomonen in Ireland. Barrington was palpably more disposed than Hamilton to celebrate the virtues of duelling, and his lucubrations on the subject have exercised greater influence on our understanding of the operation of the code of honour in Ireland than those of any other commentator.[2] It is not possible to write a history of duelling in Ireland without reference to Barrington and Hamilton, but we ought not be guided in our reconstruction of this diagnostic feature of early modern Irish society by the testimonies of two witnesses with axes to grind. Both wrote at a time when duelling, though still commonplace, was in decline, and both drew heavily on lore and on memory rather than on contemporary documentary evidence for their reconstructions and interpretations. For this reason, their accounts cannot be depended upon to provide a clear and accurate perspective on the operation of the code of honour in Ireland during the three hundred or so years that it was observed.

Hamilton and Barrington and the clusters of historians, popular chroniclers and social observers that have drawn on them (compared with Barrington, Hamilton is rarely cited) provide a window on the climacteric of duelling in Ireland in the late eighteenth century and useful insights into its decline in the early nineteenth. They have little to say about its emergence in the sixteenth and seventeenth, and its diffusion in the early and mid-eighteenth centuries. This is why one will search in vain in their work and in that of Michael MacDonagh, Constantia Maxwell, Michael Barry, V. G. Kiernan and others who have drawn on them for a convincing account of the emergence and development of the duelling phenomenon.[3] John Edward Walsh, the author of the influential excursus into popular history *Ireland sixty years ago*, was more forthcoming; and he went closer to offering a convincing overall interpretation:

> This [duelling] mania seems to have commenced after the battle of the Boyne, and terminated with the Union. The effect of the first was to disband a number of military men . . . who wandered about the country without employment or means of living, yet adhering with tenacity to the rank and feelings of gentlemen. They were naturally susceptible of slight and insult, and ready, on all occasions, to resent them by an appeal to their familiar weapons — the sword or pistol. Their opponents, the Williamites, had been soldiers likewise, and not likely to treat with due respect ruined and defeated men. These causes, acting on temperaments naturally hot and irritable, brought on constant collisions which were not confined to the parties, but soon extended through all classes. Since the Union, the sober and wiser modes of thinking of our English neighbours have corrected many of our own unstable and more excitable habits.[4]

Walsh's linkage of the emergence and decline of observance of the code of honour in Ireland to the Williamite conquest and the Act of Union is not sustainable, but he is correct in highlighting the importance of the military to its popularisation. A more rewarding area of investigation, and one to which Walsh and J. Fitzgerald Molloy (who noted that duelling was in vogue before the battle of the Boyne but who, like Walsh, attributed its dissemination to Williamite soldiers)[5] both allude but do not pursue, is the impact of the establishment of a new social elite in Ireland between 1550 and 1660. The formation, as a consequence of the revolutionary political and economic changes wrought in Ireland in the sixteenth and seventeenth centuries, of a landowning elite whose thought-processes, mores and behaviour had much in common with the *ancien régime* aristocracies of Britain and Europe, among whom duelling was already firmly rooted, provides the key to the origins of duelling in Ireland. Similarly, the decline in the phenomenon in the early nineteenth century, like the concurrent decline of Dublin, cannot simply be ascribed to the Act of Union. It must be linked, as Walsh's later remarks imply, to fundamental social changes at work in the nineteenth century — to the reformation in attitude and manners that paralleled the emergence of a more interventionist state, to the rise of a politically influential and economically dynamic middle class, and to the reanimation of evangelical religion.

As this indicates, the temporally narrow perspective on duelling provided by Barrington, Hamilton and most modern commentators is misleading.[6] It is a fact, none the less, that duelling flourished for a shorter period in Ireland than in most western European countries.[7] Duelling was practised in Ireland for less than three centuries; it was practised for somewhat longer in Britain, and for longer still on mainland Europe where it originated. Duelling came to Ireland via Britain, which for geographical as well as political and economic reasons exercised a formative influence on cultural behaviour in early modern Ireland, and the closest points of comparison with the Irish experience are to be found in Britain. In view of this, it is ironic that after Barrington, Walsh and nineteenth-century Irish novelists like Samuel Lover and Charles Lever, those responsible for moulding Ireland's reputation as a duellists' paradise were Englishmen with little knowledge of Ireland, or Irishmen who made England their home. *Litterateurs* as diverse as Richard Steele, the Earl of Chesterfield, Horace Walpole, Richard Brinsley Sheridan, Samuel Johnson, Arthur Young, C. T. Bowden, Sir John Carr and William Makepeace Thackeray all contributed to the creation of an image of Irish gentlemen as inveterate duellists. Given the pervasiveness of this tradition, it is hardly surprising that later observers, less well-circumstanced to judge, should perpetuate similar stereotypes.[8]

The elaboration of the stereotype of the duelling Irishman is an interesting issue in its own right, but it is not a central concern of this work. Its object is to trace the history of the practice of duelling in Ireland in an attempt to advance firm conclusions in the place of the conjecture that is all too prominent in writings on this subject. For instance, because many of the best-known duelling incidents concluded without injury, some have concluded, with Michael MacDonagh, that 'a fatality was happily a rare occurrence in a duel. There was no desire to kill in these encounters; "good hits but no lives lost" was the bulletin most hoped for.'[9] Hoped for or not, this was not the case in a significant though varying percentage of cases. Likewise, there is no evidence to sustain the oft-repeated claim that egregious eighteenth-century politicians, such as John Scott and John Toler, deliberately contrived to pick quarrels to rid themselves of rivals.[10]

In order to expose such misimpressions and to present a more sustainable picture of the duelling phenomenon, I have sought to build this study around a reconstruction of the duelling phenomenon during the main phases of its Irish history based on a close study of those encounters that occurred and a statistical analysis of the main features of the phenomenon —

frequency, personnel, causes, weapons, injuries, geography, etc., — during the eighteenth and early nineteenth centuries, when adherence to the code of honour was at its most intense. The data for this statistical exercise is derived from a variety of manuscript and primary printed sources. But in an attempt to make it representative of duelling as it was conducted in Ireland, at least one newspaper, and in many instance two or more, were surveyed for every year between 1716 and 1810. Despite this, the resulting file must be seen as an aggregation of examples rather than a sample in a strict statistical sense. Eighteenth- and early nineteenth-century newspapers were too inconstant in their reportage of events and too Dublin-centred to allow one to treat figures compiled from their pages as statistically representative. However, the complementary nature of the evidence derived from a variety of sources suggests that the figures provided offer an *accurate guide* to the pattern of duelling in the eighteenth century, and that in tandem with the qualitative approach offered elsewhere in this work it is possible to provide a history of duelling in Ireland in the early modern era, when thousands of gentlemen felt compelled to take up arms in defence of what one of their number referred to as 'that damn'd thing called honour'.[11]

Notes and References

1 Joseph Hamilton, *The only approved guide through all stages of a quarrell* . . . (Dublin, 1829), p. iv.
2 Jonah Barrington, *Personal sketches of his own times* (3 vols, London, 1827–32), passim.
3 Michael MacDonagh, *Irish life and character* (London, 1905); Constantia Maxwell, *Country and town in Ireland under the Georges* (London, 1940), pp. 20–22; idem, *Dublin under the Georges, 1714–1830* (London, 1936), pp. 87–9, 189, 271; Michael Barry, *An affair of honour: Irish duels and duelists* [*sic*] (Fermoy, 1981); V. G. Kiernan, *The duel in European history* (Oxford, 1988).
4 [J. E. Walsh], *Sketches of Ireland sixty years ago* (Dublin, 1847), p. 31. Versions of this work have been reprinted as *Ireland ninety years ago* (Dublin, 1885); *Ireland one hundred and twenty years ago* (Dublin, 1911) and *Rakes and ruffians: the underworld of Georgian Dublin* (Dublin, 1979).
5 J. Fitzgerald Molloy, *The romance of the Irish stage* (2 vols, London, 1897), i, 45–6.
6 Joep Leerssen, for instance, gives the impression that duelling was already in decline in Ireland by the 1770s (*Mere Irish and Fíor-Ghael* (Amsterdam, 1986), pp. 160–61).
7 Kiernan, *The duel*, passim; François Billacois, *The duel: its rise and fall in early modern France* (Yale, 1990), passim.
8 John Beresford, *Mr Du Quesne and other essays* (Oxford, 1932), p. 157.
9 MacDonagh, *Irish life and character*, pp. 34–5.
10 John O'Donovan, *Life by the Liffey* (Dublin, 1986), p. 84.
11 Letters and papers on the Browne–Miller duel, Kilmaine County Mayo, 1747 (Bowen-Miller of Milford Papers, N.L.I., microfilm p. 3793).

PART I

DUELLING TAKES HOLD

The code of honour which sustained the practice of duelling originated on continental Europe and was introduced into Ireland from England by the anglophone elite that was put in place in the sixteenth and seventeenth centuries. Because of this, the emergence of duelling in Ireland parallels the emergence of this elite. Thus the first recorded invocations of the code of honour in Ireland date from the late sixteenth century, when the Tudor conquest was still in train and the New English interest was demographically small. They were few in total, if the modest number of contemporary reports are an accurate guide, and they seldom proceeded to hostilities.

In the decades that followed the completion of the Tudor conquest there was a perceptible increase in the disposition of members of the Protestant New English interest to appeal to their weapons to repel insult to their reputations. Despite this and the striking enhancement of the size of the New English elite by plantation and immigration, the number of rencontres that took place in the early seventeenth century remained modest until the economic and demographic base and the political influence of the New English interest was enhanced substantially by the draconian Cromwellian confiscation of the 1650s. The intensified disposition to duel visible in the 1660s and the decades that followed was also promoted by the example of the Caroline court and by the return to the country of Old English Catholic royalists who spent the 1650s in exile on the continent, where they were well schooled in the precepts of the code of honour. Once back, they did not mask their disenchantment with the uncongenial political environment in which they were obliged to live, and religious and political differences provided the stimulus for many of the duels that took place in Ireland between then and the early 1690s, when the victory of the Williamite armies resulted in the effective exclusion of Catholic gentlemen from the ranks of those enabled to appeal to arms in defence of their honour.

The sword was the duellist's weapon of choice during the seventeenth century. Moreover, seconds frequently fought side by side with principals during this period. Because of this, duelling incidents sometimes degenerated into bloody affrays in which seconds as well as principals were killed and injured. This practice had died out by the early eighteenth century, when seconds restricted their role to that of adviser and helper. That said, a significant proportion of duellists continued to let their tempers get the better of their judgment, and a striking number of encounters in the first half of the eighteenth century manifested little of the disciplined self-control recommended by duelling experts. Few were punished for their excesses or took any notice of the religious and lay critics who condemned duelling as immoral and illegal. The indulgence of the authorities dovetailed with further refinements in practice, the displacement of the sword by the pistol as the man of honour's weapon of choice, and the growing confidence of the ruling Protestant elite as the Jacobite threat receded, to ensure that the number of duels that took place increased rather than diminished as the mid-eighteenth century drew closer.

1

Background and Beginnings: the sixteenth and seventeenth centuries

Although antecedents for the ritualised engagement involving two adversaries termed a 'duel' can be found in the tournaments, jousts, single combats and judicial trials by combat practised by Europe's military and nobility in the Middle Ages, it is not possible to trace an *unbroken* connection between the two phenomena in Ireland or in England. Tournaments involved two teams of knights engaging in what were, in effect, miniature wars. By the late Middle Ages in England they had given way to jousts in which two individuals competed for pre-eminence, and single combats and judicial trials by combat involving two men in which guilt or innocence was determined by martial skill. These encounters had royal sanction, but they seldom occurred after the fifteenth century.[1]

The situation on continental Europe was analagous, though not as clear-cut. Jousts, single combats and trials by combat flourished there when chivalric values were strong in the Middle Ages; they went into decline thereafter, and were an 'extremely rare and rather outdated phenomenon in the fifteenth century'. As in England, a tradition of single combat and judicial trial by combat survived in an attenuated form into the sixteenth century. However, according to François Billacois, both remained intensely alive in the 'imaginary sphere' because they served as 'an essential anchoring point for aristocratic attitudes'. In other words, though the ritualised, sanctioned combats of the Middle Ages declined, the sentiments that impelled them remained vibrant; and distinct links can be established at the levels of both practice and theory between them and the unauthorised private duels fought by the nobility of western Europe in the early modern period.[2]

Richard Talbot, Duke of Tyrconnell, after Hyacinthe Rigaud (courtesy of the National Gallery of Ireland).

Historically, duelling emerged in Europe in the sixteenth century. It was, therefore, the product of an era during which martial valour and personal honour were extolled and fundamental political and military changes were taking place. Europe was subject to prolonged warfare; unprecedentedly large standing armies were constituted; and the old decentralised aristocratic order that prevailed during the Middle Ages was under mounting pressure to give way to centralised states ruled by absolutist monarchs. With their traditionally extensive liberties under challenge from the encroaching power of monarchy and their value as soldiers diminished by technological, organisational and strategic developments, Europe's nobles were obliged to accede to the contraction of their sources of privilege and authority. The large bands of retainers they had once commanded were reduced or displaced, and with them went much of their independence *vis-à-vis* monarchy.[3] However, the nobility were too wealthy, too independent and too attached to their role as warriors to acquiesce completely, and they affirmed their determination to preserve their elite status by, among other things, asserting the right to continue to determine personal differences on matters of honour privately by recourse to arms. According to Maurice Keen, 'the most important legacy of chivalry to later times was its conception of honour' because it was a key influence on the 'fashioning of the idea of a gentleman who was the "type" figure of the dominant social and political estate of the *ancien régime*'. By this means, social elites throughout Europe, in effect, asserted their right to be above the law to which the absolutist monarchs of the new dynastic states of the early modern era made increasing appeal to bulwark their authority.[4]

The European origins of the duel

In the fifteenth and sixteenth centuries, as the social structure and values which had inspired and sustained the jousts and combats of the late Middle Ages broke down, differences between nobles in Europe were regularly determined in 'killing affrays'.[5] These were ill-regulated and frequently bloody encounters involving principals and their retainers in which the likelihood of death or serious injury was high. Gradually, however, a more formal and less irregular pattern of combat emerged. This drew on the French judicial and single combat tradition of the Middle Ages and on fifteenth- and sixteenth-century Italian juridico-ethical theory which justified individual combat and extolled honour as the motive force of civilisation. Duelling first emerged in Italy, where the art of fencing (which involved teaching people how to kill) was at its most developed[6] and discourse on the subject of honour at its most sophisticated.[7] It spread quickly to France, and thence radiated to most of the rest of Europe, where it synergised with vestigial feudal codes of combat.[8]

Duelling cannot be comprehended independent of the code of honour which gave it its *raison d'être*. Responsibility for developing this concept of honour belongs to the 'honour culture' of early modern Italy which sustained an elaborate discourse on the issue of 'defining . . . winning . . . maintaining . . . losing . . . and regaining' honour and its converse 'shame'.[9] This debate was complex because honour is a multifaceted concept which appertains to some of the most sensitive aspects of human behaviour and conduct, as the working definition of the social anthropologist Julian Pitt-Rivers attests:

> [Honour] is a sentiment, a manifestation of this sentiment in conduct, and the evaluation of this conduct by others, that is to say reputation. It is both internal to the individual and external to him — a matter of his feelings, his behaviour and the treatment he receives.

In other words, honour encapsulates 'the value of a person in his own eyes, but also in the eyes of his society', and it derives its compelling authority from the fact that it reflects 'the values of the group with which a person identifies himself'. But honour is a fact as well as sentiment; it applies and relates to behaviour, and just as appropriate behaviour can be interpreted as conferring honour, so inappropriate behaviour can confer 'shame'. 'Honour and dishonour, therefore, provide the currency in which people compete for reputation and the means whereby their appraisal of themselves can be validated and integrated into the social system, or rejected' with all the penalties that may bring.[10]

Such convictions and beliefs may be held generally by a society or they may be particular to a social group or class within a society. An example of the former is provided by the Greek-Cypriot mountain community studied by John Campbell where known infractions of their code of honour, which was equated with manliness in males and the avoidance of 'sexual shame' by women, could result in punishments as severe as ostracism and death and as slight as 'the withdrawal of full recognition or response'.[11]

A broadly similar range of sanctions were applied against those who infringed the code of honour embraced by gentlemen (which included all male members of the nobility, substantial landowners and men of proven worth and social standing) in early modern Europe. This code was founded on the conviction that the public reputation of a gentleman had to be free of stain or slight, otherwise he had no entitlement to be regarded as part of the social and political elite to which all gentlemen were deemed automatically to belong. As far as those who justified as well as those who observed the code of honour were concerned, honour and the right to take up arms to defend one's reputation against insult were privileges exclusive to the upper classes. Consequently, the honour of a gentleman could not be tarnished by the conduct, no matter how offensive, of a social inferior. A gentleman who was challenged by a social inferior could choose whether or not he wished to meet his antagonist, and he was more likely to enhance his reputation by declining to accept an inappropriate challenge than by demonstrating his bravery by agreeing to meet the individual who issued it.

Strictly speaking, then, those duels that took place in the early modern period should have involved only gentlemen, since only gentleman were expected to fight to uphold their honour. If this convention was *strictly* observed, duelling might have become the exclusive preserve of a relatively small ennobled and landed aristocracy and military *corps d'élite*. In practice, the values of the code of honour were shared, though not always warmly, with lesser members of these landed elites and with emerging professional and commercial interests, which broadened the social basis of the duelling phenomenon during the *ancien régime*. Moreover, since the definition of what constituted a gentleman (particularly in Ireland) was not always unambiguously clear, and as cowardice was deemed especially dishonourable, many men of honour fought duels with individuals of inferior rank they need not have embarked upon because they feared the consequence of doing otherwise. Perhaps the commonest cause of a gentleman challenging another to a duel was the accusation that he had lied. This was not founded on the moral conviction that lying *per se* was dishonourable. It was quite in order for a man of honour to lie to deceive, but it was an affront to an individual's reputation if he was publicly accused of having lied. In the event of this happening, an encounter would almost certainly follow, because if an individual charged with uttering an untruth did not challenge his accuser to withdraw the remark or meet him with weapons, he was accepting the truth of the accusation and the public loss of face and reputation that flowed from this. What the duel represented in this context was the arbitration by force of a quarrel between two 'individuals who competed for precedence and repute in the eyes of a public composed of their social equals'.[12] Thus the refusal of a gentleman to respond to a dishonourable insult implied either that his word could not be relied upon or that he was a coward. These were accusations no gentleman could endure if he wished to be regarded as a man of honour, and since this was something every well-born male believed was his birthright and those born to a lower social station envied and aspired to, the loss of honour was of enormous consequence. It implied that an individual was not worthy of belonging to the pre-eminent social group in society.

Such issues were of vital concern to the upper classes of Ireland and the rest of early modern Europe, as they manifested by tenaciously defending the right to duel. They did this though it meant defying two of the most powerful institutions of early modern society — the churches, which condemned duelling on religious grounds, and the courts, whose arbitrative methods were incompatible with the perceived needs of men of honour to cleanse their reputations of injury without delay. By this means, Europe's aristocratic and landed elites contrived to affirm not only their social superiority but also their distinctiveness as a social group and their identity as an elite.

The form and context of the early modern code of honour, and of duelling which was its most visible and celebrated manifestation, were shaped by the milieu and era which produced them. Both originated in an environment in which the power of the feudal nobility, the combats they had devised and practised and the concept of honour they espoused were in decline but in which they were determined to preserve as many of their traditional privileges as possible. The one they valued most was the right to bear and to use arms in defence of their reputations as well as of their lives, since they operated in an environment which was characterised by what Mervyn James has termed 'competetive assertiveness' and in which 'violence or the ever-present possibility of violence was a way of life'.[13] As Lawrence Stone makes clear, men felt at liberty during this era to indulge their tempers and to engage in behaviour that was characterised by 'ferocity, childishness and lack of self-control':

> Impulsiveness was not reproved, readiness to repay an injury real or imagined was a sign of spirit, loyalty to a friend in a quarrel was a moral duty, regardless of the merits of the case.[14]

Parallel with this, the continued development of what V. G. Kiernan terms 'individual consciousness' created a milieu in which gentlemen became increasingly inclined to perceive insult, and to appeal to arms to defend their reputations against calumny, be it real or imagined.[15] This was facilitated by the fact that virtually all men of an elevated station were schooled in the use of weapons. Most members of Europe's nobility regarded themselves as warriors, and they extolled the virtues of martial skill and interpersonal combat. The displacement of the broadsword by the rapier (which was much better suited to personal as opposed to military usage) was also significant, as was the general bellicosity of early modern society. Given a milieu in which violent confrontation was commonplace, in which the carrying of arms was *de rigueur*, in which civilians, aristocrats and military officers were 'fixated' by questions of status and precedence, and in which the state was unable to police its people,[16] it was only to be anticipated that the code of honour that evolved should place physical violence at its heart, and that its adherents should profess themselves ready to sacrifice their lives in defence of their honour.

The patriarchal nature of early modern society also facilitated this process. Honorific concerns are not exclusive to men, but because honour provides 'a nexus between the ideals of a society and their reproduction in the individual through his aspiration to personify them',[17] it was inevitable that the already dominant male point of view should prevail. If 'steadfastedness' or 'manliness' — qualities which were perceived to embrace the emblematic male attributes of truthfulness and courage — were prerequisites for male honour, then sexual purity was defined as the 'essence of honour in women'. The process whereby sexuality was defined as the litmus of female honour is beyond the scope of this work to explore, but it is clear that in the early modern period it was men who charged themselves with guarding their dependent females' honour and with avenging the shame incurred if a female family member's purity was compromised.[18] Women, in short, could be the subject of disputes of honour; but had little or no influence on its form and content.

From the outset, critics of duelling denied repeatedly and insistently that the readiness of men to take up arms in defence of their own or their family's reputation was an honourable action. Lodowick Bryskett, the English commentator who wrote penetratingly on the subject in the early seventeenth century and who, incidentally, lived much of his life in Ireland, advanced this argument forcefully in his *Discourse of civill life*:

> Honour there is none to be gotten by the combat; yet because among other things they say the combat hath bin devised for cause of honour, I must let you know that in true and sound philosophie, they that respect honour as the end of their actions, are not onely unworthy to be accounted vertuous men, but deserve blame and reproch . . . Actions are commendable but those that are honest, and where honestie is not, there can be no honour. And honestie in truth there is none (as before hath bin said) in such as fight contrary to all vertue, odious to all lawes, to all good magistrates, and to God himselfe; though the folly of the favourers of this divellish device seeke most wrongfully to draw the summe of all vertues to this injustice.

From Bryskett's vantage-point, 'the reasons which are set down in defence of this foolish custome and wicked act' were 'false and absurd' because

> there can be nothing more contrary to good discipline in a wel-ordered commonweale, than this wicked and unjust kind of fight, which destroyeth, so farre foorth as it beareth sway, all civill societie. For it breedeth the contempt of God and his commandements, of Religion, of lawes, constitutions and civill governement, of Princes, of magistrates, and finally of countrey, parents, friends and kindred: to all which men are bound by reason naturall and civill, and for defence of them to spend their lives in maner aforesaid; but not at their owne appetite, instigated by rage and furie to be prodigall thereof, or for revenge of private quarrels or injuries.

As a convinced proponent of the necessity of upholding the law of man as well as God, Bryskett urged those who felt aggrieved by the ill-behaviour of others on matters of honour to affirm their humanity as well as their Christianity by relying on the law rather than on a practice as 'odious and offensive' as duelling for recompense:

> What more glorious revenge can a man desire, or what more notable testimonie of his virtue, then to have him corrected, and rest infamous by the punishment which law shall inflict upon him who hath done him injury? Or what else do these furious minded men seeke in fine by their combat?[19]

Such arguments, repeatedly and insistently articulated by critics of the code of honour, were lost on its devotees. Indeed, the two sides became so entrenched in their respective positions that neither comprehended the point of the view of the other. This is particularly true of the critics of the code of honour, who not alone refused to accept that it was honourable to duel, but who sought, by implication, to deny that those who argued otherwise experienced real feelings. This was to fail to recognise reality. It is demonstrable that the concept of honour was keenly felt and that many duels were fought by individuals who were convinced that they were better off dead than dishonoured and alive. The eighteenth-century English aesthete Horace Walpole, for example, articulated a fear common to adherents of the code of honour that he could not bear even to think that he would be made to appear ridiculous. Voltaire, by contrast, appealed to God that his enemies would be made ridiculous, having personally experienced this misfortune in 1726 when the Chevelier Rohan-Chabot insulted him grievously by refusing to take up his offer of a challenge.[20] The nineteenth-century English statesman Sir Robert Peel shared these concerns. He was so sensitive to any 'reflection on his courage and integrity' that his 'sharp and sometimes unreasonable resentment at insult' prompted him to offer several unnecessary challenges.[21]

Such convictions might suggest that the aristocratic milieu which sustained duelling was as much preoccupied with appearance and honour as with real feeling and genuine sentiment, but this would be to underestimate the strength of the convictions of adherents of the code of honour. Moreover, honour was more easily lost than won, and once lost it was not easily regained, as is attested by the inscription on an eighteenth-century Irish duelling medal: 'Honour to him to whom honour is due'.[22] One way for a gentleman to prove he was a man of honour was by risking his life in defence of his reputation even if the challenge that prompted the encounter was unsustainable, because this was seen as the essence of bravery. *Per contra*, to decline a challenge was to risk being labelled a 'coward' or a 'poltroon', which meant disgracing not just oneself but also one's family and the social elite to which one claimed to be a part, with all the personal and social consequences this entailed.[23]

Once elaborated, the dissemination and embrace of the values of the code of honour and the rules of duelling were facilitated by the disinclination of European monarchs to take punitive action against those of their nobility that duelled. Based on his examination of the fitful efforts to regulate combats in Italy and the writings of lawyers and jurists on the subject there and in France, François Billacois has concluded that duelling was not really regarded as a crime by the state in the sixteenth century. Some attempts were made by successive French monarchs to moderate the enthusiasm with which their nobility welcomed the emerging code of honour, but they were either counterproductive or they registered little impact. Henri II (1547–59), for example, encouraged the embrace of the code of honour by mishandling the Jarnac affair (1547) and by effectively recognising duelling as a 'private procedure of superior authority to that of royalty'. His successors were less indulgent. But the efforts of Charles IX (1560–74) and Henri III (1574–89) to arbitrate quarrels were destined to fail because of their irresolution and the endemic disorder that prevailed during the wars of religion. Henri III, for example, issued decrees prohibiting duelling, but they were rarely enforced because 'he loved the nobility'.[24] Despite this broadly permissive attitude, the tide of official opinion became increasingly hostile as Henri IV (1589–1610) demonstrated by issuing two stern decrees against duelling in the first decade of the seventeenth century. A host of similar edicts were promulgated in the decades that followed, but none had the desired impact.[25] Successive French monarchs in the sixteenth and early seventeenth centuries were compelled to put up with duelling because they could not eradicate it. It was part of the price they had and, on the whole, were prepared to pay to keep their potentially restive aristocratic elites content. Henri IV, like his predecessors and most of his *ancien régime* contemporaries and successors, was dependent on his nobility; with them he could strengthen his own and his country's influence; without them he could be reduced to ruling a divided and vulnerable kingdom.

At the same time, it gradually became more attractive to duel because the duelling encounter was regularised and made uniform. The century after 1550 in France witnessed the abandonment of such vestigial feudal practices as requesting a field from the crown and the sending of heralds. The duel became simpler and shorter, and began to assume its familiar early modern form. In the first place, it was transformed from a public event to a private encounter in response to the efforts of monarchs in the early seventeenth century to proscribe it. As a result, the preferred meeting place of duellists moved from built-up public locations to secluded but, generally, convenient sites where antagonists could settle their quarrels with little fear of interruption. One consequence of this was the emergence of popular duelling fields such as the Prè aux Clercs outside Paris. Secondly, the equipment and deportment of duellists was equalised. Increasingly duels were fought on foot and *en chemise*, without armour or other protection, in contrast to sanctioned trials by combat which betrayed their medieval origins by the fact that they were still fought in full armour and on horseback. In some instances duellists even fought bare-chested to ensure against cheating. Weapons too were systematised. The pike, the musket and the broadsword were abandoned and, though the rapier remained the gentleman's weapon of preference for some time, pistols fired at a distance of ten or twelve paces became increasingly popular in the late seventeenth century. Thirdly, there was the definition of a distinct and non-combative role for seconds. In the late Middle Ages battle pledges involving teams of combatants were not unusual. There are distinct echoes of this tradition in the sixteenth-century affrays in which principals and their supporters fought each other, but by the beginning of the seventeenth century it was not unusual for seconds to attend principals solely in a supportive and advisory capacity. This was by no means standard practice. Seconds had not yet abandoned participation, and there were many incidents throughout the seventeenth century in which seconds (numbering two, three, four or more) fought and died.[26] Nevertheless, the trend was for seconds to disengage from actual combat. The process of defining a supportive role for seconds, which continued until the nineteenth century, was under way. The effect of this development, combined with advances in weaponry and procedure, which reduced the likelihood of serious injury (particularly to seconds), facilitated the embrace by nobles, gentry and others throughout early modern Europe of a code of conduct which afforded honour and the duel a pre-eminent place. In short, the early modern period witnessed the forging of a new set of essentially aristocratic sensibilities around the code of honour at the very time that the emergence of absolutist monarchy gave rise to a sustained attempt by crowned heads throughout Europe to confine the powers and privileges of their nobility and to subordinate them, like other interests, to the rule of law.

The ability of the upper classes to defy the law in a matter as important as the taking of life represents one index of the limit of the authority of absolute monarchs in the early modern period, and of the depths of the reservoirs of influence and dominion still possessed by landed and noble elites. The initiative, however, remained with the state. Europe's *ancien régime* elites were unable to build on their success in this and other spheres to exact further privileges. Indeed they had to withstand serious and, sometimes, sustained attempts to prevent them exercising the privileges of the code of honour.

Throughout the sixteenth and early seventeenth centuries rulers in every country where the duel became prominent tried to outlaw it. As we have seen with reference to France, their efforts were generally ineffectual, but this did not deter them from trying, and their intensified efforts in the seventeenth century proved more impactive. That said, only the most secure and resolute monarchs and ministers implemented the draconian penalties their decrees provided for. One such figure was Gustav Adolph (1611–32), the powerful King of Sweden, who responded to a rash of duelling in his armed forces by making it a capital crime, and who reputedly nipped it in the bud by informing two senior officers on the eve of their meeting that he would have the survivor executed.[27] Both Louis XIII of France (1610–43) and his chief minister, Cardinal Richelieu (whose brother was killed in a duel), could be equally stern. When François de Montmorency, Comte de Bouteville, and his cousin, the Comte des Chapelles, challenged the authority of the crown in 1627 by defying an edict against duelling shortly after Richelieu had embarked on the road to absolutism, Louis and Richelieu resisted all entreaties for mercy and both offenders were executed.[28] However, neither this, nor the disgracing of the bodies of duellists by hanging them on a gallows, nor the execution of the Chevalier D'Andrieu in 1638 was sufficient to curb enthusiasm for the code of honour. The edict of 1626, like previous anti-duelling ordinances, could not be enforced rigorously because French aristocrats continued to fear dishonour more than death, with the result that when royal authority was weakened during the Fronde (1648–53) duelling enjoyed an immediate upsurge in popularity. It was forced into decline again in the late seventeenth century when Louis XIV (1643–1715), the quintessential absolutist monarch, oversaw the stricter enforcement of the law following his promulgation of an edict in 1679 reaffirming the anti-duelling prohibitions sanctioned by Henri IV and Louis XIII. Louis's firm stand resulted in a sharp diminution in the number of challenges sent and the number of duels fought, but it did not result in the eradication of adherence to the code of honour in France. He did not grant pardons with the same readiness as his predecessors; but he did exonerate some offenders, with the result that though his reign encouraged important sections of French opinion to oppose the code of honour before their equivalents did so in Britain or Ireland, it also demonstrates that duelling could not be legislated out of existence. It re-emerged during Louis XV's minority (1715–26).[29]

The duel in England in the sixteenth and seventeenth centuries

The societal and political circumstances which facilitated the embrace of the code of honour on continental Europe also prevailed in England. And because the landowning elite put in place in early modern Ireland was primarily of English origin, and the intersections between the elites that provided most duellists in the two kingdoms so multifarous, the history of duelling in England throws much light on its emergence and development in Ireland.

Duelling was introduced into England, with fencing and the rapier, from the continent in the late sixteenth century, and it was embraced with such enthusiasm by the Elizabethan aristocracy that the crown soon felt compelled to intervene. Queen Elizabeth (1558–1603) did what she could to control it, but not even the threat of banishment from court deterred her nobility.[30] As a result, by the time James I (1603–25) ascended the throne, duelling was a well-established feature of the social landscape. Lodowick Bryskett observed in 1606 that young men 'feare no perill nor danger of their lives, but boldly and rashly undertake to fight',[31] and, if the examples of challenges issued in consequence of differences at cards and tennis are not wholly misleading, this was an accurate observation.[32]

Duellists in early seventeenth-century England fought with swords or with swords and daggers, which produced a high percentage of fatalities and/or serious injuries.[33] This attracted much adverse comment, but since neither the trenchant contemporary criticism of figures like Bryskett, Francis Bacon, William Howard and Walter Ralegh nor the disapproval of the crown deterred would-be duellists, James I felt compelled to have recourse to prohibition.[34] He authorised a 'severe' royal edict in July 1609 outlawing duelling and providing for the exemplary punishment of transgressors. This had some impact, but his nobility's disposition to duel was not curbed; and once it was established that the edict did not include 'rencontres' and 'frays', the number of such incidents rose.[35] James was not to be outmanoeuvred so easily. In July 1611 he reaffirmed his determination to curb enthusiasm for the code of honour by directing that the body of one gentlemen who had died as a result of a rencontre should be hanged by the feet from a gallows and that his goods should be sequestered. Two years later, in an attempt to stem the flow of British duellists travelling to the Low Countries to evade domestic anti-duelling regulations, he appealed successfully to the Dutch and Flemish authorities to take supportive action.[36] At the same time the 1609 edict against duelling was renewed, and a lengthy proclamation was authorised which called on justices of the peace and assize judges to take the necessary steps to prevent 'powerfull persons . . . turninge murder into manslaughter', directed the Court of Star Chamber to make examples of those brought before it, and authorised the Earl Marshal's court to mediate quarrels. An undertaking was also given to close such legal loopholes as existed in the law, but though calls for parliamentary legislation resulted in the presentation in

1613 of 'An act [*sic*] to prevent the impunity of foreign murders in some cases', this did not become law.[37] In the following April James appeared to give parliament the green light to legislate against duelling when he deemed the suggestion 'a godly action' in a speech to the assembled Lords and Commons, but once again no legislation was enacted.[38] Part of the reason for this was the disinclination of the peers and gentlemen in parliament to interdict a practice many of them approved of, but just as significant was James's lack of resolution at crucial moments.

The most important such moment occurred in mid-1613 when Sir Edward Sackville, who had killed Lord Bruce in a highly publicised encounter in the Low Countries, was given a royal pardon and allowed to return to court.[39] Given King James's incapacity to enforce his own anti-duelling strictures, it is no surprise that the House of Commons declined to approve bills to end 'all trial by battle' in 1620 and in 1625, or that the crown's anti-duelling regulations were soon discredited. Indeed, duelling became such a rage that one French observer maintained that England and not France was the true centre of the duelling mania.[40] This is an exaggeration, but evidence that the early Stuarts had given up the contest for lost is provided by the decision of the court of Charles I (1625–49) to direct two Scots, Sir James Ramsey and Lord Ray, to settle a dispute by recourse to arms.[41] Furthermore, such efforts as were made by the Privy Council and the Earl Marshal's court in the 1620s and 1630s to prevent individuals delivering or accepting challenges did not impact much on the generality of gentlemen, as the House of Commons further demonstrated by declining to approve legislation against duelling presented to it in 1629, 1640 and again in 1641.[42] James I had ceded the initiative in the war against duelling by the mid-1610s, and the early Stuarts never regained it.[43] In this milieu, it was entirely predictable that the duelling ethic should also penetrate the New English ruling elite in Ireland during the early Stuart period.

With the rise to power of Oliver Cromwell, the broadly permissive attitude towards duelling that prevailed in England during the reign of Charles I came to a sudden halt. Cromwell and his followers regarded duelling as a courtly vice and duellists as 'incarnate devils', and spurred on by their messianic desire to create a 'Godly Commonwealth', they endeavoured to eradicate it.[44] Their intentions were clearly indicated by the recommendation of a committee of the House of Commons, set up in 1651, that duellists suffer the penalties of forfeiture of property, banishment of person and the loss of their right hand.[45] These were harsh penalties even by the retributive standards of the day, and parliament balked at implementing them. In the absence of legislation, the onus for combating duelling was assumed by the Council of State, which underlined its commitment to the task by ordering the arrest and imprisonment of several notables involved in duelling incidents in the early 1650s. The seriousness with which the council treated duelling offences contrasts vividly with the irresolution of the early Stuarts. But even their stern actions, which resulted in the imprisonment of those who issued challenges, and the binding of aspirant duellists by bonds of £1,000 and sureties of £500 and £1,000 to keep the peace, were insufficient.[46] Fatal encounters continued to take place, albeit less frequently than before, while those cases that went to court seldom produced verdicts that were sufficiently penal to deter the duelling impulse. For example, when Lord Chandos and Lord Arundel, his second, were tried for killing Henry Compton in May 1652, the jury at Kingston-upon-Thames, where the case was initially heard, and the Upper Bench at Westminster Hall both returned verdicts of manslaughter. The Westminster decision included an instruction that the two peers 'be burnt on the hand', but since, as one contemporary observed, this 'was don[e] to them both a day after but very favourably', it is clear that the courts could not be depended upon to enforce anti-duelling legislation.[47]

Perturbed by their failure to eradicate duelling by these means, Cromwell and his advisers determined to proclaim it. An ordinance to this effect was promulgated in July 1654 and renewed in June 1656,[48] but though those who infringed these anti-duelling regulations were prosecuted, the code of honour easily survived the efforts of the Protectorate to eradicate it.[49] As far as can be established, there was a decline in the number of duels fought in England during the 1650s.[50] However, there is no evidence of a parallel decline in the commitment of the nobility and gentry to the code of honour. Quite the contrary; it was simply driven underground, and the relaxation in social control that followed the restoration of the Stuart monarchy in 1660 prompted a rapid escalation in the number of duels fought in England and, as we shall see, in Ireland.

The active reign of Charles II (1660–85) possesses a well-deserved reputation for licence and libertinism. It is certainly true that duelling was more commonplace in England in the 1660s and 1670s than it had been previously.[51] However, it is unfair to blame Charles II personally for this, because he too aspired to curb the enthusiasm of his nobility for duelling. He had sought, without success, to inhibit duelling among the royalist exiles in Europe in the 1650s. On his return from exile, one of his first acts was to issue a proclamation forbidding the fighting of duels and the carrying of challenges on pain of banishment from court and loss of employment.[52] These penalties were strikingly less severe than those employed during the Protectorate, but it was less the inadequacy of the penalties than the failure to enforce them that proved Charles II's undoing.

Instead of insisting that offenders were punished in accordance with his proclamation, Charles was prone to pardon transgressors who appealed to him for exculpation.[53] The most infamous instance of this took place in January 1668 following an encounter between the Duke of Buckingham and Lord Shrewsbury, as a result of which Shrewsbury's second, Captain William Jenkins, was killed and Shrewsbury was so badly injured that he died. This incident created a sensation because of the eminence of the participants, but also because the probable cause, Lady Shrewsbury, was Buckingham's mistress. To add to the drama, Charles pardoned the three survivors with indecent haste less than ten days after the rencontre.[54] It was an inconsistency for which Charles has rightly been criticised, because it inaugurated an era several decades long in which duelling went virtually unregulated outside of military circles.[55] However, Charles II was not solely to blame for this state of affairs. Parliament was equally unwilling to curb the aristocratic predilection for duelling. In 1666 and 1667 bills 'to prevent the sending and carrying of challenges and fighting of duels' were presented to the House of Commons, but neither proceeded beyond the committee stage.[56] It is not entirely clear what happened, but it is not difficult to understand why M.P.s and peers were loath to approve legislation which threatened each and every one of them with social ostracism and economic ruin if they sent, accepted or carried a challenge, as the following extract from a bill prepared in 1668 suggests:

> [A] person who sends, accepts or carries a challenge shall be made incapable of holding any degree or title of honour or precedency he has then or which shall afterwards come to him by descent; [he] shall be disabled from sitting in parliament and from holding any office, ecclesiastical, civil or military, and shall be reputed a person of dishonour and infamy . . . The not making known the receiving of a challenge within forty hours shall be considered an acceptance thereof; the killing of either punishable with death and any principal or second who takes part in a duel, though no death ensure, shall forfeit all his property, real and personal, besides the penalties above imposed upon challengers and acceptors of challenges. The like punishment shall be inflicted on any person who sends or who accepts a challenge to fight a duel beyond seas.[57]

The unease excited by Charles's pardon of Buckingham in January 1668 and the appointment in February of a Committee of Council 'to consider the ways of preventing the frequent mischief of duelling' seemed to augur better for anti-duelling legislation on this third attempt.[58] But once again the bill, which was considered by the Commons in February and presented to the Lords by the Duke of York on 6 April with a declaration from the king that he would not in future pardon anyone responsible for killing another in a duel, did not reach the statute book.[59] In the absence of firm laws, the courts had few options open to them. Indeed, in some instances, as the 1667 rencontre in which the playwright Thomas Porter killed Sir Henry Belasyse emphasises, duellists were not even brought to court because coroner's juries were not prepared to bring in an appropriate verdict to facilitate their prosecution.[60]

Given the reluctance of the king,[61] parliament and the law to take a firm stand, and the continued disposition of gentlemen to have recourse to weapons to defend their 'honour'[62] over minor as well as major matters, it is no surprise that the number of duels that took place in England rose during the reign of Charles II.[63] It is hardly surprising either, given their cultural as well as geographical proximity, that it was at this moment that the code of honour became an established feature of the lifestyle of the new order that was now ensconced as the dominant economic, political and social force in Ireland.

The introduction of duelling into Ireland

Although the code of honour was firmly established in England before the end of the reign of Elizabeth I, sixteenth-century Ireland represented less fertile soil for such modes of behaviour. The kingdom did have a tradition of single combats and trials by combat extending into the sixteenth century,[64] but the comparative paucity of reference to them in the surviving record would suggest that they were not as popular in medieval Ireland as they were in medieval England and Europe. Furthermore, because the Gaelic and Anglo-Norman ruling elites that dominated Irish society during the late Middle Ages were largely cut off from the new political and social order emerging in Renaissance and early modern Europe, they were unversed in developments in the area of juridico-ethical theory and single combat. Late medieval Ireland was dominated by 'warlords', each with his own territory and clan, whose honour tradition demanded that he defended and protected these interests and, if he was strong and skilled enough, that he conquered and pillaged those of his neighbours as well. The absence of a central source of authority in Ireland ensured that Irish society remained traditional and essentially centrifugal. As a consequence, the concept of honour that prevailed remained distinctively different, and for as long as it continued thus Ireland remained unreceptive to duelling and the social precepts and beliefs that gave rise to it.[65]

But no society is immune to change, and when the Tudor monarchy embarked in the 1530s upon its long and fitful conquest, in the process of which it destroyed the traditional foci of political and military power in

Ireland,[66] it paved the way for the emergence of a new elite whose outlook, thought-processes and mores were palpably different to those of their predecessors and more in tune with contemporary European aristocratic norms. The Tudor conquest was effectively completed when Hugh O'Neill and Lord Mountjoy concluded the Treaty of Mellifont in 1603, but the full social as well as economic implications of their military triumph remained to be felt. The New English, the military and administrative representatives of the crown resident in Ireland, were few in number and only at the outset of forging a distinctive identity that reflected their newly acquired status in Ireland. This represents one reason for the paucity of evidence for duelling in Ireland in the late sixteenth and early seventeenth centuries.

There was no intrinsic reason, of course, why the emerging anglophone ruling elite in Ireland should imitate the aristocracies of other western European countries and embrace the code of honour and the practice of duelling. The boyars of Russia, for example, refrained from duelling until the eighteenth century.[67] But if the particularities of Irish history provide an explanation as to why duelling did not become a prominent feature of Irish life in the second half of the sixteenth century when it did so in England, there were clear signs that it was but a matter of time. William Palmer has argued that honour played an important part in the mental and political worlds of both Irish lords and the English conquerors in the sixteenth century. But the cultural definitions of honour applied by the 'lineage society' in place in Ireland and the 'civil society' of the New English were so fundamentally different there was no way the former could serve as a basis for the dissemination of the emerging *ancien régime* code of honour. Only the New English were familiar with this, and it was their determination to introduce modern European and English social as well as economic, legal and political practices that provides the key to the introduction and popularisation of duelling.[68]

The most salient indicator that the code of honour would become an intrinsic feature of social relations within the new hierarchial order being put in place in Ireland is provided by a number of honorific incidents in the late sixteenth century. In 1571, during James Fitzmaurice's rebellion, the President of Munster, Sir John Perrot, became so frustrated by his failure to bring Fitzmaurice to heel that he challenged him 'to finish the same with combate or single fight'. Fitzmaurice toyed with the idea for a time and indicated his readiness provided certain conditions were met, but he did not turn up on the day appointed and no encounter took place.[69] Sixteen years later, Perrot made another appeal to the code of honour. By 1587, relations between two of the most prominent representatives of the New English, Sir John Perrot, who was now Lord Deputy, and the

President of Connacht, Sir Richard Bingham, had deteriorated to such an extent that Bingham was reported to have asserted that 'he would have . . . combat' with Perrot if he was 'out of office'. Outraged by this and by the 'untruths' he claimed Bingham was spreading about him, Perrot sent the constable of Dublin Castle, Stephen Seagrave, 'one of his greatest cutters or fighters', to challenge his antagonist and to inform him of his readiness to meet him immediately. Bingham responded that he believed it would be 'a very strange thing' if he accepted the challenge, and, once again, no encounter took place.[70] However, four years earlier, on 12 September 1583, Conor MacCormac O'Connor and Teige MacGillapatrick O'Connor were ordered by the Lords Justices and Privy Council at the prompting of the Master of the Rolls, Sir Nicholas Whyte, to settle differences arising out of mutual accusations of treason by force of arms. The 'trial by combat' took place in the inner court of Dublin Castle before a crowd that consisted of 'the lords justices, the judges and the councellors'. During the contest each man displayed 'great courage', and Conor O'Connor was killed and beheaded.[71]

As indicated above, judicial trials by combat were occasionally sanctioned by the Tudor and Bourbon courts in the late sixteenth century to settle differences between members of their nobility. Historically, they bear closer comparison to the jousts and trials by combat of the Middle Ages than to the self-policing private duels practised by the aristocracy of early modern Europe, and the 1583 encounter at Dublin Castle belongs to this tradition rather than that of the early modern private duel.[72] However, we cannot dismiss it simply as a vestigial hangover of an earlier period. Billacois notes that the duel in France borrowed from the trial by combat, and the official sanction forthcoming for the 1583 encounter, Perrot's challenge to Fitzmaurice, the threatened Perrot–Bingham altercation and the frequent appeals of Bingham to 'his honour' in his account of the dispute suggest that both the code of honour and duelling were part of the value system of those of the New English resident in Ireland, even if they generally forbore from practising it.

If the unstable condition of late sixteenth-century Ireland did not offer an environment as conducive to the observance of the code of honour as England and Europe, the gradual extension by the New English ruling elite of its economic and political foothold in the seventeenth century slowly removed this obstacle. The key events in the process whereby the small New English interest present in Ireland at the end of the sixteenth century was able to assume more of the trappings of an aristocratic elite were the replantation of Munster and the plantation of Ulster, Wexford, Longford and elsewhere in the first four decades of the seventeenth century.[73] The remodelling of the social, economic and political order which this prompted was complex and long drawn out, and it had only arrived at an interim stage when the outbreak of rebellion in 1641 threatened to bring the whole process to a crashing halt. For this reason, it is not surprising that there is comparatively little evidence of duelling in Ireland in the early seventeenth century.[74] The challenge facing the many thousands of English and Scottish settlers, who became tenants, and the smaller number of undertakers, servitors and speculators who became landlords, was to create a society and economy similar to that with which they were familiar in Britain, and to protect themselves from the aggrieved population they had displaced. Most settlers carried, or had access to arms, but these were primarily for defensive purposes; duelling was an indulgence they were disinclined to allow themselves. It is noteworthy, for instance, that the differences that kept Bishop James Spottiswood of Clogher and Lord Balfour at loggerheads during the 1620s and 1630s did not produce a single challenge, though a similar disagreement a century and a half later, even one involving a bishop, would probably have invited a recourse to arms.[75]

Needless to say, not everyone possessed such forbearance and self-discipline. Sir Nicholas Bagenal, the constable of Leighlin, and Sir William St Leger fit this category. They met in 1607 in an ill-documented encounter as a result of which Bagenal died of his wounds.[76] There is more information on the affray that took place in November 1609 between the irascible Lord Howth and Roger Jones, the son of the Lord Chancellor and Archbishop of Dublin, Thomas Jones. Their disagreement arose out of Jones's alleged participation, with his brother-in-law, Gerrott Moore, and a number of others, in an attempt in 1608 to assassinate the son of Sir Robert Dillon, the former Irish Chief Justice of the Common Pleas, for supporting Howth's prosecution of 'some notorious malefactors' who were Moore's retainers. Howth also alleged that Jones attempted to subvert the course of justice by providing character references and by accepting bribes to intercede with his father on behalf of 'two kerne' he (Howth) was convinced were guilty of treason. Howth pursued his grievance with such intemperate zeal at the Privy Council and elsewhere that the disagreement soon degenerated into an unseemly squabble as both sides endeavoured to blacken the other's reputation with increasingly scurrilous allegations. This reflected badly on the Irish administration, but though Sir Arthur Chichester, the Lord Deputy, made a number of efforts to 'reconcile' the two enemies he was unable to report any progress. Indeed, the quarrel worsened when Roger Jones 'in the presence of divers persons of good rank and fashion, termed him [Howth] a coward' in the summer of 1609. Determined to uphold his honour against slight, Howth sought out Jones in order to 'cudgell' him and thereby to redeem himself or to provoke Jones into a duel. Attended by ten or twelve retainers, he finally encountered Jones at a tennis court in Thomas Street on 27 November. Swords were drawn, and in the confrontation that ensued Simon Barnewell, one of Jones's colleagues, was fatally injured by one of Howth's party. Howth and his retainers were committed to custody as a consequence, but they were released when the coroner's court returned a verdict of manslaughter.[77]

The attempts by Chichester to reconcile both Jones senior and Jones junior with Lord Howth amply attests to the anxiety of the authorities in the early seventeenth century to prevent disputes on matters of honour proceeding to hostilities. Much depended on the disposition of the opponents; for example, the intervention of a Jesuit priest was sufficient to prevent two Kilkenny gentlemen resolving a difference with weapons in 1619. However, there was little anybody, lay or religious, could do to dissuade individuals determined to fight.[78]

Soldiers were the group most disposed to press matters to a violent conclusion. And it is an indication of the importance of the military in disseminating the practice of duelling that, notwithstanding the small and underdeveloped state of the army in Ireland in the early seventeenth century, they were probably the most enthusiastic observers of the code of honour at this time. Thus in the winter of 1629–30, Lieutenant-Colonel Sir Francis Willoughby, who commanded at Limerick, was challenged to a duel by Sir Lucius Cary following his appointment to lead a 'company' which Cary regarded as his own. Willoughby was anxious not to fight, and he may well have evaded a showdown by appealing to Lord Dorchester to mediate.[79] According to tradition, duelling was sufficiently commonplace among the military to prompt the foundation, some time in the reign of James I, of an association known as the Friendly Brothers of St Patrick which committed its members not to accept challenges. Nothing is known of its activities, and it may be that the claim by the Friendly Brothers to an early seventeenth-century origin has no basis in fact.[80]

In view of the modest number of duels known to have taken place in Ireland in the early seventeenth century, and the strong antipathy of the Cromwellians towards the code of honour, there is, as might be expected, little evidence of a significant increase in duelling in Ireland in the crisis-torn decades of the 1640s and the 1650s. This notwithstanding, these years are important in the history of duelling in Ireland because they created an environment in which the code of honour could flourish. The rising of 1641 and the wars that followed transformed Ireland into an international battleground, which attracted soldiers of diverse backgrounds from England, Scotland and continental Europe, who adhered keenly to the code of honour.[81] More significantly in the long term, the impact of the Cromwellian conquest, land confiscation and of the attempts in the 1650s to shape Ireland according to English precepts significantly altered the structure of Irish society by decimating the native Irish and Old English interests that had posed such a formidable threat in the 1640s.[82] In addition, the Cromwellian land settlement, which oversaw the emplacement of approximately 8,000 new Protestant landowners, the reinforcement of the New English already *in situ* with confiscated land, and substantial immigration from England and Scotland significantly increased the size as well as the self-assurance of the landowning elite.[83] Ireland now possessed the basic social structure of an *ancien régime* society; it had reached a stage in its evolution when it could sustain the code of honour and the practice of duelling.[84] The task now is to trace how this was brought about.

The code of honour was reinforced as a feature of Irish life in the mid-seventeenth century through a number of different routes. These were the activities of the various military forces in Ireland in the 1640s, the experiences of Irish royalists in exile with Charles II in Europe during the 1650s, and the influence of the more relaxed attitude to duelling that prevailed in England during the Restoration period.

The presence in the 'orders of warre' drafted for the Confederate army in 1643 of two articles (nos 19 and 20) which deemed 'private quarrel[s] and private fight[s]' without as well as within 'the camp or garrison' a capital offence, and another (no. 44) that provided for the 'imprisonment, publike disarming and banishment from the army' of officers that offered or accepted 'challenges' indicates that duelling was a problem among the Confederate armies in Ireland in the 1640s.[85] This is hardly surprising given the continental experiences of many of the soldiers in the armies of the Confederation, but the royalist commander, the Marquis of Ormond, had a similar problem which he was no less anxious to eradicate, for he provided for equally stern punishments. When Sergeant Walter Kyle killed Lieutenant William Baird in a rencontre conducted by moonlight at Portaferry, County Down, in February 1642 following a disagreement the two men had embarked upon while drinking, Kyle was court-martialled, found guilty and sentenced to 'be shott att a poste till death'.[86] Capital punishment may have served to confine the disposition to duel evident among the soldiery present in Ireland in the 1640s, but it did not eradicate it.[87] Moreover, once the fighting was over, military discipline relaxed, most visibly among those who fled the kingdom for the peripatetic court of Charles II.

Exile to the continent was an acutely frustrating experience for the adherents of the House of Stuart following their defeat in the Civil War. Excluded from the power and influence they believed was rightfully theirs, they endeavoured to pass the time as best they could, but were prone to faction and petty bickering which precipitated quarrels that frequently culminated in rencontres. Duelling was particularly prevalent during their time in Flanders in the late 1650s, and Irish royalists in exile were as disposed as their English colleagues to risk their lives on the altar of honour. In one notable case, Theobald, Viscount Taaffe, who was eventually sent from court for repeated acts of aggression, his second Richard Talbot and three others fought Sir William Keith, a Scotsman, and his seconds at Amiens in Northern France in 1658 over 'three royals and a half at tennis', as a result of which Keith was slain by Taaffe, and Dick Hopton wounded by Talbot.[88] On another occasion Talbot, who clearly merited the soubriquet 'Fighting Dick', challenged Lieutenant-Colonel MacCarty to a duel after he rejected his application for a military promotion. We do not know the outcome on this occasion;[89] but Talbot's reputation and the preparedness of seconds to risk their lives in other people's quarrels indicate that the code of honour took firm root among the royalist exiles in Europe in the 1650s, and that this represented one of the chief means by which, on the restoration of the monarchy, it was established as a feature of upper-class Catholic behaviour in late seventeenth-century Ireland.

The upsurge in enthusiasm for duelling in England which followed the restoration of Charles II to the throne also encouraged its practice in Ireland. The geographical contiguity of the two islands made this likely in any event, but the fact that the ruling Protestant elites in the two kingdoms shared common origins, a common recent history, a common social network and many common precepts facilitated its transmission. This is vividly illustrated by a number of notable duelling incidents in England in the 1660s, 1670s and 1680s involving prominent members of the Irish aristocracy.

The most celebrated of these encounters took place in October 1666 when Lord Ossory, the Duke of Ormond's son, took exception to the assertion by the Duke of Buckingham in the House of Lords that those who opposed a bill prohibiting the importation of Irish cattle into England possessed either 'an Irish interest or an Irish understanding'. This was, as Samuel Pepys acknowledged, a serious insult; Buckingham was all but calling the bill's Irish critics fools,[90] and Ossory, who felt his honour impugned, responded by challenging the duke to defend his remarks by recourse to arms. This put Buckingham in a difficult position. He was disinclined to fight, but he could not be seen to decline the challenge; so drawing on all his diplomatic experience and his knowledge of the code of honour, he outmanoeuvred his opponent by going to the wrong field, by accusing him of not turning up at the appointed place, and by informing the House of Lords of Ossory's challenge. Ossory was charged with a breach of parliamentary privilege which effectively precluded him pursuing the affair, and both he and Buckingham were sentenced to spend three days in the Tower of London as a punishment.[91] The sentence had little effect. Eleven years later Ossory was in the wars once again when he and one of his McCarthy cousins were challenged by Buckley and Grant as a result of a difference over Buckley's wife. McCarthy and Grant were both wounded in the rencontre that followed.[92] A similar fate awaited Americus de Courcey, Lord Kingsale; he and his second, Patrick Sarsfield — then an unemployed soldier — were both seriously wounded in an encounter with Charles, Earl of Newburgh, in December 1681.[93] Sarsfield was run 'through the body near the shoulder, very dangerously', but it did not dissuade him from duelling. Indeed, this was his second affair of honour in four months; he was the aggressor in an incident in September 1681 with the English peer Lord Grey of Warke which arose out of slighting remarks the latter had made about Irishmen. No duel took place on this occasion because Grey reported the matter to the Privy Council, and Sarsfield was lucky to escape prosecution.[94] Undaunted by these experiences, Sarsfield continued to get into scrapes. He was still recovering from a serious wound incurred in another duel in the spring of 1683 when a difference with Sir John Parsons, an erstwhile 'friend and accomplice', over a warrant protecting him from prosecution caused him to challenge Parsons. The two men met on 29 April behind Montague House; both were run through the lungs and seriously injured, but once again both lived to tell the tale.[95]

In view of the willingness of Irish peers and Irish soldiers in the 1650s, 1660s, 1670s and 1680s to flout royal wishes on duelling when abroad,[96] it is no surprise that they did likewise at home. Recent events in England might tempt one to conclude that its devotees were more likely to come from among those with a royalist rather than a Cromwellian background, but such a distinction is unsustainable. The newly arrived adventurers, officers and soldiers of Cromwellian background, were as willing as their predecessors of New as well as of Old English ancestry to demonstrate that they were men of honour. Duels in this period were not 'an everyday occurrence', as MacLysaght and Kiernan contend,[97] but the comparative laxity of the authorities' response to the participants in those that did take place did nothing to discourage the practice.

When informed of an impending duel, the authorities were inclined to intervene to prevent it taking place if possible. For example, when Lord Chichester (son and heir to the Earl of Donegall) challenged Lord Roscommon in 1667, the Duke of Ormond, who was Lord Lieutenant, ordered Roscommon to be confined for a night. In the following year when Sir Hercules Langrishe and Mr Luttrell quarrelled in a tavern, both men were taken up by the guard to prevent them proceeding with their planned rencontre.[98] Likewise, when the Earl of Essex was Lord Lieutenant in the 1670s, he went to considerable lengths to prevent Richard Power, the Earl of Tyrone, Colonel Edward Villiers and the Earl of Clanricarde and Colonel Duggan settling their differences by recourse to arms. Essex was not prompted to take this action by principled opposition to the code of honour. When he was insulted in 1677 by Captain Edward Brabazon, it was with great reluctance that he declined 'takeing that satisfaction . . . gentlemen in like cases doe'.[99] Moreover, the authorities responded indulgently to those peers and soldiers who duelled. When Wentworth, seventeenth Earl of Kildare, fought a duel with Talbot, the secretary to the Earl of Shrewsbury who was Treasurer and Receiver General of Ireland, in December 1662, he was banned 'from the council table'. However, the sentence was not long maintained, and he was soon reinstated.[100]

The failure of the authorities in Ireland as in England to take a firm stand against duelling meant that the law did not serve as a deterrent in either kingdom to determined duellists. Moreover, because duelling in Ireland was not the sanitised and ritualised encounter of legend, it was quite normal for seconds to support their principals by fighting by their side. One consequence of this was that seconds were as likely to get killed or injured as the principals. A good illustration of this type of duel is provided by the 1664 encounter that arose from 'a difference between Colonel Dempsey and Mr Luttrell', as a result of which Ensign Buckley (Luttrell's second) was 'dangerously wounded' and his opposite number was injured.[101] This refusal to adhere to prescribed procedures meant that duellists were vulnerable to allegations of misconduct such as those levelled in 1663 at Loftus, the nephew of Lord Cork and Orrery, who, it was claimed, killed Bromley, Sir Nicholas Armorer's ensign, before he had removed his sword from its scabbard.[102]

It is impossible to establish a reliable statistical overview on the cause or outcome of duelling in late seventeenth-century Ireland because of the fitfulness of the surviving record. But many were prompted by differences that appear so banal in hindsight that they give strength to Lawrence Stone's claim that gentlemen in the early modern era were possessed of very short tempers. For instance, in December 1667 the Earl of Roscommon and the Earl of Clancarty's brother quarrelled over their place at the funeral of Captain Harman of the Guards, and would have resolved their difference by force of arms but for the arrival of the Lord Lieutenant's guard as they were readying themselves for confrontation.[103] Three years later the Lord Lieutenant was unable to prevent a six-man meeting in the Phoenix Park involving on one side Lord Brabazon,

Captain Fitzgerald and Ensign Slaughter, and on the other Captain Savage, Lieutenant Bridges and Ensign Trevor Lloyd. The cause in this instance was a difference 'at play . . . at the Castle Tavern'; in the rencontre Slaughter was killed and Lloyd, Bridges, Brabazon and Fitzgerald all wounded. This was an exceptionally high casualty list even by seventeenth-century standards. But instead of exploiting it for all that it was worth to arrest the growing disposition to duel, the Court of King's Bench returned a verdict of manslaughter when Lloyd was brought to trial for the murder of Slaughter. Brabazon received a royal pardon.[104] In 1679 Captain Douglas killed Captain Campbell in a duel that resulted from 'some words' that passed between them while hunting.[105]

As these last two encounters, and another in 1677 involving Colonel McDonnell and Richard Coote in which the former was killed, bear witness, the law in Ireland continued to be as ineffectual as it was in England to combat duelling. The normal practice was to adhere scrupulously to all the legal formalities, but in no instance that I have discovered did a verdict other than manslaughter result. The McDonnell–Coote affair is a case in point. It had a complex gestation, but its immediate origins lay in the rival claims of Richard Coote, the son and heir of Lord Colooney, and Captain Arthur Forbes, the son and heir of Lord Granard, to the hand of Mary, the eldest daughter of Sir George Rawdon of Moira, County Down. For reasons that remain unclear, but which may well be connected with an existing difference, McDonnell, who was a friend of Forbes, challenged Coote and was worsted in the ensuing encounter. Everybody involved was utterly convinced that Coote had, in Sir George Rawdon's words, 'behaved with honour'. However, there were legal procedures to be observed, so that even when Lord Colooney accepted the coroner's verdict of '*homicida se defendendo*', Rawdon anticipated the case would still be heard by the Court of King's Bench.[106]

There is no evidence that Coote did stand trial for the murder of McDonnell, but the fact that Rawdon was so anxious to ensure that all legal procedures were followed in a case that was virtually a textbook instance of manslaughter provides a warning against exaggerating the disposition to duel and the frequency with which differences were settled by recourse to arms in late seventeenth-century Ireland. That said, it is clear that among the military, at least, duelling was reasonably commonplace and that this reflected landed society at large, because the army in Ireland was 'interwoven with the very fabric of the country's whole society. Its officers came from the best of the Irish gentry.'[107] In one short period during the summer of 1679 there were six or seven duels, at least one of which resulted in a fatality, between soldiers garrisoned at Youghal.[108] The predisposition of soldiers to duel can partly be accounted for by reference to their profession. But since one of the features that distinguished a gentleman was the right to bear arms, and all did so, this on its own does not explain why soldiers figure so prominently in the duelling record for the late seventeenth century. A more convincing explanation as to why the army in Ireland became so prone to duelling, in the 1680s at least, can be found in the tensions between those of an Old English background, who were Catholic, and those of New English or Cromwellian background, who were Protestant.[109] The latter grew increasingly perturbed when, towards the end of his reign, Charles II and, after him, James II (1685–8) were seen to favour Catholics over Protestants.

It is not always easy to establish precisely which duels can be attributed to internal politico-religious cleavages within the army, but there can be no question but that it was an important causative factor.[110] In 1671, for instance, when Robert Leigh reported a duel involving Sir Henry Ingoldsby and Richard Talbot's nephew, Thomas Cusack, from which both emerged unhurt, his main concern was that it would 'breed much greater animosities'.[111] The same anxiety was articulated with greater cause fourteen years later when Talbot, now the Earl of Tyrconnell, was one of the most powerful figures in the land. As a result of some 'words' at table, Captain Tory Hamilton and Esquire Nugent, another relation of Tyrconnell, and their seconds — Lord Forbes and Sir Robert Maxwell on Hamilton's side and Captain Nangle and another Nugent on Nugent's — met in a bloody affray at Lisburn in which all six combatants were injured, one of them 'dangerously'.[112]

But political and religious tensions were not the only source of military duels in the 1680s. Simple disagreements led to so many disabling injuries that James II felt compelled in July 1685 to direct the Lords Justices of Ireland 'to cashier all officers sending, receiving or delivering any challenge to a duel . . . or giving any real affront to any other'.[113] A proclamation to this effect was promulgated shortly afterwards.[114] But if it encouraged caution among some, it had little effect on the four officers from the Irish Foot Guards who fought two separate duels in August 1685. It had little effect also on Captain Tom Flower and Captain Sankey of the regiment of Guards, who met at the public exchange in Dublin in the same month; and on Henry Jones and his cornet, Ambrose Jones, who were so inflamed by a difference of opinion in October that they fought by candlelight at their quarters at Carrick-on-Shannon, wounding each other so desperately that they both died.[115] The enforced Catholicisation of the army resulted in a fall-off in the number of duels fought in the late 1680s, but the code of honour was too firmly entrenched in the military and in Irish landed society to be eradicated by royal decree. This is confirmed by the fact that as well as military officers,[116] local legal officials did not hesitate appealing to arms to resolve grievances. In October 1690 a disagreement at dinner in County Down between the High Sheriff, Bernard Ward and Jocelyn Hamilton, his neighbour, led to a duel with swords *and* pistols as a result of which both participants died: one was shot dead; the other was run through.[117]

As these examples indicate, MacLysaght's interpretation of the role and practitioners of the duel in late seventeenth-century Ireland needs modification. The stereotypical duellist, if such a being can be said to have existed, was more likely to be a soldier or a peer than a 'feckless, hard-drinking, fearless, fox-hunting, fire-eating landlord'.[118] The era of the latter had still to come; late seventeenth-century Irish society was too unstable and immature, and still in the process of definition. The Protestant interest that had emerged some decades earlier did not yet feel sufficiently secure from threat; while the existence of a restless Catholic landowning class, whose numbers had been increased as a consequence of the revision of the Cromwellian land settlement in the 1660s, and whose political ambitions were encouraged by James II,[119] provided cause and occasion for the ill-will and resentments that were ideal breeding-grounds for animosities that culminated in duelling encounters. It was not until victory was achieved over the Jacobites in 1690–91 that the Protestant ruling elite in Ireland could begin to feel secure, and that duelling in Ireland could become the preserve of civilians rather than of soldiers.

Notes and References

1 Richard Barber, *The knight and chivalry* (Ipswich, 1974), pp. 159–82; J. R. V. Barker, *The tournament in England, 1100–1400* (Woodbridge, 1986), pp. 188–90; Donna T. Andrew, 'The code of honour and its critics: the opposition to duelling in England, 1700–1850', *Social History*, v (1980), pp. 409–10; A. R. Ferguson, *The Indian summer of English chivalry* (Durham, 1960), pp. 13–15; Billacois, *The duel*, pp. 15–17, 26–7 cites a number of sixteenth-century trials by combat, but acknowledges they were unusual.

2 Billacois, *The duel*, pp. 17–18.

3 Kiernan, *The duel*, pp. 6–53; Billacois, *The duel*, passim; Geoffrey Parker, *The military revolution: military innovation and the rise of the west, 1500–1800* (Cambridge, 1988); Lawrence Stone, *The crisis of the aristocracy in England, 1558–1641* (Oxford, 1965).

4 They also preserved a range of fiscal, judicial, political, honorific and seigneurial privileges (M. L. Bush, *Noble privilege* (Manchester, 1983), passim); Maurice Keen, *Chivalry* (Yale, 1974), pp. 248–9.

5 The phrase is Andrew's ('The code of honour', p. 410).

6 Sydney Anglo, 'How to kill a man at your ease: fencing books and the duelling ethic' in idem, ed., *Chivalry and the Renaissance* (Woodbridge, 1990), pp. 6–8, 11–12.

7 Peter Burke, *The historical anthropology of early modern Italy* (Cambridge, 1987), pp. 13–14; Antonio Massa, *Contra l'uso del duello* (Venetia, 1555); Giovanni Possevini, *Dialogo dell' honore* (Vinegia, 1553); Dario Attendoli, *Discorso intorno all' honore* (Vinegia, 1552); idem, *Il duello* (Vinegia, 1552).

8 Billacois, *The duel*, pp. 18–26, 33–48.

9 Burke, *Historical anthropology*, pp. 13–14.

10 This paragraph draws on Julian Pitt-Rivers, 'Honor' in *International encyclopaedia of the Social Sciences* (17 vols, New York, 1968), vi, 503–4; idem, *The fate of Shechem or the politics of sex: essays in the anthropology of the Mediterranean* (Cambridge, 1977), p. 1.

11 J. K. Campbell, *Honour, family and patronage* (Oxford, 1964), pp. 268–73.

12 Pitt-Rivers, 'Honor', p. 508; see also Stone, *The family, sex and marriage in England, 1500–1800* (London, 1977), p. 503; Mervyn James, 'English politics and the concept of honour 1485–1642' in *Society, politics and culture: studies in early modern England* (Cambridge, 1988), p. 325.

13 James, 'English politics and the concept of honour', pp. 309–13.

14 Stone, *The family, sex and marriage*, p. 234; idem, *Crisis of the aristocracy*, pp. 223–4; Kiernan, *The duel*, pp. 79–80.

15 Kiernan, *The duel*, p. 77; Stone, *Family, sex and marriage*, p. 234.

16 M. L. Bush's review of Kiernan, *The duel* in *English Historical Review*, cvi (1991), pp. 1071–2; Billacois, *The duel*, pp. 191–6; Stone, *Crisis of the aristocracy*, pp. 242–3; Anglo, 'How to kill a man', pp. 2–3, 9.

17 Pitt-Rivers, 'Anthropology of honour', p. 1.

18 James, 'English politics and the concept of honour', p. 325; Pitt-Rivers, 'Honor', p. 505; Campbell, *Honour, family and patronage*, pp. 269–74; Stone, *Crisis of the aristocracy*, p. 503.
19 Lodowick Bryskett, *Literary works*, ed. J. H. P. Pafford (London, 1972), pp. 64–84, especially pp. 65–6, 70, 75–6, 78–80.
20 Bush, *Noble privilege*, passim; Brian Fothergill, *The Strawberry Hill set: Horace Walpole and his circle* (London, 1983), p. 20; Theodore Besterman, *Voltaire* (Oxford, 1976), pp. 113–16; Pitt-Rivers, 'Anthropology of honour', p. 10.
21 Norman Gash, *Sir Robert Peel* (London, 1972), p. 187.
22 National Museum of Ireland.
23 Kiernan, *The duel*, pp. 11, 15–16; M. Corr, 'Reminiscences of duelling in Ireland', *Macmillan's Magazine*, xxix (1873–4), p. 313. I wish to thank Dr W. E. Vaughan for the second reference.
24 Billacois, *The duel*, pp. 45–6, 49–56, 95–6; Kiernan, *The duel*, p. 69; Michael Bush, *Rich noble, poor noble* (Manchester, 1988), p. 92; Charles Mackay, *Extraordinary popular delusions and the madeness of crowds* (New York, 1972), pp. 661–5.
25 Billacois, *The duel*, pp. 98–103; idem, *Le duel dans la societé française* (Paris, 1986), pp. 418–19; *Receuil des édits, declarations des arrests de le cour de parlement contre les duels publiez depuis l'année 1599 jusques à present* (Paris, 1660); Ode Trelon, *Advis sur la presentation de l'édit de sa majesté contre la damnable coustume des duels* (Paris, 1604); Jean Savaron, *Traité contre les duels* (Paris, 1610).
26 Billacois, *The duel*, pp. 59–68; Mackay, *Extraordinary popular delusions*, p. 671; Stone, *Crisis of the aristocracy*, pp. 225–7, 243–4; Anglo, ed., *Chivalry*, pp. 3–4.
27 Kiernan, *The duel*, p. 69; Michael Roberts, *Gustavus Adolphus: a history of Sweden, 1611–32* (2 vols, London, 1953–58), ii, 242.
28 Kiernan, *The duel*, pp. 76–7; Billacois, *The duel*, pp. 97–105, 107–11, 144–62; Mackay, *Extraordinary popular delusions*, pp. 668–70.
29 Kiernan, *The duel*, pp. 96–7; Billacois, *The duel*, pp. 165–88; Mackay, *Extraordinary popular delusions*, pp. 672–3.
30 Billacois, *The duel*, pp. 26–9; Stone, *Crisis of the aristocracy*, pp. 244–5; idem, *The family, sex and marriage*, pp. 93–4; Kiernan, *The duel*, p. 53; Andrew, 'The code of honour', p. 410.
31 Cited in Kiernan, *The duel*, p. 81.
32 Billacois, *The duel*, pp. 27–30; Stone, *Crisis of the aristocracy*, p. 247. In April 1610 the Earls of Southampton and Montgomery were only prevented from duelling as a result of a 'difference' during a game of tennis by the intervention of the Lord Chamberlain; and in October of the same year Sir Walter Chute wounded Mr Beecher in two places as a result of a disagreement over cards (H.M.C., *Downshire*, ii, 280, 371, 373).
33 For example, in November 1609, Sir George Wharton and James Stuart both died as a result of a duel fought with daggers (H.M.C., *Downshire*, ii, 182).
34 Bryskett, *Literary works*, pp. 65–85; Stone, *Crisis of the aristocracy*, pp. 246–7; Lord William Howard, 'A treatise against duelling' (H.M.C., 15th Report, appendix 6, *Carlisle MSS*, p. 5); Kiernan, *The duel*, pp. 82–3; Mackay, *Extraordinary popular delusions*, pp. 675–6.

35 H.M.C., *Downshire*, ii, 189, 476; iii, 100, 230–31.
36 Ibid., iii, 108; iv, 205–06, 212; James I, *A publication of His Maties edict and severe censure against private combats and combatants* (London, 1611); A brief of two proclamations and His Majesty's edict against duells, 4 Feb., 15 Oct. 1613 (B.L., folio volume of heraldic precedents and collections, Add. MS 6297 f.284); J. F. Larkin and P. L. Hughes, eds, *Stuart royal proclamations* (2 vols, Oxford, 1973–83), i, 295–7, 302–08; Mackay, *Extraordinary popular delusions*, pp. 676–7.
37 Stone, *Crisis of the aristocracy*, pp. 247–8; H.M.C., *Downshire*, ii, 86; iv, 21, 59; H.M.C., 3rd Report, appendix, *House of Lords MSS*, p. 14.
38 King's speech, Apr. 1614, in H.M.C, *Hastings*, p. 233. See also Minutes of King James's speech and judgment in the Star Chamber concerning duels, 1616 (B.L., Lansdowne MS 160, no. 91, f. 302).
39 H.M.C., 3rd Report, appendix, *Duke of Devonshire MSS*, p. 38; H.M.C., *Downshire*, iii, 181, 186, 190, 196; Kiernan, *The duel*, p. 83.
40 Billacois, *The duel*, p. 27; H.M.C., *Downshire*, iii, 201, 207; Stone, *Crisis of the aristocracy*, pp. 249–50; Billacois, *The duel*, p. 407.
41 H.M.C., *Mar and Kellie*, p. 191. It is also instructive that no anti-duelling proclamations date from Charles I's reign (Larkin, ed., *Stuart royal proclamations*, ii, passim).
42 *C.S.P.D., 1623–6*, pp. 315, 366; ibid., *1637–8*, p. 213; Billacois, *The duel*, p. 27.
43 The interpretation advanced here conflicts with that of François Billacois (*The duel*, pp. 29–30). He maintains that duelling declined in the reign of Charles I and rose again in the mid-seventeenth century, but he provides insufficient evidence to substantiate this interpretation.
44 John Sym, *Life's preservative against self-killing*, ed. Michael MacDonald (London, 1988), pp. 114–16.
45 Kiernan, *The duel*, p. 94.
46 *C.S.P.D., 1651*, p. 69; ibid., *1651–2*, pp. 240, 461, 498, 507; ibid., *1652–3*, pp. 9, 21, 319, 350, 371; ibid., *1654*, p. 115 and passim.
47 *C.S.P.D. 1651–2*, p. 240; diary of events, May 1653, in H.M.C., *De L'Isle and Dudley*, vi, 616.
48 *C.S.P.D., 1654*, pp. 115, 227, 244; H.M.C., 14th Report, appendix iv, *Kenyon MSS*, p. 65.
49 *C.S.P.D., 1657–8*, pp. 258, 290–91; ibid., *1658–9*, pp. 52, 62, 66.
50 This observation rests on a survey of the *C.S.P.D.* for the 1650s, which will dispel the view that duelling in England was eradicated in the 1650s only to be revived during the reign of Charles II.
51 *C.S.P.D., 1660–85*, passim; Robert Latham, ed., *The diary of Samuel Pepys* (11 vols, London, 1970–83).
52 'Declaration against duells', 1658 (B.L., Nicholas Papers, Egerton MS 2542, f. 278); H.M.C., 5th Report, appendix, *Duke of Sutherland MSS*, p. 168; *C.S.P.D., 1660–61*, p. 189.
53 Concern was frequently expressed at court about duelling (*Pepys diary*, iii, 157), but pardons were quite commonplace. For example, Lord Chesterfield was pardoned in January 1660 for killing Francis Wooley in a duel (ibid., i, 202 note).

54 *Pepys diary*, ix, 26–7; *C.S.P.D., 1667–8*, p. 192; Mackay, *Extraordinary popular delusions*, p. 678.
55 Kiernan, *The duel*, p. 99; *Pepys diary*, viii, 140–41.
56 *C.S.P.D., 1666–7*, p. 209; *Commons' Jn. (England)*, viii, 652; ix, 1, 5.
57 'Bill on duelling', 6 Apr. 1668 in H.M.C., 8th Report, appendix, part 1, *House of Lords MSS*, p. 122a.
58 *Pepys diary*, ix, 53; H.M.C., 12th Report, appendix vii, *Le Fleming MSS*, p. 52.
59 *Lords' Jn. (England)*, xii, 216; H.M.C., *House of Lords*, p. 122a.
60 *Pepys diary*, viii, 363–4, 377.
61 See also Charles II to Lichfield, 28 Oct. 1682, in H.M.C., 2nd Report, appendix, *Dillon MSS*, p. 32.
62 The term is used by Pepys in his account of the Montagu–Cholmely duel of 1662 (*Pepys diary*, iii, 157). Kiernan, *The duel*, p. 99.
63 As well as those cited above see H.M.C., 2nd Report, appendix, *Spencer MSS*, p. 22; H.M.C., *Le Fleming MSS*, pp. 121, 129–30; H.M.C., *Rutland*, ii, 32, 35, 36; H.M.C., *Ormonde*, vi, 117 for further examples.
64 James Mills, ed., *Calendar of the justiciary rolls or proceedings in the Court of the Justiciar of Ireland* (2 vols, London, 1905–14), ii, 415; Preparations for a duel, *c.* 1445 (B.L., Royal MS 10B, ix, f. 59v); *Ancient Irish histories: the chronicles of Ireland* (2 vols, Dublin, 1809), ii, 29; J. G. Crawford, *Anglicizing the government of Ireland: the Irish Privy Council and the expansion of Tudor rule 1556–1578* (Dublin, 1993), pp. 194–5.
65 Katharine Simms, *From kings to warlords* (Suffolk, 1987); Brendan Bradshaw, *The Irish constitutional revolution of the sixteenth century* (Cambridge, 1979), chapter 1.
66 S. G. Ellis, *Tudor Ireland: crown, community and the conflict of cultures* (London, 1985); Ciaran Brady, 'Court, castle and country: the framework of government' in Ciaran Brady and Raymond Gillespie, eds, *Natives and newcomers* (Dublin, 1986), pp. 22–49.
67 R. O. Crummey, *Aristocrats and servitors: the boyar elite in Russia, 1613–89* (Princeton, 1983), pp. 138, 170.
68 William Palmer, 'That "insolent liberty": honor, rites of power and persuasion in sixteenth-century Ireland', *Renaissance Quarterly*, xlvi (1993), pp. 308–27. The terms 'lineage' and 'civil' societies are derived from Mervyn Jones, *Family, lineage and civil society: a study of politics and mentality in the Durham region, 1500–1640* (Oxford, 1974), p. 182ff.
69 *The history of Sir John Perrot, Knight of Bath and Lord Lieutenant of Ireland* (London, 1728), pp. 60–63; Palmer, 'That "insolent liberty"', pp. 311–12; Richard Bagwell, *Ireland under the Tudors* (3 vols, London, 1885), ii, 209–10; *C.S.P.I., 1509–73*, pp. 460, 466.
70 *C.S.P.I., 1586–8*, pp. 270–71; J. S. Brewer and William Bullen, eds, *Calendar of the Carew Manuscripts preserved . . . at Lambeth* (6 vols, London, 1868), ii, 442. I wish to thank Dr Raymond Gillespie for bringing these sources and the works cited in note 68 to my notice.
71 Lord Walter Fitzgerald, 'The duel between two of the O'Connors of Offaly in Dublin Castle on the 12th of September 1583', *J.R.S.A.I.*, xl (1910), pp.

1–5; *C.S.P.I., 1574–85*, p. 468; Holinshed's Chronicles, cited in T. and V. Pakenham, eds, *Dublin: a travellers' companion* (London, 1988) pp. 58–9.

72 Billacois, *The duel*, pp. 26–7, 49–56.

73 Michael MacCarthy-Morrogh, *The Munster plantation* (Oxford, 1986), p. 136ff; Philip Robinson, *The plantation of Ulster* (Dublin, 1984); Raymond Gillespie, *Colonial Ulster: the settlement of east Ulster, 1600–41* (Cork, 1985).

74 This conclusion is based on a survey of the *Calendar of State Papers* for the reigns of James I and Charles I.

75 Raymond Gillespie, 'The trials of Bishop Spottiswood, 1620–40', *Clogher Record*, xii (1987), pp. 320–33.

76 P. H. Bagenal, *Vicissitudes of an Anglo-Irish family, 1530–1800* (London, 1925), p. 80; J. P. Prendergast, 'The plantation of the barony of Idrone, County Carlow', *J.R.S.A.I.*, vi (1861–20), p. 187. I wish to thank Dr Christopher Woods for the latter reference.

77 *C.S.P.I., 1608–10*, pp. 107–13, 320–23, 326–8, 330–31.

78 J. J. Corboy, 'The Jesuit province in Ireland, 1595–1626' (M.A. thesis, U.C.D., 1941), p. 151; see also P. F. Moran, ed., *Spicilegium Ossoriense* (3 vols, Dublin, 1874–84), i, 118.

79 *C.S.P.I., 1625–32*, p. 503. I wish to thank Dr Raymond Gillespie for this and the previous reference. For the army see P. A. Morris, 'Ormonde's army: the Irish standing army, 1640–69' (Ph.D. thesis, Vanderbilt, 1980), pp. 12–16.

80 R. F. Pollock, *The ancient and benevolent order of the Friendly Brothers of St Patrick: history of the London knots, 1775–1973* (privately printed, London, 1973), p. 1.

81 David Stevenson, *Scottish Covenanters and Irish Confederates* (Belfast, 1981); J. I. Casway, *Owen Roe O'Neill and the struggle for Catholic Ireland* (Philadelphia, 1984).

82 Ian Gentles, *The New Model Army in England, Ireland and Scotland, 1645–53* (Oxford, 1991); T. C. Barnard, *Cromwellian Ireland* (Oxford, 1975); K. S. Bottigheimer, *English money and Irish land* (Oxford, 1971).

83 Bottigheimer, *English money and Irish land*, chapter 5; Raymond Gillespie, 'Landed society and the interregnum in Ireland and Scotland' in Rosalind Mitchison and Peter Roebuck, eds, *Economy and society in Scotland and Ireland, 1500–1939* (Edinburgh, 1988), p. 45.

84 S. J. Connolly, *Religion, law, and power: the making of Protestant Ireland, 1660–1760* (Oxford, 1992), passim; T. C. Barnard, 'The political, material and mental culture of the Cork settlers, *c.* 1650–1700' in Patrick O'Flanagan and Cornelius Buttimer, eds, *Cork: history and society* (Dublin, 1993); idem, 'Gardening, diet and improvement in late seventeenth-century Ireland', *Journal of Garden History*, x (1990), pp. 71–85.

85 C. P. Meehan, *The Confederation of Kilkenny* (Dublin, 1905), pp. 299–303.

86 Report of court martial, 2 Mar. 1643 (N.L.I., Ormonde papers, MS 2307, ff 321–25); G. S., 'Court martial held two centuries ago, at Portaferry, County Down', *Ulster Journal of Archaeology*, 3rd series, viii (1960), pp. 62–9.

87 H. F. Berry, ed., *The registers of the Church of St Michan's, Dublin, 1635–85* (Dublin, 1907), p. 26.

88 R. N[ ] to Sir Andrew Newport, 4 Sept. 16[58] in H.M.C., 5th Report, appendix, *Duke of Sutherland MSS*, pp. 146–7; Ronald Hutton, *Charles II: King of England, Scotland and Ireland* (Oxford, 1989), pp. 122–3; H.M.C., *Bath MSS*, ii, 130–31.

89 P. W. Sergeant, *Little Jennings and fighting Dick Talbot* (2 vols, London, 1913), i, 85.

90 According to Pepys: 'the Duke of Buckingham . . . said . . . that whoever was against the bill was there led to it by an Irish interest and an Irish understanding, which is as much as to say he is a fool' (*Pepys diary*, vii, 342–3).

91 *Pepys diary*, vii, 342–3; John Beresford, *Mr Du Quesne and other essays*, p. 157.

92 Camden to Loos, 4 Dec. 1677, in H.M.C., *Rutland*, ii, 42.

93 Camden to Rutland, 8 Dec 1681, ibid., p. 62.

94 Piers Wauchope, *Patrick Sarsfield and the Williamite wars in Ireland* (Dublin, 1992), pp. 17–22.

95 Ibid., p. 26.

96 As well as the above, three Irish gentlemen, at least one of whom was a soldier, met three Englishmen in Liège in a duel in 1684 in which one died and one was wounded (H.M.C., 7th Report, appendix, *Graham MSS*, p. 302). In another incident two Irish soldiers named Burke and Moore fought at Ratisbon in May 1686 (H.M.C., *Ormonde*, vii, 422).

97 Edward MacLysaght, *Irish life in the seventeenth century after Cromwell* (London, 1939), pp. 95–6; Kiernan, *The duel*, p. 106.

98 Boyle to Cork and Burlington, 15 June 1667; Roscommon to Cork and Burlington, 9 [July] 1667 (B.L., Althorp Papers, MS B.5–6); *C.S.P.I., 1666–9*, p. 573. (I wish to thank Dr Toby Barnard and Dr Raymond Gillespie for these references).

99 C. E. Pike, ed., *Essex Papers, 1675–77*, Camden Society, 3rd series, vol. 24 (London, 1913), pp. 78–9, 109, 132–3. I wish to thank Dr Raymond Gillespie for drawing this source and that cited in the following note to my attention.

100 Entry sub 11 Dec. 1662 (B.L., Ware Papers, Add. MS 4784, f. 247 v).

101 Newsletter, Nov. [1664] in H.M.C., *Heathcote*, p. 170; *C.S.P.I., 1663–5*, p. 449.

102 *C.S.P.I., 1663–5*, p. 30.

103 Stone, *Crisis of the aristocracy*, pp. 223–4; *C.S.P.I., 1666–9*, pp. 526–7.

104 *C.S.P.I., 1669–70*, pp. 321, 322, 326; *C.S.P.D., 1671*, p. 169.

105 H.M.C., *Ormonde*, n.s., v, 138–9.

106 *C.S.P.D., 1677–8*, pp. 479–80, 510, 533. For further evidence of adherence to legal proceedings see H.M.C., *Ormonde*, n.s., v, 138–9.

107 Morris, 'Ormonde's army', p. 146.

108 H.M.C., *Ormonde*, n.s., v, 138–9, 173. As well as the incidents cited, duels were fought by military personnel in September 1666 and February 1671 (*C.S.P.D., 1666–9*, p. 206; ibid., *1671*, p. 86).

109 Morris, 'Ormonde's army', p. 89.

110 It was in England; see John Childs, *The army, James II and the Glorious Revolution* (Manchester, 1980), pp. 43–5.

111 *C.S.P.D., 1671*, p. 86.

112 Ellis to [Rawdon], 27 June 1685; Farewell to Rawdon, 30 June 1685, in H.M.C., *Hastings*, ii, 395–7.
113 H.M.C., *Ormonde*, ii, 365, n.s., vii, 353; *C.S.P.D., 1685*, p. 272; Childs, *The army, James II*, p. 72. Individuals like Lord Orrery had long been recommending 'severe penalties' (H.M.C., *Ormonde*, n.s., v, 138–9).
114 *C.S.P.D., 1685*, p. 284; H.M.C., *Ormonde*, vii, 355–6.
115 Roscommon to Ormond, 12 Oct 1685 in H.M.C., *Ormonde*, n.s., vii, 355–6, 371; Fairfax to Arran, 25 Aug. 1685 (N.L.I. Ormonde Papers, MS 2444, f. 369); Childs, *The army, James II*, p. 72.
116 Patrick Melvin, ed., 'Sir Paul Rycaut's memoranda and letters from Ireland, 1686–7', *Analecta Hibernica*, no. 27 (1972), pp. 138–9.
117 Newsletter, 21 Oct 1690, in H.M.C., *Le Fleming MSS*, p. 299.
118 McLysaght, *Ireland in the seventeenth century*, pp. 90–91.
119 T. C. Barnard, 'Crises of identity among Irish Protestants, 1641–85', *Past and Present*, no. 127 (1990), pp. 38–83; K. S. Bottigheimer, 'The Restoration land settlement in Ireland: a structural view', *I.H.S.*, xviii (1972), pp. 1–21; John Miller, *James II: a study in kingship* (London, 1989), pp. 210–33.

2

'Powder and Steel': the early eighteenth century

The trend identified during the Restoration era of intensified observation of the code of honour was continued in the first half of the eighteenth century. It is hazardous to offer a perspective on this process, but following a probable fall-off in the number of duels in the quarter-century after 1690, there was an increase in the disposition to duel in the late 1720s. As far as can be ascertained, the level of duelling remained fairly constant until the middle of the century, when there was a further palpable and visible increase. This occurred despite the high casualty rate that was a feature of duelling at this time and the existence of a current of opinion which repeatedly and insistently decried the code of honour as unchristian and uncivilised.

Duelling at a low ebb: the 1690s and afterwards

The ostensible relish with which military officers and landed gentlemen in Britain and Ireland endangered their lives in defence of their honour in the second half of the seventeenth century was a source of acute disquiet to many in both countries who disliked the code of honour and all it represented. Criticism of duelling rested on traditional religious and secular foundations. The former was represented by a diffuse group of moralists and clergymen who condemned duelling and the code of honour because it upheld a 'false religion' that was contrary to the law of God. One of the most forthright was John Hales, the Eton-based clergyman,

Richard Steele (courtesy of the National Library of Ireland)

who denounced the code of honour forthrightly as 'a great and hainous sin' and an affront to divine will:

> It is part of our profession, as we are Christians, to suffer wrong and disgrace . . . To set up another doctrine, and teach that honour may plead prescriptions against Christ's precepts, and exempt you from patient enduring of contumely and disgrace, you withstand Christ, and deny your vocation and therefore are unavoidable apostates.[1]

From Hales's vantage-point, and that of such clerical critics as Jeremy Taylor, Thomas Combar and Edward Wetenhall, those who sought to defend duelling as the legitimate response of gentlemen whose honour had been impugned were merely justifying sin and immorality. '*Drinking*, *gaming*, and *whores*, these are the rotten bones that he hid under *painted sepulchre* and title of *honour*,' Hales proclaimed defiantly.[2] Jeremy Taylor, the Church of Ireland Bishop of Down and Connor (1661–7) was more restrained. He condemned duelling as 'in fact . . . uncharitable, and . . . unreasonable, so much against all laws of God and man . . . that nothing can excuse it', while Edward Wetenhall, Bishop of Cork and Ross (1679–99), simply identified it as 'a sin now [1686] too prevalent'.[3] The observations of Hales, Taylor, Wetenhall and others reflect the implacable hostility of many clergy to duelling, but it had negligible influence on the aristocracy and military who were its main practitioners. This is true also of the Catholic Church, which condemned duelling as a hellish and detestable practice encouraged by the devil for the destruction of body and soul, and provided, at the Council of Trent, for the excommunication of duellists, seconds and spectators and forbade them burial in consecrated ground. The Society of Jesus incorporated opposition to duelling into its mission in early seventeenth-century Ireland, but because Tridentine doctrine on this issue registered little impact in Catholic France, it could not be expected to act as a deterrent in the less receptive climes of Ireland and England.[4]

As a consequence, the task of containing duelling remained, where it had rested for over a century, with the state. Like their predecessors, the later Stuarts continued to rely on sanction to keep the predilection of their nobility and military for duelling within bounds.[5] When, for example, the Duke of Ormond founded the Royal Hospital at Kilmainham in the 1670s to provide for invalid soldiers, one of its by-laws stipulated that 'any officer or soldier' that went 'forth to fight privately . . . shall be turned out of the hospital'.[6] As this indicates, military duelling remained a persistent and serious problem in the late seventeenth century, and in an effort to contain it James II's instruction to the Lords Justices in July 1685 to cashier officers involved in duelling incidents was subsequently included in the 'instructions' given to successive Lords Lieutenant and to Lords Justices on their appointment.[7]

There is some evidence to suggest that the authorities sought to take a stiffer line with duellists in the late 1680s,[8] but, like his predecessors, James II undermined his anti-duelling stance by responding favourably to appeals for clemency. In 1686 he ordered the reversal of an outlawry decree imposed on David Stanier for killing Sir William Throckmorton in a duel because the encounter was occasioned by 'a very high provocation'.[9] William III (1689–1702) did likewise. In 1697 he pardoned William Drummond for his role in a duel in Edinburgh in which two men died; four years later he reversed an outlawry imposed on John Young for killing John Carey in a duel because of his military record.[10]

The inability of successive monarchs to dissuade the aristocracy, gentry and military in Britain and Ireland from duelling demonstrates that the code of honour could not be legislated or prosecuted out of existence.[11] It would only wither and die when people chose not to duel. This was an option embraced by only a small minority in Ireland in the 1690s. It has been suggested that the only known Irish organisation to include opposition to duelling among its objectives — the Friendly Brothers of St Patrick — was reconstituted in the wake of the Williamite wars. The seventeenth-century origins of this body remain obscure, but it is believed a number of 'knots' were established by disbanded Williamite troops in order to encourage a less belligerent approach to the resolution of differences. The absence of records makes it impossible to assess the impact of the organisation in the early eighteenth century, but the increase in the number of challenges presented indicates that its impact was negligible.[12]

Compared with what was to follow, the number of recorded duels fought in Ireland in the quarter-century after the battle of the Boyne was modest. One of the main reasons for this was the exodus of thousands of Jacobites who had contributed to the creation of the tense political atmosphere in the 1670s and 1680s in which duelling flourished. Obviously, all of the so-called 'Wild Geese' were not enthusiasts of the code of honour, but some certainly were, as is demonstrated by the career of Peter Drake, the Jacobite adventurer and soldier, who was involved in five duelling incidents in France and Spain between 1706 and 1714. Most of these involved other soldiers. Three concluded without serious injury; one at Dunkirk in 1707 resulted in the death of a sergeant, while the most bloody was an affray at Tournai in 1706 involving thirteen soldiers in which three died and two were wounded.[13] Moreover, Drake's experiences pale into insignificance compared with those of Thomas Macnamara of County Clare, who, legend has it, fought thirty duels, mostly in France and Flanders, before he reached his twenty-fourth birthday. Most of what is written about Macnamara is undocumentable, and it is unlikely that he embarked on more than a fraction of the affairs of honour attributed to him.[14] However, his career and that of Peter Drake suggest strongly that the exodus of thousands of Jacobites was important in ensuring that *relatively* few duels were fought in Ireland in the three decades after 1690. A further factor was the decision of the Irish parliament in 1695 to debar Catholics by law from carrying arms without a licence.[15]

The religious and political tensions which had provided the stimulus for many duels in which Catholics participated in the 1670s and 1680s did not vanish after the surrender of the Jacobites at Limerick, but Catholics were involved in a small and diminishing percentage of encounters after that date. In 1695 at Mitchelstown Captain Newell, a Jacobite who had served in the army of James II, killed Edward Raymond, a local Protestant, in a duel that arose out of an altercation between Edward's father, Anthony Raymond, and Newell. In the following year two prominent Jacobites, Henry, Viscount Dillon, and Judge Denis Daly, met in Dublin, but their rencontre concluded without injury or loss of life when Daly disarmed his opponent. Some years later, on 14 May 1710, John Mandveille killed John Slatterie in a duel in County Tipperary; while John Fitzgerald, the brother of the Knight of Glin who was an active supporter of the Jacobite cause, earned the nickname *Seán na gComharc* (John of the Combats) because of his martial disposition.[16] These were not the only Catholics to take up arms in the cause of honour, but because those that did so were seen by Protestants to be behaving provocatively, and were frowned upon by their co-religionists,[17] only the most resolute or foolhardy were prepared to take the risk. As a consequence, with relatively few exceptions, the duels that took place in Ireland until the prohibition against Catholics bearing arms was relaxed in 1793 involved only Protestants.[18]

The fall-off in the number of duels fought in Ireland in the quarter-century after the battle of the Boyne was primarily the result of diminished opportunity rather than of diminished inclination, as the readiness of Irishmen in European armies to take up arms in defence of their honour attests. The same was true of Irishmen resident in England and its dependencies.[19] In November 1698 Colonel Richard Coote died as a result of a sword-thrust to the throat when he became embroiled in a duel with the notorious Lord Mohun.[20] Charles, fourth Earl of Orrery, fought and wounded Worthly, his fellow member of parliament for Huntingdon, in Hyde Park on 27 March 1701. Over a decade later the Belfast-born general, George Macartney, was Lord Mohun's second in the infamous Hyde Park encounter of November 1712 when Mohun and his opponent, James Douglas, the fourth Duke of Hamilton, were both fatally wounded. Indeed, it was alleged that Macartney was responsible for Hamilton's death, and a reward of £500 was offered for information leading to his arrest. Macartney managed to exculpate himself in 1716, after a four-year exile, but because he and Hamilton's second had also crossed swords, he was unable to eradicate the impression that he was an unprincipled duellist.[21] Elsewhere, Colonel Eldrington, the governor of the Caribbean island of Nevis, was too strong for Captain Chambers, a soldier on the Irish army establishment, when they disagreed over a bottle in Antigua in 1702. Others had worse experiences. In March 1713 a Mr Pyne from Ireland was killed in a duel in Chelsea Fields in London; while some months later Lucius O'Brien of Dromoland, the M.P. for County Clare, killed his companion and friend Colonel William Hickman in a duel on Hampstead Heath.[22] The O'Briens were enthusiastic duellists; in 1710 Christopher O'Brien, an army captain, dispatched Major Syms in Minorca. Another Irish officer fared less well when he drew on a gentleman following a jostling incident in London in 1724; he escaped with his life, but he was 'taken up' by the constable 'seriously injured'. Irish civilians had similar experiences. When Fitzpatrick and Grantham, 'two Irish gentlemen students in the law', fought a duel in Garden Court in the Temple in 1721, the former was killed and the other so severely wounded that his life was endangered.[23]

Incidents such as these, and that in which Richard Steele, the essayist, found himself embroiled in June 1700 when an Irish army officer named Harry Kelly threw a glass of wine in his face,[24] so influenced English consciousness as to give Irishmen the reputation of being inveterate duellists by the early eighteenth century.[25] Steele, of course, was of Irish background himself, and his encounter with Kelly ended without fatality, but the incident had a lasting impact on him, for he was ever afterwards a harsh critic of the code of honour in the *Spectator* and the *Tatler* magazines.[26] Steele's criticism of the emotionalism and irrationality that fuelled contemporary enthusiasm for what he called the 'tyrant custom' and 'false notions of honour' was strikingly different to the primarily religion-based criticism that had prevailed in the seventeenth century. But like it, he found that his celebration of Louis XIV for his ostensible triumph over duelling within his realm,[27] his censure of those monarchs who did not do likewise, and the harsh punishment he recommended for those who did duel, won him few converts.[28]

Slow recovery: duelling in early Georgian Ireland

In Ireland, meanwhile, the combination of political and military factors that contrived to keep duelling at low ebb in the aftermath of the Williamite wars gave way in the reign of George I to more visible enthusiasm for what James Trail of Belfast (echoing Steele) termed the 'false notion of honour'.[29] A survey of the main newspapers and a selection of manuscript and published primary material for the late 1710s and 1720s produced six reported duels in the four years 1716–19 and sixteen in the five years to 1730 (Table 2.1). This may not appear particularly significant, but the number of encounters in the late 1720s was greater than ever previously reported.

As this suggests, early Georgian Ireland was a relatively disorderly society in which the law struggled to prevail over the lawless,[30] and the disorderly character is reflected in the manner in which duels were fought. Early eighteenth-century duels were seldom precise *pro forma* observances of the duelling ritual. On the contrary, they were generally bloody and, not infrequently, vicious encounters in which ill-temper usually triumphed over etiquette. For example, when the Dublin justice of the peace Adam Cusack engaged his relation Lieutenant Brice following a disagreement at dinner in December 1716, the two men made no attempt to await until the following day as duelling etiquette recommended; they simply picked up their weapons, went outside and fought to a standstill; Brice died of his wounds the next day, and Cusack a few days later.[31] In May 1726, when Lieutenant James Smith quarrelled late one night in a tavern with Pat Kelly, the son of a prominent Dublin brewer, the two antagonists made their way to Ormond Quay, where they drew their swords and fought till Smith was run through the heart and Kelly so badly wounded he was adjudged past recovery.[32] These were exceptional events in that it was unusual for both principals in an encounter to lose or to run the risk of losing their lives. More characteristic were cases like that which took place in March 1718 when Scott, an attorney, and Eames, the son of an army major, met in Stephen's Green following 'some words . . . the night before' and Scott was killed by Eames' 'first push'.[33] Two weeks later, also in Stephen's Green, Duncan Spike died as a result of an encounter with a goldsmith named Young after the two had disagreed while drinking.[34]

In the last two incidents some attempt at least was made to follow the code of honour. This was not always the case. In the final years of Queen Anne's reign Thomas Mathew of Thomastown, County Tipperary, and his second *both* fought and seriously wounded two soldiers, Pack and Creed, who had provoked a quarrel in a tavern in Dublin. In April 1728, following a particularly divisive election in County Tipperary, a young ensign named Jones walked up to Colonel Dawson, struck him on the shoulder with his naked sword and 'bid the old rascal draw'. Dawson had little option but to comply, and he bested his antagonist in the swordplay that followed with a 'run through' the groin. Four years earlier a more blatant breach of duelling etiquette occurred in Dublin when a soldier worse for drink accosted Paul Reily, the son of Alderman Terence Reily, on Arran Quay in the company of a number of women whom he alleged were 'persons of ill fame'. Reily was incensed; he drew his sword and stabbed the soldier to death.[35] This was murder, and Reily, whose ultimate fate is unknown, was lucky if he escaped the gallows.

In less than clear-cut cases, it was normal practice for the survivor in a fatal duel to submit to due legal process. Theoretically this involved a coroner's inquest within a day or so of the duel's occurrence, and a full trial, generally before the Court of King's Bench or the local assizes, some months later. In all instances in which the duel was deemed to have been conducted within the rules that governed such encounters (as they were understood and practised in Ireland), the survivor was acquitted or found guilty of manslaughter in his own defence and set free. This was the experience of Peter Daly, the son of Judge Denis Daly, who killed Francis Power in 1718; of Henry Smith, an attorney from Smithfield, who killed the eldest son of Captain Richard Lee, a County Westmeath landowner, in 1719; of Henry Bellingham, who killed one of the Tisdalls of Dunleer in November 1725; and of James Burnsides, who killed John Cashel in Dublin in 1732.[36] In less straightforward cases, such as the quarrel in Waterford in which a customs officer named Charles Young killed his controller, Edward Harrison, and was found guilty of homicide in his own defence, the offender was pardoned.[37] In general, the legal procedures following a fatal duel in the 1710s, 1720s and 1730s were straightforward and, generally, lenient.

This was not how contemporaries perceived matters, however, and individuals on the margins of respectability who duelled could anticipate a testing experience. For instance, Young, the goldsmith who vanquished Duncan Spike in 1718, was kept in custody to await trial when he surrendered himself to Alderman Quin, though there was no allegation of unfair play. Many magistrates and sheriffs were inclined as a matter of course to commit the survivor in duels involving fatalities to prison, and for this reason many chose to go into hiding and to surrender themselves to the authorities only when it was clear that they need not await their date in court in confinement.[38] Indeed, in 1728 Colonel Dawson took flight when he learned from Ensign Jones's doctor that his opponent's life was in danger. Given the appalling condition of most Irish prisons, this was an understandable response. Moreover, since there was no automatic provision for bail and only the best-connected duellists (Hamilton Gorges of County Meath is one instance) did not experience problems in this respect, it is not surprising that many chose to delay their surrender to the authorities.[39]

In circumstances such as these, it paid to be well-connected, or to have influential friends to intercede on one's behalf. An especially well-documented example of this took place in 1725 when the leading English Whig William Pulteney, later Earl of Bath, interceded with the Lord Chancellor of Ireland, Richard West, on behalf of a young army captain, Nicholas Jones, who had killed the Hon. Colonel Nugent in a duel at Lucas's coffee shop in Dublin. According to Pulteney, Jones was 'forced to fight' by repeated provocations, and he requested West to ensure that he came to no harm as he was 'a particular friend of mine'.[40] It is not clear if West did as he was requested, but the court's decision was certainly acceptable; Jones was found guilty of manslaughter, which was virtually equivalent to an acquittal, since the defendant was released as a matter of course after such a verdict. Four years later, when John Mills of Nantes was imprisoned to await trial for killing a young Catholic hothead named Mullenaux in Galway, he had reason to be grateful for the help of Lord St George, who used his influence with Judge Michael Ward and others to secure his release on bail (in the teeth of protests from the prosecution) and the postponement of his trial until the arrival of witnesses from France.[41]

From these and the other cases referred to above, it is clear that few duellists found themselves in serious trouble with the law if they observed the code of duelling and followed the correct legal procedures. Nobody, be they peer or peasant, could take the law for granted, but in all cases in which the code of honour was broadly adhered to, the courts did not return a verdict other than manslaughter. However, the law was less supportive of those who sought to decline a challenge, as Jonathan Swift's *intime*, Knightly Chetwode of Woodbroke, Queen's County, learned to his cost. He appealed to the law authorities for support in 1721, during a difficult moment, and he was appalled by the apathetic response.[42]

The involvement in duels of individuals who made their living from goldworking, brewing, the law, trade and the revenue in the 1710s and 1720s indicates clearly that observance of the code of honour in early eighteenth-century Ireland was not confined to the Protestant landed elite which provided the bulk of the country's aristocracy. This was a testimony to the relative openness of the Protestant ruling elite that dominated Irish life in the eighteenth century, as well as to the less than rigid attitude of that elite to the practice of duelling. This is not to say there were no prominent casualties. Tisdall of Dunleer was killed by Henry Bellingham in an encounter which had its origins in an electoral row in Louth in 1725; John Slattery, the M.P. for Blessington, was killed in a duel fought with swords and pistols by Stephen Moore, the M.P. for Clonmel, in November 1726. Another parliamentarian, Samuel Boyse, the M.P. for

Bannow, was dangerously wounded in a duel in Waterford in 1729; while Henry Hayes, the son and heir of Captain William Hayes, a wealthy Dublin brewer, was killed by an army captain in a churchyard at Mornington, County Meath, in the same year.[43] The most socially eminent casualties were Brice Leeson, the eldest son of Joseph Leeson, the Dublin brewer and father of the Earl of Milltown, who was killed in Holland in November 1728 and Robert Southwell, the son of Thomas, first Baron Southwell, who was killed by Henry Luttrell in London in 1724.[44] However, if the reported cases represent an accurate guide to the pattern of duelling in the early eighteenth century, the number of craftsmen, professionals, middle-ranking soldiers and modest gentry who forfeited their lives in duels comfortably exceeded that of the upper gentry and aristocracy.[45]

Duelling was by no means open to all Protestants, however, for not alone did duels involving craftsmen and professional men receive greater attention from the authorities, they also attracted greater public censure. This can be illustrated by reference to the altercation, which caused a sensation at the time, between William Todd, an attorney, and his relative, Pierce Rice, in 1730. Rice's occupation and social status cannot be definitely established, but considering that the row which ended with his death began over a card game at the Golden Bottle Inn in St Nicholas Street and that the two came to blows there, it is fair to conclude that the adversaries did not conform easily to the contemporary definition of what constituted a gentlemen. This evidently was the view of the authorities, because they charged Todd with murder. However, when it emerged in court that Rice was the aggressor, that he had slapped Todd and accused him of attempting 'to wrong' him, and that Todd, in return, had endeavoured to heal the breach, the jury had no hesitation in returning a 'not guilty' verdict.[46]

It could be argued that because the Irish Protestant ruling elite was small and still developing in confidence in the early eighteenth century, it was inevitable there should be some uncertainty, particularly at the intersection between the upper and middle classes, as to precisely who was permitted the privilege of resolving differences by recourse to arms. This may account for some duels, but the unique social structure of Ireland was more important. Because of the privileged position their religion guaranteed them in Ireland, each male Irish Protestant was encouraged to perceive himself as part of a political and social elite, and this served to encourage a wider social catchment to duel than might otherwise have been the case. This probably accounts for the presence of pettifogging attornies and minor customs officials on the duelling roll of honour. However, it should also be noted that elsewhere in eighteenth-century Europe duelling was not the exclusive preserve of an aristoctratic *corps d'élite*. In France, for example, duelling became reasonably commonplace among elements of the rising middle class as the once definite barriers separating the aristocracy from the rest of society grew progressively less rigid.[47]

A further convincing pointer to the extent of the embrace by Irish Protestants in the early Georgian era of what Dr Allured Clarke termed 'the shadow of honour and the silly tyranny of custom'[48] is provided by the readiness with which they cited the concept of 'honour' in cases of personal slight. Lord Mayo did so in 1719 when he demanded, and received, an apology from Arthur Ormsby for an allegation made during the hearing of an election petition in the House of Commons that Mayo's supporters were in the 'Popish interest'.[49] James Trail in Belfast noted the same disposition among gentlemen in the north-east in the same year, while the young William Wray demonstrated that this disposition was equally strong in County Donegal by demanding 'speedy satisfaction' from his neighbour Charles Stewart of Horn Head because, he claimed, he had 'been affronted publicly in the face of my county' by a less than neighbourly gesture by Stewart. Wray's upset stemmed specifically from his conviction that because his 'honour is att stake', the only way he could 'have justice done' was by challenging and meeting his traducer.[50] There is no evidence that Stewart took up Wray's challenge. But the preparedness of a young man (he was twenty-four) with a university education to call out his elderly neighbour confirmed what most already realised, that the code of honour was firmly established in the value system of the ruling Protestant interest in Ireland before the end of the reign of George I.

'The shadow of honour': duelling in the 1730s and 1740s

Despite the high percentage of fatalities arising from the duels fought in Ireland during the early Hanoverian period, the conduct of Irish duellists remained a long way short of the refinement recommended by the custodians of the code of honour. A significant number of the thirty or more duels fought between 1730 and 1750 corroborate Sean Connolly's observation that Irish society in the second quarter of the eighteenth century was tolerant of, if not indulgent towards, the 'habits of violence among sections of the social elite'.[51] For some, indeed, the duel was less a means by which a gentleman could defend his reputation against insult, than an opportunity to exact vengeance. In a small number of instances what passed for duels bear closer comparison with assassinations than with ritualised combats. In a further and larger number duelling etiquette was more honoured in the breach than in the observance.

One of the commonest means by which Irish duellists in the 1730s and 1740s infringed the code of honour was by failing to allow a decent interval to elapse between the issuing of a challenge and the holding of the encounter. The rationale for delay was that it distanced duelling from criminal behaviour and demonstrated the principled nature of gentlemen and the code of honour they observed. However, many individuals who conceived of themselves as gentlemen found this provision impossible to observe, and they generally escaped punishment because of the willingness of the legal system to give them the benefit of every doubt. A good illustration of this is provided by the encounter that took place at Arklow in October 1738 when George Johnston and Sir William Baker clashed after church and Johnston insisted that Baker 'fight or die'. Baker fought and killed his antagonist, and was absolved by the jury at the County Wicklow assizes, which returned a verdict of manslaughter in his own defence, when the case came for trial.[52] Two years later John Lynch, a Galway merchant, was found guilty of the more serious offence of manslaughter-at-large and ordered to be burnt in the hand following a row at the playhouse between himself and Charles Lewis, a stock officer, which resulted in a duel at the theatre door in which Lewis was killed.[53] Such incidents were always likely to happen, because not alone did gentlemen carry weapons, but many, like the gentlemen of Youghal described by Aland Mossom, were 'so quarrelsome that they never walk[ed] the streets without a case of pistols in their pockets and . . . they . . . won't be bound over'.[54]

This disposition to quarrel was not exclusive to gentlemen. It permeated virtually all levels of male society. In 1733 a difference over a greyhound culminated in 'a bloody action' near Mitchelstown between Newall, who was Lord Kingston's gamekeeper, and one of the Raymonds. There was a long tradition of ill-feeling between these two families, and these two antagonists were so incensed on this occasion that

> they entered the lists on horseback with sword and petronel; . . . [Newell] having discharged at and missed . . . , the other rid up to his breast but missed fire, whereupon he [Raymond] immediately dismounted and drew, as Newell did the like, and having made some sasas at each other, both received some slight wounds, but still the combat lasted, till at length one of Raymond's spurs got hold of his stockings, whereby he fell on his face to the ground, at which the other stabbed him through the back, and [he] not long after expired.[55]

Engagements of such viciousness were rare. But they were the inevitable product of a society in which the law was applied unevenly, and individuals, particularly landlords, were able not merely to set the law at defiance but, on occasions, to ensure it was applied in a manner that benefited them.[56] For instance, when Harry St Lawrence visited Kilbrew, County Meath, the family seat of the Gorges, in January 1737, he was so offended when Hamilton Gorges called a companion of his sister-in-law, Lady Howth, silly, that he challenged him to a duel. Unwilling to wait till dawn, the two antoganists engaged at midnight behind closed doors without seconds present. Luckily for St Lawrence, Gorges, who was fatally wounded, lived long enough to absolve him of any wrongdoing, with the result that both the coroner's inquest and the courts returned verdicts of manslaughter in his own defence and St Lawrence went unpunished.[57] In view of this, it should come as no surprise that retainers like Raymond and Newall should imitate their superiors' disposition to resolve differences by recourse to arms. In another incident in County Armagh in April 1740, Lorimer, the receiver of Sir Arthur Acheson, died as a result of a duel with an army officer at Market Hill.[58]

A more blatant and infamous breach of duelling etiquette took place in Galway in July 1733 when Robert Martin killed Lieutenant Henry Jolly. The occasion was this. Martin was walking past a coffee-house and billiard-room when he was hit by expectoration which came from within the building. Enraged by what he believed was a deliberate insult, he stormed into the coffee-house, sword in hand, and demanded satisfaction from whoever was responsible. Captain Edward Southwell, who was playing billiards with Lieutenant Jolly, confessed he was the guilty party and offered his apology. Martin refused to accept it and, insisting he was owed 'further satisfaction', demanded that Southwell (who was unarmed) return to his barracks to retrieve his sword so that the two of them could settle the matter like gentlemen. Southwell did as requested, but in his absence Jolly made some derisive comments which prompted Martin to approach him threateningly. Jolly felt so intimidated that he held up a chair in a defensive posture between Martin and himself, but this only provoked Martin to thrust his sword repeatedly at and through the chair. As a result, Jolly received several fatal wounds from which he died.

Martin's conduct was so outrageous that the authorities authorised a crown prosecution for murder. However, there were a number of obstacles in the way of a fair trial. If the case was heard in County Galway, where Martin owned extensive property, it was anticipated that no jury that could be assembled would return a guilty verdict. The sheriff, for one, was determined that Martin should be acquitted, and the panel of jurors he nominated for the trial reflected this. According to one report, it consisted 'chiefly of relations . . . Papists, or such Protestants as were either . . . confined to their houses by sickness or absent from the kingdom'. Because of this, the law officers at Dublin Castle determined that the trial should be transferred to the capital. Martin was brought to Dublin under armed guard in January 1735 to face an unusually long trial (eleven hours), at the end of which the Dublin jury brought in a not guilty verdict though it 'went directly against the charge of the court' and elicited 'severe reprimands from every one of the judges'. Upon Martin's fulfilling the bail requirement, he was released on 10 May 1735 to plead His Majesty's pardon.[59]

Robert Martin was lucky. The law authorities had ordered the transfer of his trial to Dublin in the belief that a Dublin jury would find him guilty. Things did not work out as they hoped in this instance, but ten years later a jury might have taken a less lenient attitude. In April 1744 James Farlow was tried at Limerick assizes for the murder of John Warwick in a duel. Farlow protested his innocence. He claimed that 'Mr Warwick, giving him the lye, took up a pistol before he touched his and presented it at him before he shot'. The judge and jury was not persuaded by his testimony; they found Farlow guilty and sentenced him to death.[60] This was unusual. Most eighteenth-century juries were inclined to return verdicts sympathetic to the survivor, regardless of whether the duel was irregular or not. However, at some point in the late 1730s or early 1740s the authorities may have determined that they could no longer indulge abuses of the code of honour. If so, James Farlow was a little-known victim of this policy; the prosecution of Richard, Earl of Anglesey, at the County Kildare assizes at Athy in August 1744 for assaulting James Annesley and three of his retainers, Daniel Mackercher, Hugh Kennedy and William Goostry, at a race-meeting at the Curragh in the previous September indicated that the authorities were disinclined to look more favourably upon the excesses of those of a higher social station.

This is not the place to review the labyrinthine course of the bitter struggle between the Earl of Anglesey and James Annesley to secure possession of the Anglesey title and estates.[61] What is significant for present purposes is that at the Curragh meeting the Earl of Anglesey tried to provoke his opponent into a duel and encouraged his followers to attack and assault Annesley and Mackercher in an attempt to settle the matter once and for all. The trouble began when Anglesey publicly described Mackercher as 'a rogue, scoundrel and villain' in second-hand finery. In normal circumstances this insult would have been enough to prompt a challenge, but Mackercher declined to be provoked. This only caused Anglesey and his retainers to behave more offensively. His coachmen, in particular, persisted in calling Annesley a 'shoeboy'. Mackercher was so convinced that Anglesey had authorised this insulting behaviour for a reason that he approached the peer and asked to speak to him. Anglesey evidently interpreted Mackercher's actions as a challenge (Mackercher was wearing a pistol), for he asserted that the moment was not opportune as he was unarmed. Mackercher, for his part, was ready, as he admitted in court, to settle the matter with weapons, so instead of withdrawing he demanded that the earl strip his coachman of his livery and turn him off the course for insulting his client. Anglesey was so enraged by what he deemed a gross impertinence that he took up his coachman's cry and publicly labelled Annesley 'a shoeboy, a blackguard and a thief'. Matters were now very tense, and they were exacerbated by the intervention, while Anglesey and Mackercher were trading insults, of Francis Annesley of Ballysax, one of Lord Anglesey's retainers, who struck Mackercher with his whip. This was a traditional invitation to an opponent to issue a challenge, but instead of accepting the opportunity Mackercher responded in kind, and recognising that an already ugly situation could only get worse if he stood his ground (he had been given information that Lord Anglesey planned to kill him and James Annesley), he slipped away to look for the claimant. He found him, and the two men rode off pursued by a number of Anglesey's retainers, who had been exhorted by their patron to 'follow the son of a ———, and knock his brains out'. Annesley escaped, but it was a close-run thing, as he was knocked unconscious by a fall from his horse while in full flight.

This extraordinary sequence of events highlights once again just how close at times the connection could be between blatant criminality and legitimate duelling in the first half of the eighteenth century. No duel actually took place on this occasion, but it was clearly identified by the Earl of Anglesey as a potentially useful means to rid himself of a problem that threatened his patrimony. Matters did not work out as he had hoped, however, and the courts took a dim view of his actions at the trial that followed. That said, the decision simply to bind him to keep the peace for assaulting Mackercher and two others was hardly sufficient to deter him from similar behaviour in the future.[62]

A further illustration of how narrow the margin could be in the first half of the eighteenth century between legitimate duelling and conspiracy to murder, and of the resolve of the law to punish abuses in the way duels were conducted, is provided by the affair of honour between John Browne of the Neale and Robert Miller of Milford that took place at Kilmaine, County Mayo, in January 1747. The cause of this altercation was John Browne's objection to the rule of the loyalist True Blue Club of Kilmaine which prohibited membership to anyone 'who had a great grandfather of the popish religion'. Browne was a first-generation Protestant (he conformed in 1729), and he took violent exception to the regulation, which he deemed personally slighting. He informed his relation Robert Miller, one of the founders and a former president of the club and a former high sheriff of the county, on 20 January 1747 that he was 'as favourably attached to the present establishment in church and state as anyone of your Club', and he requested him to have the rules amended so that he and others like him could become members. This put Miller in a difficult position, and he attempted initially to make light of the matter. The club, he stated in his reply to Browne, was simply a social group that met once a year. More pertinently, he pointed out that though he and the other founders had not intended to insult or to exclude Browne when they had drafted the rules, it was not in his power to change them. This did not appease Browne. Indeed, he was so angered by Miller's reply, which, he maintained, was 'an affront to me and my family', that he requested Robert Lyndsay to present Miller with a challenge to meet him at Turlough if he did not resign from the club or have its rules altered.

While he awaited Miller's answer, Browne readied himself for the encounter he anticipated would follow. He had no bullets, so he melted down and cast some shot into slugs, though this was an infringement of duelling etiquette. He also practised his shooting, though this too was contrary to rule, while his retainers scoured the locality for whatever weapons they could lay their hands on. This too was not normal practice, but Browne, who according to Robert Lyndsay was 'quite mad' with anger, was determined that Miller would not leave Turlough alive. And to ensure this he gave instructions to ten of his retainers to take up positions around the duelling field and to kill Miller if he failed to accomplish the task himself.

When Browne and Miller gathered at the appointed place at 2 p.m. on the afternoon of Thursday 21 January, Browne reiterated his demand that the rules of the True Blue Club be amended. Miller replied that it was not in his power to do this, whereupon Browne raised his pistol and fired before Miller was ready. He missed, but so too did Miller's reply, whereupon Browne raised his second pistol, once again before Miller was ready, and this time he scored a direct hit, and his opponent fell to the ground fatally wounded. However, instead of manifesting concern, as was expected of duellists in these circumstances, Browne was unable to conceal his feelings of anger and contempt; he threw his pistol at his dying opponent, leaped on his horse and rode away.[63]

Browne's conduct, like that of Robert Martin, posed the authorities with a problem. They were increasingly irritated by the abuses of the code of honour and by the failure of duellists to operate within the generous parameters allowed them. The sentencing of James Farlow to death in 1744 had not persuaded the military or the nobility to mend their ways, and they were determined for this reason that Browne should not escape unpunished lest his example tempted others to similar actions. The

Attorney General, St George Caulfield, was persuaded, on reviewing the evidence, that Browne was 'in strictness guilty of murder', and he determined that Browne and a number of his retainers should be brought to trial. Eaton Stannard, the Recorder, concurred and advised that because Browne had fled the country for The Hague, the case should be heard before the Court of King's Bench in Dublin, where the jury would be less disposed to acquit the defendant.[64] Once the trial date was determined, Browne returned from abroad in January 1749 and surrendered himself to the high sheriff of County Mayo to await his court appearance. The trial itself was unremarkable. Browne was 'attended by a great number of nobility and gentry', and the jury brought in the hoped-for verdict of not guilty of murder. However, he was found guilty of manslaughter-at-large. This was a more serious offence than manslaughter in self defence, which was the usual verdict in duelling cases, and the judge sentenced him to spend six months in prison and be burnt in the hand.[65]

By the standards normally applied in such cases, this was a stern sentence. It indicated that in cases where the rules of duelling were infringed, judges in the late 1740s were not prepared to let offenders escape unpunished. And if there were any doubts about this in gentlemen's minds, they must have been dispelled a few months later when the judge at Roscommon assizes sentenced Lieutenant Tucker to be burnt in the hand and to ten months' imprisonment for killing Lieutenant Weeks in a duel. Tucker and Weeks had quarrelled at Athlone, but instead of waiting until the next morning to settle their differences, they fought there and then with knives, as a result of which Tucker died. The local coroner returned a verdict of 'wilful murder' when the case came before him, but this judgment was overturned in favour of manslaughter-at-large at the assizes.[66] A year earlier, another coroner, this time in County Tipperary, returned a verdict of 'wilful murder' against Edward Nugent Shanaghan for killing John Perry, because the attempt of Perry's second to reconcile the parties had been obstructed by Thomas Long, Shanaghan's second. However, when this case came to trial, a specially 'packed' jury of gentlemen found Shanaghan guilty of manslaughter only and acquitted Long 'after a very short stay'. There was never any question that Long would be penalised, since the Lord Lieutenant, the Earl of Harrington, had signalled before the court case that he would pardon him should the jury find him guilty.[67]

In the absence of the relevant legal records, it is not possible to say for certain if the sterner than usual verdicts returned by coroner's and the law courts in the late 1740s flowed from a decision by the law authorities to clamp down on abuses of the right to duel as a consequence of an increase in the number of encounters coming to public notice (Table 2.1). There is certainly evidence to suggest that this was not so. We have, for example, the evidence of the preparedness of the authorities to offer pardons and to show no disfavour towards duellists who were well-connected. For instance, when Sir Robert King and Captain Johnston exchanged shots without effect in May 1748, Johnston was not only not prosecuted but was observed 'at the Castle' within a few days of the incident.[68] As against that, it is striking that 11 of the 34 duels known to have taken place between 1731 and 1750, went to trial, compared with two out of a total of 50 cases in the fifteen years 1751–65 (Table 2.6). It is true that in virtually all of the cases that were tried, juries returned verdicts of manslaughter; indeed, in a number of instances the accused was 'honourably acquitted' or described by the judge as having behaved in a manner 'becoming a man of honour'.[69] However, the ordeal of having to flee the country to avoid imprisonment if the duel was irregular, or of awaiting trial in prison if flight was rejected, and the possibility, remote though it was, of a hostile verdict, may have led some to decline presenting or accepting challenges. It is hardly completely fortuitous that the rise in the number of duels taking place after 1750 coincides with a reduction in the prosecution of duellists. The authorities at Dublin Castle in the 1730s certainly perceived a connection, as they advocated the prosecution of those who challenged law officers as a matter of course. Thus when Arthur Rochfort, a justice of the peace in County Meath, was challenged in 1737 by Thomas Nugent of Donore, a convert to Protestantism, and his second Hugh Maguire, 'a papist', following Rochfort's conviction of one of Nugent's servants for poaching and carrying arms, the Attorney General initiated a prosecution, backed by the Lords Justices. For a number of years thereafter, it became official policy 'for preserving the peace of the country, to prosecute any persons indifferently that demand satisfaction of any magistrate for putting the laws in execution'.[70]

It is not clear if this policy was responsible for the high proportion of prosecutions in duelling cases in the 1740s. There certainly appears to have been a change of heart by the early 1750s, since such prosecutions had all but ceased and pardons were readily available. When Ensign Shaw was threatened with prosecution for his role as second in a controversial duel in Cork in 1752 in which a local merchant lost his life, the Lord Lieutenant, the Duke of Dorset, was persuaded by the Duke of Cumberland, who took up Shaw's case, to signal his intention to grant him 'a reprieve' should he be tried and found guilty.[71]

High-level representations, such as occurred in this and other cases,[72] provide a salutary caution against expecting too much from the Irish judicial system in the early eighteenth century. As the Martin–Jolly, the Browne–Miller and other incidents bear witness, many gentlemen possessed a distinctly ambivalent attitude towards the law. The perceptive mid-century Chief Baron of the Court of Exchequer, Edward Willes, described this well when he lamented 'the frequent practice of disobedience to the civil process of law and an open and violent resistance to the civil magistrate'. Willes endeavoured to counter this by 'convinc[ing] gentlemen that it is for the public service . . . to be assisting to putting the laws in force and of requiring obedience to them', but he registered only modest success.[73] The legal system of itself could not change society nor the law change attitudes in those parts of the country where the law was flouted and obstructed virtually as a matter of course. In large parts of Iar-Chonnacht, where Robert Martin's estates lay, 'neither the law nor the gospel do', the Archbishop of Tuam, Josiah Hort, observed dolefully in 1749. The commissioners of the revenue concurred; they declined even to put the area 'under their care and inspection'.[74]

This disposition to obstruct the legal system which inhibited any attempt the authorities might undertake to eradicate illegal behaviour among gentlemen was manifested even more vividly in County Tipperary. In 1738 five local 'gentlemen (as gentlemen go in this part of the country)', who chased Lieutenant John Hume round a tavern in Roscrea before slashing him to death, were able for a time to frustrate the law because of the protection afforded them by their neighbours and the disinterest of the sheriff, despite the judgment of the coroner's inquest that this was a case of 'wilful murder'.[75] David Hepburne, who was an acquaintance of the deceased, explained:

> I . . . perceive a strong tendency to that partiality most people have to their friends and neighbours in the country to the prejudice of justice . . . It is too well known how easily evidences to serve a turn are to be had . . . I greatly question the appearances of those for the crown . . . at next assizes. The maid of the house who knew more of the matter than anyone was spirited away the morning the coroner's inquest sate, nor is there any but personal security required of those that appear'd at the inquest to appear at the tryal, which, God knows, is little to be depended on . . . The friends of the murtherers are beginning already to tamper with the evidence for the Crown. They have rais'd a story that Mr Hume was kill'd by our own people and I doubt not of their finding evidence to swear it.[76]

However, the authorities were not completely bereft of public support or resources, and previous accounts of this incident have failed to note that they not alone pursued those responsible for Hume's death but secured the capital punishment of his main assailant. Their first action in November/December 1738 was to issue a proclamation offering a reward for the apprehension of John Leadwell, who had wielded the murder weapon. This did not produce immediate results, but the net gradually tightened round Leadwell and he was captured in February 1740 (some eighteen months after Lieutenant Hume's murder) in a house at Clouneykenny, near Roscrea, after a violent struggle in which one of his pursuers was killed. A month later he was brought to trial and was sentenced to be executed and gibbetted.[77]

The capture and conviction of Leadwell, like the trials of Robert Martin and John Browne, emphasises that gentlemen, for all their influence and privileges, were not above the law. There were, as already acknowledged, areas like Iar-Chonnacht, parts of south Kilkenny, south Tipperary, west Kerry and mid-Tyrone where the law was not properly enforced.[78] But their number and significance should not be over-emphasised; they were the geographical equivalent of exclusive social interests like the Protestant ruling elite who chose to defy the law by duelling, and like duellists they existed because the authorities were able to reconcile themselves to the imperfection of a situation in which the writ of law did not prevail equally geographically or socially. There is plenty of evidence to demonstrate both habitual defiance of and disregard for the law by members of the Protestant elite in early eighteenth-century Ireland, but it never threatened to degenerate into general lawlessness, perhaps because its perpetrators included some of the most influential figures in the land. This was one of the reasons duelling was tolerated. Thus in May 1745 the former M.P. for the borough of Carysfort, Viscount Allen, died as a result of wounds he received in a rencontre with one of the guards at Dublin Castle, while in the following year Robert, Lord Belfield, was involved in a duel with Richard Herbert, the M.P. for Ludlow, in London over a 'debt of honour' in which the latter was seriously injured. Four years later, in April 1750, one of the Commissioners of the Revenue, John Burke, was only dissuaded on the duelling field from fighting Colonel Butler as a result of a difference over spinning-wheels. Also in 1750, Viscount Allen's cousin and successor, Lord Allen, and Captain Eustace were tried at the County Kildare assizes for their part in an affray which cost another Butler his nose and which threatened, Under-Secretary Waite apprehended, to provoke a feud between Allen's and Butler's relations, while in 1751 Edward Deane of Terenure, the M.P. for Inistiogue, was killed in an encounter with Major General Thomas Pigott of Knapton, Queen's County. Meanwhile, in County Kerry, Richard, Knight of Glin, who conformed to the Church of Ireland in 1740, fought a number of duels and cultivated the 'hero' image it gave him.[79] In the light of this and the incidents considered above, the most striking feature of mid-eighteenth-century Irish society was not the inability of the law authorities to control the aggressive propensities of their landed and military elites but the unstable equilibrium that existed between law and order and lawlessness and disorder in society as a whole.

Public opinion and duelling in the early eighteenth century

The inability of the law to do much more than encourage duellists to eradicate abuses in the way they conducted themselves in duelling encounters if they wished to avoid legal complications pained the rather slim ranks of the opponents of the code of honour in early and mid-eighteenth-century Ireland. Occasionally a bishop of the Church of Ireland would include duelling with infidelity and profanity among a list of transgressions of 'God's ordinances' which all self-respecting Christians should endeavour to eradicate, but the church was too closely bound to the Protestant elite that sustained duelling to engage in an energetic campaign of opposition.[80] The Presbyterian Church was less confined in this respect, and it played an important part in forging the ethos which ensured that Ulster produced the smallest number of recorded duels of the four provinces (Table 2.2). But even Presbyterians were not completely immune to the duelling impulse. The General Synod felt compelled in 1744 to rebuke William Armstrong of the presbytery of Strabane for 'scandalous' conduct for 'having challenged, or accepted a challenge to a duell and going to the place of combat armed with sword and pistol'.[81]

In the main, opposition to duelling was founded on the conviction that its eradication would benefit society. Only the occasional misanthrope felt it should be allowed to continue. Dean Swift, for example, was so little concerned with the fate of duellists that he felt they should be allowed continue exterminating each other.[82] More orthodox expressions of unease were articulated by the fifth Earl of Orrery, who resided in Ireland for most of the 1730s and 1740s. A refined and rather sensitive figure who seems out of place in the rough and tumble of Irish life, Orrery deplored the enthusiasm Irishmen showed for alcohol as well as for duelling, which made him fear for his own life. 'Mars must resign to Bacchus in blood and slaughter,' he observed despondently in the aftermath of the St Lawrence–Gorges encounter.[83] Taking the refinement and sophistication of the salons of London as his standard, Orrery attributed the Irish enthusiasm for duelling to the fact that the two countries were at different and unequal stages of development. He outlined his views to one of his English acquaintances in May 1736:

> You are slaves amidst civil'd people; we are slaves amidst bears and tygers; arts and sciences flourish with you; ignorance reign with us. Your island is fill'd with woods, fine seats, and ornaments collected from all parts of the world, but here we see nothing but bogs, desert plains, or an awkward imitation of what is now distinguish'd by the word taste. Yet this, bad as it

> is, may be borne more patiently than the manners and customs of the people. Drunkenness is the touchstone by which they try every man, and he that cannot or will not drink has a mark set upon him . . . It is a Yahoo that toasts the glorious and immortal memory of William III in a bumper without any other joy in the Revolution, than that it has given him a pretence to drink so many more daily quarts of wine. The person who refuses a goblet to this prevailing toast is deemed a Jacobite, a Papist, a Knave . . . Commonsense is as dangerous here as temperance, and both are utter obstacles to preferment or interest in this kingdom.[84]

Though the contrasts are clearly overdrawn, Orrery was, in effect, attributing the enthusiasm of the Protestant ruling elite in Ireland for duelling to what Sean Connolly maintains was the intrinsic provincialism of early eighteenth-century Irish Protestant society. It was, Connolly contends, a society whose key feature was 'the uneven penetration of a provincial elite by the standards of metropolitan society', with the result that the behaviour of that elite 'lagged some distance behind that seen in the main centres of taste and refinement'.[85] For this reason, the practice of duelling provides as accurate and as partial a mirror to early eighteenth-century Irish society as the better-known drawing-room milieu chronicled by Mary Delany and others. Ireland and Irish society in the 1730s and 1740s, when Orrery made his observations, was struggling to cast off the seventeenth-century legacy of war and rebellion and to overcome the enormous economic travails visited upon it in the second quarter of the eighteenth century. It was a society that was perched between confidence and caution, recession and recovery, famine and plenty, law and anarchy, refinement and boorishness. Economic conditions and public confidence improved markedly once the country escaped the clutches of famine in the 1740s, and this resulted in more rather than fewer affairs of honour. As Table 2.1 indicates, the number of duels rose in the late 1740s as the code of honour was embraced by ambitious gentry, aspiring middlemen and men on the make, who were anxious to be accepted as gentlemen by their peers.

These 'half-mounted gentlemen', to appropriate Barrington's celebrated later phrase, led pretty rough-and-ready existences, as Richard Cumberland, Mrs Delany and Dudley Bradstreet (who was not unrepresentative of the type) bear witness. Though generous hosts, they frequently lived in ramshackle residences because they had neither the money to pay for improvements nor the inclination to imitate metropolitan fashions.[86] Their milieu was the antithesis of the literary salon frequented by the likes of the Earl of Orrery; indeed, Richard Cumberland noted that the County Clare gentlemen he visited had few or no books. Consequently, they were unlikely to be aware of, never mind receptive to, the criticism of the code of honour incorporated into works like Richardson's *Clarissa* and *Sir Charles Grandison* which were avidly read in more polite circles.[87]

Samuel Madden, who in 1738 published the influential reformative tract *Reflections and resolutions proper for the gentlemen of Ireland* in which he deplored the fact it was, in his words, 'safer to kill a man [in a duel] than [to] steal a sheep or a cow', attributed this want of refinement of Irish gentlemen to the fact that they were the descendants of 'soldiers' and had 'inherited their stomachs as well as their courage'.[88] This is unsustainable, but it remained a popular point of view, as it was repeated in the *Freeman's Journal*, which was strongly critical of duelling, in the 1760s.[89] What is indisputable is that substantial numbers of gentry or gentlemen in early-eighteenth century Ireland found intellectual endeavour unappealing. They were men of action who were happier doing than thinking, and whose life revolved around their estates, their horses, their claret, their guns and, in some instances, their cards and their mistresses, and the diversions they brought — hunting, riding, drinking, gambling and womanising. This lifestyle was not to the taste of improvers like Madden and 'Jack Wildair' who deemed duelling 'ridiculous' and irrational, or to the religious-minded who deemed it a 'most audacious insult upon the laws of God and man',[90] but all calls for a 'reformation of manner' which would result in the eradication of gaming, swearing, sexual profligacy, excessive drinking and duelling fell on deaf ears. Indeed, there was no refuge for those who desired to abandon vice for 'religion, benevolence, generosity, affability and self-denial'[91] until the revival of the Friendly Brothers of St Patrick in 1750.

There is so little information on the history and personnel of the Friendly Brothers in the early eighteenth century that it is impossible to say with any confidence why it was reanimated at this time, but it may be that it was connected with an observable increase in the disposition to duel in the late 1740s and early 1750s. From what is known, it appears that the organisation was sustained in the early eighteenth century by Robert Broughton of Athenry, and that he played a key part in the reanimation that resulted in no fewer than twenty-one knots or branches being established in Ireland between 1750 and 1754. This process commenced at Athenry in 1750, but Dublin, which became the home of the prestigious General Grand Knot, quickly emerged as the headquarters of the order.[92] The formulation in 1750 and the publication in 1751 of the *Fundamental laws, statutes and constitutions* of the brotherhood, which defined the purpose of the society as 'to promote and encourage among men, the just observance of private and singular friendships', provided its *raison d'être*. And in keeping with this aspiration, it sanctioned a rule which decreed that 'no friendly brother shall affront or quarrel with a *continued member* of the order', and that all disputes should be resolved by mediation:

> If any member of this order, through the frailty of human nature, should have the misfortune so far to forget the love he owes his brother, and the obedience due to these statutes, as to proceed to anger with a *continued friendly brother*, and disturb the peace and tranquillity of the order, he shall not presume to decide his own quarrel, according to the laws of pretended honour, by the barbarous practice of duelling, unknown to the politest and bravest nations; but shall peaceably and with due obedience, submit his differences to the decision of his knot, who shall cause the offender to make sufficient and honourable attonement for his error, and the parties on both sides shall renew their friendship and, in all points, submit themselves to the friendly admonition and determination of their brethern, who shall judge on such occasions, without prejudice or favour.

Those who refused to observe this or the other rules of the order were liable to expulsion.[93]

This regulation against duelling, which survived the many revisions and amendments made to the brotherhood's rules over the next hundred years,[94] offered a peaceful way of resolving disputes of honour, but there is nothing to suggest that it was called into frequent use.[95] This is not to say that the order simply functioned as a social club. The various knots spread about the country attracted a socially eminent membership. As well as a substantial number of clergy and military officers, among those who became 'prefects' in the brotherhood between 1751 and 1794 were Sir Arthur Gore, Sir Richard Cox, Peter La Touche, Lord Knapton, Lord Mountgarrret, Earl Wandesford, the Duke of Leinster, Sir John Parnell, Henry Monk Mason, Richard Westenra, Sir Vesey Colclough, the Earl of Tyrone, Lord Kingsale and Cornelius Grogan. The most active members of the organisation came from the ranks of the gentry, higher professions and luxury trades rather than the peerage and large estate owners, but the brotherhood did include such well-known aristocrats as the Earls of Clanricarde, Aldborough and Arran, Lord Cavan and Sir Lucius O'Brien among its members.[96] The membership of the County Kildare knot, for example, reads like a 'who's who' of local life in the late eighteenth century. The Duke of Leinster, Lord Valentia, Thomas Conolly, Sir Fitzgerald Aylmer, Sir Kildare Burrowes, Sir Michael Cromie, Thomas Burgh of Oldtown, Sir James Tynte, Walter Hussey Burgh and Lords Henry, Charles and Edward Fitzgerald were all members of the brotherhood at one time or other, and since most members took its rules seriously, it seems reasonable to conclude that it offered some at least a modicum of protection from the harsh dictates of the code of honour.[97]

The nature of duelling in the mid-eighteenth century

Although the surviving evidence represents an incomplete record of what actually took place, an examination of a range of primary sources indicates that duelling increased in popularity during the eighteenth century. A tabulation of a sample of cases (Table 2.1) collected between 1716 and 1770 suggests that the level of duelling remained fairly constant until the 1750s, when there was an appreciable increase in the number of affairs of honour that proceded to term, and that this trend was sustained. There is no obvious explanation for this, but it was probably connected with the improving economic fortunes of the Irish ruling elite. By 1750 the country was well on the road to recovery from the experiences of famine and scarcity, depopulation and economic stagnation that characterised much of the twenty-year period 1725–45. In the third quarter of the eighteenth century substantial economic growth and buoyant exports boosted the financial position of landowners, middlemen and merchants, and this, in turn, prompted accelerated investment in building, infrastructural development and service industries.[98] The mid-eighteenth century also witnessed a dramatic rise in the number of pamphlets (including reprints of accounts of notorious English duels)[99] and newspapers seeking readers, as well as an increase in the number of playhouses and taverns competing for custom, and a growth in the consumption of everything from fashion to fine wines.[100] The Protestant ruling class in Ireland in the mid-eighteenth century exuded the confidence of an aristocratic elite by allocating a substantial percentage of their growing economic surplus to the replication and emulation of the style and tastes of their British and European neighbours.

Parallel with and indivisible from this, the mid-eighteenth century witnessed the invigoration of the urban mercantile interest and the emergence in the countryside of substantial numbers of middlemen who benefited considerably from the increase in economic activity and price inflation that accompanied it.[101] As a result, there was a substantial increase in the number of individuals who aspired to live the life of a gentleman and who possessed the wherewithal to sustain such pretensions.

As this implies, the main practitioners of duelling in the mid-eighteenth century were gentlemen. This pattern had been established in the early eighteenth century, when individuals so described provided one or both principals in 69 per cent of a sample of sixty-one duels recorded for the period 1716–50. Members of the military who had provided the bulk of duellists in the more militarised conditions of the late seventeenth century were involved in 30 per cent of these encounters, while individuals with a definable middle-class background (crafts and professional men) provided one or both principals in 21 per cent of these cases.[102]

This pattern underwent only marginal change in the mid-eighteenth century. Of the eighty-three duels involving Irishmen known to have taken place in the 1750s and 1760s, gentlemen provided one or both participants in 75 per cent of instances. Soldiers were involved in 23 per cent of cases, while members of what we can call the middle class (7 per cent) which includes lawyers (who had done nothing as yet to deserve their later reputation as notorious duellists) and the lower classes (6 per cent) were each involved in a modest percentage of the reported duels (Table 2.1). There are, of course, problems in defining precisely what these labels mean. Contemporaries used the word 'gentleman' in an elastic manner, and there is evidence to indicate that some of those in Ireland who deemed themselves gentlemen and who claimed the privileges of that status were barely able to keep up appearances. The *Dublin Evening Post* pointed out some years later:

> It is observable that in the remote parts of the kingdom, every man who is a degree above the plebian, looks upon himself as a gentleman — of course unquestionably qualified to fight any man . . . There are so many gentlemen it is amazing there are any yeomanry at all. The ill effects of this may be seen on contested elections when a party spirit breaks out and appeals are too often made to the pistols instead of the laws.[103]

It is certainly true that a significant proportion of those who duelled in Ireland in the mid-eighteenth century were not of the first rank of the nobility or gentry. Some of Barrington's 'half-mounted gentlemen', for example, were perched precariously on the lowest rung of the landed ladder. Unable with ease to maintain a genteel lifestyle and all that went with it (university education, foreign travel, a country mansion, a town house, political involvement, dowries, jointures and portions), they compensated for their lack of style with an exaggerated eagerness to risk their lives over trivialities. The fact that they were allowed to do so gave them a sense of belonging to the elite, though, paradoxically, most peers and politicians were more than willing to extricate themselves from 'scrapes' rather than risk their lives unnecessarily over a trifle. In the case of the dispute between the Earl of Kildare and George Faulkner in February 1754, this was entirely within the rules of the code of honour because of the disparity in rank between the two men; but in other cases in which political differences were at the root of disagreements, discretion clearly triumphed over valour.

The Kildare–Faulkner row was prompted by the publication by George Faulkner, the proprietor of the *Dublin Journal*, of a list of toasts drunk at a meeting in Dublin at which the Earl of Kildare was present, which included a toast to the Duke of Dorset, to whom Kildare was deeply antipathetic, but omitted 'the Glorious Memory'. Kildare was so upset by this misrepresentation that he 'charg'd [Faulkner] severely for daring to insert falsehoods with his name, and . . . solemnly threatened he would break what bones he [Faulkner] had left in his body if he did not . . . retract his error and publish the D[uke] of D[orset]'s health was not drunk'. Faulkner declined to accede to the demand, and a duel seemed the only possible outcome. However, the earl forbore to present a challenge, as he was entitled to do, and no duel ensued.[104]

As Table 2.1 indicates, the fervid political atmosphere in Ireland in the early 1750s contributed to the increase in the number of affairs of honour, though many of these were negotiated without the participants endangering their lives. For example, when Richard Boyle, the son and heir of Speaker Boyle, pulled Digges La Touche's nose and kicked him for some slighting reflections he made about his father, a duel seemed inevitable, but because La Touche chose not to take umbrage, no encounter resulted.[105] Some months later Arthur Rochfort, the M.P. for County Westmeath, challenged Edmund Sexton Pery, the M.P. for Wicklow, because Pery had insulted him, but once again no duel ensued because Primate Stone, Pery's mentor, successfully counselled caution.[106]

Pery was one of a new generation of ambitious politicians sharply critical of existing vested interests, and he found himself in trouble once again in January 1759 when he incautiously questioned the motives of Lord Drogheda, Sir Ralph Gore and others in raising regiments to support the crown's war effort against France. Informed of this, Lord Drogheda demanded 'an explanation' from Pery in the chamber of the House of Commons on the following day. This provoked a furore. M.P.s accused the peer of 'the highest insult and a breach of privilege in giving a member a challenge for what he spoke in the House', but a duel seemed unavoidable. Pery agreed under pressure from the assembled members not to challenge Drogheda, but refused to commit himself to 'decline any challenge' communicated to him. Eventually the whole unedifying episode was brought to an end when the Speaker, John Ponsonby, who was Drogheda's uncle, apologised to the house for his nephew's behaviour and assured M.P.s that he would 'not call upon Pery'.[107]

As this and Pery's previous difference with Arthur Rochfort attest, politicians who quarrelled were generally amenable to mediation if it could be accomplished in a manner that ensured they did not lose face. On occasions this necessitated the intervention of the most powerful figures in the land. In 1760 the Privy Council in London had to intervene to prevent a potentially momentous encounter between the Earl of Clanricarde and the Duke of Bedford. Clanricarde injudiciously maintained that when Bedford was Lord Lieutenant of Ireland he had engaged in a 'diabolical attempt' to effect a union. This was untrue, and the duke was so incensed by the allegation that he determined to seek satisfaction, and he would have done so but for the decision of the cabinet, which was informed of the affair by Richard Rigby, Bedford's former Chief Secretary, to order the Attorney General to prosecute Clanricarde for libel. The government did not want to see one of its highest office-holders being forced to risk his life over an unsubstantiatable allegation because of the alarming precedent it would set for all incumbents of political office. However, Rigby was not content to let the matter rest at that. He was determined to uphold his patron's dignity in the time-honoured fashion, and he dispatched a messenger to Clanricarde on 8 October inviting him to meet with pistols at Holyhead. The challenge was delivered, but no duel ensued because of Clanricarde's suspicion that it was a ruse to get him onto English soil where he would be arrested and brought to trial. There was no such plan and no prosecution, but Clanricarde did not escape scot-free. He was removed from the Privy Council in July 1761 and the dispute was eventually concluded three years later when Clanricarde tendered an apology.[108] Despite his provocative behaviour, Clanricarde was evidently at one with those who believed that it was not worth risking one's life over a quarrel. When Lord Kerry and Mr Leeson had a 'violent quarrel' at a *soirée* in 1762, everybody present feared it would end in a duel, but, once again, wiser councils prevailed.[109]

Examples such as these indicate that members of the Irish Protestant elite did not reach for their pistols at every available opportunity, and highlight that it was among the aristocracy that the greatest forbearance was shown. This point must be kept in perspective. There are too many well-established instances of influential and wealthy landowners duelling in the mid and late eighteenth century to invalidate facile conclusions, based on the above examples, that the cream of the Irish aristocracy ritually observed the code of honour but ensured that disagreements were not pushed to the extent that recourse to weapons became necessary. This was the outcome in a large number of political quarrels involving commoners and peers in the 1750s. However, in areas other than politics, Irish landlords had few qualms about appealing to arms if they believed the occasion warranted it. Loughlin O'Malley of Mayo, and Robert Martin and Stratford Eyre of Galway, for example, each got themselves into many duelling scrapes. According to a family memoir, which probably exaggerates, O'Malley fought nine duels, while the irrepressible Martin pursued Eyre to London on one occasion to defend his honour. Despite their broad acres, figures like O'Malley and Martin were closer in outlook and attitude to Barrington's 'half-mounted gentlemen' than to the peers and politicians that dominated the salons and corridors of power in Dublin, and they shared their ambivalent attitude towards the legal system.[110] The same is probably true of Jack St Leger who fought and killed Jack Hill on the Curragh in December 1753 following an altercation over 'an old play debt', though he came from a well-established family and was eventually to achieve judicial office.[111]

The problems associated with establishing the social station of those who duelled caused by the elastic contemporary usage of the term 'gentleman' pose fewer difficulties in the case of the military. In the main, duelling in the army was the preserve of low- and middle-ranking commissioned officers. Common soldiers and top-rank officers did duel on occasions, but both were less disposed to do so than lieutenants, captains, ensigns and cornets. Military duellists were as prone to fight each other as civilians, and they did so with the connivance of the military authorities, who made little effort to combat or to eliminate duelling from within the ranks. This was not a consequence of low casualties. On the whole, military duels tended to produce an above-average number of fatalities because the combatants were less disinclined to leave the field of fray until one was incapacitated or killed. Furthermore, because they were trained in the use of firearms and were generally skilled swordsmen, soldiers inflicted more injuries. This point can be illustrated by example,[112] but it is more vividly highlighted by Table 2.8, which summarises the outcome of twelve military duels which took place in the 1750s. Seven fatalities, four mortal wounds, six cases in which both parties were injured, and only one case in which there were no injuries was a heavy toll from twelve encounters. More than half of these duels involved only soldiers, but the military did not avoid civilians, and five of the twelve duels involved military and civilian participants. The civilians proved more than a match for their military opponents. As a result of the five encounters involving civilians and military, two soldiers were killed and two were mortally injured.[113] When Peter Daly esquire met Lieutenant John Lyons in the Phoenix Park in March 1754, Lyons was shot dead;[114] six months later William Sproule, a Dublin attorney, mortally wounded Lieutenant Alexander Jameson with a shot in the belly at the same location.[115] In only one of these encounters was a gentleman wounded, and then not seriously.[116] One concluded without injuries.[117]

The highest-ranking officer to fight a duel in the 1750s and 1760s was a lieutenant-colonel; he was seriously injured in his encounter with a captain.[118] At the other end of the military hierarchy, a small number of ordinary soldiers sought to imitate their superiors by having recourse to powder or steel to determine differences of opinion. For instance, when two horse soldiers, who disagreed at Maryborough in 1755, appealed to their pistols to settle a difference of opinion, one was killed. In September 1761 two soldiers from a light horse regiment stationed at Drogheda came to blows, as a result of which one (Christopher Mooney) was mortally wounded.[119] Duels between privates were of comparatively rare occurrence, and the military did what they could to discourage them. As well as that, there is evidence to suggest that rank- and-file soldiers were not as eager as their superiors to appeal to the judgment of weapons. They had their own ways of resolving disputes that did not necessitate recourse to firearms. When a dispute broke out between two soldiers at Cork in September 1756, they chose to settle it with fisticuffs rather than with weapons. The result was just as serious; one soldier died from the beating he received.[120]

As the last incident indicates, duelling was not a privilege of the elite imitated by all. However, there were plenty of people on the fringes of the social elite who chose to settle differences by duelling even though they could not be described as 'gentleman' by the application of even the most elastic definition of the term. A good illustration is provided by the duel that took place at Eyrecourt, County Galway, in January 1759 between 'two eminent tradesmen', Nicholas Donnelan and Laughlin Minican, in which the latter was killed.[121] Four years later a dispute between an engraver and a clockmaker in Dublin in which both parties conducted themselves 'with the greatest spirit' was concluded without injury.[122] Approving comments such as this seldom appear in the published reports of such encounters. By and large, news reports of duels sought to affirm the widely shared conviction that duelling was the preserve of the landed and ennobled elite, because they alone knew how to conduct themselves appropriately. And duelling reports, like the following example, reinforced such beliefs:

> This evening [16 March 1767] a duel was fought at the upper Red House between two young men, bakers; the pistols were charged before their faces with powder and ball; they both trembled shockingly before they fired, but to their agreeable surprise, their lives were saved by their humane seconds, who took the opportunity of drawing the balls and putting dough in their stead.[123]

This was not a unique incident. A year previously a journeyman baker and a journeyman hairdresser charged their pistols with dough and hard pometum when they met in the Phoenix Park.[124]

Most of the reported rencontres between individuals who were not gentlemen took place in Dublin. This accords with what we can establish of the geographical distribution of duelling generally in the eighteenth century, though any attempt to identify regional patterns must be received with some caution because of the metropolitan origin of many of the newspapers from which the sample of duels on which this conclusion is based is drawn. Bearing this reservation in mind, Table 2.2 suggests that there was an identifiable regional character to the duelling impulse in the early eighteenth century.

Just over half the sample of duels which can be definitely located for the thirty-five years to 1750 were fought in Leinster (51 per cent), with Dublin city and county playing host to the majority — 33 per cent as against the rest of the province's 18 per cent. Munster contributed just over 16 per cent of the total, while Connacht (8 per cent) and Ulster (6.5 per cent) were not receptive duelling territories (Table 2.2). Dublin was the epicentre of duelling in the country. This was the inevitable consequence of the fact that it was the main social and political centre of the kingdom, which made it a magnet for most of the social *corps d'élite* that duelled. Somewhat unexpectedly, as Table 2.3 highlights, virtually all reported duels were fought in the city. In the years 1716–50 15 (75 per cent) of the 20 duels known to have taken place within the boundaries of County Dublin took place in the city. By contrast, only one took place in the Phoenix Park; none took place in the North Lotts or Merrion Fields, which emerged as favourite duelling venues in mid-century, while four were held in other parts of the suburbs or county.[125] However, during the years 1751–70 just 52 per cent of the total of 27 duels recorded as having occurred within the Dublin county boundary took place in the city; 11 per cent took place in the North Lotts, 18.5 per cent in the Phoenix Park, and a similar percentage elsewhere in the county (Table 2.3). It could be suggested that the decision of duellists to engage in open areas like the Phoenix Park and the North Lotts, which were at some remove from the city boundaries, indicates that duelling was being marginalised. But the rise in the number of duels taking place demonstrates that this is not so. More importantly, the increased embrace by Irish duellists of such aspects of the ceremony and convention of the code of honour as seconds, formal challenges and waiting overnight between the issuing of challenge and the fighting of a duel demanded more space.[126] For these reasons, it is preferable to see the move to the Phoenix Park and other open areas as a manifestation of the increased discipline and order that became a feature of duelling from the mid-eighteenth century.

The duellist's weapon of choice in the first half of the eighteenth century was the sword (Table 2.4). In duels involving swords the antagonists seldom disengaged before one party was seriously injured or killed. This partly accounts for the high fatality ratio during the early eighteenth century (Table 2.5). The figures are incomplete, but those that can be assembled suggest that only a small percentage of duels fought between 1716 and 1750 ended without the death or injury of one of the principals. The recorded mortality/encounter ratio was 61 per cent (37 duellists died in 61 recorded duels), and this may well be an underestimate because if we incorporate the instances in which a duellist received what contemporary reports call 'mortal wounds', the figure rises to 69 per cent. However, since two duellists were involved in every encounter, the overall duellists' mortality ratio in the period 1716–50 was substantially lower. Thirty-four per cent of duellists were either killed or mortally wounded 'blazing'; a further 15 per cent were injured. These are substantial percentages, but given the number of duels fought in early eighteenth-century Ireland without seconds in attendance (Table 2.6), and the readiness to play fast and loose with the rules for conducting a duel, they are not entirely unexpected. These percentages fell in the mid-eighteenth century as duelling became more orderly.

One reason for this was the increased presence of seconds. Statistical evidence for this remains thin, but such as exists indicates that fewer duels were fought without seconds in attendance in the 1750s and 1760s than before (Table 2.6). Following their active participation in encounters in the seventeenth century in Ireland,[127] there is little reference to the actions of seconds in most accounts of duelling in the early eighteenth century. They re-emerge in the record in the mid-century to perform a quite different role from that which they had played in the seventeenth century. Their main function now was to ensure fair play; they conveyed the challenge; they agreed the time, place and weapons to be used in association with the principals; and, on the field, they sought to ensure that combat was entered into in accordance with the spirit of the code of honour. By this means, they served to mitigate the undisciplined character of so much Irish duelling in the early eighteenth century. Indeed, if they did their utmost to reconcile the adversaries, as recommended, they could well ensure that honour on all sides was satisfied without loss of life. Of course, not all seconds were men of integrity. Some inflamed rather than dampened the martial ardour of the principals, but, on the whole, they brought more regularity to duelling and, as a result, contributed to a decline in the mortality/encounter ratio.[128]

Of equal importance in reducing the level of mortality was the eclipse of the sword by the pistol as the duellist's weapon of preference. This was as much a result of behavioural as technological developments. In the early eighteenth century virtually all gentlemen wore swords, because to do so was, as the playright Farquhar observed, 'a distinguishing mark of honour'. However, from 1730 an increasing number of English gentlemen opted to carry a malacca cane instead. Given the environment in which they lived, Irish gentlemen may have been less keen to abandon wearing swords, but the fact that the emergence of the pistol as the duellist's weapon of preference occurred at the same time in Ireland as it did in England cautions one against making a strong case for Irish exceptionalism.[129] Of 42 duels fought in Ireland for which there is evidence of the weapons used in the period 1751–70, 81 per cent were fought with pistols, and only 17 per cent with swords. Only one duel involved use of both weapons. The figures for the period 1716–50 are almost the complete reverse; then 58 per cent of the duels for which evidence survives were fought with swords, 15 per cent with pistols and swords, and only 27.5 per cent with pistols (Table 2.4). A pistol demanded less skill to use, but more skill to use *accurately* than a sword. Moreover, pistols were more elegant-looking than they were technologically efficient. As a consequence, an unskilled duellist stood a better chance of inflicting or escaping serious injury in a duel involving the use of pistols than he did in an encounter involving swords.[130]

The implications of these developments for duelling were enormous, as a consideration of mid-eighteenth-century casualty rates makes clear. All told, there were twenty deaths from eighty-three duels in the twenty years January 1751 to December 1770. This works out at 24 per cent, which represents a sharp reduction on the corresponding figure for a sample of duels collected for the period 1716–50, which was 61 per cent. Even when we add in the number of instances in which contemporary reports maintain that a duel produced 'mortal' wounds, the percentage of fatalities (35 per cent) remains strikingly less than the respective figure for the years 1716–50 (69 per cent). However, this is not the full story, as the figures for total injuries reveal. Approximately 24 per cent of the duels in the sample gathered for the years 1751–70 concluded without injury to either party. This represented a dramatic improvement on the early eighteenth-century figure; but a substantial 18 per cent of duels (10 per cent more than was the case during the thirty-five years 1716–50) resulted in the death or injury of both participants. Put another way, if the tabulated sample of encounters is representative, there was a 76 per cent chance that one or both parties would be killed or injured in every duel that took place in the 1750s and 1760s; 50 per cent of *all* duellists in these two decades were either killed or injured as a result of their resolve to uphold their honour with weapons (Table 2.5). These figures differ strikingly from Wilkinson's findings for Britain. Based on a sample of two hundred cases, he has calculated that one in fourteen duels produced a fatality, and one in six an injury; in Ireland in the mid-eighteenth century the former figure is closer to one in four, and the latter to three in four. Interestingly, the percentage of total injuries (that is, inclusive of deaths) varies little over the period 1716–70; in this respect at least duelling changed little.[131]

Although these figures support the impression that duelling became a more orderly, less sanguinary affair in the mid-eighteenth century, the virtual constancy in the overall casualty rate warns against exaggerating this trend. A direct hit from a pistol shot to any major organ was almost invariably attended with fatal consequences, as the Fullarton–Uniacke and Jameson–Sproule duels in 1752 and 1754 emphasise.[132] This was an inevitable consequence of the lack of knowledge of basic techniques of sterilisation, which meant that it was virtually impossible to extract a pistol ball safely. Indeed, a direct shot in the limbs could also be acutely dangerous, and amputation was not an uncommon result. This was the experience of Cornet Nugent, who lost his arm as a result of his encounter with Captain Hamilton at Gort, County Galway, in April 1752.[133] Over a year later the life of Thomas Lloyd was endangered when his shin bone was smashed by a ball fired by Robert Franklin when they met in County Limerick; while the prognosis for the young gentleman who had his thigh-bone broken in a duel at Oxmantown Green in March 1768 was equally gloomy.[134]

Each of these duels was, as far as can be ascertained, fought fairly. The injuries that resulted were of the kind every man of honour could anticipate when he raised his weapon in anger. In cases where the combatants refused to observe recommended procedures or refused to desist until one party was unable to fight any longer, the consequences were likely to be more serious. When Captain Cuthbertson and Lieutenant Vanlewin met in Galway in May 1753, Vanlewin was wounded twice and Cuthbertson five times; not surprisingly, Cuthbertson died.[135] A few days earlier at Waterford, Lieutenant Collonwood and Lieutenant Walsh were so badly injured as a result of their duel that Collonwood died within a few days and Walsh lay 'dangerously ill'.[136] A quite extraordinary encounter took place in Queen's County in 1759 between Colonel Jonah Barrington of Cullenaghmore and a gentleman named Gilbert as a consequence of a longstanding grudge. Having concluded that the only way to resolve their differences was by recourse to arms, they determined to meet on horseback with pistols and swords on Maryborough Green. As in medieval jousts, the two men galloped towards each other weapons at the ready, except in this instance both parties employed guns rather than lances. Having missed each other first time round, they faced each other once more; this time Barrington was hit in the face, but not so seriously as to prevent the encounter continuing with swords. During the swordplay Barrington was cut in three places, twice on the arm and once on the head, while Gilbert was cut on the thigh and side. Realising that the fight was slipping away from him, Barrington switched his attention from his opponent's person to his steed, which he brought down with repeated thrusts. Having gained the initiative in this way, Barrington was able to take advantage of his opponent's weakened state to compel him to beg for his life or die. Gilbert chose the former course, which concluded one of the most remarkable encounters that took place in eighteenth-century Ireland.[137]

Clearly this incident has little in common with the carefully regulated duels that became the norm in Ireland in the mid-eighteenth century. Jonah Barrington, who recounts his father's experience, claimed it was in accordance with 'the ancient mode of duelling in Ireland',[138] but there is little evidence to sustain this. That said, a considerable percentage of duels continued to infringe the rules of the code of honour. For instance, when Amyas Griffith, the mercurial controversialist and pamphleteer, was employed as a revenue gauger at Wexford in the 1760s, he responded to some insulting remarks by an excise officer named Robert Wi——es in the unlikely surrounds of the club room of the Friendly Society by challenging him to a duel there and then. Wi——es was evidently as tempestuous as Griffith, for, rather than insist they waited until the following morning, he grabbed his pistol and followed Griffith to an 'inner chamber' where the two men took their places a mere seven yards apart. Griffith fired first and missed; whereupon Wi——es marched up to his opponent and, pointing his pistol at him, ordered him to beg for his life. Griffith refused, but said he would receive Wi——es's fire as he was honour-bound to do. Wi——es resumed his place and took aim, but when he pulled the trigger his gun did not go off. Undeterred by this, both men determined to resume their places, and would have done so but for the intervention of bystanders, who insisted that the encounter was concluded.[139] A similar incident took place in Essex Street, Dublin, in May 1759, when two gentlemen who had exchanged some sharp words drew their swords and would not have ceased fighting till one died or gave up, though both were soon injured, but for the intervention of several gentlemen.[140] Temper, such as that displayed by the principals on this and on the former occasion, was incompatible with the proper conduct of a duel, but it was not uncommon notwithstanding the fact that a duel fought under these circumstances was more likely to result in serious injury.

Because most reports of affairs of honour are brief, it is difficult to establish precisely their cause, as the modest number of cases tabulated in Table 2.7 illustrates. The fact that many duels took place in or arose out of differences that occurred in taverns would lead one to believe that the heavy consumption of alcohol, for which Irish gentlemen were famous, may have played a more decisive role than Table 2.7 indicates. One is certainly struck by the number of duelling incidents in the city of Dublin which arose from altercations in taverns and coffee-houses. The most notorious venue was Lucas's coffee-house, which was located next door to Dublin Castle on Cork Hill. This opened its doors in the 1680s, and it was established as one of the haunts of the Dublin fast set by the 1720s.[141] The first duel known to have taken place within its precincts dates from 1725.[142] By the late 1740s it was the duelling epicentre of the country, though its colloquial designation, 'Surgeon's Hall', is misleading; it was *not* usual to find the bodies of deceased duellists laid out on the house's table. Likewise, the claims of Maxwell, Swift, Molloy, McCracken and others that eager duellists paraded its floors inviting challenges have little basis in fact, though it was not a place to frequent if you wished to avoid trouble.[143] Many clearly did not, and much of the appeal of Lucas's centred on the vicarious excitement it brought to otherwise humdrum lives.

Few duels took place within the four walls of the coffee-house, but the yard at the rear was washed by the blood of a significant number of Irish gentlemen. At least seven encounters are known to have taken place in Lucas's in the ten years 1748–58, when the duelling reputation of the coffee-house was at its height. Two of these resulted in fatalities. In January 1748 Francis Hamilton was fatally wounded by Arthur Mervyn; and in November 1755 Patrick Kerwin of Creggs, County Roscommon, and Edward Brereton, the deputy serjeant-at-arms in the House of Commons, met with swords in a more acrimonious and bloody enounter, as a result of which both parties were injured, and Kerwin died within a few days from a wound to the abdomen.[144] The names of the participants in the five other duelling incidents that took place in the coffee-house are not known, but three produced injuries — in one instance serious injuries — one concluded without injury, while in the final case the principals were put under arrest to prevent the encounter taking place.[145] Thereafter Lucas's seems to have attracted a less duelling-disposed clientèle; it faded from view in the mid-1760s, and it was eventually demolished to make way for the Royal Exchange in 1768.

If Lucas's reputation as the most notorious duelling spot in mid-eighteenth century Dublin has survived the harsh test of time, it was not the only coffee-house or tavern to play host to the code of honour. At least four other duels fought between July 1754 and June 1763 took place in similar locations, and all produced injuries. This is not unexpected. Because of space restrictions, duels with pistols in such confined environments could not be fought at the recommended distance of ten or twelve paces, and the closer the combatants the greater the risk of serious injury. This was highlighted in June 1763 when an encounter in an unnamed tavern resulted in one participant being killed, and the other receiving serious injuries when he was struck by a ball in the mouth.[146] Duelling with swords in such restrictive environs was also extremely dangerous. Of the six participants in three other tavern duels in the 1750s, two were 'mortally' or 'dangerously' wounded; three received slight or non-serious injuries; only one emerged unscathed.[147]

Given this lengthy list of casualties, it is not surprising that there was a move away from such loci in the 1760s. Duellists were frequently impetuous, but the trend was to minimise the chances of serious injury or death, and experience revealed that it was safer to duel with pistols in the open air than with pistols indoors or with swords in any location. This should not be interpreted as indicating any lessening in the level of commitment to the code of honour, as Edmund Burke discovered.

According to James Boswell, who recorded the incident, when Burke pointed out to one of his countrymen (almost certainly Robert Martin), who had travelled from the west of Ireland to London to pursue a quarrel, that it was contrary to his religion to duel, he met with a baffled response: 'The gentlemen said he could not believe GOD almighty meant that we should bear to be insulted, or would be angry at a man's taking revenge if he did it like a gentleman'.[148] As this indicates, as far as most of the ruling Protestant elite in Ireland were concerned, the most precious possession of any man was his honour. The citation by a correspondent in the *Freeman's Journal* in the 1760s of the example of a father who maintained that he would prefer to see his son dead than decline a challenge bears further witness to this point of view. Of course, not everybody felt so strongly, but few were willing to bear 'the odious apellation of scoundrel' or 'poltroon' which attached to anyone who declined to fight.[149] Every self-respecting eighteenth-century gentleman believed himself a man of honour and was guided in his daily activities by this perception. Thus, for example, we find Lord Chancellor Lifford pronouncing that 'my honour . . . is dearer to me than my life' when his judgment was questioned, while his predecessor, Lord Bowes, avowed in 1767 that he would retire only if he could do so 'with honour'.[150] Given the conviction with which such views were held, neither religion, law nor the, by now, routine instructions to Lords Lieutenant to cashier military officers who were involved in duels had any visible impact.[151] Duelling was to become much more popular before it was even to commence to decline.

Table 2.1: Duelling, 1716–70 – number of duels; social status of principals

Date	Number of duels sampled	Averted duels	Gentlemen	Military	Middle class	Lawyers	Lower class
1716–20	6	1	4	2	1	2	—
1721–25	5	1	2	2	—	—	—
1726–30	16	—	10	7	4	2	—
1731–35	5	1	4	—	—	—	1
1736–40	8	2	5	2	3	—	—
1741–45	7	—	5	2	—	—	—
1746–50	14	1	12	3	1	—	—
1751–55	22	4	12	8	1	1	—
1756–60	14	3	12	5	—	—	1
1761–65	14	2	10	3	2	—	—
1766–70	33	1	28	3	—	1	4

Table 2.2: The geography of duelling, 1716–70

Date	Number of duels sampled	Dublin city and county	Rest of Leinster	Munster	Ulster	Connacht	Irishmen duelling abroad
1716–20	6	5	—	—	1	—	—
1721–25	5	1	1	—	—	—	3
1726–30	16	5	1	4	1	3	1
1731–35	5	—	—	2		1	
1736–40	8	1	3	1	1	—	—
1741–45	7	3	1	2	1	—	—
1746–50	14	5	5	1	—	1	2
1751–55	22	14	1	5	—	2	—
1756–60	14	4	1	2	—	3	1
1761–65	14	3	3	4	—	—	2
1766–70	33	6	6	8	—	8	2

Table 2.3: Duelling in Dublin, 1716–70

Date	Number of duels sampled in Dublin area	Dublin city	Phoenix Park	North Lotts	Dublin county and suburbs
1716–20	5	3	—	—	2
1721–25	1	1	—	—	—
1726–30	5	3	1	—	1
1731–35	—	—	—	—	—
1736–40	1	1	—	—	—
1741–45	3	3	—	—	—
1746–50	5	4	—	—	1
1751–55	14	6	4	1	3
1756–60	4	4	—	—	—
1761–65	3	1	—	—	2
1766–70	6	3	1	2	—

Table 2.4: Duelling, 1716–70 – weapons; shots fired

		Weapons				Shots fired		
Date	Number of duels sampled	Pertinent sample	Sword	Pistol	Sword and pistol	Pertinent sample	Two shots fired	More than two shots
1716–20	6	5	5	—	—	—	—	—
1721–25	5	3	3	—	—	—	—	—
1726–30	16	13	8	1	4	3	3	—
1731–35	5	2	1	—	1	—	—	—
1736–40	8	5	3	2	—	1	—	1
1741–45	7	4	—	3	1	—	—	—
1746–50	14	8	3	5	—	2	1	1
1751–55	22	11	1	10	—	4	1	3
1756–60	14	4	2	2	—	1	—	1
1761–65	14	8	1	7	—	4	3	1
1766–70	33	19	3	15	1	5	3	2

Table 2.5: Duelling, 1716–70 – mortality and injuries

Date	Number of duels sampled	Fatalities	Mortal wounds	One wounded	Two wounded	No injuries	Total injuries
1716–20	6	6	—	1	1	1	9
1721–25	5	3	1	1	—	—	5
1726–30	16	9	2	4	1	—	17
1731–35	5	4	—	—	—	—	4
1736–40	8	5	—	1	2	—	10
1741–45	7	4	1	1	—	—	6
1746–50	14	6	1	1	1	—	10
1751–55	22	7	—	9	5	4	26
1756–60	14	2	2	3	7	1	21
1761–65	14	4	2	6	1	2	14
1766–70	33	7	5	6	2	13	22

Table 2.6: Seconds; the law and duelling, 1716–70

	Seconds			The law and duelling				
Date	No seconds	Seconds intervene	Reconciliation	Law intervenes	Coroner's court hearing	Number of trials	Manslaughter	Murder
1716–20	2	—	—	—	1	2	2	—
1721–25	—	—	—	—	1	1	1	—
1726–30	2	—	—	—	—	4	4	—
1731–35	—	—	—	—	1	2	2	—
1736–40	2	—	—	2	1	3	2	1
1741–45	—	—	—	—	1	3	3	—
1746–50	1	2	—	—	—	3	3	—
1751–55	—	—	—	2	1	1	1	1
1756–60	1	1	2	3	—	—	—	—
1761–65	—	3	3	1	—	1	1	—
1766–70	2	5	1	2	—	4	3	—

Table 2.7: The causes of duelling, 1716–70

Date	Pertinent sample	Politics and elections	Religion	Playhouse	Insult/ argument	Jostling/ grudge, feud	Women
1716–20	4	—	—	—	4	—	—
1721–25	3	1	—	—	1	1	—
1726–30	4	1	—	—	3	—	—
1731–35	2	—	—	—	2	—	—
1736–40	4	—	—	1	3	—	—
1741–45	2	—	—	—	2	—	—
1746–50	3	—	1	—	2	—	—
1751–55	3	1	—	1	1	—	—
1756–60	6	2	—	—	2	2	—
1761–65	7	2	—	—	4	—	1
1766–70	5	3	—	—	—	1	1

Table 2.8: Military duelling in the 1750s

	Participants		Consequences			
No. duels	Military only	Military and civilians	Fatalities	Mortal wounds	Both wounded	No injuries
12	7	5	7	4	6	1

Notes and References

1 John Hales, *Golden remains of the ever memorable Mr John Hales* (London, 1673), p. 140, cited in Andrew 'The code of honour', p. 416.

2 Hales, *Golden remains*, pp. 87–8.

3 *The whole works of Jeremy Taylor* (3 vols, London, 1835), iii, 444; Edward Wetenhall, 'The Christian law of the sword' in *Hexapta Jacobaea: a specimen of loyalty to . . . James II* (Dublin, 1686). (I wish to thank Dr Toby Barnard for the latter reference.) For further religious-based criticism of duelling see Thomas Comber, *A discourse of duels showing the sinful nature and mischievous effects of them* . . . (London, 1687); John Cockburn, *The history and examination of duels shewing their heinous nature and the necessity of suppressing them* (London, 1720); A speech in convocation against duelling . . ., 1711 (B.L., Lansdowne papers, MS 846, no. 37, f. 148); Thomas Milner, *The life, times and correspondence of Isaac Watts* (London, 1834), p. 421.

4 Above, p. 29; Billacois, *The duel*, pp. 83–4.

5 *C.S.P.D., 1686–7*, p. 45.

6 *Abstract of the by-laws, rules and orders made by the governors of the Royal Hospital of King Charles the Second* . . . (Dublin, 1828), p. 56; Kiernan, *The duel*, p. 133.

7 Above p. 35; *C.S.P.D., 1685*, pp. 272, 284, 397; ibid., *1690–91*, p. 178; ibid., *1694–9*, p. 457; ibid., *1702–3*, p. 651; P.R.O., S.P., 67/2 ff. 22, 77, 104. I wish to thank John Bergin for the latter reference.

8 H.M.C., *Ormonde*, n.s. vii, 355–6; *C.S.P.D., 1686–7*, p. 348; ibid., 1700–2, pp. 496, 529; Lapthorne to Coffin, 1690–97 in H.M.C., 5th report, appendix (*Pine Coffin MSS*), pp. 381–4.

9 *C.S.P.D., 1686–7*, p. 306.

10 Royal warrant, 1 Mar. 1697, in *C.S.P.D., 1697*, p. 48; warrant, 1701, in *C.S.P.D., 1700–2*, p. 363. In other instances, court martials returned 'not guilty' verdicts on soldiers charged with infringing the articles of war by duelling (Report of two court martials, 7 Aug. 1696 (N.L.I. Ormonde Papers, MS 2456, ff. 279–83)).

11 Evidenced by the continuing practice of duelling in the 1690s; see notes 8, 9 and 10; John Childs, *The British army of William III, 1689–1702* (Manchester, 1987), pp. 44–6; H.M.C., *Rutland*, ii, 118; *C.S.P.D., 1698*, pp. 55, 381; H.M.C., 12th Report, appendix 9 (*Beaufort MSS*), p. 96; H.M.C., 15th Report, appendix iv (*Portland MSS*), pp. 59, 208–09; H.M.C., *Mar and Kellie*, p. 234; Yard to Blathwayt, 23 Aug. 1698 (Beinecke Library, Osborn Collection, Blathwayt Papers, Box 20); J. D. Aylward, 'Duelling in the eighteenth century', *Notes and Queries*, clxxxix (1945), pp. 32–3.

12 A. M. Fraser's account of 'The Friendly Brothers of St Patrick' in *Dublin Historical Record*, xiv (1955–8), pp. 34–40 has little on this. A similar organisation — the Brotherhood of the Passion — was founded in France in the 1650s (Billacois, *The duel*, pp. 167–9).

13 Sidney Burrell, ed., *Amiable renegade: the memoirs of Captain Peter Drake, 1671–1753* (Stanford, 1960), pp. 14–5, 82–3, 88–9, 228, 325–7.

14 N. C. MacNamara *The story of an Irish sept* (London, 1896), p. 259.
15 Catholics were forbidden to carry weapons by 7 Will. III, c. 5.
16 Courtenay Moore, 'Some account of a fatal duel fought at Brigown, Mitchelstown, in 1695', *J.C.A.H.S.*, ii (1903), pp. 83–5; John Ainsworth, ed., *Inchiquin MSS* (Dublin, 1943), p. 43; W. P. Burke, *History of Clonmel* (Waterford, 1907) p. 153; J. A. Gaughan, *The Knights of Glin* (Listowel, 1978), p. 58.
17 Michael Manning, 'Dr Nicholas Madgett's *constitutio ecclesiastica*, 1758', *Journal of the Kerry Archaeological and Historical Society*, ix (1976), p. 82.
18 In February 1729 in Galway, John Mills of Nantes killed a young Catholic named Mullenaux in an irregular encounter (Gallagher to St George, 19 Feb. 1729, 9 Apr. 1730 (P.R.O., C110, Box 56, ff 720, 757)). In December 1730 Ensign Goddart was challenged and wounded by a Catholic named Blake (*Dublin Weekly Jn.*, 2 Jan. 1731). Another duel, possibly involving Catholics, took place in Dublin in 1710, when Florence MacNamara of Clare wounded his opponent (Ainsworth, ed., *Inchiquin MSS*, pp. 102–3).
19 Ainsworth, ed., *Inchiquin MSS*, p. 93; Burrell, ed., *Amiable renegade*, pp. 365–9; D. W. Ressinger, ed., *Memoirs of the Reverend Jaques Fontaine, 1658–1728* (London, 1992), pp. 188–9.
20 *C.S.P.D., 1698*, pp. 410–11; Mackay, *Extraordinary popular delusions*, p. 682.
21 G.E.C., *The Complete Peerage*, x, 179 note 7; *D.N.B.*; *Dublin Gazette*, Nov.-Dec. 1712, 17 Jan. 1713; N.A., Proclamations, 1690–1800, 16 Jan. 1712; *Dublin Intelligence*, Nov.–Dec. 1712; J. L. Rayner and G. T. Cook, eds, *The complete Newgate Calendar* (5 vols, London, 1926), ii, 224–5; *Needham's Postman*, 1 Oct. 1724; Aylward, 'Duelling', pp. 33–4.
22 *Flying Post*, 29 June 1702; *Dublin Intelligence*, 18 July 1702; Berkeley to Stratton, 6 Mar., 26 June 1713, in J.J. Cartwright, ed., *The Wentworth Papers, 1705–39* (London, 1883), pp. 324, 339; Ainsworth, ed., *Inchiquin MSS*, p. 113.
23 Ainsworth, ed., *Inchiquin MSS*, pp. 104–5; *Dublin Courant*, 3 Nov. 1724; *The Weekly Journal or Saturday Post* (London), 1 July 1721.
24 Calhoun Winton, *The early career of Richard Steele* (Baltimore, 1964), pp. 54–5; Barry, *An affair of honour*, p. 23.
25 David Hayton, 'Anglo-Irish attitudes: changing perceptions of national identity among the Protestant ascendancy in Ireland, *ca* 1690–1750' in *Studies in Eighteenth Century*, xvii (1987), pp. 145–57; idem, 'From barbarian to burlesque: English images of the Irish *c.* 1660–1750' in *Irish Economic and Social History*, xv (1988), pp. 6, 21; Burrell, ed., *Memoirs of Peter Drake*, pp. 330–31. Writers such as John Dunton contributed to the forging of this image.
26 Austin Dobson, ed., *Steele: selections from the Tatler, Spectator and Guardian* (Oxford, 1896); D. F. Bond, ed., *The Spectator* (5 vols, Oxford, 1965).
27 This was an established theme in English anti-duelling writing; see *The laws of honour; or an account of the suppression of duels in France* ([London], 1685).
28 Bond, ed., *The Spectator*, i, 358–60, 418–19, 410–12.
29 M. A. K. Garner, 'James Trail, his journal' in *Proceedings of the Belfast Natural History and Philosophical Society*, 2nd series, ix (1970–77), pp. 47–8.

30 See Owen Gallagher's account of his visit to County Limerick in April 1728 (P.R.O., St George Papers, C110, Box 46, f. 531); Ressinger, ed., *Memoirs of Fontaine*, pp. 162–3.
31 *P.O.*, 4 Jan 1717.
32 *Dublin Intelligence*, 28 May 1726; *Dublin Courant*, 28 May 1726; *Dublin Weekly Journal*, 28 May 1726; *A full and true account of a duel . . . between Lieutenant James Smith and [Pat] Kelly, the brewer's son of Proper Lane . . .* (Dublin, [1726]).
33 *P.O.*, 22 Mar 1718. For other examples see *An account of a battle fought between Mr Smith, an attorney in Smithfield, and Mr Lee, son to Captain Lee in the county of Westmeath* (Dublin, 1719); *An account of a desperate duel fought at Talla-Green in the county of Catherlow between Lieutenant Barkley . . . and Mr Edward Culling, steward to the late Lord Chief Justice Doyn's eldest son* (Dublin, 1719).
34 *P.O.*, 1 Apr. 1718.
35 John Gilbert, *A history of the city of Dublin* (3 vols, Dublin, 1859–61), iii, 296–8; *Walker's Hibernian Magazine*, 1796, pp. 36–7; *Hume's Dublin Courant*, 25 Jan. 1724; Gallagher to St George, 27 Apr. 1728 (P.R.O., St George Papers, C110, Box 46, f. 531).
36 *An account of a battle . . . between Mr Smith . . . and Mr Lee; P.O.*, 29 Apr. 1718, 31 Jan., 14 Feb. 1719, 19 Dec. 1732; Anthony Hewitson, ed., *Diary of Thomas Bellingham, an officer under William III* (Preston, 1908), p. xvi.
37 *Dublin Intelligence*, 12 Oct. 1728; *Dublin Gazette*, 24 May 1729.
38 For other examples see the cases of Edward Dempsey of Granard, County Longford (*Dublin Intelligence*, 2 July 1726) and James Burnsides (*Dublin Gazette*, 8 July 1732); *An account of a battle . . . between Mr Smith . . . and Mr Lee*; *An account of a desperate duel fought at Talla-Green.*
39 J.W[ard] to R. Ward, 15 Jan 1737, in H.M.C., *T. H. G. Puleston*, pp. 312–13; Gallagher to St George, 27 Apr. 1728 (P.R.O., St George Papers, C110, Box 46, f. 531).
40 *Dublin Weekly Jn.*, 13, 27 Nov. 1725; Pulteney to West, 2 Nov. 1725 (Yale University, Sterling Library, Burnet Papers, file 4).
41 Gallagher to St George, 19 Feb., 10 Mar. 1729, 9 Apr. 1730 (P.R.O., St George Papers, C110, Box 46, ff 720, 721, 757).
42 Harold Williams, ed., *The correspondence of Jonathan Swift* (5 vols, Oxford, 1963–5), ii, 384, 386, 450–2, 455.
43 Hewitson, ed., *Diary of Thomas Bellingham*, p. xvi; *Dublin Weekly Journal*, 19 Nov. 1726; Worthington to St George, 17 Nov. 1726 (P.R.O., St George Papers, C110, Box 46, f. 451); *A full and true account of a bloody duel fought between Henry Haze and — Peper, Esqrs at Drogheda on Saturday 22 Feb. 1729 . . .* (Dublin, 1729); *Dublin Gazette*, 26 Feb.,20 Sept. 1729; *Dublin Intelligence*, 25 Feb., 22 Mar. 1729; Burke, *Clonmel*, pp. 115, 153.
44 *Dublin Intelligence*, 26 Nov., 10 Dec. 1728; *D.N.B.*
45 As well as the above, a revenue gauger killed a young gentleman in County Roscommon in 1727 (P.R.O., C110, Box 46, f. 471).
46 *Tryal and examination of William Todd, attorney, for the murder of Pierce Rice, 20 February last at the Golden Bottle . . .* (Dublin, 1730); See also *An account of*

a barbarous and bloody murder committed on . . . Mr Huddleston, innkeeper in Ballagh . . ., Friday 3 Sept. 1725 by one Byrn, a sollicitor (Dublin, 1725).

47 Kiernan, *The duel*, p. 98.

48 Mrs Thompson, ed., *Memoirs of Viscountess Sunden* (2 vols, London, 1847), ii, 120.

49 *P.O.*, 14 Nov 1719.

50 As note 29; C. V. Trench, *The Wrays of Donegal* (London, 1945), pp. 132–6. Another illustration of the extent to which the concept of honour was entrenched is provided by the suicide of John Deseray, the son of Alderman Deseray of Kilkenny, as a result of 'the slight he had received from one of his friends' (*P.O.*, 23 May 1738).

51 S. J. Conolly, 'Violence and order in the eighteenth century' in Patrick O'Flanagan *et al.*, eds, *Rural Ireland: modernisation and change, 1600–1900* (Cork, 1987), p. 49.

52 *P.O.*, 7 Oct. 1738, 17 Mar. 1739.

53 *P.O.*, 15 Dec. 1739, 8 Apr. 1740; Raymond Hughes, 'Galway town, 1692–1750: a study in local administration and society'(M.A. thesis, University College, Galway, 1985), pp. 65–6.

54 Mossom to Alcock, 22 Nov. 1740 (Villiers Stuart Papers, P.R.O.N.I., T3131/B/4/14).

55 Ross to Price, 13 Apr. 1733 in H.M.C., *Puleston*, p. 314; Connolly, 'Violence and order', pp. 49–50; above, p. 48.

56 For example, in 1729 the sheriff of County Antrim had to admit his inability to raise a 'posse' to deliver possession of the Mansion House in Portglenone to the Bishop of Down and Connor ('Calendar of Church miscellaneous papers, 1652–1795' in *P.R.O.I., 58th Report of the Deputy Keeper* (Dublin, 1951), p. 83).

57 W[ard] to Ward, 15 Jan. 1737 in H.M.C., *Puleston*, pp. 312–13; *P.O.*, 8, 11 Jan., 26 Mar. 1737.

58 *P.O.*, 22 Apr. 1740.

59 *P.O.*, 10 July 1733, 18, 25 Jan., 1, 10 May 1735; Tickell to Cary, 5 May 1735 (P.R.O.N.I., Wilmot Papers, T3019/ 150); *The whole tryal and examination of Mr Robert Martin who was try'd at the King's Bench on Friday 2 May 1735 for the murder of Lieutenant Henry Jolly* (Dublin, 1735); Roderic O'Flaherty, *A chorographical description of West or h-Iar Connaught* (Dublin, 1846), pp. 118n, 295–6; *Galway Reader*, ii (1950), pp. 205–6; Connolly, 'Violence and order.', pp. 49–50; Hughes, 'Galway town, 1692–1750', p. 65.

60 *F.D.J.*, 22 May 1744.

61 *The trial in ejectment . . . between Campbell Craig, lessee of James Annesley . . . and Richard Earl of Anglesey before the Barons of His Majesty's Court of Exchequer in Ireland . . .* (London, 1744); Maurice Craig, *Dublin, 1660–1860* (Dublin, 1969), pp. 150–53; Andrew Lang, ed., *The Annesley case* (London, 1912).

62 Lang, ed., *The Annesley case*, pp. 16–19.

63 Letters and papers on the Browne–Miller duel, Kilmaine County Mayo, 1747 (Bowen-Miller of Milford Papers (N.L.I., microfilm, p.3793)), documents 1–9; two examinations, Feb. 1747 (Northumberland Record Office, Potter Papers, MS 650/C/25); *Dublin Courant*, 30 Jan. 1747.

64 Letters and papers on the Browne–Miller duel, no. 10; *Dublin Courant*, 19 July 1748.

65 Letters and papers on the Browne–Miller duel, nos 11–21; *Dublin Courant*, 19 July 1748, 9 May, 25 Nov. 1749; *F.D.J.*, 14 Jan., 18, 22, 25 Apr., 9 May 1749.

66 *F.D.J.*, 25, 29 Apr. 1749; *Dublin Courant*, 22 Aug. 1749.

67 *Dublin Courant*, 6 Sept. 1748; *Dublin Weekly Jn.*, 24 Sept., 22 Oct. 1748; Wood to Price, 16 Oct. 1748, in H.M.C., *Puleston*, p. 337.

68 [ ] to Whyte, 18 May 1748; Waite to Wilmot, 21 May 1748 (P.R.O.N.I., Wilmot Papers, T3019/1037–8).

69 *P.O.*, 24 Aug. 1742; *F.D.J.*, 6 July 1745; *Dublin Courant*, 18 Mar. 1746; A. P. I. Samuels, *The early life, correspondence and writings of Edmund Burke* (Cambridge, 1923), p. 76.

70 Lords Justice to Devonshire, 23 May 1737 (P.R.O.N.I., Shannon Papers, D2707/A1/8 pp. 6–9); Statement of case between Rochfort and Hugh Maguire [c.23 May 1737](P.R.O.N.I., Chatsworth Papers, T 3158/23–5); Boulter to Devonshire, 7 June 1737, in *Letters addressed to His Excellency Hugh Boulter* (2 vols, Dublin, 1739), ii, 178.

71 Sackville to Wilmot, 1, 22 July 1752 (P.R.O.N.I., Wilmot Papers, T3019/1927, 1934).

72 Above, pp. 51–2.

73 Sir Edward Willes, 'Miscellaneous observations on Ireland' (P.R.O.N.I., T2855/1, pp. 20–25).

74 Hort to Belcher, 8 Aug. 1749, in 'Calendar of Church Miscellaneous Papers, 1652–1795' in *Public Record Office of Ireland, 58th Report of the Deputy Keeper*, p. 87; Commissioners of the Revenue to Lords Justices, 4 Feb. 1755 (P.R.O.N.I., Wilmot Papers, T3019/2504); James Kelly, ed., *The letters of Lord Chief Baron Edward Willes to the Earl of Warwick, 1757–62* (Aberystwyth, 1990), pp. 85–6.

75 The true state and circumstance . . . of killing of Lieutenant John Hume, October 1738 (Northumberland Record Office, Potter Papers, MS 650/C/25); Tickell to Potter, 27 Oct. 1738 (P.R.O.N.I., Wilmot Papers, T3019/178); Hepburne to Campbell, 3 Oct. 1738; Campbell to Marchmont, 17 Oct. 1738; Johnstone to Marchmont, 3 Nov. 1738, in H.M.C., *Polwarth*, v, 152–8; Connolly, 'Violence and order', pp. 49–50; idem, *Religion, law, and power*, p. 70.

76 Hepburne to Campbell, 3 Oct. 1738, as note 75.

77 N.A., Proclamations, 1701–1800, nos 109–110; *Dublin Gazette*, 26 Feb., 29 Mar. 1740; Connolly, 'Violence and order', pp. 49–50; idem, *Religion, law and power*, p. 69.

78 Grand jury of Tyrone, 14 Apr. 1752 (N.A., Calendar of Miscellaneous Letters and Papers prior to 1760, f. 293); Commissioners of the Revenue to Lords Justices, 5 Feb. 1755 (P.R.O.N.I., Wilmot Papers, T3019/2504); Gaughan, *Knights of Glin*, pp. 61, 72–3.

79 *Gentleman's Magazine*, 15 (1745), p. 332; 16(1746), p. 348; Romney Sedgwick, ed., *The House of Commons* (2 vols, London, 1970), ii, 130; *Dublin Courant*, 2 Sept. 1746; Waite to Weston, 1 May, 1750; Weston to Lindon, 21 July, 11 Aug. 1750 (P.R.O.N.I., Wilmot Papers, T3019/1567, 1603, 1613); Vaughan, *Knights of Glin*, p. 73; G. D. Burtchaell, *Genealogical memoirs of the members of parliament for the county and city of Kilkenny, 1295–1886* (London, 1888), p. 138.

80 *A sermon preach'd at Christ-church Dublin before their excellencies the Lords Justices on Friday 23 December 1720 . . . by Henry Downes, Lord Bishop of Elphin* (Dublin, 1721), p. 24. I wish to thank Dr Raymond Gillespie for this reference.
81 *Records of the General Synod of Ulster* (3 vols, Belfast, 1890–98), ii, 307.
82 Kiernan, *The duel*, p. 173.
83 The Countess of Cork and Orrery, ed., *The Orrery Papers* (2 vols, London, 1903), i, 150; see also pp. 189–90.
84 *Orrery Papers*, i, 156–8.
85 Connolly, *Religion, law, and power*, pp. 66, 71.
86 Lady Llanover, *The correspondence of Mrs Delany* (3 vols, London, 1861), i, 351; Richard Cumberland, *Memoirs, written by himself* (2 vols, London, 1807), i, 258–63; G. S. Taylor, ed., *The life and uncommon adventures of Captain Dudley Bradstreet* (London, [1929]), passim; Pole Cosby, 'Autobiography of Pole Cosby', *Journal of the Kildare Archaeological Society*, v (1906–8), p. 258.
87 R. C. Cole, *Irish booksellers and English writers, 1740–1800* (London, 1986), p. 66; G. J. Barker-Benfield, *The culture of sensibility: sex and society in eighteenth century Britain* (Chicago, 1992), p. 80.
88 Samuel Madden, *Reflections and resolutions proper for the gentlemen of Ireland* (Dublin, 1816), p. 141; Constantia Maxwell, *Dublin under the Georges*, (London, 1936), pp. 88–9; see also *F.J.*, 21 Feb. 1764, 24 Feb. 1767.
89 Connolly, *Religion, law, and power*, p. 66.
90 J[ack] Wildair, *Three letters to the young gentlemen of the present age* (Dublin, 1748), pp. 44–50; *F.J.*, 7 Apr. 1764. I wish to thank Eamonn O Ciardha for the former reference.
91 *F.J.*, 24 Feb. 1767.
92 Portlock, *The Friendly Brothers of St Patrick*, pp. 1–2; *P.O.*, 2 Mar. 1751, 24 Mar. 1753; *F.D.J.*, 14 Mar. 1758; *Universal Advertizer*, 20 Jan. 1759; Tigheran Mooney and Fiona White, 'Dublin winter season' in David Dickson, ed., *The gorgeous mask: Dublin, 1700–1850* (Dublin, 1987), p. 13.
93 *The fundamental laws, statutes and constitutions of the ancient and most benevolent order of the Friendly Brothers of St Patrick* (Dublin, 1751), pp. 11–12.
94 See the editions of the *Fundamental laws* published in Dublin in 1763, 1787, 1814, 1820, 1823 and 1847.
95 Proceedings of the Select Grand Knot in Dublin, 1751–94 (Friendly Brothers of St Patrick, 22 St Stephen's Green, Dublin), passim.
96 Proceedings of Select Grand Knot, 1751–78, 1780–94, passim; Minute book of the General Grand Knot, 1763–78, passim; A.T.Q. Stewart, *A deeper silence: the hidden origins of the United Irishmen* (London, 1993), p. 169.
97 Minutebook of the County Kildare knot, 1777–91, passim.
98 L. M. Cullen, *An economic history of Ireland since 1660* (London, 1972), chapter 3; idem, 'Economic development, 1691–1750' and 'Economic development, 1750–1800' in Moody and Vaughan, eds, *A New History of Ireland*, iv, pp. 146–95.
99 *The trial of Captain Edward Clark, commander of His Majesty's Ship the Canterbury, for the murder of Captain Thomas Innes, of His Majesty's Ship the Warwick, in a duel in Hyde Park, March 12 1749 . . .* (Dublin, 1750); *The tryal*

of William, Lord Byron . . . for the murder of William Chaworth esq. before the Right Honourable the House of Peers in Westminster Hall (Dublin, 1765).

100 Robert Munter, *The history of the Irish newspaper, 1685–1760* (Cambridge, 1967), pp. 131–88; E. K. Sheldon, *Thomas Sheridan of Smock Alley* (Princeton, 1967); W. S. Clark, *The Irish stage in the county towns* (Oxford, 1965); John Stevenson, *Life in County Down over two centuries* (Belfast, 1917), pp. 276–7.

101 David Dickson, 'Middlemen' in Thomas Bartlett and D. W. Hayton, eds, *Penal era and golden age* (Belfast, 1979), pp. 162–85; idem, 'Catholics and trade in the eighteenth century' in T. P. Power and Kevin Whelan, eds, *Endurance and emergence: Catholics in Ireland in the eighteenth century* (Dublin, 1990), pp. 85–100.

102 The percentages are expressed in terms of the total number of duels; this amounts to over 100 because some duels involved individuals from more than one category — gentlemen and military, or gentlemen and members of the middle class etc.

103 *D.E.P.*, 24 June 1786.

104 *Orrery Papers*, ii, 120–23; P.R.O.N.I., Harrowby Papers, T3228/1/65; Malcomson, ed., *Eighteenth-century Irish official papers*, ii, 53.

105 Barry to Orrery, 14 Mar. 1754 in *Orrery Papers*, ii, 256.

106 H.M.C., *Stopford-Sackville*, i, 230.

107 Memorandum on debates, 1759–60, pp. 28–30 (Warwickshire Record Office, Willes Papers); R. E. Burns, *Irish parliamentary politics in the eighteenth century* (2 vols, Washington, 1989–90), ii, 279–80.

108 *Copy of a letter from the E[arl] of C[lanricarde] to the D[uke] of B[edford]* (Dublin, 1760). There is a copy in P.R.O., Chatham Papers, 30/8/83, ff 48–9; James Kelly, 'The origins of the Act of Union, 1650–1800', *I.H.S.*, xxv (1987), p. 248; A. P. W. Malcomson, ed., *Eighteenth-century Irish official papers, ii* (Belfast, 1990), pp. 247, 250, 267; Burns, *Irish parliamentary politics*, ii, 297–8; Halifax to Pitt, 7 July 1761 (P.R.O., S.P. 63/419); Printed letters of Clanricarde and Rigby, 11 Aug., 8 Oct. 1760, 21 Jan., Wilmot to Devonshire, 4 Aug. 1761 (P.R.O.N.I., Chatsworth Papers, T 3158/1623–4, 1632, 1636); Clanricarde's apology, 1763 (P.R.O., Privy Council papers, P.C. 1/7/55).

109 Brian Fitzgerald, ed., *Correspondence of Emily, Duchess of Leinster* (3 vols, Dublin, 1949–57), i, 230.

110 History of the Belvedere branch of the O'Malleys in the eighteenth century (N.L.I., O'Malley Papers, MS 5619); Ida Gantz, *Signpost to Eyrecourt* (Bath, 1975), pp. 144–5.

111 Adderly to Charlemont, 29 Dec. 1753, in H.M.C.,*Charlemont*, i, 190; *P.O.*, 29 Dec. 1753; *Hibernicus, or memoirs of an Irishman now in America* (Pittsburgh, 1828), pp. 86–8.

112 Waite to Wilmot, 22 Feb. 1752 (P.R.O.N.I., Wilmot Papers, T3019/1851); *P.O.*, 18 Apr. 1752, 29 May 1753.

113 Lieutenant Sheldon was twice wounded in 1757 in an encounter with a Mr Wilkinson (*P.O.*, 11 June 1757). In February 1756 an unnamed gentleman

seriously wounded a soldier in the chest; the gentleman was slightly wounded in the arm (*P.O.*, 2 Mar. 1756).

114 *P.O.*, 26 Mar. 1754. The coroner's verdict was 'willful murder' (*P.O.*, 30 Mar. 1754), but since there are no further reports, it is safe to assume that Daly was not punished.

115 *P.O.*, 28 Sept., 1 Oct. 1754.

116 *P.O.*, 2 Mar. 1756.

117 *Universal Advertizer*, 7 July 1759.

118 *Freeman's Journal*, 5 May 1764.

119 *P.O.*, 17 May 1755; *Public Gazetteer*, 12 Sept. 1761.

120 *P.O.*, 14 Sept. 1756; *Corke Journal*, 9 Sept. 1756.

121 *Universal Advertizer*, 20 Jan 1759.

122 *Public Gazetteer*, 19 Feb. 1763.

123 *F.L.J.*, 21 Mar. 1767.

124 *Dublin Mercury*, 5 Aug. 1755. As well as this and incidents cited, two journeymen brogue-makers preparing for a duel in 1769 in Ennis were interrupted by magistrates and put in the stocks (*F.L.J.*, 19 Aug. 1769).

125 Table 2.3.

126 On this see Kiernan, *The duel*, pp. 135–6. A similar development had taken place in seventeenth-century France (Billacois, *The duel*, pp. 62–4).

127 See above, pp. 33–35.

128 See Kiernan, *The duel*, pp. 63–4, 137–41, 298.

129 Aylward, 'Duelling in the eighteenth century', p. 34; Barker Benfield, *The culture of sensibility*, p. 80; 'Description of Dublin, 1732' in Gilbert, ed., *Calendar of ancient records of Dublin*, x, 524.

130 As well as Tables 2.4 and 3.4 see Kiernan, *The duel*, pp, 140–42.

131 This paragraph is based mainly on an analysis of Table 2.5. Wilkinson's figures are taken from Kiernan, *The duel*.

132 In the Fullerton–Uniacke duel, which took place in Cork in March 1752, William Uniacke died as a result of a shot in the 'belly' (*P.O.*, 31 Mar. 1752). Lieutenant Alexander Jameson died from a similar injury secured in his encounter with William Sproule (*P.O.*, 28 Sept., 1 Oct. 1754). For other examples see *F.D.J.*, 17 June 1758; *F.J.*, 5 May 1764.

133 *P.O.*, 18 Apr. 1752.

134 *P.O.*, 18 Sept. 1753; *F.L.J.*, 6 Mar. 1768.

135 *P.O.*, 29 May 1753. Vanlewin was tried for murder, but the jury returned a verdict of manslaughter in his own defence (*P.O.*, 4 Sept. 1753).

136 *P.O.*, 29 May 1753.

137 Barrington, *Personal sketches*, ii, 54–7.

138 Jonah Barrington, *Recollections* (Dublin, n.d.), pp. 311–12.

139 *F.J.* 3 Aug. 1765; J. F. Fuller, 'Amyas Griffith: a chequered career', *Kerry Archaeological Magazine*, iii (1914–16), pp. 172–4. A decade later, Griffith fought another duel with Cornelius O'Driscoll of Cork; once again there were no injuries (*F.L.J.*, 17 May 1775).

140 *F.D.J.*, 19 May 1759.

141 Gilbert, *Dublin*, ii, 9–11; Jonathan Swift and Thomas Sheridan, *The Intelligencer*, ed. by James Woolley (Oxford, 1992), pp. 74–5, 77.

142 *Dublin Weekly Journal*, 13 Nov. 1725; above, p. 52.
143 John Swift, *History of the Dublin bakers and others* (Dublin, [1948]), p. 131; Walpole to Ossory, 16 Mar. 1773, in W. S. Lewis *et al.*, eds, *The correspondence of Horace Walpole* (42 vols, New Haven, 1938–80), xxxii, 107; Maxwell, *Dublin under the Georges*, p. 189; Molloy, *Romance of the Irish stage*, i, 50–53; J. L. McCracken, 'The social structure and social life, 1714–60' in W. E. Vaughan and T. W. Moody, eds, *A New History of Ireland*, iv, 49–50.
144 *Dublin Weekly Journal*, 9, 16 Jan. 1748; *Dublin Courant*, 2 Feb. 1748; *P.O.*, 25 Nov., 6 Dec. 1755.
145 *P.O.*, 6 Mar., 11 Dec 1753, 6 Dec. 1757; *F.D.J.*, 24 Jan., 22 July 1758.
146 *Public Gazetteer*, 11 June 1763.
147 *P.O.*, 20 July 1754, 2 Mar., 3 July 1756.
148 I. S. Lustig and F. A. Pottle, eds, *Boswell: the applause of the jury, 1782–85* (London, 1981), p. 156. See above p. 71.
149 *F.J.*, 21 Feb. 1764, 20 Aug. 1765.
150 Lifford to Eardley-Wilmot, 20 Apr. 1785 (Beinecke Library, Osborn Collection, Lifford files); Bowes to Willes, 27 June 1767 (Warwickshire Record Office, Willes Papers, 8); for further examples see Fitzgerald, ed., *Leinster corresp.*, i, 9; Connolly, *Religion, law, and power*, p. 91; Llanover, ed., *Delany corresp.*, iii, 152–3.
151 See the instructions of Viscount Weymouth, 12 June 1765 in *C.H.O.P.*, *1760–65*, p. 559.

Part II

DUELLING AT ITS ZENITH

In the late 1760s and early 1770s a number of highly publicised duels involving some of the most eminent political figures in the land had a profound impact on the history of duelling in Ireland. Like the Jarnac affair in sixteenth-century France, they served to confer increased respectability on the code of honour and, thereby, to encourage others to emulate their example. The intensified observance of the code of honour this fostered was promoted further by the confrontational political climate of the late eighteenth century as fundamental cleavages within the Irish ruling elite significantly increased the political temperature and the frequency with which acrimonious political disagreements resulted in invitations to a duel. Most of the affairs of honour that originated within the precincts of the houses of parliament were defused without bloodshed, but the example set by M.P.s encouraged others 'out of doors' where less reticence was manifest. As a result, both locally and nationally, the number of affairs of honour pursued annually reached record levels during the 1770s and 1780s. It was during these decades that the cream of the Irish landed and political elite felt most compelled to appeal to their pistols to defend their reputations from even the imputation of insult. Representatives of this elite had engaged in affairs of honour in the early eighteenth century, but with less ardour than middle- and lower-ranking gentry and middle-ranking military officers. The eagerness of the latter interests to assert their honour by recourse to arms did not diminish after 1770. If anything it increased, and their continued disposition to duel, combined with the readiness of unprecedented numbers of prominent social and political figures to do likewise, make the last three decades of the eighteenth century the apogee of duelling in Irish history. Perhaps the best known feature of this phase of Irish duelling history is the 'fire-eaters'. These were individuals who became so enraptured with the excitement and, in the case of a number of notorious aficionados, *with the opportunity duelling offered to dispose of unwelcome rivals that they created a duelling sub-culture which extolled the code of honour and celebrated the deeds of those who observed it. The activities of the 'fire-eaters' have been described at some length in Barrington's celebratory memoir; he devotes strikingly less space to the modest but persistent flow of criticism from those who deplored duelling as sinful, unnatural and criminal. This had little impact during the 1770s or early 1780s, but by the late 1780s there were already signs that the accommodating attitude of the law authorities which had facilitated duelling and had enabled it to permeate deeply into Protestant society was beginning to wear thin. The most unambiguous evidence for this is provided by the trial in the late 1780s of a number of individuals for serious abuses of the privilege of duelling and of others for simply issuing challenges. These developments did not stop appeals to the code of honour; even the anti-aristocratic United Irishmen could not disencumber themselves sufficiently of the dictates of honour to avoid offering or accepting challenges. However, there were signs before the end of the century that duelling had passed its acme and that the new century was likely to represent a more fruitful era for its critics and opponents.*

3

'Knee-Deep in Blood': 1769–1773

By the late 1760s duelling was more firmly established in Ireland than ever. A survey of a range of newspapers, printed primary sources and manuscripts for the period 1766–70 has produced thirty-three duelling incidents — more than ten greater than similar surveys have revealed for any preceding five-year period, and nearly twenty greater than for the quinquennium 1761–65 (Table 2.1). However, this increase was dwarfed by what happened in the 1770s and afterwards (Table 3.1). For this and for other reasons, the late 1760s and early 1770s represent a turning-point in the history of the duel in Ireland; they represent a watershed between an era when duelling, though firmly established and quite widely practised, was not yet an everyday event, and an era when duelling was both fashionable and commonplace.

Many factors contributed to the growth in enthusiasm for duelling in Ireland in the late 1760s and 1770s. The social and attitudinal effects of economic prosperity, already referred to,[1] were at work *a fortiori* by the end of the 1760s; while the disinclination of the authorities to use the law to confine the enthusiasm for duelling meant that there was little by way of legal obstacles in their path. Table 2.6, which summarises the response of the law to the recorded duelling incidents that constitute our sample for the years 1716–70, indicates that there was an identifiable decline in the proportion of duellists taken to court in the mid-eighteenth century. By the 1760s the authorities no longer prosecuted duellists as a matter of course, even in cases in which there were fatalities, if the duel was deemed to have been conducted within the code of honour, because judges and

Henry Flood (courtesy of National Library of Ireland)

juries routinely returned verdicts of manslaughter in self-defence which ensured the defendant's prompt release.

But the relaxation in the recourse to the courts was not the main reason for the rise in the number of duels that took place in the late 1760s and afterwards. The law followed opinion; it did not shape it. We need to look elsewhere for an explanation of the increased disposition of men to have recourse to arms to defend their honour. The answer is to be found in the changes in the political milieu that followed the breakdown of the broad consensus that prevailed in Irish politics during the heyday of the undertaker system and that paralleled the emergence of a younger generation of more aggressive politicians who aspired to make government in Ireland more responsive to the wishes and needs of Protestant opinion at large.

As Table 2.7 illustrates, it is impossible to arrive at any conclusion, other than the most general, as to the cause of duels in Ireland between 1716 and 1760. Contemporary reports are generally uninformative, and when they do venture a causal explanation, they are usually perfunctory. 'A difference', 'some words', 'a quarrell' or some equally banal formulation are the usual explanations proffered,[2] and it is possible only in a small number of instances to penetrate this veil of obscurity. Matters improved somewhat after 1760, but despite the substantial increase in the numbers of newspapers carrying reports of affairs of honour, press reports are seldom forthcoming on this aspect of duelling. As Tables 2.7 and 3.9 attest, it is possible to throw light on the cause of no more than 40 per cent of the duelling incidents known to have taken place between 1761 and 1800. This issue will be considered more fully below,[3] but the most striking feature of these tables is the rise in prominence of electoral and parliamentary politics as a causative factor. Exceeded only by 'arguments' — a catch-all category which embraces such vague and ultimately unsatisfactory contemporary explanations as 'some words', 'a difference' and so on — political and electoral disagreements had emerged as the main identifiable cause of duelling by the 1770s because of the changing pattern of Irish politics from the 1750s.

The money bill dispute, which erupted on the Irish political stage in December 1753, had an important destabilising impact upon domestic political activity. It signalled the beginning of the end of the 'undertaker era', during the *floruit* of which political differences, both personal and principled, were sacrificed on the altar of political brokerage, and personal gain was the litmus of political ambition. These tendencies did not disappear from Irish political life, of course, not least because the undertaker system which enshrined them emerged from the money bill dispute intact if not unscathed. But the political playing-field became less predictable and less manageable as a consequence of the emergence of such talented and vigorous 'Patriot' politicians as Edmund Sexton Pery, Charles Lucas and Henry Flood, and the reluctance of Lords Lieutenant during these decades to resort to the old practice of relying on one parliamentary undertaker.[4] The upshot was that though Irish politics calmed down in the late 1750s and early 1760s compared with the eventfulness of the early and mid-1750s, there was no return to the political quietude of the 1730s and 1740s. Uncertainty, disagreement, controversy and frustrated ambition were among the most visible features of the political milieu in these years, and they combined to ensure that the number of actual and averted duels that took place was significantly higher than it had been in the 1730s and early 1740s. The death of George II in 1760 and the amendment of the electoral law in 1768 to provide for general elections every eight years also contributed by offering young and ambitious politicians increased opportunity to become members of parliament; while the radicalising impact of events in the American colonies and the emergence of a strong reform movement in Britain also played a part by providing Irish politics with an agenda for change which many believed worthy of imitation.[5]

Until the Octennial Act of 1768 the Irish parliament was dissolved only on the death of the ruling monarch. This meant that there was no general election between the accession of George II in 1727 and his demise thirty-three years later.[6] This contributed to the general uneventfulness of political life during much of this period. It also ensured that the 1761 general election, the first since the money bill dispute, was keenly contested in a range of county and borough constituencies. In the absence of provision for regular general elections, political influence for a generation was seen to be at stake, and tempers ran high. They ran highest in County Tipperary, where Daniel Gahan, the election agent of Sir Thomas Maude of Dundrum, a staunch Protestant of the 'red-hot' variety strong in that county,[7] fought and killed Thomas Prendergast, the agent of Thomas Mathew, a member of the largely Catholic Mathew family of Thomastown who had converted to Protestantism, in a duel that arose out of Gahan's assertion that Prendergast's wife was a Catholic.[8] Seven years later, when the first general election was called in accordance with the recently ratified Octennial Act, the political temperature in the country at large had become decidedly warmer.

The appointment of George, Viscount Townshend, who was widely perceived in Ireland as an acolyte of the reviled Lord Bute,[9] as Lord Lieutenant in 1767 lifted Irish politics out of the torpor into which they had descended in the mid-1760s because of the non-residence and disinterest of successive Lords Lieutenant. Townshend was not sent to Ireland with a programme for radical change. He was simply instructed to secure parliamentary approval for the augmentation of the Irish army establishment, but this became an intensely controversial measure because his refusal to meet what he believed were the avaricious demands of the undertakers for their support for the proposal had an acutely disruptive effect on the prevailing political order in Ireland. Part of the price Townshend paid to get his way with the augmentation bill was the ratification of an Octennial Act. This measure had been urged for some time by the Patriots; its ratification now was due only in part to their pressure. This notwithstanding, the fact that it came into force at a time when the management structures in place in the House of Commons were also under threat and the level of popular political agitation continued to increase meant that parliamentary elections became more fraught affairs. This led inevitably to confrontations, and, beginning with the general election of 1768, electoral duelling became a regular feature of Irish political life.

The 1768 election was not especially violent, though contemporaries were taken aback by what they observed. Robert Harrison, Lord Fingall's estate agent, reported to his employer in September that 'the country . . . has been all in flames everywhere by means of the elections . . . Thank God they are all over with a few duels but very little hurt.'[10] Harrison was exaggerating. The country was not 'in flames', though the number of duelling incidents reported in 1768 was significantly up on preceding years. A survey of the surviving files of *Pue's Occurrences* and *Finn's Leinster Journal* suggests there were at least eleven duelling incidents in the calendar year 1768. Only four of these can be attributed definitely to electoral rivalry,[11] but others almost certainly originated in similar circumstances.[12] Whatever their precise origins, the number of duels that took place in 1768 was significantly above the level recorded for any previous year. However, as Harrison noted, none of the election duels resulted in the death of any of the participants. A number were wounded, but nobody's life was endangered.[13]

If general elections every seven to eight years between 1768 and 1797 provided increased opportunity for disagreement and hence for more duels, neither regular general elections nor the more confrontational political mood of the times provide a full explanation for the striking escalation in the number of duels that took place in Ireland in the early 1770s. There is one other factor. This is the example set for the generality of the Irish landed and ruling elite by their peers. Unlike the early eighteenth century, when relatively few duellists came from the pinnacle of Irish society, several highly publicised disputes involving the cream of British and Irish society took place between 1769 and 1773 and these had the effect of giving duelling unprecedented publicity and respectability.

The Flood–Agar duel, 1769

The first such encounter took place at Dunmore, County Kilkenny, in August 1769 and involved Henry Flood, then the most prominent Patriot and talented orator in the Irish House of Commons, and James Agar of Ringwood, whose nephew became the first Viscount Clifden. This is not the place for a detailed account of the struggle for control of the Callan borough that locked the Floods and the Agars in bitter emnity for several decades, but some background is necessary.[14] The roots of the disagreement that led to the duel can be traced to the breakdown in the working agreement arrived at by the Flood, Agar and Wemys families in 1715 to share the representation of the borough between them. Despite this, the Floods sought and managed to establish themselves as the dominant force in the constituency during the reign of George II because the Rev. Henry Candler, who served as sovereign of the borough without interruption for twenty-two years from 1735, allied himself with them. However, Candler's death in 1757 loosened the allegiance of some freeholders in his interest, with the result that the Floods were soon precipitated into a desperate struggle to prevent the borough passing out of their control and into that of their most resolute and determined opponent — James Agar of Ringwood. Matters simmered uneasily for a time after Candler's death, but flared up violently in 1759 (the year Henry Flood was first elected to parliament) when a 'desperate quarrell', following the controversial re-election of Charles Flood of Ballymack as sovereign of the corporation, resulted in the deaths of two men. Francis Flood of Paulstown (Henry's uncle) and Francis junior (his cousin) were brought to trial for their involvement in the incident, but they were acquitted. Despite this, the Flood-Agar rivalry for control of Callan was renewed the following year (1760), when it made headlines once again. This time Charles Flood, Henry's second uncle, was tried for his part in the events that led to the death of Matthew Keogh, but he too was acquitted.[15]

By now the struggle for Callan was almost out of control, and the authorities seemed powerless to do anything to stop it. Following a contested general election return in 1761–2, further acrimonious elections for the office of sovereign of the borough in the early 1760s, and legal proceedings initiated on Agar's behalf which challenged the very basis of the Floods' command of the borough, relations between Henry Flood and James Agar deteriorated to such an extent that James Agar was bound over in 1763 'to keep the peace towards all his Ma[jes]ties subjects and in part[icu]lar Henry Flood Esqr for one whole year'. Neither Henry nor any of the Floods was similarly confined, and, after a family dinner during which, it was reported, the Floods collectively affirmed that they 'would go knee-deep in blood for Callan', Charles Flood endeavoured to take advantage of this fact by provoking Agar into a duel. Agar did not respond as anticipated; instead Charles Flood was charged, tried and found guilty in August 1763 of waylaying and assaulting James Agar. Two years and several legal setbacks later, the Floods' control of Callan became even more tenuous when James Agar purchased the extensive Callan estate of the financially embarrassed peer Lord Desart. This meant that Agar now commanded most of the lands in the borough as well as a substantial interest in the corporation, and it was probably the realisation that control of the borough was slipping irrevocably from his grasp that caused Henry Flood to assault Agar 'in an inhuman manner openly in the street of Dublin' in May 1765. This was a *casus duelli*, and Agar, as anticipated, issued a challenge. However, before the two men could proceed to an exchange of shots in the Phoenix Park the sheriff of Dublin 'interposed' and bound them both over. This interruption angered Flood, who maintained that Agar could have avoided being bound over with little difficulty, and his irritation was heightened ten days later when he received a request via Thomas Adderly, Agar's second, that he should accompany Agar out of the country to settle the matter in a foreign jurisdiction. Flood declared he was ready 'at an hour's notice' to go wherever necessary, despite the advice of 'the most punctilious in duelling' that he was no longer bound even to respond to such messages because Agar had facilitated the imposition of the recognisance to keep the peace. However, instead of interpreting Flood's response as reason to press on with the arrangements to bring the dispute to an early climax, Agar and Adderley procrastinated. Matters remained in this unsatisfactory state for a number of days until Agar determined that 'Calais or somewhere out of his majesty's dominions' was a suitable location, but Flood's second, Sackville Gardiner, demurred, preferring, like Flood, to go to England. The two principals did embark finally for Holyhead in early June, where they proceeded to an exchange of shots, as a result of which, according to one source, Agar was slightly wounded.[16]

The readiness of Henry Flood and James Agar to risk their lives in a duel indicates just how bitter and how personalised the battle for control of Callan had become by 1765. And with several cases pending against John, George and Charles Flood in both the Irish and English courts for exercising illegal control over the office of sovereign of Callan, there was no let-up in the inter-family rivalry. Indeed, things worsened as a series of court decisions in 1767–8, which went the way of Agar, further undermined the legal basis of the Floods' claim to command the borough.[17]

The Floods' control now depended primarily on their ability to preserve their precarious majority among the burgesses. Every vote was vital, so when it was suggested in October 1768 that Francis Knapp, the 'deputy sovereign', who 'usualy voted in the interest of Mr Flood', was contemplating quitting his farm at Burnchurch, which he rented from Henry Flood, for a farm on Agar's estate, the Floods determined to stop him. Control of the borough was seen to rest on Knapp's vote, and they did their utmost to persuade him to maintain his traditional allegiance. They were only partly successful. Knapp vacillated, but his wife, who was made of sterner stuff, refused to change her mind, and she invited James Agar to visit their home to assure her husband. Agar was persuaded by friends of the inadvisability of entering what was now virtually enemy territory, and requested the Catholic landlord of the Red Lion Inn in Callan, Michael Keogh, go in his place. He even gave him his pistols for the journey to Burnchurch, though it was illegal for a Catholic to bear arms without a licence. When Keogh and Bridget Knapp, who accompanied him, arrived at their destination, they were met by some of the Floods' retainers who shot at them, forced the chaise in which they were travelling to stop, smashed it to pieces and assaulted the chaise-boy. Keogh was slightly wounded by a pistol ball, but he managed to escape serious injury by fleeing the scene and abandoning Agar's pistols. This was a setback, but with control of the borough within his grasp, Agar was not prepared to let the matter rest. He directed Keogh to place an advertisement in *Finn's Leinster Journal* in October offering a £40 reward for the discovery and prosecution of those who assaulted him. Not to be outdone, Henry Flood had George Huson, his mother's servant, publish a counter-advertisement a few days later claiming that Keogh was hurt attempting to break and enter Knapp's home in 'pursuance of a corrupt bargain' he had entered into with 'a certain gentleman [i.e. James Agar]'; the advertisement sought information on the owner of the pistols Keogh had left behind and offered £40 to any person who would 'prosecute to conviction' those who, it alleged, had attacked Francis Knapp's house.[18]

In the short term, the Floods' defiant response paid dividends. Their candidate was victorious once again in the election for sovereign of Callan borough in 1769, but James Agar refused to back down. He filed an information in the Court of King's Bench in June 1769 against Flood and others concerning the events at Burnchurch in the previous October, and he sent Richard Roth on 22 August to Flood to demand the return of his pistols. Flood denied they were in his possession. Agar refused to accept his word and demanded that Flood meet him to settle the matter like men of honour. Given Agar's offensive attitude and determination to fight (he repulsed all suggestions by Roth that he should let the matter drop), Flood had no alternative but to agree a time and a place if he was not to be ridiculed publicly by his rival as a liar and a coward. Dunmore was the agreed location, and, with their seconds, Gervase Parker Bushe and Richard Roth, in attendance, the two men lined up at fourteen paces at two o'clock on the afternoon of Friday 25 August. As had been the case throughout this phase of their dispute, Agar was the more aggressive of the two adversaries on the field. He declined all suggestions of mediation, and once he had been cautioned by Bushe against using his free arm as a 'rest' for his pistol, he was the first to fire. His first shot missing, he took up his second pistol in readiness to use it if Flood's shot was also off-target. It was not. With Agar's words 'Fire, you scoundrel' echoing round the ground, Flood's ball penetrated Agar's left breast; he slumped to the ground and died within minutes.[19]

Because the duel had been conducted in the presence of seconds, and because Agar had issued the challenge, there was little likelihood that Flood would be found guilty of murder should the case be brought to court. Gervase Parker Bushe, for one, was convinced that 'no man ever was more compelled to defend his honour and his person, and no man ever did it with more temper and steady courage than Mr Flood'.[20] Lord Townshend, who had planned to visit Flood at his seat at Farmley on his way back to Dublin from his Munster tour, was also persuaded that 'Flood stands fair'.[21] Inevitably, the Agars saw things differently. Relations between the two families had been so poisonous for so long that they determined to prosecute for murder, and the coroner's inquest gave them some grounds for optimism. Instead of returning a verdict of 'manslaughter in self defence' or of 'wilful murder', as was usual in such circumstances, the coroner simply recorded the facts as they were presented and left it to the law courts to decide. Flood was 'charged with the killing of . . . James Agar . . . in defence of the life of . . . the said Henry Flood which . . . James Agar had attempted and was again prepared and about to attempt'. This was unusual but, because of the influence of the Agar family in County Kilkenny, it was not wholly unanticipated. There was no question of Flood being held in custody. He was bound by his own recognisances and those of his uncles John and Charles to await trial at the spring assizes in 1770.[22] Flood would have preferred an earlier court appearance. He appealed to Townshend 'for a special commission to be tried immediately', but the Lord Chancellor, Lord Lifford, rejected the idea on the grounds that it would set an unwelcome precedent others would seek to imitate.[23] Counsel for the Agars meanwhile prepared as strong a case as they could assemble to prosecute Flood. However, they had little with which to work, except the longstanding animosity of the combatants,[24] because Flood had conducted himself impeccably on the duelling field and fulfilled every legal requirement expected of him in its wake.[25] The outcome was never in question; when the case came to trial, Flood was found guilty of manslaughter in his own defence and set free.

Because of the long history of antagonism between the two families and the national profile of the participants, the Flood–Agar duel excited an enormous amount of public attention. It was the talk of the salons as well as of the coffee-houses, the subject of private correspondence and public discourse. Counsel for the Agars alleged in court that the Floods manipulated the press coverage in order 'to intimidate magistrates from doing their duty', but there was little reason for them to do this, as the press eagerly published every scrap of information on the duel that came their way. Flood was an immensely popular figure — a hero alike to the increasingly politicised urban middle classes, who applauded his oratory in the House of Commons, and to the country gentlemen, who admired his abilities. He was their champion, and they anxiously followed every twist in this dramatic saga. As a consequence, the Flood–Agar encounter gave the code of honour unprecedented publicity.[26] Its profile and image was boosted further in the years that followed by a number of sensational encounters involving other members of the Irish and English political and aristocratic elites.

*

Within a couple of months of the Flood–Agar duel, Dublin was gripped by a report that Sir George Macartney, Lord Townshend's Chief Secretary, had met Lord Mountnorres in a duel in December 1769 and that both men had been wounded. The report was false.[27] No duel took place, but the alacrity with which people accepted that it had and the lack of censure in their observations indicated that the report had done Macartney's reputation as a political trouble-shooter no harm at all; indeed, it had probably enhanced it.

The facility with which bravery under fire could establish or rehabilitate an injured reputation at this time is best illustrated by the response to the encounter that took place in London a year later between Lord George Sackville, the so-called 'coward of Minden', and Captain George Johnstone. Sackville, who had served for a time as Chief Secretary in Ireland in the early 1750s, was a sad and lonely figure in English political circles in the 1760s because of the imputation of cowardice that had followed his tardiness in following orders at the battle of Minden in 1759.[28] Johnstone sought to exploit this, and he was more than surprised when, following 'some scurrilous expressions' he made at Sackville's expense in the House of Commons in December 1770, Sackville challenged him to a duel in Hyde Park and 'behaved with much cool and real courage under fire'. Like the Flood–Agar encounter, the Sackville–Johnstone duel was the talk of polite society in Dublin as well as London, and since Johnstone was one of the first to acknowledge his opponent's bravery and was, by all accounts, more nervous on the field, the reputation of the so-called 'coward of Minden' was instantly redeemed.[29] Colonel Smith, one of Townshend's many London correspondents, summed up the position up well when he observed on 18 December that 'Lord George is much praised and Johnstone blamed', and that he (Sackville) had atoned for his lapse of judgment in 1759. This news was warmly welcomed in Ireland, where Sackville had many friends and where his disgrace had shocked leading figures in the Irish administration.[30]

Such a clear-cut example of the facility with which courage in a duel could rehabilitate an injured reputation is rare, but it demonstrates the potency of the code of honour in British and Irish society at this time more clearly than a dozen unexampled assertions. The point can be demonstrated further by reference to the incident reported by William Hull of Bandon to Edward Lees at Dublin Castle some months later:

> Little Bernard [Francis Bernard junior] is one of his [Townshend's] votaries . . . The other day in a mixed company, one of them threw out something slighting which Bernard took up very smartly and said it was very ill bred to animadvert on his crest. The affair went so far that Bernard threw a glass of wine in his face and instantly drew his sword, but by the interposition of the company the matter was reconciled. The father was a little uneasy when he heard it; but on second thoughts he told me he was glad to find Frank had so much spirit, and that he would be very ungrateful if he should suffer anything to pass unnoticed which reflected on Lord Townshend . . . [The incident] has got the young man great credit.[31]

These remarks bear witness to the positive image enjoyed by the code of honour in the 1760s and 1770s which contributed to the heightened disposition to duel. This disposition was facilitated by the continuing disinclination of the authorities in Britain as well as Ireland to take the steps necessary to contain the martial ardour of their nobility. For example, when Lord Milton struck Lord Paulet in London on 26 January 1771 in order to get him to fight, a company of horse guards intervened to prevent the incident leading to a duel. However, the civil authorities declined to take any legal action, with the result that within three days of their release the two men met and fought a duel in which Milton was injured.[32] Six years earlier when Lord Byron was brought to trial for killing William Chaworth in a duel, he was found guilty of manslaughter by the House of Lords, but was released unpunished because of his rank. This was the usual response in such cases. According to V. G. Kiernan, only eighteen of ninety-one fatal duels fought in England during the reign of George III gave rise to court proceedings.[33] This leniency exasperated the upholders of the law as well as the opponents of duelling. In his seminal *Commentaries on the laws of England*, which was first published in the 1760s, Sir William Blackstone delineated the legal options open to judges if they wished to combat duelling. He acknowledged the right of an individual to kill in self-defence (*se defendendo*) 'in the event of being attacked', but denied that this could be extended to include duelling. Blackstone perceived 'malice and concerted design' in most duels, which meant, he affirmed, they should be denominated 'felonious' rather than 'excusable homicide':

> Express malice is when one, with a sedate deliberate mind and formal design doth kill another: which formal design is evidenced by external circumstances discovering that inward intention; as lying in wait, antecedent menaces, former grudges, and concerted schemes to do him some bodily harm. This takes in the case of deliberate duelling where both parties meet avowedly with an intent to murder: thinking it their duty as gentlemen, and claiming it as their right, to wanton with their own lives and those of their fellow creatures, without any warrant or authority from any power either divine or human, but in direct contradiction to the laws both of God and man and therefore the law has justly fixed the crime and punishment of murder on them, and on their seconds also.[34]

However, one can only gain a clear perspective on a law when one assesses it in terms of the society that validates it, and Blackstone's analysis of statute law on the subject of duelling is vitiated by the fact that both aristocratic sensibilities and current practice were predisposed to avow that duelling should be indulged.[35] As a consequence, as Blackstone himself acknowledged, the law could not ensure the abandonment of duelling without a palpable revolution in manners:

> It requires such a degree of passive valour to combat the dread of even undeserved contempt, arising from the false notions of honour too generally received in Europe that the strongest prohibitions and penalties of the law will never be intirely effectual to eradicate this unhappy custom; till a method be found out of compelling the original aggressor to make some other satisfaction to the affronted party which the world shall esteem equally reputable as that which is now given at the hazard of the life and fortune as well as of the person insulted as of him who hath given the insult.[36]

Such a time was still some way off in Britain. It was even further away in Ireland, where enthusiasm for duelling blossomed in the confrontational political atmosphere fostered by the Townshend administration.

The Townshend–Bellamont duel, 1773

A peer by birth and a soldier by training, Lord Townshend was a decisive, strong-willed man of firm convictions who found it difficult to indulge the self-importance of Irish politicians. His primary object in Ireland was to affirm Britain's imperial authority.[37] This was not a popular policy, and Townshend was not a popular Lord Lieutenant as a result. Although he was gregarious and convivial, Townshend's relations with many prominent Irish political figures was far from easy. Unable to curb his instinctive impatience[38] or to bear with fortitude the forbidding chore of balancing the rival demands for patronage from an endless series of Irish *and* English supplicants he was inclined, on occasions, to let his emotions cloud his judgment. As a consequence, he found himself embroiled in difficulties with several prominent Irish gentlemen.

Townshend's most celebrated disagreement was with Charles Coote, Earl of Bellamont. Bellamont was an unpredictable man whose punctiliousness, vile temper, poor judgment and self-importance plunged him into numerous scrapes and cost him the friendship and affections of many who were close to him during his incident-filled life.[39] Relations between the two peers got off to a bad start when Bellamont's impolitic request for an extension to the leave of absence allowed to Colonel James Gisborne, shortly after Townshend's acceptance of his Irish posting, obliged the new Lord Lieutenant (to his manifest displeasure) to bend military regulations to accommodate the Irish peer.[40] This achieved, Bellamont urged his own claim to be raised to the rank of lieutenant-colonel in the army. One of Townshend's viceregal predecessors, the Earl of Hertford, had promised him it would 'be done', Bellamont maintained when he presented his case in 1767, but Townshend could do little to meet his wishes as there were no vacancies, and the matter was still unresolved three years later.[41] Meanwhile in 1768 Bellamont had proffered what he believed was a small request. He sought a vacant state trumpeter's place for Henry Cornelius of Dublin, but because the place had been filled by the time Bellamont presented his request to Townshend at his country retreat at Leixlip, he was promised the next vacancy. Unfortunately for Bellamont, he pressed his case with too much ardour. In January 1769 he responded to a rumour that the state trumpeter, Rowly Gibbons, had died, by recommending the suit of Cornelius once again. Anxious to be rid of the importunate peer, Townshend ordered the appointment to be made, only to be informed that Gibbons was not dead.[42]

By now Townshend was so out-of-humour with Bellamont that he did not want even to meet him, and he declined repeated requests for an audience in 1769. He referred Bellamont instead to Thomas Waite, his efficient Under-Secretary, but the punctilious peer was not prepared to be fobbed off. He insisted that his business was 'simply with your excellency' and expressed his willingness to wait until the Lord Lieutenant was free.[43] Townshend must have agreed to see him, because relations between the two men had mellowed a year later when Bellamont submitted an application 'in writing' for a military transfer which the Lord Lieutenant forwarded to London. Such matters commonly took time to arrange, but Bellamont could not resist the temptation to put his oar in to speed things up.[44] It is not clear if it was this that was responsible for alienating Townshend once again; it certainly did little to advance Bellamont's subsequent request for an exchange with Colonel William Burton, and at the end of January 1772 he was once again to be found knocking on Townshend's door. The Lord Lieutenant had evidently had his fill of Bellamont by now, for he declined to meet him on each occasion he called at Dublin Castle, and on the 24th directed his *aide de camp*, Lieutenant-Colonel Walsh, to inform the waiting peer that he could not see him 'at an earlier day than this day se'nnight'. This was quite unusual, and Bellamont was incensed at what he perceived as Townshend's unparalleled rudeness. He immediately dispatched a letter to the Lord Lieutenant protesting at 'the unexpected refusals which I have formerly had and the extraordinary difficulties and delays which have on this last occasion been thrown in my way', withdrawing his request for an exchange with Colonel Burton, and affirming his determination to sell his employment of deputy quartermaster-general.[45]

Bellamont was not the only Irish peer at odds with Townshend early in 1772, as the Lord Lieutenant struggled to make the inadequate patronage he had at his disposal stretch to satisfy the apparently insatiable Irish appetite for preferment. Henry Loftus, the ambitious Wexford borough magnate, antagonised the Lord Lieutenant when he failed to display sufficient gratitude for his appointment to the Board of Accounts and his son's promotion to a cornetcy. Loftus, who had also applied for a position for his brother (with whom he currently divided his official salary), gave the credit for his son's good fortune to Lord Ely rather than to the Lord Lieutenant. Townshend was so irritated by Loftus's lack of graciousness that he directed Sir George Macartney to write to him to ask him if he wished to surrender his position. Loftus naturally declined, but he was so 'injured' by the communication that he requested Townshend to withdraw the charge that he (Loftus) had 'used you ill'.[46] This was the sort of situation that seemed tailor-made to precipitate a duel if Loftus had the courage to press the matter to such a resolution. He could not do so, obviously, while Townshend was Lord Lieutenant, but Townshend's term in Ireland came to a close in the autumn of 1772. However, by this time Loftus's irritation had subsided; he had no wish to reanimate an old quarrel, and he let the matter rest.

Others were not so forgiving, and rumours abounded throughout 1772 and 1773 that Sir Edward Newenham, George Rochfort and the

Earl of Belvedere each awaited an opportunity to call Townshend to account. Sir Edward Newenham was aggrieved because Townshend had dismissed him from a lucrative position in the revenue;[47] while the Earl of Belvedere and his son, George Rochfort, were offended by a letter in which Townshend criticised Rochfort for not supporting a parliamentary address of thanks.[48] None of these was to receive an opportunity to call the former Lord Lieutenant out. Hardly had Townshend returned to England than Lord Bellamont deputised the Earl of Charlemont to wait on him with a paper which contained an account of the 'intentional indignity wantonly cast' on him on 24 January[49] by Townshend's instruction to his *aide de camp* to inform him (Bellamont) publicly that he could not see him that day, though others were given an audience. In accordance with Bellamont's instructions, Charlemont demanded an apology. Townshend declined to respond on the grounds that if he did so he would be acknowledging an offence he claimed he never intended. This did not satisfy Bellamont who increased the temperature of the dispute by instructing Charlemont to inform Townshend that he considered him 'divested of every principle that constitutes the character of a man of honour'. Such an uncompromising insult made a duel virtually certain if Townshend did not offer the required apology. He did not do so, but he did the next best thing; he sent his second, Lord Ligonier, to Bellamont on Saturday 20 December with a note assuring him that he had 'never meant to offend you'. This gave Bellamont an ideal opportunity to extricate himself from the quarrel with his honour intact, but he declined to avail of it. Instead he returned Townshend's letter, claiming it was 'not yet entirely sufficient'. Now guided by Lord Ancram, he demanded that the apology 'be fully expressed', and he transmitted a draft which called on Townshend to disavow the thoroughly 'offensive' message delivered by his *aide de camp* and to state that it was not his desire 'to give Lord Bellamont any offence'. This was going too far. Although Lord Charlemont had opined in an account of the affair he sent to Henry Flood on 30 December that the matter was near resolution, he had misjudged. Townshend was simply not prepared to offer a 'a submissive apology' which he deemed 'humiliating'.[50]

By this date matters had reached a point of no return. Having seized the initiative as a result of a mistake by Ligonier over the issue of the written apology, Bellamont resolved to press home his advantage by publishing an account of the affair. Townshend was determined the dispute should not become a matter of public debate. He had most to lose if he was forced to enter into a public discussion on the merits or otherwise of his actions, so he determined to bring matters to a speedy conclusion. He had no fear of duelling. On his return from America after leading the storming of Quebec in 1759, he had become involved in an altercation with Lord Albemarle which was only concluded when both men were arrested on the duelling field. Ten years later, he all but invited Charles Lucas to challenge him 'at the mayor's feast' in Dublin.[51] Convinced that the matter had dragged on long enough, he offered Bellamont the challenge he seemed so determined to provoke. Bellamont accepted, and the two men and their seconds met in the afternoon of 2 February in Marylebone Fields. Both combatants carried small swords as well as pistols, but the encounter did not last long enough for the swords to be called into play. Bellamont was incapacitated by Townshend's first shot; he was hit in the groin and had to be carried from the field in a chair.[52]

Given the eminence of the participants, it was entirely predictable that the Townshend–Bellamont duel would cause a sensation in both kingdoms. Although a number of Lords Lieutenant had been threatened with challenges, none of them had yet been induced to fight a duel to justify his actions while in office, and it was a topic of conversation with everybody from peers to paupers. Interest in the duel in Ireland was heightened by the fact that Townshend was *persona non grata* with most of the press, politicians and public. The Dublin popular press had echoed to the sounds of anti-Townshend sentiments throughout 1771 and 1772, and they were solidly pro-Bellamont in 1773.[53] The duel itself was given unprecedented press coverage. Column-inch after column-inch in popular papers like the *Hibernian Journal* and *Finn's Leinster Journal* were given over to extensive reports of all aspects of the affair,[54] and support for the Irish peer grew as it emerged that he had acquitted himself with dignity and bravery on the duelling field.[55] The fact that he had allowed Townshend to fire first and that he bore stoically the futile efforts of his surgeons to extract his opponent's ball impressed many; others were simply concerned for his recovery.[56] Within weeks the incident had become politicised as opposition interests strove to exploit the event for their own ends, as the popular toast 'may we never want a Bellamont to chastise the insolence of a viceroy' bears witness. Supporters of Lord Townshend, for their part, rushed to his defence with a toast of their own: 'may the friends of government never want a Townshend to defend their cause'.[57] When Bellamont had recovered sufficiently to return to Ireland in October, he was afforded an effusive welcome.[58] In the popular mind at least, his duel with Townshend was seen as a patriotic rather than a personal quarrel:

> The call which brought him to the field of honour was not the idle whim of a modern duellist, nor the instantaneous spirit of blood thirsty revenge; it was the cool deliberation of many months; it was the determined result of serious thought, actuated by a love for his country, which would not bear that even the representatives of majesty should, unpunished, insult the dignity of a subject.[59]

This was, of course, a deliberate and dangerous example of special pleading, which distracted the public's attention from the more disturbing aspects of the Bellamont–Townshend incident. These were not lost sight of in Britain. It was a cause of acute concern in political circles there that a retired Lord Lieutenant should be obliged to risk his life in a duel arising out of decisions he had taken while in office.[60] Such concerns did not elicit comment in Ireland, probably because attention was soon distracted by news of another encounter involving a major politician. A mere three days after the Townshend–Bellamont duel in London, the new Chief Secretary, Sir John Blaquiere, met Beauchamp Bagenal of Dunleckney, M.P. for County Carlow, in the Phoenix Park.

The Blaquiere–Bagenal duel, 1773

Beauchamp Bagenal possesses the reputation of being a keen duellist. He was reputed to relish the company of his pistols so much that it was said that he kept a loaded pair by his side even when dining. During the viceroyalty of Lord Townshend he declined to support the administration even though it favoured his friends with places and positions,[61] and spent most of his time abroad. While in Paris, where John Blaquiere was *chargé d'affaires* in the British embassy, he requested to be presented to the King of France, but Blaquiere declined to advance his request on the grounds that Bagenal was not known to him. Angered by this slight, Bagenal applied for and secured a declaration of his *bona fides* from Lord Rochford, who served as ambassador in Paris for a time; but even this did not secure his admission to Versailles, and there the matter rested. However, Bagenal did not forget the incident, and when Blaquiere accepted the invitation to move to Ireland to act as Lord Harcourt's Chief Secretary in 1772, it did not take long for ill-feeling to emerge. The cause of the difference this time was a misunderstanding over Bagenal's request for leave for a kinsman serving with the army in America. Bagenal believed the misunderstanding was sufficiently malicious to warrant the presentation of a challenge, and the two men met with their seconds in the Phoenix Park on the morning of Saturday 5 February 1773. Bagenal fired his two pistols, though one of them needed a change of flint and seven snaps before it fired, and grazed his opponent. Blaquiere fired only once and missed; he reserved his second shot, whereupon the principals were reconciled by their seconds and, according to one contemporary report, 'parted good friends'. The authorities, who were not alerted to the affair until it was over, also obliged both men at the Court of King's Bench to 'pledge their honour severally that nothing further should pass'.[62]

As in the case of the Bellamont–Townshend encounter, the public's response to the Blaquiere–Bagenal duel was uncritical. The Chief Secretary was almost universally praised for his bravery under fire, with figures as diverse as Henry Flood, Edmond Malone and Lord Harcourt singling him out for special mention.[63] Those in office, or with experience of office, were more reproving. Robert Waller, one of Macartney's Irish correspondents at Dublin Castle, was particularly disturbed by the incident. He concluded apprehensively that it might soon become necessary for 'persons receiving appointments . . . [to] . . . provide good pistols and learn to fence'. Henry Seymour Conway, the former English Secretary of State, empathised; he urged greater 'civility' in public affairs in Ireland, as 'too nice resentment of all words and actions in such cases would make public office impracticable'.[64] Conway was, in effect, urging that some distinction should be drawn between public and private grievances to protect office-holders against challenges arising from their work, but few in Ireland saw the need for it. Duelling was fast becoming such an everyday feature of life that it was more usual to animadvert on the details of a duel than to consider the implications of its occurrence. It is striking that Blaquiere's altercation with Bagenal did his career little harm. Indeed, within weeks of his encounter in the Phoenix Park, George III approved a request made on his behalf by Lord Harcourt that he be allowed to sell his commission.[65]

Duelling in the early 1770s

The combined impact of the Flood–Agar, Townshend–Bellamont and Blaquiere–Bagenal duels on Irish public consciousness was considerable. These encounters did more to create an environment in which duelling was acknowledged as part and parcel of normal life than all previous incidents. The most striking evidence for this is to be found in the rise in the number of reported duelling incidents. From its previous high of 33 for the quinquennium 1766–70, the number of reported duels involving Irishmen climbed dramatically to 81 during the first five years of the 1770s.[66] In broad terms, the character of duelling in the early 1770s was pretty much the same as it had been in mid-century. But there were a number of noteworthy developments which made the increase in the disposition to duel more bearable and which may have contributed to the increase that took place, as an analysis of the pattern of duelling in the early 1770s reveals.

As in the early and mid-eighteenth century, gentlemen provided the overwhelming bulk of duellists in the early 1770s, with members of the military, the middle and lower classes making up the remainder (Table 3.1). The distributional pattern too registered only small changes from the situation in the early and mid-eighteenth century (Table 3.2).[67] Indeed, the most visible geographical trend in the early 1770s was the continued decline in the percentage of duels that were fought within the city of Dublin and the emergence of suburban venues like the Phoenix Park (Table 3.3).[68] This process was still incomplete, but seen in the context of the virtual eclipse of the sword as a duelling weapon of choice by the pistol (Tables 3.4 and 3.5)[69] and the greater reliance on seconds (Table 3.8), it is not surprising that the mortality/encounter ratio fell appreciably in the early 1770s. A total of twelve people died as a consequence of the eighty-one duels that comprise our sample for the years 1771–5. This means that there was a 15 per cent chance that one of the principals would die in every encounter, and if this appears low compared with the figure for the early eighteenth century, the percentage of total injuries, which provides a clearer perspective on the nature of duelling during this period, are distinctly less reassuring. In all, 59 per cent of duels produced injuries of some sort to one or both parties, which meant that just over 31 per cent of all duellists were injured or killed as a result of their recourse to arms (Table 3.7). Though still high, these figures represent a palpable improvement on the situation in the early eighteenth century and reflect the fact that a record percentage of encounters (41 per cent) concluded without any injuries, which suggests, in turn, that the increasingly orderly conduct of duelling may have contributed to its rising popularity.

Statistical analysis of this kind provides a bird's-eye view of the changing pattern of duelling in the early 1770s. A closer look at the eighty-one duels that constitute the sample for this period reinforces the impression conveyed by the figures that the rise in the level of duelling was accompanied by a visible improvement in the behaviour of duellists. Seconds were certainly more active in the early 1770s than previously; they ensured that duels were conducted in the proper spirit, and were generally ready to intervene to reconcile the principals once honour had been satisfied by an exchange of shots.[70] It is impossible to state with precision the percentage of recorded duels in which seconds participated because of the lack of information on this point in many cases, but what there is attests to a striking increase in their involvement *and* to their increased readiness to intervene to reconcile hostile principals. Indeed, there are only two recorded instances in which it is clear that there were no seconds present; *per contra*, seconds attempted to reconcile the contending parties in 23 per cent of known cases. They were not always successful, but 16 per cent of the reported duels fought in Ireland between 1771 and 1775 ended in reconciliation because of the mediation of seconds

(Table 3.8). As a result, there are few of the brutal incidents, commonplace earlier in the century, when principals endeavoured to maim and kill their opponents by whatever means they could.

This is not to say there were no bloody encounters in the early 1770s. There were some, but none emulated the viciousness apparent in earlier decades. A good example of a duel in which the antagonists were determined to spill blood took place at Thurles, County Tipperary, in 1773 when two troopers, who failed to settle their differences with pistols, unsheathed their swords and 'cut each other in so desperate a manner that . . . both their lives are in danger'.[71] The same tendency, but with a different outcome, is also illustrated by the encounter involving two attornies which took place in Dublin in 1772 in which an estimated forty shots were fired without one hitting its target.[72] An only slightly less bizarre encounter took place in County Monaghan some years later when William Coulson met a local man named Griffith. Neither was a skilled marksman, since they expended their four shots and all their powder without effect. Anxious that matters should not conclude so unsatisfactorily, Griffith suggested the they should continue the quarrel with swords, but Coulson declined. Unwilling to let matters rest, Griffith went to his home, which was nearby, for a fresh supply of powder and ball, and on his return the two men exchanged twelve more shots before Coulson hit Griffith in the thigh and they agreed to conclude proceedings.[73] Compared with these, Thompson and Young who met in the Phoenix Park in 1773 were the very essence of decorum; they submitted to the suggestion of their seconds to conclude their quarrel after six shots when Young's fourth pistol failed to fire.[74]

Such prolonged encounters could only take place when the principals chose to fight with pistols. A more familiar infringement of duelling etiquette occurred in November 1773 when two gentlemen, who had exchanged 'some words' at the Dublin assizes, hired a room in a tavern and took their places at three yards' distance. Somewhat surprisingly, only one party was injured, and then not seriously.[75] Lieutenant Reynolds of the 45th Regiment of Foot was not so lucky. He quarrelled with Lieutenant Ruxton at Limerick barracks on the evening of 20 April, but instead of waiting until the next morning to fight, Reynolds insisted they did so there and then. It was not a wise decision. He was wounded in the side and died on the following day, having previously absolved his opponent of any wrongdoing by acknowledging the fault was his.[76] Incidents such as these were proportionately less common in the 1770s than they were earlier in the century.[77] This is further testimony to the penetration of duelling etiquette which encouraged duellists to leave a decent interval between the issuing of a challenge and the taking up of arms in order to refute allegations of their critics that duelling was nothing other than the legitimisation of such base emotions as anger, revenge and rage. This was never entirely possible because it was precisely these emotions that prompted many to duel. When, for example, Ryan was killed by Shannon in July 1773 following a disagreement over his failure to repay a loan, the two men fired their first shots in anger in Drumcondra, and their second, which led to Ryan's death, some time later in Glasnevin.[78]

Press accounts of the Shannon–Ryan encounter were harshly critical of their seconds for failing to prevent the principals resuming their quarrel in Glasnevin. But this was hardly fair. Seconds could only do so much, and they were not helped by the failure of the authorities (specifically, the political and judicial authorities) to take appropriate steps to counter the rise in the number of duels taking place. Occasionally local officials did intervene to prevent a duel,[79] but in most instances, as the Bagenal–Blaquiere affair attests, they simply did not know an encounter was scheduled to occur until it was over. In cases in which the parties were intercepted or interrupted, the usual procedure was to bind them to keep the peace. This worked well enough within the Irish legal jurisdiction, but since it did not extend to Britain, a steady trickle of Irish duellists made the journey to Holyhead to do there what they were prohibited from doing in Ireland.[80] The extent of the law's disengagement from the task of combating duelling is emphasised by the fact that the number of duellists who were tried in court for their actions dwindled virtually to nothing in the early 1770s. Moreover, those that were sent for trial all secured 'honourable acquittals' (Table 3.8).[81] Indeed, the law not only tolerated, it frequently indulged duellists. This is indicated by an incident in Sligo in 1770 in which a 'notorious duellist', apprehended for killing another, refused to go to the local jail because 'it was a dirty place . . . not fit for a gentleman'. He was permitted to take lodgings in an inn instead; however, when a local landowner was informed of this arrangement, he made the offender's acquaintance and was so taken by him that he invited him to stay in his own house until the trial was over.[82]

In circumstances in which landlords were willing to offer 'notorious duellists' shelter, it is hardly surprising that juries were not disposed to return guilty verdicts in those cases that did go to trial. But it was not just the landed aristocracy but the very apparatus of the law itself that was disposed to protect duellists. This was brought home with startling vividness in 1772 by the court martial of Captain Garstin of the 17th Dragoons for cowardice. Garstin had had a disagreement with Major Birch of the same regiment which, Birch contended, could only be settled with weapons. The two men and their seconds fixed the time and the place, but when the seconds called upon them to fire, Garstin 'burst into a flood of tears . . .

kept his pistol close by his side, the muzzle pointed to the ground, and said he [Birch] might do with him whatever he pleased, but that he would not fire upon him'. Birch was so appalled by what he deemed the pusillanimous conduct of his opponent that he departed the ground 'like a man of honour' and promptly initiated the proceedings that were to result in Garstin being brought before a general court martial for cowardice. As it happened, Garstin got off on a technicality because the court martial was improperly constituted, but not before he had been reprimanded, and everybody from the Lord Lieutenant (Townshend) to the English Secretary of State (Rochford) concluded he had behaved in a most 'unmilitary' fashion.[83] This was an extraordinary outcome given that Lords Lieutenant were instructed 'to cashier . . . all such officers as shall send, receive or deliver any challenge, or give any real affront to any other'.[84] However, the experience of Garstin and of Captain David Roche, who was only persuaded to accept the challenge of a Scots officer by the disapproval of his colleagues when they learned he intended to decline it, reveals clearly that army officers placed more store on observing the code of honour than the law.[85]

If military law, which was tougher in most respects than civil law, was unable to contain duelling within the ranks of the army, it was not to be expected that the civil courts would act differently in cases involving soldiers, and it did not. Thus, for example, when Captain Samuel Williams of the 11th Regiment of Foot was tried before the Dublin commission of Oyer and Terminer in July 1773 for the murder of Lieutenant Wolsely in a duel two months earlier, he was 'honourably acquitted'.[86] The duelling ethos was so deeply inculcated in society at large by the 1770s that those, like Captain Garstin, who declined to duel were arguably as brave as those who conformed and who accepted and issued challenges. However, few contemporaries accepted this, and as a result few dared risk the opprobium that would result from such behaviour. Thus when the M.P. Sir John Conway Colthurst refused to call out St Leger St Leger in 1771 after the latter had assaulted him, he was described in a confidential government list as 'a mere paltry fellow'.[87] Similarly, when Colonel George Browne, briefly M.P. for County Mayo, declined to meet a fellow-soldier while serving in America, he was deemed a coward by a hostile critic who concluded that 'to bestow on you the title of a soldier is to prostitute that honourable name'.[88]

The dictates of the code of honour spread its tentacles wider than the military and political establishments. Though not significant statistically, enough members of the middle classes duelled to indicate that the code of honour was as firmly established among certain sections of the professions by the mid-1770s as it was among the aristocracy and gentry.[89]

More revealing still, the concept of honour, though not duelling with weapons, was taken on board by artisans and skilled labourers. Their preferred method of settling scores was boxing, and their encounters could be as deadly as if they used weapons. When James Warren, a weaver, and Charles Clarke, a sailor, met near Newtown, County Waterford, in December 1774, Warren killed his opponent with 'a punch under the short ribs'. Some months later a 'duel' at Sligo between a weaver and a brogue-maker was not concluded until the seconds 'boxed it out to the full satisfaction of the honour and injury of all parties'.[90] These were not fortuitous happenings. They were the lower class's response to the growing enthusiasm for duelling throughout society. It might be suggested that such incidents owe more to the rising interest in pugilism than to the code of honour, but this is too simplistic. Newspapers, for instance, went out of their way to connect the two practices, and frequently cited the willingness of individuals of lower-class background to fight to the death when they disagreed as reason for 'people in the higher walks of life' to desist from duelling. Indeed, the *Hibernian Journal* in 1774 went so far as to describe boxing as a superior means of settling disputes because, it observed pointedly, it resulted in fewer fatalities.[91] This observation may have had some bearing on the rising popularity of boxing encounters. By the late 1780s, when pugilism was better established, there was a distinct willingness on the part of members of the lower professions to have recourse to fisticuffs rather than to weapons to determine disputes, though the outcome in the instances that were reported could be just as deadly. Thus in May 1789 Morrissey, a carman, and Quirk, a labourer, fought with their fists in a field near Clonmel till Morrissey was fatally injured. A few weeks later the report of an altercation in Dublin involving two hackney coachmen indicated that one of the participants was very seriously hurt as a result. In September there were two more incidents with equally grim outcomes; one man was killed, and another was so seriously injured that he was expected to die. And similar reports continued to appear at irregular intervals in Irish newspapers in the late eighteenth and early nineteenth centuries.[92]

By the mid-1770s, then, the code of honour in Ireland was certainly not the exclusive preserve of gentlemen. Gentlemen and soldiers represented its main constituency, but artisans, attornies, merchants, farmers, even brothel-keepers,[93] were prepared to risk their lives in defence of their honour. That this was so is due, in large part, to the impact on the public of the celebrated encounters between Henry Flood and Charles Agar, Lord Townshend and Lord Bellamont, and Sir John Blaquiere and Beauchamp Bagenal. Once they had entered the lists, it was to be some time before the practice of duelling was to return to the *comparatively* cloistered context in which it had existed in the early and mid-eighteenth century.

Table 3.1: Duelling, 1771–1790 – number of duels; social status of principals

Date	Number of duels sampled	Number of averted duels	Gentlemen	Military	Middle class	Lawyers	Lower class	Clergy
1771–75	81	8	63	14	4	4	4	—
1776–80	78	8	59	17	6	3	3	1
1781–85	69	23	57	12	4	6	2	1
1786–90	78	5	51	21	9	8	4	—

Table 3.2: The geography of duelling, 1771–90

Date	Number of duels in sample	Dublin city and county	Rest of Leinster	Munster	Ulster	Connacht	Irishmen duelling abroad
1771–75	81	41	9	13	3	7	5
1776–80	78	29	8	18	6	8	5
1781–85	69	15	9	18	5	13	2
1786–90	78	28	12	14	7	8	4

Table 3.3: Duelling in Dublin, 1771–90

Date	Number of duels sampled from Dublin area	Dublin city	North Lotts	Phoenix Park	Merrion Fields	Dublin county and suburbs
1771–75	41	15	1	13	—	12
1776–80	29	7	1	14	2	5
1781–85	15	5	1	6	2	1
1786–90	28	5	—	11	1	11

Table 3.4: Duelling in Munster, 1751–1810

Date	Number of duels sampled	Munster total	County Cork	County Tipperary
1751–55	22	5	2	—
1756–60	14	2	—	—
1761–65	14	4	1	3
1766–70	33	8	—	—
1771–75	81	13	6	5
1776–80	78	18	6	8
1781–85	69	18	17	—
1786–90	78	14	3	5
1791–95	50	12	4	1
1796–1800	61	17	3	1
1801–05	42	13	5	2
1806–1810	39	20	7	1

Table 3.5: Duelling, 1771–1790 – weapons

Date	Number of duels sampled	Pertinent sample	Sword	Pistol	Sword and pistol
1771–75	81	67	3	61	3
1776–80	78	65	2	61	2
1781–85	69	46	3	42	1
1786–90	78	67	3	63	1

Table 3.6: Duelling, 1771–90 – pistol shots fired

Date	Number of duels sampled	Pertinent sample	One shot	Two shots	Three shots	Four shots	More than four shots
1771–75	81	39	3	15	3	15	3
1776–80	78	41	4	15	1	18	3
1781–85	69	28	5	10	1	9	3
1786–90	78	35	8	11	—	14	2

Table 3.7: Duelling, 1771–90 – mortality and injuries

Date	Number of duels sampled	Fatalities	Mortal wounds	One wounded	Two wounded	No injuries	Total injuries
1771–75	81	12	1	25	6	33	50
1776–80	78	18	7	23	4	27	56
1781–85	69	14	2	17	8	21	49
1786–90	78	21	6	29	6	17	68

Table 3.8: Seconds; the law and duelling, 1771–90

	Seconds			The law and duelling				
Date	No seconds	Seconds intervene	Reconciliation effected	Law intervenes	Coroner's court hearing	Number of trials	Manslaughter verdict	Murder verdict
1771–75	2	19	13	5	1	2	2	—
1776–80	—	14	8	1	—	1	1	—
1781–85	—	14	3	2	1	3	3	—
1786–90	3	17	5	1	4	8	6	2

Table 3.9: The causes of duelling, 1771–1810

Date	Pertinent sample	Politics	Elections	Religion	Law Cases	Money	Gambling
1771–75	25	6	1	1	—	2	4
1776–80	28	2	7	—	—	1	—
1781–85	29	1	9	—	5	—	—
1786–90	40	1	9	—	2	2	—
1791–95	23	4	1	—	2	1	—
1796–1800	30	10	2	1	2	—	—
1801–05	15	4	—	—	3	1	—
1806–10	16	1	4	—	—	—	—

Date	Pertinent sample	Alcohol	Playhouse	Insult/ argument	Jostling	Grudge/ feud	Women
1771–75	25	—	—	9	1	—	1
1776–80	28	1	2	6	—	1	8
1781–85	29	1	—	9	2	—	2
1786–90	40	3	1	20	—	—	2
1791–95	23	3	2	10	—	—	—
1796–1800	30	3	2	6	1	—	3
1801–05	15	—	2	4	—	—	1
1806–10	16	3	1	5	—	—	2

Notes and References

1 See above, p. 68.
2 For examples, see *Dublin Courant*, 28 June 1748; *F.D.J.*, 21 Mar. 1749; Adderly to Charlemont, 29 Dec. 1753, in H.M.C., *Charlemont*, i, 190.
3 Below, pp. 139, 265.
4 Burns, *Irish parliamentary politics*, ii, passim.
5 S. A. Cummins, 'Opposition and the Irish parliament 1759–71' (M.A. thesis, St Patrick's College, Maynooth, 1978); idem., 'Extra-parliamentary agitation in Dublin in the 1760s' in R. V. Comerford, *et al.*, eds, *Religion, conflict and coexistence in Ireland* (Dublin, 1990), pp. 118–34; James Kelly, 'Parliamentary reform in Irish politics, 1760–90' in David Dickson, *et al.*, eds, *The United Irishmen* (Dublin, 1993), pp. 74–6.
6 E. M. Johnston, *Great Britain and Ireland, 1760–1800* (Edinburgh, 1963), part 2; J. L. McCracken, *The Irish parliament in the eighteenth century* (Dundalk, 1971).
7 Kelly, ed., *The Willes Letters*, p. 46.
8 *Public Gazetteer*, 12 May 1761; Burke, *Clonmel*, pp. 154, 365–6; Philip O'Connell, 'The plot against Fr Nicholas Sheehy' in *Proceedings of the Irish Catholic Historical Committee, 1965–7* (Dublin, 1968), p. 50; M. McDonnell Bodkin, *Grattan's parliament: before and after* (London, 1912), p. 375; Kevin Whelan, 'Catholic mobilization, 1750–1850' in L. M. Cullen and L. Bergeron, eds, *Cultures et pratiques politiques en France et en Irlande* (Paris, 1991), p. 248.
9 From their surviving correspondence in the Townshend Papers in the Lewis Walpole Library, it is clear that Bute did not and did not seek to influence Townshend.
10 Harrison to Fingall, 3 Sept. 1768 (N.L.I., Fingall Papers, MS 8021/10).
11 At Phillipstown, King's County, in July (*P.O.*, 16 July 1768), and two in Cork, also in July (*P.O.*, 23 July 1768); *F.D.J.*, 27 July 1768.
12 At Cork (*F.L.J.*, 6 Sept. 1768); Clonmel and Galway (*P.O.*, 30 July 1768).
13 *P.O.*, 23, 30 July 1768.
14 See Joe Kennedy, 'Callan: a corporate town, 1700–1800' and Thomas Power, 'Kilkenny politics in the eighteenth century' in William Nolan and Kevin Whelan, eds, *Kilkenny: history and society* (Kilkenny, 1990), pp. 296, 303–4, 324–7; James Prim, 'Documents re Flood duel', *Journal of the Historical and Archaeological Society of Ireland*, 3rd series, x (1868), pp. 234–41; David Dickson, 'Henry Flood and the eighteenth-century Irish patriots' in Ciaran Brady, ed., *Worsted in the game: losers in Irish history* (Dublin, 1989), pp. 97, 101.
15 As note 14; *F.D.J.*, 30 June 1759; Brief for the prosecution in the trial of . . . Henry Flood (N.A., Prim Collection, MS 37).
16 Flood to Burke, 30 May 1765 (Sheffield City Libraries, Wentworth Woodhouse Muniments, Burke Papers, P.1/47); *Dublin Gazette*, 8 June 1765; J. L. Clifford, ed., *Dr Campbell's diary of a visit to England in 1775* (Cambridge, 1947), pp. 35–6, 109–10.
17 Brief for the prosecution in the trial of . . . Henry Flood (N.A., Prim Collection, MS 37); P.R.O., K.B.7/7 (1763–4), 7/8 (1771–2).

18 Brief for the prosecution . . . of . . . Henry Flood (N.A., Prim Collection, MS 37); James Prim, 'Documents re Flood duel', pp. 234–41; idem., 'Kilkenny inns and taverns', *Journal of the Kilkenny and South-East of Ireland Archaeological Society*, n.s., iv (1862–3), pp. 166–7 and notes; *F.L.J.*, 9, 22, 29 Oct. 1768; *P.O.*, 8 Oct. 1768.
19 As note 18; 'An affair of honour a hundred years ago', *Dublin University Magazine*, lxxviii (1871), pp. 376–7; 'A letter on a fatal duel', *Journal of Royal Historical and Archaeological Society of Ireland*, 4th series, ii (1870–71), pp. 13–14; Bushe to Grattan, Sept. 1769, in Henry Grattan Jr, *Memoirs of the life and times of Henry Grattan* (5 vols, London, 1839–46), i, 140–42.
20 Bushe to Charlemont, 26 Aug. 1769, in *J.R.H.A.S.I.*, 4th series, ii (1870–71), pp. 13–14.
21 Townshend to Macartney, 31 Aug. 1769, in Thomas Bartlett, ed., *Macartney in Ireland, 1768–72* (Belfast, 1978), p. 41.
22 'Flood's bail bond, 1 Sept. 1769' in *Journal of the Kilkenny and South East of Ireland Archaeological Society*, iii (1854–5), pp. 316–17.
23 Flood to Townshend, 29 Aug. 1769 (N.A., Townshend Papers, MS 724); Waite to Macartney, 11 Sept. 1769 (Beinecke Library, Osborn Collection, Waite–Macartney Letters); Lifford to Charlemont, 10 Sept. 1769 in T[homas] R[odd], ed., *Original Letters . . . to . . . Henry Flood* (London, 1820), p. 49.
24 Brief for the prosecution of Henry Flood (N.A., Prim Papers, MS 37).
25 *F.L.J.*, 28 Mar. 1770.
26 *F.L.J.*, Sept. 1769–May 1770.
27 Peter Roebuck, ed., *Macartney of Lisanoure* (Belfast, 1983), p. 133; Anne Macartney to George Macartney, 26 Dec. 1769, 8 Jan. 1770, in Bartlett, ed., *Macartney in Ireland*, p. 266.
28 Piers Makesy, *The coward of Minden: the affair of Lord George Sackville* (London, 1979).
29 *Biographical, literary and political anecdotes of several of the most eminent persons of the present age* (3 vols, London, 1797), iii, 274–8; Allen to Townshend, 18 Dec. 1770 (N.A., Townshend Papers, MS 730/49); *F.L.J.*, 26 Dec. 1770.
30 Smith to Townshend, 18, 19 Dec. 1770 (Beinecke Library, Osborn Collection, Smith Letters, nos 17, 18); Bowes to Dodington, 21 Mar., 17 Apr. 1760, in H.M.C., *Reports on various collections*, vi: *Eyre Matcham MSS*, p. 74.
31 Hull to [Lees], 16 Aug. 1771 (Beinecke Library, Osborn Collection, Townshend Papers, Box 10).
32 Smith to Townshend, 26, 29 Jan. 1771 (Beinecke Library, Osborn Collection, Smith Letters, nos 26, 29).
33 Walpole to Montagu, 19 Feb. 1765, in W. S. Lewis, *et al.*, eds, *Walpole corresp.*, x, 148n; *The tryal of William Lord Byron . . . for the murder of William Chaworth esq. before the Right Honourable the House of Peers in Westminster Hall* (Dublin, 1765); Mackay, *Extraordinary popular delusions*, p. 683; Aylward, 'Duelling in the eighteenth century', *Notes and Queries*, clxxxix (1945), p. 46; Kiernan, *The duel*, pp. 143–4.

34 Sir William Blackstone, *Commentaries on the laws of England* (4 vols, Oxford, 1765–69), iv, 176–200. The quotation is from p. 185.
35 See Kiernan, *The duel*, pp. 104–5 for similar observations on Scottish law.
36 Blackstone, *Commentaries*, iv, 185.
37 Thomas Bartlett, 'The Townshend viceroyalty, 1767–72' (Ph.D. thesis, Q.U.B., 1976); idem, 'The Townshend viceroyalty' in Thomas Bartlett and D. W. Hayton, eds, *Penal era and golden age* (Belfast, 1979), pp. 88–112.
38 In a letter to his brother, dated 20 Jan. 1746 (Lewis Walpole Library, Townshend Papers), he admitted to having a strong temper.
39 Desmond Guinness and William Ryan, *Irish houses and castles* (London, 1971), pp. 44–6; Brian Fitzgerald, *Lady Louisa Conolly* (London, 1950) pp. 82–4, 141–2.
40 Bellamont to Townshend, 17 Aug. 1767 (Lewis Walpole Library, Townshend Papers).
41 Townshend to Shelburne, 16 Dec. 1767; Townshend to Weymouth, 17 Aug. 1770, in *Calendar of Home Office Papers, 1760–75* (4 vols, London, 1878–99), iii, 232; iv, 57.
42 Bellamont to Townshend, 21 Jan. 1769 (Lewis Walpole Library, Townshend Papers).
43 Bellamont to Townshend, 1 June 1769 (ibid.).
44 Bellamont to Townshend, 30 June, 29 Sept. 1770 (ibid.).
45 Bellamont to Townshend, 24 Jan. 1772 (ibid.); W. G. Wood-Martin, *History of Sligo county and town from the close of the revolution of 1688 to the present time* (3 vols, Dublin, 1892), iii, 315.
46 Loftus to [Macartney], 27 Mar. 1772; Loftus to Townshend, 22 April 1772 (Beinecke Library, Osborn Collection, Townshend Papers, Box 10).
47 See Lifford to Townshend, 28 Apr. 1771, enclosing Newenham to Lifford, 26 Apr. 1771 (Lewis Walpole Library, Townshend Papers); Bartlett, ed., *Macartney in Ireland*, pp. 270, 300–1.
48 *H.J.*, 7 Dec. 1772; *F.L.J.*, 13, 17 Feb. 1773. Rochfort reportedly sent Townshend a challenge, but the Lord Lieutenant declined to accept it.
49 In the copy of this paper printed in *Biographical, literary and political anecdotes*, iii, 291–4, the incident is dated February 1770. But as the original correspondence cited above reveals, it took place in January 1772.
50 'Account of the duel between the Marquis Townshend and the Earl of Bellamont' in *Biographical, literary and political anecdotes*, iii, 291–302; Charlemont to Flood, 30 Dec. 1772 in H.M.C., *Charlemont*, i, 313; Conolly to Leinster, 15 Jan. 1773, in Fitzgerald, ed., *Leinster corresp.*, iii, 65.
51 Walpole to Montagu, 4 Nov. 1760, in Lewis *et al.*, eds, *Walpole corresp.*, ix, 318–19; Boyle-Walsingham to Shannon, [Nov. 1760] (P.R.O.N.I., Shannon Papers, D2707/A1/10/21); Kiernan, *The duel*, p. 123; Waite to Weston, 28 Nov. 1769 in H.M.C., *Weston Underwood MSS*, p. 417.
52 *Biographical, literary and political anecdotes*, iii, 298–302; Maurice Craig, *The Volunteer earl* (London, 1948), pp. 154–6; Walpole to Ossory, 4 Feb. 1773, in *Walpole corresp.*, xxxii, 93; Ogilvie to Leinster, [Feb. 1773] (N.L.I., Fitzgerald Papers, MS 623, f. 2a).

53 See *Hibernian Journal*, *Freeman's Journal* and *Finn's Leinster Journal* in 1771 and 1772.
54 For example, the 13 February 1773 issue of *Finn's Leinster Journal* devoted a full page to the duel.
55 *H.J.*, 12 Feb. 1773.
56 *Annual Register*, xvi (1773), pp. 72, 85; Ogilvie to Leinster, [Feb. 1773] (N.L.I., Fitzgerald Papers, MS 623, f. 2a); Foster to Holroyd, 11 Mar. 1773 (East Sussex Record Office, Add. Sheffield Papers (P.R.O.N.I., T3465/19)); Lord Charles Fitzgerald to Leinster, 8 Mar. 1773 (N.L.I., Fitzgerald Papers, MS 13022/122).
57 *H.J.*, 22 Feb. 1773.
58 *H.J.*, 29 Oct. 1773.
59 *H.J.*, 22 Oct. 1773.
60 Conway to O'Hara, 21 Feb. 1773 (N.L.I., O'Hara Papers, MS 20391).
61 William Hunt, *The Irish parliament in 1775* (Dublin, 1907), pp. 2–3; Bagenal to Macartney, 8 Oct. [1769] (Beinecke Library, Osborn Collection, Townshend Papers, Box 8); below p. 150.
62 Barry, *An affair of honour*, p. 10; Bagenal, *Vicissitudes of an Anglo-Irish family*, pp. 151–3; Hunt, *Irish parliament in 1775*, pp. 2–3; Waller to Macartney, 5 Feb. 1773, in Bartlett, ed., *Macartney in Ireland*, p. 165; Harcourt to Rochford, 8 Feb., 4 Mar. 1773, in *C.H.O.P.*, iv, pp. 15, 25–6; *F.L.J.*, 10 Feb. 1773; *H.J.*, 8 Feb. 1773; Edmond to Richard Malone, 8 Feb. 1773 (Malone Papers (N.L.I., microfilm p.1561)); Heron to Heron, 19 Nov. 1776 (N.L.I., Heron Papers, MS 13034/2).
63 Flood to Charlemont, 5 Feb. 1773, in H.M.C., Charlemont, i, 314; Malone to Malone, as note 62; Harcourt to Rochford, 4 Mar. 1773, in *C.H.O.P.*, iv, pp. 25–6.
64 Waller to Macartney, 5 Feb. 1773, in Bartlett, ed., *Macartney in Ireland*, p. 165; Conway to O'Hara, 21 Feb. 1773 (N.L.I., O'Hara Papers, MS 20391).
65 Harcourt to Rochford, 4, 19 Mar. 1773, in *C.H.O.P.*, iv, pp. 26, 31.
66 If the observation of the Rev. J. Burrowes is correct, this may be an underestimate. He claimed that no less than fifteen duels took place in Dublin in the winter of 1772–73 (Burrowes Diary, P.R.O.N.I., T3551/1).
67 Sixty-two per cent of locatable duels took place in Leinster (51 per cent in Dublin), 17 per cent in Munster, 9 per cent in Connacht, 4 per cent in Ulster, and 6 per cent abroad. Three duels cannot be geographically fixed.
68 Thirty-seven per cent of duels fought within the Dublin county boundary were fought in the city, 32 per cent in the Phoenix Park, and 29 per cent in other locations in the county (Table 3.3).
69 Pistols were used in 91 per cent, swords in just less than 5 per cent, and swords and pistols in less than 5 per cent of the sampled duels (Table 3.5).
70 For examples from 1775 see *F.L.J.*, 29 Mar., 25 Oct., 30 Dec.; *H.J.*, 3 Apr. 1775.
71 *F.L.J.*, 15 Dec. 1773.
72 *H.J.*, 4 Mar. 1772.
73 *F.L.J.*, 12 Nov. 1774; *H.J.*, 16 Nov. 1774.

74 *F.L.J.*, 20 Oct. 1773.
75 *F.L.J.*, 24 Nov. 1773.
76 *H.J.*, 28 Apr. 1775; *F.L.J.*, 29 Apr. 1775.
77 For another example see *F.L.J.*, 30 Dec. 1775.
78 *F.L.J.*, 7 July 1773; *H.J.*, 5, 7 July 1773.
79 For examples see *F.L.J.*, 28 June 1775; *H.J.*, 11 May 1772.
80 *F.L.J.*, 28 Jan. 1769; Clifford, ed., *Dr Campbell's diary*, pp. 35–6.
81 For examples see Wood-Martin, *History of Sligo*, iii, 315; *F.L.J.*, 1 Sept 1770.
82 Wood-Martin, *History of Sligo*, iii, 315.
83 Townshend to Rochfort, 15 Aug., 18 Sept. 1772, in *C.H.O.P.*, iii, pp. 534–6, 546.
84 Instructions of Harcourt, 17 Oct. 1772, in W. E. Harcourt, ed., *Harcourt Papers* (10 vols, privately printed, 1888–1905), ix, 29.
85 Extract of a letter of Captain David Roche, 20 Nov. 1773, cited in *H.J.*, 20 Mar. 1774.
86 *F.L.J.*, 22 May, 10 July 1773.
87 M. Bodkin, ed., 'The Irish parliament in 1773', *P.R.I.A.*, 48C (1942), p. 182.
88 *H.J.*, 5 Aug. 1771.
89 See Table 3.1 and, for examples, *H.J.*, 25 Nov. 1772; *F.L.J.*, 15 June 1774.
90 *H.J.*, 28 Dec. 1774; *F.L.J.*, 13 May 1775.
91 Ibid.; *Dublin Weekly Journal*, 27 June 1730; *F.L.J.*, 15 June 1774.
92 *D.E.P.*, 17 May 1768; *D.C.*, 12, 28 May, 5, 10 Sept. 1789; *F.J.*, 4 Feb. 6 May 1802.
93 Browne, the keeper of a brothel in Fishamble Street, was killed in a duel in March 1775 by an unnamed mason (*H.J.*, 1 Mar. 1775; *F.L.J.*, 4 Mar. 1775).

exact Portrait of G.R.Fitzgerald Esq
Drefs in which he chose to be executed
fhed as the Act directs by J.Ridgway in Piccadilly; Aug.10.1786.

G. R. Fitzgerald (courtesy of the National Library of Ireland)

4

The Era of the 'Fire-Eaters': the 1770s and '80s

Duelling peaked in Ireland in the 1770s and 1780s. This is the period which dominates Sir Jonah Barrington's chronicle of Irish duelling and all subsequent treatments. Assuming, as I believe we can, that the sampling procedure utilised in this work offers a *broadly accurate guide* to the history of duelling in the country, it is obvious why. A survey of at least one newspaper and a selection of manuscripts and primary printed sources for every year between 1771 and 1790 has produced a sample of 306 duels. This is more than double the size of the sample gathered by a similar survey for the fifty-five years 1716–70, and substantially more than occurred in the whole of the preceding century or in any subsequent two decade period. The 1770s and 1780s, in short, represent the period in the history of the code of honour in Ireland when it was most enthusiastically observed. Neither the law nor public criticism posed a significant deterrent, and such efforts as were made to contain the passion to 'blaze' did not have much impact. It was during this period also that the most infamous Irish duellists — George Robert Fitzgerald, Alexander English and others — were active.

Political duelling in the 1770s and 1780s

'We have no news here. The town was the week before last amused with duels and *rencontres*,' Lord Townshend mused in a letter to Sir George Macartney shortly before he handed over the reins of power to Lord

Harcourt.[1] As Townshend's bantering remark attests, duels were matters of intense public interest, and the unprecedented concentration of duelling incidents that occurred in the 1770s and 1780s figure prominently in private and official correspondence as well as in the public media. The most widely talked about involved politicians. This is attributable to the fact that the extensive coverage given to political debate afforded political figures a higher public profile than others of equal rank, and to the fact that a substantial proportion of duels and duelling related incidents involved well-known politicians. As argued above, the main reason for this was that Irish politics became more confrontational. The abandonment of the undertaker management system in the House of Commons paved the way for the emergence of two broadly opposing political interests. The better known of these, Protestant nationalists or 'Patriots', espoused a popular and broadly reformist programme against a Castle-organised interest, usually numerically stronger, which supported the policies of the British government. These were not hard-and-fast divisions; some M.P.s steered a middle course between both, while still others voted according to issues. As a consequence, one cannot facilely categorise the duels involving politicians as just another aspect of the rivalry of the Patriot and Castle interests, because many do not fit neatly into such a simple pattern. Rather the increase in the political temperature in the 1770s and 1780s produced a more aggressive mood which, every so often, prompted M.P.s to appeal to arms to defend their honour against calumny.

The impact of the emergence of a more confrontational political environment on duelling patterns was clearly manifested during the 1773–4 parliamentary session.[2] During an acrimonious committee meeting on public expenditure in the House of Commons on 2 November 1773 the prominent Patriot Benjamin Chapman took exception to an irreverent intervention by John Scott, one of the Castle's leading spokesmen, in which he queried the aptness and relevance of opposition amendments. Chapman accused Scott of having recourse to 'severe . . . sarcasm' and 'ill-timed jocularity' and of seeking to reduce the debate on 'these serious matters into redicule'. Scott indignantly rejected the charge, and retorted that Chapman had succumbed to 'the green-eyed canker of melancholy'. The exchange became so unwarrantedly personal by this stage that the assembled members intervened and adjourned the debate. This did not conclude the disagreement, however, and shortly afterwards when the house was in full session Sir William Mayne, the M.P. for the borough of Carysfort, was observed talking separately to the two opponents. Mayne had been invited by Chapman to act as his second and to arrange a time and place for himself and Scott to meet to settle their differences with pistols. Barry Barry, the M.P. for County Cavan, noted what was happening and brought it to Speaker Pery's attention. Pery, who had been in a similar situation himself on a number of occasions, took immediate action. He ordered the house to be cleared of 'strangers', had the doors locked, and ordained that neither Scott nor Chapman would be allowed leave until 'they should each pledge his honour to the house, that they would not proceed any further in consequence of that day's altercation'. Unwilling to challenge the authority of parliament, both men acceded to the Speaker's request, and there the matter ended.[3]

Pery's strict enforcement of the standing order which provided that 'when any altercations had arisen as portended disagreeable consequences between any two members . . . the members should be called upon and not suffered to depart the house till they had assured the house they would not proceed further' prevented a potentially fatal encounter between Scott and Chapman.[4] However, it did not have the hoped-for rehabilitative impact on the behaviour of M.P.s. Just over two weeks later Chapman was in trouble once again when he animadverted critically during a debate in the committee of supply on the cost to the exchequer of providing for Thomas Allan, Lord Townshend's agent, and moved that he should not be paid the £350 in expenses he sought. Allan was enraged by remarks he deemed untruths, and he was about to set matters in train to uphold his honour when Speaker Pery again intervened. Unfortunately, because the house was in committee and because Chapman denied all knowledge of a challenge, he could do little but alert the city sheriffs to bind both men to keep the peace. This was done, but it was not until the following Friday, 26 November, that the Speaker was in a position to extract a promise from Allan that he would not pursue the matter further.[5]

It was unusual for an M.P., even one as vocal and outspoken as Benjamin Chapman, to find himself in trouble with the Speaker on two occasions within such a short space of time. Heated exchanges were part and parcel of debate in the House of Commons, and M.P.s were unwilling to confine their right to speak their mind. This explains why it was Commons' policy to do everything possible to ensure that disagreements within the chamber did not conclude in encounters outside, because of the conviction, articulated memorably by John Ponsonby, Pery's predecessor in the Speaker's chair, that 'if challenges and duels were to be the consequence of members speaking their sentiments, then there would be an end to all parliamentary freedom of speech and . . . gentlemen would be afraid to urge their opinions'.[6] The Lords operated a similar policy. When relations between Lord Irnham and Charles Agar, the Bishop of Cloyne, became so fragile in 1774 that a few ill-chosen words prompted both to contemplate an appeal to arms, the mediation of Lords Shannon, Bellamont and Crosbie and Sir John Blaquiere reconciled the hostile peers.[7]

The disposition of lords as well as commoners to intervene between members in dispute ensured the number of political duels arising out of differences in parliament was kept within reasonable bounds. However, the readiness of peers and M.P.s to appeal to arms to resolve differences that arose outside parliament indicates that they had little hesitation in backing up their words with deeds when circumstances demanded. Local political rivalries were fertile causes of duelling incidents, as we shall see, but politics was not the only source of confrontation between politicians, and non-political disputes were generally more likely to culminate in confrontation. Thus the outspoken Castle loyalist John Scott, who had almost come to blows with Benjamin Chapman in 1773, was unable to avoid a meeting with James Cuffe, the M.P. for County Mayo, a year later when (it was alleged) he was 'shamefully detected in a criminal conversation' with Cuffe's wife. Neither party was injured in the duel, though Cuffe pledged himself dissatisfied with the outcome.[8] George Ogle, the M.P. for County Wexford, had even less reason to be satisfied than Cuffe with the outcome of his encounter in November 1773 with Richard Moore of Marlfield, County Tipperary, for he received a hit square in the body that was at first deemed mortal.[9] In fact he made a full recovery. But this incident, and another a few weeks later in which rival claimants to the mayoralty of Galway, Patrick 'Galway' Blake and Charles French, were both wounded in an encounter in which they fired at a mere five yards' distance, and another in March 1774 when Francis Mathew, M.P. for County Tipperary, was wounded in the leg by Wray Palliser, indicate that duelling was as likely to interrupt a promising political career as it was to advance it.[10]

Someone who had little to prove, but who was to find himself immeshed in one of the most extraordinary duelling sagas of the eighteenth century was the former Prime Serjeant, John Hely-Hutchinson. Hutchinson had ascended the greasy pole of political preferment in the 1760s through a combination of application and avariciousness. He had begun his political career as a Patriot, but switched allegiance subsequently and was, by the early 1770s, a key figure in Castle circles and the *bête noir* of the Patriots, who singled him out for virulent criticism in the House of Commons.[11] One such incident in the 1760s almost precipitated a duel with Charles Lucas, the M.P. for Dublin city and favourite of the Dublin populace. Hutchinson was declaiming with some animation in the House of Commons when Lucas was overheard, during a pause, to comment: 'Rest, rest perturbed spirit.' Instead of accepting the interjection as part of the normal cut-and-thrust of political debate, Hutchinson took offence and sent Lucas a challenge. Seconds were chosen, and everything was set fair for an encounter when the arrival of a number of Privy Councillors on the field as the two principals were about to take position halted proceedings, and the seconds availed of the interruption to reconcile the two adversaries.[12]

Hutchinson took this in his stride, and on the death of the Provost of Trinity College, Francis Andrews, in 1774, he crowned his already enviable record in securing high office by winning the nomination to succeed him. The appointment excited almost universal surprise and precipitated Hely-Hutchinson into the greatest political roller-coaster ride in his eventful life. Although he was subject to intense press criticism from the moment he took up his Trinity appointment, the Provost's tribulations did not begin in earnest until the winter of 1774 when his attempts to secure the election to parliament of his eldest son, Richard, to represent the college met with intense resistance from a combination of fellows and Dublin liberals. Their candidate for the vacancy, occasioned by the demise of Provost Andrews, was William Doyle, a Master in Chancery. The campaign was tense from the start, but it became downright confrontational in November when Doyle published an address to 'the independent electors of Trinity' in which he reproved the Provost for 'arbitrarily' dispersing a 'constitutionally assembled' meeting of fellows. Hutchinson took strong exception to this and challenged Doyle to justify his allegation on the duelling field. Doyle accepted the challenge, but he was unable to agree a day and a time because of an eye infection. Instead he signalled his preparedness to meet the Provost as soon as his eyesight improved, which he calculated would be in about five weeks. Meanwhile, Richard Hely-Hutchinson, who had also felt his honour impugned by Doyle's address, was not prepared to leave it to his father alone to defend the family name, and he too presented the Master in Chancery with a challenge. This was a most unusual turn of events, and Doyle sought to decline this second invitation to defend his sentiments with weapons on the grounds that his quarrel was with the Provost alone. However, Hely-Hutchinson junior was not to be put off. He posted his challenge, which left Doyle no option but to agree to a meeting if he wished to avoid the imputation of cowardice.[13] First, however, he had to survive his encounter with Hely-Hutchinson senior, who was convinced, as he informed his wife, that he too had no choice but to go through with his challenge if he was to 'live honourably' and refute the 'unprovok'd malignity' of his opponent.[14]

Doyle's eye infection had cleared up sufficiently by early January 1775 to enable the affair to proceed. The venue was the back garden of a house in Summerhill, and because neither participant was in full health, it was a perfunctory affair. Both men fired one shot; both missed their target, after which they were quickly reconciled by their seconds.[15] Doyle had still to meet the younger Hely-Hutchinson, who, the newspapers reported, had been practising in anticipation of the day. However, since the affair had become a *cause célèbre* by this point, it was no surprise when the authorities intervened on 20 January, as Hely-Hutchinson junior awaited the arrival of Doyle at a prearranged location, and bound him to keep the peace.[16] This was an appropriate moment for both men to call a halt to their quarrel with honour satisfied, but neither was prepared to let the matter rest. Obliged now, if they wished to evade prosecution and, possibly, imprisonment, to fight outside the country, they chose to go to Breda in the Dutch Republic. They met there in July; both fired a case of pistols without inflicting any injuries.[17]

This encounter in Breda ended one of the most complex and bizarre duelling sagas in Irish history. The three principals had emerged with their honour intact, but none could claim to have enhanced his reputation. Indeed, there was a general feeling of unease that the differences between the parties were not resolved in some manner other than by recourse to arms. George III expressed his 'surprise and concern' at events. Lord Townshend, who had forged a personal as well as a professional relationship with John Hely-Hutchinson while he was in Ireland, was astonished that Hely-Hutchinson fought with 'such a character as Mr —— I forget his name'; the incident proved to him that 'among other qualifications for public station [in Ireland], the gladiatorial is one of the most essential'.[18]

The confrontational nature of Irish politics evident in the mid-1770s became even more marked in the late 1770s as the Patriots and Dublin Castle struggled to establish themselves in the ascendant in the House of Commons. This gave rise to fewer duels than one might have anticipated given previous events, but there were a number of headline-creating encounters which mirrored political divisions. One of the most publicised took place in 1778 and involved the aristocratic Commissioner of the Revenue, John Beresford, and the earthy Protestant liberal, Sir Edward Newenham. Beresford and Newenham held diametrically opposing views on most of the key political issues of the day, but the cause of their disagreement was as much personal as political. Following his controversial dismissal from the revenue establishment by Lord Townshend in 1771, Newenham harboured deep resentments which he lost no opportunity to exercise in public. In March 1778 he took advantage of a debate on a financial motion to condemn what he termed 'the oppressive proceedings of government in former times' to single out the Commissioners of the Revenue for special criticism and, Beresford reported, to say 'everything he could to raise a commotion on the subject'. Unwilling to allow misrepresentation to stand unchallenged, Beresford responded by relating what he regarded as the true version of events. Newenham accused the Commission of the Revenue of misrepresentation and demanded an apology. None was forthcoming, so Newenham responded with 'a most serious and imprudent paragraph' which he had inserted in the *Hibernian Journal*. Beresford's options now were limited. He had no wish, as he explained to Thomas Allan, 'to risk my life on an equal footing with such a man, because I had the imprudence to support Government measures'; but to decline to avenge his insult would mean transgressing the rules of honour. The result was that the two men did meet. Newenham, who was no stranger to such occasions,[19] fired his two pistols without effect. Beresford fired only one (it slightly grazed his opponent); and by declining to fire his second pistol he was seen to have achieved a moral victory in the encounter with an antagonist he plainly regarded as beneath him.[20]

Beresford's perception that Newenham was not his social equal and that it was unreasonable, therefore, that he should have to risk his life to defend his honour against such a man echoes Lord Townshend's dismissive reference to William Doyle. Such views ran deep. It was precisely such perceptions which had prompted the Marquis of Kildare to decline to call out George Faulkner in 1754.[21] However, this option was less available to the country's leading aristocratic families in the 1770s because of the duelling fever that gripped the country. Obviously, every challenge did not precipitate an exchange of shots, as the incidents in the House of Commons discussed above demonstrate, but the surviving evidence would suggest that few duels were averted because one of the principals was not the social equal to the other. In the Beresford–Newenham incident, for example, this option was simply not open to the Commissioner of the Revenue, because the challenge came from a baronet and an M.P. of considerable standing, which tipped the scale of social prejudice sufficiently to oblige Beresford to fight. If he had failed to do so, he would have run the risk of damaging his reputation. This was not an invariable rule, however; it was quite possible, as John Fitzgibbon demonstrated in 1784, to decline a duel with a perceived social inferior and emerge with honour intact.

The major issue of public debate in 1784 was parliamentary reform. This was advocated by an alliance of radical Protestants and Presbyterians led in Dublin by James Napper Tandy and opposed by the Dublin Castle administration, which was guided on this issue by the Attorney General, John Fitzgibbon. Never one to mince his words, Fitzgibbon laid the blame for the unusually high level of civil disorder in the city of Dublin in 1784 at the feet of Tandy, whom he sought to discredit by alleging he was unable to pay his bills. Tandy was appalled by this scurrilous suggestion, and he responded by publishing an advertisement describing the allegation as 'an infamous falshood'. This was virtually the equivalent of sending Fitzgibbon a challenge, and to ensure there was no ambiguity as to his meaning, Tandy paraded ostentatiously before the Houses of Parliament wearing a sword. To everybody's surprise, Fitzgibbon simply ignored the newspaper column and dealt a body-blow to Tandy's reputation and self-esteem by letting it be known that he was not prepared to meet him because he was not a gentleman.[22]

Few people had sufficient self-confidence or sufficient contempt for their opponents to make such a stand. In Fitzgibbon's case, it worked very well because most of those whose judgment mattered shared his views. Things were much less clear a few years earlier when the punctilious Sir Henry Cavendish threatened the recently retired Lord Lieutenant, the Earl of Buckinghamshire, with a challenge if he did not deliver on a promise made while in office. Cavendish had been given an assurance by Buckinghamshire, in return for his support in the House of Commons, that the Lord Lieutenant would provide for him 'before he left the kingdom', and he had voted steadily with the administration for this reason. However, when news of Buckinghamshire's recall was announced in 1780, Cavendish maintained that he had not been suitably provided for, and he did not hesitate to remind the Lord Lieutenant of his promise. He received no reply and, believing the worst, he wrote to Buckinghamshire accusing him of having treated him with 'silent contempt' and having 'deceived and injured' him, and threatened him with a challenge unless a satisfactory answer was forthcoming before Buckinghamshire left Ireland for his home in England. The crown's law officers were informed, and they took a dim view of Cavendish's threat, but since no challenge was actually presented and no duel followed, there was little they could do. The matter eventually slipped from view without Sir Henry Cavendish receiving the provision he anticipated, but with the law once again displaying its ineffectiveness in respect to duelling.[23]

Some three years later one of the best-known affairs of honour in Irish history took place when Henry Flood and Henry Grattan, two of the oratorical gladiators of the House of Commons, clashed in bitter and acrimonious fashion. Following the concession of legislative independence in the early summer of 1782, fissures emerged in Patriot ranks between the moderates led by Henry Grattan, who were satisfied with the constitutional concessions recently conceded by the British government, and the more exigent led by Henry Flood, who demanded that the government should go further and renounce its rights to legislate for Ireland.[24] The divisions this fostered within Patriot circles heightened the ill-feeling, already barely concealed, between Grattan and Flood. And relations disimproved further in 1783 when the British government yielded to Flood's demand and Grattan attached his colours to Dublin Castle by throwing in his lot with the Whig administration of Lord Northington. As a result, Flood was enabled to supplant Grattan in the affections of the populace. The change in the fortunes of the two men was quite dramatic.

From being the darling of the popular press, which had hung on and relayed his every word, Grattan was now eyed suspiciously. The newspapers which had formerly been effusive in his praise now levelled brickbats. Worse, they held up and applauded Henry Flood as the true defender of the aspirations and interests of Ireland. These developments rankled with Grattan, whose own relationship with the Northington administration was far from trouble-free. This is all quite clear. What is not clear is what prompted him to launch a vitriolic *ad hominem* attack on Flood in the House of Commons on 28 October during a debate on a financial motion, most notable up to this for a rather tetchy exchange between Flood and John Ponsonby. Whatever his precise thinking at this time, Grattan was given the floor and in a series of contributions, punctuated only by Flood's interjections, offered an interpretation of his rival's political career that portrayed him in the most unflattering of lights.

According to Grattan, Flood's political life could be divided into three phases. At the outset, Grattan averred, Flood pursued an intemperate course on the opposition benches. Subsequently he embarked on his 'corrupt' phase, which coincided with his acceptance of government office; currently his behaviour was 'seditious' because of his partisan advocacy of 'renunciation' and reform. Unable to harness his resentment Grattan condemned Flood personally as well as politically as a selfishly motivated opportunist desperate for popularity. And in one of the most memorable, and most vicious, pronouncements ever made in the Irish House of Commons, he directed the full force of his formidable oratorical powers into an unrestrained and deeply personalised assault on Flood:

> Sir, your talents are not so great as your life is infamous; you were silent for years, and you were silent for money. When affairs of consequence were debating, you might have been seen passing these doors like a guilty spirit, just waiting for the moment of putting the question, that you might hop in and give your venal vote; or, at times with a vulgar brogue aping the manner, and affecting the infirmities of Chatham; or, like a kettle-drummer, fathering yourself into popularity to catch the vulgar; — or you might be seen hovering over this dome, like an ill-omened bird of night with sepulchral notes, a cadaverous aspect and broken beak, ready to stoop and pounce on your prey. You can be trusted by no man — the people cannot trust you — the minister cannot trust you; you deal out the most impartial treachery to both. You tell the nation that it is ruined by other men, while it is sold by you. You fled from the embargo, you fled from the mutiny bill, you fled from the sugar bill! I, therefore, tell you in the face of your country, before all the world, and to your beard, *you are not an honest man.*[25]

By any standards, this was an apostrophe of unusual vituperation. But the abuse was not all one way. Flood was too skilled and experienced a parliamentary performer not to be able to respond in kind. Perhaps his most wounding observation was that Grattan was a 'mendicant patriot who was bought by his country for a sum of money and sold his country for prompt payment'. Grattan endeavoured to shrug this off; however, he could not ignore Flood's ominous pronouncement that he would meet him 'anywhere, or on any ground by night or by day'.[26] Even without these words, a duel was the likely result of the preceding exchanges. There was no way either man could wear such insult and not demand that his opponent back it up with weapons. Most M.P.s were aware of this, but both they and the Speaker were too captivated by the confrontation to intervene to stop it. Flood had the support of the packed galleries; Grattan had the silent backing of a majority of M.P.s, but his most important spur, Edward Cooke observed perceptively, was his personal need 'to justify his conduct' because of the constant flow of public and private criticism which had lost him the accolade of most popular politician to Flood.[27] Eventually, when Grattan had finished and Flood was 'coolly defending himself' against Grattan's allegations and having the better of things, the Speaker intervened and, overruling Flood's request to be heard, instructed him to say no more. Flood was so upset that he left the chamber and could not be found when John Foster, the M.P. for County Louth, secured the support of the house for his call that the two men should be taken into custody by the serjeant-at-arms or the sheriff of Dublin to prevent them resuming their confrontation on the duelling field.[28] The former option was impossible because Flood had left the precincts of the Houses of Parliament, but when he was called upon at his Dublin residence by Alderman Exshaw, he gave the alderman to believe that he respected the Commons' decision and had no plans to leave home. Flood was being disingenuous. He was determined to fight whatever the consequences, as his cousin Sir Frederick Flood later admitted. Grattan, for his part, had gone underground, and while the city authorities sorted out a jurisdictional tangle with the officials of the House of Commons, Flood communicated a challenge and the two men agreed to meet to settle their differences with weapons on Thursday 30 October.[29]

The duel never took place. Because of the enormous publicity the affair had engendered, the sheriff stationed lookouts on all the main roads leading from the city. One of these spotted the duelling party as it headed for a predetermined location at Blackrock, and they were interrupted by the sheriff before they could accomplish their object. Flood and Grattan were brought before Lord Chief Justice Annaly, who bound them to official recognisances of £2,000 each to keep the peace.[30]

To everybody's surprise, this represented the end of the affair. Both men accepted the decision of the Lord Chief Justice and sought, in their own ways, to put the matter behind them. Relations remained strained, but because Flood made a convincing speech in vindication of his career in the Commons on 1 November when he received the permission of the Speaker to respond formally to Grattan's allegations, there was widespread agreement that he had emerged best from this unhappy episode.[31] On balance, this is probably true. Grattan's initial attack on Flood was almost certainly premeditated and carefully prepared. Flood, for one, was convinced that Grattan's attack was deliberately conceived 'to do me the utmost mischief', but given his satisfaction with the outcome, it would have been injudicious as well as impolitic of him to have prolonged the affair.[32]

There was genuine surprise in many quarters that this confrontation — one of the most sensational and publicised political altercations of the eighteenth century — ended so tamely. John Hotham, Bishop of Clogher, spoke for many when informed the quarrel was over: 'How it can be so according to the code of honour, as it is called, I confess, tho' a dealer in mysteries, I cannot comprehend.'[33] Indeed, it surprised many that Grattan and Flood did not follow the example of other disputants bound over by the courts and make the short journey to Holyhead to settle the matter there. Neither man was opposed in principle to going abroad to conclude affairs of honour. Flood had travelled to Holyhead in 1765 to exchange shots with James Agar, while Grattan demonstrated his equanimity on the matter by advising Lord Mornington in 1785 that he 'must fight' to avenge a slight done him; Mornington and his antagonist, Mr Vernon, travelled to Calais to settle their differences, but concluded the affair without an exchange of shots.[34]

Flood and Grattan are merely the best-known Patriots who put their honour above their lives. There were many others. George Ogle, as we have seen, fought a duel in 1773; he was to fight another in 1802.[35] Isaac Corry, who emerged as the leading Patriot spokesman in the House of Commons in the mid-1780s when Henry Flood devoted his energies to Westminster politics, mortally wounded a man named Stannis from Carlingford in 1784; sixteen years later, when he was Chancellor of the Exchequer, he exchanged shots with Henry Grattan.[36] David Walsh, the M.P. for Fethard, who was a strong supporter of Flood in the early 1780s, fought his first duel with a soldier at Clonmel in 1764; there were no injuries then or later when he exchanged shots with another outspoken opposition figure and experienced duellist — John Philpot Curran.[37]

Curran had plenty of opportunity to display his nerve under fire. In his case, several challenges flowed directly from his inability to curb his quicksilver tongue. In 1780, during the infamous Doneraile case, he took so many liberties with Captain St Leger (a relative of the defendant, Lord Doneraile) that a challenge ensued. Even then, he could not refrain from making light of the occasion; yet he emerged triumphant, because of his refusal, after St Leger had fired his first pistol, to return fire.[38] Five years later Curran found himself at loggerheads with a more dangerous adversary — the Attorney General, John Fitzgibbon. Curran and Fitzgibbon clashed in the House of Commons on 12 August 1785 during the controversial debate on the admission of the government's bill for effecting a commercial settlement with Britain. The precise cause of their difference is variously reported, but there is agreement that it resulted from a verbal exchange, which the more loquacious Curran won. This prompted the irascible Fitzgibbon to allege that 'Curran was no lawyer and that the monstrous nonsense that came from him was fit only for Sadler's Wells'. A duel ensued, but it resulted in no injuries to either party.[39] Five years later Curran was again in the wars following an altercation in the street with John Giffard, the so-called 'dog in office'. Giffard was a hack journalist and parliamentary reporter in the employ of the Chief Secretary, Robert Hobart, who took Curran to task publicly for some remarks he made in the House of Commons. Curran was so infuriated by Giffard's effrontery that he wrote to Hobart demanding that he should be dismissed. The Chief Secretary responded with a denial that it was in his power to comply, but Curran refused to accept this. He alleged that Hobart was 'sacrificing the principles of a man of honour to political expediency' in order to maintain Giffard in his employ. This was unfair. Giffard had been employed by the Castle before Hobart came to Ireland, and besides it was hardly reasonable of Curran to extend his dispute with Giffard in this manner. How and ever, Hobart's refusal to be more accommodating prompted Curran to send him a challenge. The two men met at Luttrellstown in March 1790. Curran fired one shot; Hobart declined to fire, and there were no injuries.[40]

Despite the harsh words and bitter recrimination that prompted so many affairs of honour considered above, it is remarkable just how few political duels concluded with deaths or serious injuries. The fact that in a high proportion of instances the contending parties did not fire a shot in anger provides the key to this. It may be that some principals colluded to ensure that there were no injuries, but there is no evidence to indicate that this was a regular occurrence. Indeed, the balance of evidence indicates that all duellists, no matter what their station, entered the duelling field as equals. Their lives depended simply on the skill with which their opponents handled their weapons, and many must have been very grateful that the readiness of their opponents to appeal to their pistols was not matched by the accuracy of their shooting.

Electoral duelling in the 1770s and 1780s

Political duelling was not exclusive to the national political arena, of course. The rise in the political temperature in the 1770s also resulted in a greater number of duels at local level. One would be hard-pressed to prove that the contests to win control of individual boroughs were more intense in these years than before. What is certain is that actual and aspirant borough-owners, members of parliament and their supporters showed less reluctance to have recourse to arms to uphold their interests. The fact that general elections were held every seven to eight years after 1768 contributed to this.

Electoral rivalries emerge in the 1770s as one of the main identifiable causes of duels (Table 3.9). A considerable number of these were perfunctory affairs, but the fact that at least five people died in encounters originating from such rivalries between 1770 and 1790 indicates that this was not always the case. Indeed, it is fair to say that the political animosities at a local level which induced rivals to duel were more likely to produce bloody consequences than those resulting from differences in the House of Commons, as there was no tradition of mediation to induce antagonists to keep the peace. Furthermore, the legal authorities were too thin on the ground and, frequently, too closely identified with one or other of the participants to interrupt such incidents before they proceeded to violence.

Because national political eminence was dependent on a commanding local presence, no politician who was not content to purchase his seat could afford not to look after his constituency interests. This was particularly true of the leaders of major parliamentary connexions, whose influence was determined by the number of seats they controlled. One of the greatest of these was Henry, second Lord Shannon. He was not as politically adept as his father, Henry Boyle (created Earl Shannon in 1756), but he remained a major force in the Irish parliament because of his unrivalled command of parliamentary seats. He maintained this position by unremitting attention to the minutiae of borough management, and he was not averse, when the occasion demanded, to warn off rivals with the threat of a duel. For example, when the County Waterford magnate Lord Tyrone visited Youghal (one of the parliamentary boroughs under Shannon's control) in 1770, the latter suspected it was part of a larger scheme to wrest control of the constituency from him. Realising the potential dangers, he made it clear to Tyrone that he regarded his presence as 'intermeddling . . . [and] a high affront' and that a challenge would follow unless he desisted immediately. Lord Tyrone took the point at once and there was no need for recourse to weapons.[41] A positive stand of this kind could prove an effective means of warning off interlopers; it was of less use where two rivals were already at loggerheads. We have already seen this in the case of Callan borough. Another, less well-documented, instance is provided by Fethard, County Tipperary, where the contest to elect the sovereign in 1772 prompted a duel between Cornelius O'Callaghan and William Barton in which the latter was wounded in the thigh.[42]

Rencontres such as these were not exclusive to corporation boroughs. The reanimation of Dublin popular politics in the 1770s also produced confrontations and personality clashes which led directly to trials by arms.[43] In January 1774 Sir Edward Newenham with his second, James Napper Tandy, met Alderman Benjamin Geale at Kilbarrack church. The cause was 'a postscript at the foot of one of the alderman's late polls' to which Newenham took exception. However, nobody was hurt, as Newenham's pistol misfired and Geale reserved his shot.[44] Six weeks later, Newenham was again in the wars. On this occasion he challenged Sheriff John Tucker to a meeting at Baldoyle. Once again there were no injuries, but, as in his encounter with Geale, Newenham was the more aggressive of the two combatants. During his rendezvous with Geale he had requested new powder to remedy the problem caused by the misfiring of his pistol; during his meeting with Sheriff Tucker he drew his sword with a view to continuing the combat after both principals had fired their pistols without effect, but the intervention of the seconds persuaded both to conclude proceedings without further violence.[45]

The fact that the city treasurer (Geale) and sheriff (Tucker) both exchanged shots with the leading radical of the day (Newenham) within such a short space of time and that this did not elicit disquiet or comment in political and press circles indicates how commonplace duelling had become by the mid-1770s. It was hardly desirable, as one correspondent of the *Hibernian Journal* pointed out, that public officials, especially law officers, of their standing should behave in this manner. But in the wake of the decision of Lord Townshend and Chief Secretary Blaquiere to appeal to arms to defend their reputations in not altogether dissimilar circumstances, this argument did not carry much weight.[46]

Indeed, if anything, the disposition to duel increased in the mid-1770s as the second general election since the enactment of the Octennial Act drew close. In August 1775 Sir Richard Johnston, later M.P. for Blessington, was lucky to escape with his life when a bullet fired by Isaac Corry of Newry grazed his left breast but left him with only 'a slight contusion'.[47] Political rivalries were even more intense in Galway city because of the ongoing dispute over the control of the corporation between the Daly family, led by Denis Daly of Dunsandle, and the Blakes, led by Patrick Blake of Drum. By 1775 it was apparent to most observers that Daly had triumphed. However, Blake refused to admit defeat, and he attended Gort races in mid-1775 with the express purpose of provoking a decisive quarrel with his opponent. Daly was not present, but this did not inhibit Blake, who described him publicly as 'a scoundrel and a coward'. This was cause enough for a duel, but because he did not hear it personally and had more to lose than to gain from a rencontre, Daly ignored it. Still, Blake did not give up. A few days later when the corporation elections were scheduled in Galway, Blake and two companions, Peter Darcy and Captain Kirwan, were observed patrolling the streets of the city armed with swords and whips awaiting Daly's arrival. Realising that he could not continue to avoid his antagonist, Daly sent him a message indicating his willingness to meet him on the Parade. Whether Daly actually anticipated fighting there and then is not clear; Blake certainly did, for as soon as he was within earshot he started to insult his opponent and approached him with his sword drawn. Unable to contain their antipathy, the two men touched swords and engaged. Blake fared worst; he was wounded twice and had to be assisted from field of combat; Daly was unhurt.[48]

If the run-up to elections provided intemperate gentlemen with plenty of opportunity to exorcise their anger by force of arms, the polls themselves tended to be even more violent. Any congregation of gentlemen was likely to give rise to duels, as Jonah Barrington observed;[49] the confrontational atmosphere fostered by an election almost guaranteed them. The 1776 general election was not especially disorderly. It was described accurately in one newspaper as 'very warm' rather than hot;[50] instead of taking every opportunity to defend their honour, many gentlemen chose to exercise restraint. There were notable exceptions. In County Tipperary the hostility of Francis Mathew and Henry Prettie prompted a meeting at Kilworth. Mathew was injured by Prettie's first shot, but not dangerously so, and the intervention of the seconds prevented the affair going further.[51] In County Mayo the infamous George Robert Fitzgerald, whose father was a candidate for the county, proved a more deadly marksman. He killed Cornet Swords when the two men met at Ballinrobe. It did little to advance his father's electoral ambitions, however; Fitzgerald trailed in a poor third behind Arthur Browne and James Cuffe.[52]

The contest for County Clare was closer and, as a result, even more disputatious. There were four candidates, and it was not clear who would secure the second seat when the poll closed on 23 May. The runaway winner with 502 votes was Edward Fitzgerald; Hugh Dillon Massy was second with 365; Sir Lucius O'Brien was third with 352, while Nicholas Westby trailed in a poor fourth with a mere 138 votes. As was usual in tightly fought contests of this kind, the third-placed candidate demanded a scrutiny. While the sheriff determined the merits of Sir Lucius O'Brien's request, rival interests set about settling old scores. On the evening the poll closed, Colonel William Burton of Buncraggy called out Dillon Massy because of Massy's refusal to surrender the burgesship of Ennis borough; this encounter concluded without injury after one shot had been fired. Ten days later, when the county sheriff announced his decision to reject O'Brien's request for a scrutiny, the political temperature became even more confrontational. With Fitzgerald and Massy declared elected, O'Brien's hopes of being returned rested on his receiving a favourable hearing from the House of Commons. This would take months, and in the interval he was unable to conceal his disappointment or to avoid trouble. An advertisement he placed in the press was deemed insulting by Dillon Massy, and a riot by a pro-O'Brien mob in which George and Massy Stacpoole, two of Dillon Massy's supporters, were assaulted prompted the latter to challenge O'Brien to a duel on 4 June. O'Brien was disinclined to accept. He believed his actions were justified because the election had been fought 'unfairly'. Moreover, as a longstanding member of the Friendly Brothers of St Patrick, he disliked duelling, and he suggested a date three weeks' distant as an appropriate time for them to meet. This was unacceptable to Massy, but not even his assertion that 'he looked upon Sir Lucius as a poltroon and a coward and would horsewhip him everywhere he met him' provoked the stubborn baronet, who was, Hugh Howard contended unsympathetically, 'quite ruined in reputation', to agree to an earlier date. Indeed, Sir Lucius became more obstructive as the matter dragged on. By the end of August he simply refused to meet his frustrated challenger, who 'considered him destitute of every principle of a man of honour'.[53]

Sir Lucius O'Brien was a man of unusual resolve. Few possessed his combination of stubbornness and disregard for convention. Certainly not Henry Flood, who found himself embroiled in another affair of honour in 1777. The background to this incident is ill-documented, but there were newspaper reports in early September that Flood had been killed in a duel with John Butler, M.P. for the borough of Newcastle.[54] These were untrue, but relations between the two men were clearly close to breaking-point because of Flood's decision to petition the House of Commons against the return for County Kilkenny. Butler was so angered by the petition, which threatened to invalidate the election of his kinsman Edmund Butler, that he demanded Flood withdraw it 'in a manner he [Flood] thought very improper' because it came with the assertion that otherwise he 'should be insulted'. Flood was as determined not to give way to these bully-boy tactics as he was that the affair should not proceed to an exchange of shots, and it was at his request that the Speaker called on him in the House of Commons on 5 November to declare he would not fight with 'another gentleman'. Flood complied, but ever mindful of the *need to be seen* to have behaved honourably, he availed of the meeting of the committee appointed to consider the petition against the return for County Clare on 12 November to offer a full explanation of his conduct and to defend the rectitude of his stand on what he termed 'a dispute of right':

> I petitioned the house with regard to the County of Kilkenny. I made a reference to a judicature establish'd by act of parliament, to which we all pay the utmost deference. I did it as I thought upon good grounds. The hon. member, against whom I petition'd, applied to me upon this subject in a manner I thought very improper. He sent to me to withdraw that petition. Had I ever made any promise, or engagement of honour to do it, I should have done it instantly. I desir'd to know if I had made any promise. But in my apprehension, sir, the idea of any gentleman sending to another to say, you have a dispute of right with me, that you shall not dispute it by right, but by force is a thing so intollerable in a civilis'd country that it can't too soon meet with a rebuke. . . . It was my orginal, and unalterable determination, *that no man alive sho'd take a dispute of right and alter it to a dispute of force*; no man has a right to do that. The man that attempts to do it does not act under the laws of honour. Were a man just enter'd the world, it is a sentiment I should avoid in the face of the world. I think it becomes every man to do so; it is nothing but a pusillanimity in every man to do otherwise. I have not the smallest apprehension that any man would think I am influenc'd by personal apprehension; there is not a man of whom I am afraid. But there is a tyranny in this, that any man should be subjected to say you have a good cause and therefore the goodness of your cause shall be an injury. I do not mean to say anything disrespectful of the Hon Gent. I don't wish to think anything personally hard. I wish to have this subject stated, that the mind of gentlemen may be taken and satisfied upon it, and that it may not rest upon my private judgement.[55]

Flood's conciliatory tone helped to defuse this dispute and to ensure that no duel ensued from this difference, but, as the history of the 1783 general election amply attests, few were sufficiently impressed to emulate his example, and this was nowhere better illustrated than in Cork.

The 1783 elections for Cork city and county were among the most keenly fought contests in the country because Lord Shannon faced a coalition of opponents that threatened his longstanding domination of politics in both constituencies for the first time in decades. Those opposing his nominees, John Bagwell for Cork city and Richard Townsend for Cork county, were part of an unusual alliance of 'renegades from the Shannon connection', independents, and ambitious local magnates. Separately they were no match for the 'colossus of Castlemartyr'; combined they posed Shannon a challenge he was always struggling, and ultimately failed, to overcome.[56] Because of this, it is hardly surprising that the political temperature throughout Cork county and city in 1783 was never far from feverish, and that both the county and city contests produced an exceptional number of duelling incidents. Contemporary news reports may exaggerate, but twenty-two duelling incidents are reputed to have resulted from the contest in the county between Richard Townsend and his chief rival, Lord Kingsborough. As was usual in hot-house conditions such as these, only a small percentage of putative encounters proceeded to an exchange of shots. According to the *Dublin Evening Post*, nine Shannonites were horsewhipped (which was a common *casus belli*), and another four encounters were in embryo in early October, but the fact that fifteen apologies were forthcoming from members of the Townsend party indicates that most of those who gave offence were unwilling to push matters to their logical conclusion; and this is confirmed by the fact that only two shots were fired and no hits recorded. This suggests that the supporters of both sides ritualistically threatened duels in macho shows of bravado but studiously avoided putting their lives at risk.[57] Such an outcome is less surprising on consideration than it appears at first sight, and it may provide the key to occasional reports from county assizes or race-meeting that between five and ten duels had recently taken place. For instance, at the County Cork assizes in May 1783 it was claimed that seven duels were fought without any injuries resulting. Once again the evidence is evanescent, which suggests that most of these incidents concluded with an apology rather than an exchange of shots.[58]

The unwillingness of candidates in the constituency of County Cork to press disputes of honour to a violent dénouement was not replicated in the contest for the city. Indeed, it was claimed in one quarter that the passionate atmosphere that characterised the county election had its origins in the city constituency. Whatever its precise *fons et origo*, it is clear that the total number of duelling incidents in the city was less than in the county, but that the total number of actual duels (excluding aborted challenges and averted duels) amounted to the not inconsiderable total of seven. None produced fatalities. Indeed, in only one instance was there a 'hit'; Lord Doneraile wounded his opponent, Captain Brayer, in the leg, but the injury was not serious. The *Dublin Evening Post* described the form some or most of these incidents took:

> a warm expression, an angry task, an unpleasant gesture were sufficient cause for duelling; as the causes were trifling, the effects were not fatal; the interposition of seconds after a shot effected a reconciliation.

Given this practice, one can begin to understand how someone like Richard Hely-Hutchinson (who had rallied to his father's side during the Trinity College by-election in 1774 and sought to do so again in July

1783 when serious differences emerged between Robert Dillon and Hely-Hutchinson senior over the representation of the borough of Lanesborough) had the nervous energy to exchange shots with both Richard Longfield, his father's main opponent in the contest for Cork city, and Counsellor John Egan, later M.P. for Tallow, in the space of a couple of days in Cork in September/October 1783. Egan, who was to make his name as a lawyer specialising in electioneering cases,[59] went one better; as well as Hely-Hutchinson, he fought James Connor and Counsellor Roger Barrett, but in no instance did an injury result.[60]

If the Cork county and city elections in 1783 are unusual both for the high number of duels and the low level of casualties they produced, this was not the signal for the commencement of a new era in which duellists observed the ritual of the code of honour but sought not to kill or injure their opponents. Barrington's droll account of the encounter during the Queen's County election between Frank Skelton, a local 'half-mounted gentleman', and an excise man in which the latter was twice wounded illustrates this in its own way.[61] Four years later, in 1787, following some remarks critical of the Provost he made in the House of Lords, Lord Mountnorres was lucky to escape with an arm injury in an encounter at Donnybrook with Francis Hely-Hutchinson.[62]

An even clearer illustration was provided in the same year when Sir John Colthurst, a disappointed candidate in the County Cork election in 1783, took exception to some remarks made by Dominick Trant in a pamphlet in which he accused Colthurst of complicity in the Rightboy disturbances then racking the province of Munster.[63] John Egan, Colthurst's second, met Trant at the Four Courts on 12 February and requested Trant to disavow his libel against Colthurst. Trant refused even to offer an explanation, which caused Egan formally to issue a challenge. The two men agreed to meet at Ballsbridge, but the arrival of the sheriff forced them to abandon this plan; and when Colthurst was arrested and bound to keep the peace, it seemed that a duel would not now take place. In fact this was not the case. Trant insulted Colthurst anew on the latter's insistence to free him from the recognisance to keep the peace, and the two agreed to meet on the morning of 14 February at Ranelagh. Once again the appearance of city law officers prevented an exchange of shots, but determined not to lose the opportunity, the principals and their seconds, Egan and Richard Hely-Hutchinson, set out for Bray. When they arrived at their destination, both men fired three shots without inflicting any injuries. The seconds intervened at this juncture, but they were unable to effect a reconciliation because Trant persisted with his refusal to offer any explanation of the offending passage in his pamphlet. Rather than stand 'dishonoured', Colthurst called for more pistols. This time the two men were on target. Colthurst grazed Trant; the latter hit Colthurst square in the chest, and he died shortly afterwards.[64]

The Trant–Colthurst duel excited much public attention and debate because of the ease with which the principals circumvented the efforts of the authorities to prevent them meeting. However, what had taken place was not incompatible with the law, since the courts returned a verdict of manslaughter in self-defence when Trant was brought to trial.[65] By then prospective candidates were readying themselves for another general election, polling for which took place in May 1790. Compared with what had preceded in 1783, the 1790 general election was uneventful, but the county constituencies of Antrim, Cork, Waterford, Mayo, Tipperary and Queen's County each produced at least one duel. In Cork two candidates, Lord Kingsborough and Abraham Morris, exchanged shots without inflicting any injuries;[66] in County Tipperary John Bagwell and Colonel Henry Lysaght did likewise, as did Wray and Leslie in County Antrim.[67] The outcome elsewhere was less agreeable. In Queen's county, a gentleman named Roberts was twice wounded in a duel near Maryborough by Graves, his opponent.[68] In County Waterford the twenty-one-year-old son of Richard Power of Clashmore, who was one of the candidates for the constituency, became embroiled in a bitter row with Captain Gumbleton of the 13th Dragoons as a consequence of his allegation that Gumbleton's brothers were 'dishonourable' for not voting for his (Power's) father. Both men were impervious to all efforts at conciliation, for having failed to inflict any injuries with a case of pistols, they each took up a third, as a result of which Power was fatally wounded.[69]

Passions were even more acute in County Mayo. There were four candidates for the two seats in the county in 1790. James Cuffe, the sitting M.P., was well placed to retain his seat, but the second lay between the other sitting member, the Hon. Denis Browne of Westport, and John Bingham of Castlebar. Both Browne and Bingham were influential figures in the county but relations between the two men were less than harmonious and, as it emerged that the contest was too close to call, tempers became frayed. Before the poll was long under way three duels took place. The most serious involved Hugh O'Donel and one of the Binghams in which the former was dangerously wounded.[70] A short time later the two rival candidates quarrelled. The cause on this occasion was Bingham's public denigration of Browne as 'a Castle hack'. Neither man was injured in the duel that followed, but because Browne 'fired his last shot in the air, perceiving from Mr Bingham's position at the time, had he done otherwise, he must have mortally wounded his antagonist', he emerged from the encounter with most credit, and he went on to win the election by a narrow margin.[71]

The 1790 general election was the last before the Act of Union in which duelling figured prominently. The general election in 1797 produced few such incidents, though the phenomenon of electoral duelling remained alive. For example, in a by-election for County Kerry in October 1794, a dispute flared between Sir Barry Denny, the sitting M.P., who had pledged to keep out of the contest, and John Crosbie, one of the candidates, who took exception to Denny's unanticipated appearance on the hustings in support of his rival, the Knight of Kerry. The precise course of events remains obsure, but Crosbie evidently accused Denny of breaking his word and using undue influence. This was too much for Denny to bear, and he challenged his critic to back up his words with deeds. Crosbie agreed, and with the assistance of their seconds (the Knight of Kerry and Captain William Godfrey) a day and time was decided. Crosbie was the underdog. He had supposedly never before fired a pistol, but his first shot hit his opponent and killed him instantly.[72]

The outcome of many duels, as the Denny–Crosbie encounter vividly illustrates, depended heavily on chance. The gap between life and death on such occasions could rest on something as unpredictable as the misfiring of a pistol or on the thickness of a waistcoat, as the Derinzy–Heathley encounter in Wexford in 1775 indicates.[73] It was this uncertainty, as much as the social consequences of failing to conduct oneself on the duelling field with dignity, that demanded bravery. It was this too which prompted so many participants in electoral duels to decline to fire or to conclude proceedings after a simple exchange of shots. This pointed forward to a day when gentlemen would refuse to put their lives on the line for what were in many instances simply displays of bad-manners. But that day was still some time away, as the reaction of John Fitzgibbon, the Attorney General, to the news that his brother-in-law, Dominick Trant, had dispatched Sir John Colthurst demonstrates. Fitzgibbon had a low opinion of Trant up to this; but he was so impressed by Trant's handling of Colthurst's challenge that he rose significantly in his estimation.[74]

The 'fire-eaters'

Because they set the tone for the rest of society, at a time when public interest in politics was high, the enthusiasm Irish politicians showed for the code of honour and the general tolerance of the legal authorities facilitated the emergence in the 1770s and 1780s of the phenomonen known as the 'fire-eater'. These were individuals whose reputations derived from their enthusiastic devotion to the code of honour. It was not difficult, in truth, to acquire such a reputation, as Barrington's encomium to duelling in his lifetime bears ample testimony, but Barrington's remarks on duelling must be treated with a generous measure of caution, as he was an avowed enthusiast of the code of honour. Three successive generations of his family duelled.[75] Furthermore, he possessed a formidable personal reputation as a duellist. According to one late eighteenth-century observer, he was

> so good a *marksman* that he can repeatedly strike out a mark upon the ace of spades at twelve paces distance; he has frequently fought and never missed his man. In Ireland it is considered *not fair to fight him*.[76]

Like so much else associated with duelling, there is more than a hint of rodomontade to this description. However, it underlines the importance of not placing too much credence in the ready fund of anecdotes and incidents related with such élan by Barrington and other nineteenth-century chroniclers of the duel. Indeed, Barrington's 'short abstract . . . of official [*sic*] duellists who have figured . . . in my time' has exercised disproportionate influence on those commentators who have considered the duelling phenomenon in late eighteenth-century Ireland, just as his claim that an ability to duel was an essential qualification for social acceptance has been afforded too much uncritical attention.[77] There can be little doubt but that familiarity with a pistol was an asset; but unless there was a disproportionate volume of under-recording of duelling in eighteenth-century Ireland, many (perhaps even a majority) gentlemen never fired a pistol in anger at another.

Barrington is most valuable for the insight he gives into the *mentalité* of that late eighteenth-century phenomonen — the duelling enthusiast. It is seldom clear how many duels the best-known late eighteenth-century duellists actually fought, but in few instances fact does coincide with myth. In part, this is simply the normal consequence of the distortion due to the lapse of time and the selectiveness of memory, but there is also a element of wish-fulfillment in the readiness with which contemporaries and commentators who describe eighteenth and early nineteenth-century Ireland as a duellist's paradise maintain that George Robert Fitzgerald fought twenty-six duels and Thomas MacNamara of Clare thirty.[78] Neither claim is sustainable; and while it is undeniable that George Robert Fitzgerald displayed a disturbing proclivity for violence, few men were principals in more than five duels in their lifetime. Furthermore, it is not clear precisely what criteria were applied when individuals were singled out in this manner; it certainly appears that an unwarranted distinction was drawn between duels prompted by political differences as opposed to other issues. A number of prominent figures in late eighteenth-century Irish politics were involved in almost as many duelling incidents (though all may not have proceeded to an exchange of shots) as some so-called 'fire-eaters'. Many were no more principled in their behaviour than the notorious 'blazers' depicted with such verve by Barrington, yet they are seldom portrayed in so simplistic and stereotypical a fashion. This is the case, for example, with John Scott, the Attorney General, Chief Justice of the Common Pleas and, from 1793, Earl of Clonmel, who fought four duels, one of which resulted from his supposed liaison with Mrs Cuffe, and another (with Lord Llandaff) from a family disagreement.[79] It is true also of Marcus Patterson, the Chief Justice of the Common Pleas, who fought three country gentlemen, each of whom he wounded;[80] and of Sir Edward Newenham, the M.P. and political radical, who also fought three times, but who is not even mentioned by Barrington or by any other chronicler of the duel. It is difficult, in fact, to establish any convincing reasons, other than Barrington's selective memory and personal prejudices, for the distinction he makes between the above-mentioned and the squireens and 'fire-eaters' he singles out for special attention. This can be illustrated by comparing the duelling careers of Richard Hely-Hutchinson and John Egan. Between 1775 and 1783 Hely-Hutchinson fought at least three duels — one the highly publicised encounter at Calais with Major William Doyle, another against Egan during the 1783 general election in Cork. He was also involved in a number of incidents which did not proceed to an exchange of shots. Egan, for his part, fought five largely uneventful duels — three at Cork during the 1783 general election and one against John Philpot Curran some time later. Both men were clearly experienced and combative duellists, but it is Egan who is remembered. Hely-Hutchinson is seldom if ever referred to in the same context as Egan largely because Barrington confused his famous encounter with William Doyle with that of his father.[81]

But if the combination of Barrington's prejudice and error have resulted in some important duellists being overlooked, and others being being portrayed unfairly as conducting their lives according to the feckless standards of the 'half-mounted gentlemen' he immortalised, the fact remains that late eighteenth-century Ireland produced a number of thoroughly disreputable figures whose main claim to a presence in the historical record rests on their enthusiasm for duelling. As already indicated, they were fewer in number than is usually implied. Moreover, there is so little information on the duelling activities of such supposed 'fire-eaters' as Pat Power, Jemmy Keogh, Amby Bodkin, Crow Ryan, Bryan Maguire and others as to raise doubts as to their credentials. In several instances it would appear that their reputations owe more to their deportment and lifestyle than to their duelling exploits.[82] However, there is sufficient information on three infamous late eighteenth-century duellists — Beauchamp Bagenal,

Alexander 'Buck' English and George Robert 'Fighting' Fitzgerald — to establish a clearer image of them and their activities.

Beauchamp Bagenal of Dunleckney, County Carlow, made a dramatic entry into the duelling role of honour in 1773 when he embarked on his celebrated encounter with Sir John Blaquiere.[83] Based largely on this incident and another a few weeks later with a man named Kelly, in the course of which he was shot in the arm, his reputation as an enthusiast of the code of honour was forged.[84] Inflated claims are made on his behalf[85] that he fought twelve duels, but there is little hard evidence linking him with this number of encounters. Indeed, his reputation rests as much on his fabled eccentricity and his hard living as his love of guns. He scandalised Carlow society by living with a succession of mistresses, by drinking to excess and by general bad behaviour. However, he was not without positive qualities. He certainly did not seize every opportunity that came his way to duel, though his instruction of his better-known cousin, Beauchamp Bagenal Harvey, in the rules of duelling has led some to conclude otherwise. According to O'Neill Daunt, he was contemptuous of what he described as the 'mere duellist', but was a strong defender of the right to duel in defence of one's 'character'. It is striking that when Weld, one of his neighbours, challenged him to a duel in 1788 because he had ordered the tails of some of Weld's pigs that had trespassed repeatedly on his property to be cropped, he agreed to meet him but refused to return Weld's fire. Indeed, he inaugurated the legal prosecution of his antagonist instead. A host of stories about Beauchamp Bagenal survive, but the balance of probability is that, like Bagenal's reputation as a duellist, they contain more than a tincture of hyperbole.[86]

Alexander English of Springfield, County Tipperary, was as notorious in his day as Beauchamp Bagenal. Indeed, it is likely that it is to him rather than to any other person that Tipperary owes its reputation as a major duelling county.[87] There were other factors, of course — bitter electoral rivalry, acute denominational animosity, and the precarious financial and social circumstances of a large number of gentry and *soi-disant* gentlemen[88] — but the sheer bravado of English merits particular acknowledgment. English's first recorded encounter took place in the city of Cork in April 1774 and was with a grocer named Samuel Powell. Powell was the aggressor. He knocked English down with an undrawn sword, but it was not long before both men, swords drawn, were locked in combat. English's superior swordsmanship soon made itself felt. He broke through Powell's defences and killed him with a single thrust.[89] Having acquired the taste for combat, English found it difficult to overlook insult. In May 1775 he met Robert Bradshaw of Alleen, County Tipperary. Pistols were the chosen weapon on this occasion, but although four shots were fired there were no injuries save for a slight graze which English received from a passing bullet.[90] By now English had a reputation as a skilful and intrepid duellist who never declined a challenge. Thus when he was involved in a minor misunderstanding in London in the early winter of 1776, he had no qualms about appealing to his pistols to settle the matter. He and his antagonist, the 'swashbuckling Irishman', Captain David 'Tyger' Roche, who had recently been acquitted by 'a complaisant jury' of killing Lieutenant Ferguson at the Cape, chose to meet in Hyde Park; they fired their first shots at twelve paces and missed; they fired their seconds at six and missed again, and were about to raise their pistols for a third time when the seconds intervened and reconciled the parties. It was not necessary for English to challenge Roche, as he later admitted, but such was his obsessive anxiety to avoid losing face that he preferred to duel rather than take the risk of tarnishing his honour.[91]

By the late 1770s English's reputation was so inflated that he was widely regarded as a forbidding opponent whom most people feared to fight. This is vividly illustrated by the encounter precipitated in December 1778 by a public disagreement with a Tipperary landowner named McDowell. Both men fulfilled the requirement of the code of honour by receiving one shot, but whereas English was prepared to press the matter to a bloody resolution, his opponent had had enough and 'precipitately quit the field in spite of every remonstrance and severity of expression that could be made use of to prevent him'.[92] This was a most unusual turn of events; but it reflected what many felt about Alexander English — that he was quite simply the most dangerous opponent anybody could meet on the duelling field. If confirmation of this was needed, it was provided a few months later when, in the duelling equivalent of the clash of the champions, English and George Robert Fitzgerald met with swords in St Stephen's Green. Both were accomplished swordsmen, but English was physically stronger. He wounded Fitzgerald in several places and was about to deliver the *coup de grâce* when 'several gentlemen who were present interposed and with difficulty disarmed and separated them'.[93]

Fitzgerald had a lucky escape in this instance. But as the history of duelling reveals, luck was integral to every encounter. Fitzgerald certainly had his share during his brief existence as Ireland's most prolific and ruthless duellist. George Robert Fitzgerald enjoyed a privileged, if affectionless, upbringing. He was born in the late 1740s, probably in 1748; but his parents, George Fitzgerald of Turlough, County Mayo, and Lady Mary Hervey, daughter of Lord Hervey the memoir-writer and vice-chamberlain to George II, separated while he was young because of what Mary McCarthy describes as George Fitzgerald's 'unreasonable and puerile disposition'. As a result, George Robert spent long periods in

London with his mother and grandmother, and at Eton where he attended school. It is clear, however, that it was the manners and mores of Mayo rather than of the London salons or Eton's playing-fields that left the deeper impression, for his main activity and entertainment as a youth and as an adult was hunting, and his lifestyle and behaviour bore closer comparison to that of a Mayo squire than of an educated London aesthete. Fitzgerald hunted as he did most other things — with barely controlled fury. It seems as if his father's unreasonableness and his mother's frivolity had coalesced to create a person whose behaviour throughout his life was utterly and totally self-centred. He was, as one informed contemporary observed, 'restless and turbulent in his temper; captious and irascible in his nature; vindictive and sanguinary in his resentments'. More significantly, in an age in which duelling was commonplace, he was

> easily provoked; he would quarrel upon the most trifling occasion; and having once conceived an enmity towards another, was of that implacable, revengeful and sanguinary nature as to suffer nothing but the blood of the person from whom he supposed he had received an injury, to appease his wrath, or satiate his spirit of resentment.[94]

George Robert Fitzgerald was introduced to duelling while he was still a teenager. His earliest recorded encounters took place in Galway when he was stationed there following his enlistment in the army. His first resulted from improper liberties he took with a young milliner and concluded in a harmless exchange of shots with Michael French. Some time later he was called out by a fellow-officer, Lieutenant Thompson, following a series of petty but provocative incidents. This encounter did not go well for Fitzgerald; he was hit in the head by his opponent's ball and was not expected to live, but trepanning and the insertion of a silver plate enabled him to pull through.[95]

Having taken leave of the army, Fitzgerald applied himself to the acquisition of a wife, and he wooed and won Jane Conolly, the sister of Thomas Conolly of Castletown. Fitzgerald was able to persuade her, against her brother's advice, to elope with him and they married in 1770. She brought him a fortune of £10,000, and in the early years of their marriage they lived splendidly amid the expensive splendours of cosmopolitan Paris.[96] Fitzgerald's finances could not sustain this extravagant lifestyle, and he was only enabled to survive by borrowing. One of his creditors was a Major Baggs, who, despairing of recovering a loan of several hundred pounds, put it about that Fitzgerald refused to honour his debts. Enraged by this, Fitzgerald determined to cleanse himself of the insult and to liberate himself of the debt by provoking a duel. However, before the two men could meet, Baggs was bound over to keep the peace. This meant a trip out of French jurisdiction to the Austrian Netherlands. Accompanied by Hamilton Rowan, who was living in Paris and whom he persuaded to act as his second, Fitzgerald and his party made their way to Valenciennes, where, the preliminaries completed, the principals faced each other across a field. Both men fired their first shots together, but only Fitzgerald's was on target. His ball hit Baggs in the leg, shattering bone and forcing him to drop to the ground. In most instances this would have represented the end of the affair, but Fitzgerald was not satisfied. Determined to finish off his opponent and to free himself from the encumbrance of the loan he owed, he took aim and fired his second shot, but it missed its target. He had also underestimated his opponent. Somehow or other, Baggs raised himself to his feet, pistol in hand and hobbled towards Fitzgerald. Unwilling to act as a static target, Fitzgerald turned heel and ran. He was not quick enough; he was wounded in the thigh as he endeavoured to flee the scene.[97]

Fitzgerald's conduct on the duelling field at Valenciennes left much to be desired, but there was no legal retribution because Hamilton Rowan allayed the suspicions of the French authorities.[98] However, it was clear by now to all that made his acquaintance that Fitzgerald had as little respect for the law as he had for the niceties of the code of honour. To him duelling was a means simply to get his own way.

Having recovered from this experience and returned to London, George Robert Fitzgerald became a leading member of the group of young bucks known as the Macaronis, and he was in their company in July 1773 when he met more than he bargained for in the person of the Rev. Henry Bate, the editor of the *Morning Post* and celebrated patron of the theatre. It appears that Fitzgerald, accompanied by the raffish Lord Lyttelton and Captain Croftes, espied Bate dining with the actress Mrs Hartley and a number of friends at Vauxhall, and that they endeavoured to have fun at their expense. Bate, who was a powerfully built man, remonstrated with his antagonists and, when this failed to have the required effect, sought physically to dispatch them. In the scuffle that followed, blows were exchanged by Bate and Croftes which led to a challenge. However, instead of leaving the two to settle their difference in their own way, Fitzgerald intervened and tried to make a fool of Bate by presenting one of his footmen, a prize-fighter, in regimentals as his real antagonist. His intention was to trick Bate into a bare-knuckle fight. Bate was not taken in by this rather crass effort at deception; and to Fitzgerald's dismay he not alone soundly thrashed his footman but extracted a full confession of Fitzgerald's intentions from him.[99] Determined to press home his advantage, Bate printed a full account of the episode in his newspaper, which caused such a stir that Croftes felt compelled to resign his commission and to set sail for India. Lyttelton too chose to go abroad; Fitzgerald alone determined to brave out the scandal by remaining in London.

Inevitably, the matter did not rest there. In August a number of Guards stationed at St James's Palace were discussing the incident at dinner when one of those present, Captain John Scawen, laid the blame for the whole sorry episode at Fitzgerald's feet and 'said he ought to have had a stick laid over his shoulders or words like'. Scawen's observations were relayed by one of the company to Fitzgerald, who was so anxious to redeem his injured reputation that he sought out Scawen and, when the latter refused to deny that he had uttered the offending words or to withdraw them, challenged him to a duel. Scawen chose pistols as his weapon, as he was entitled to do, but Fitzgerald evidently insisted on swords, with the result that the two men came to blows over which weapon they would use. This was not conduct becoming gentlemen, but matters were to get worse. Scawen was intercepted by the authorities on his way to his rendezvous with Fitzgerald and bound over to keep the peace, which meant he could not keep his appointment. This was not unusual, but Fitzgerald chose deliberately to interpret it as an act of deliberate cowardice, and declined Scawen's offer to fight in France on the grounds that since he (Scawen) had failed to turn up when they had agreed to meet, he was under no obligation to do so. Perceiving desperate measures were called for to compel Fitzgerald to agree to duel, Scawen assaulted him with a stick the next time they met. A journey to Lisle in the Austrian Netherlands followed, and, once again, Fitzgerald demonstrated the lack of principle that had characterised his behaviour so far in this affair. He fired his two pistols and dropped to his knees before Scawen fired his first. Scawen's second protested, but rather than prolonging the encounter, all involved sought to bring the matter to a close. Scawen apologised for his remarks and allowed Fitzgerald to place a sword lightly on his shoulder. It was an anticlimactic ending to a most complicated affair from which Fitzgerald emerged much better than he might and, in truth, deserved.[100]

Although John Scawen rather than George Robert Fitzgerald bore most of the brickbats that flowed from their encounter in August 1773, the latter's reputation also suffered as the public became familiar with his erratic and unprincipled conduct. He was, William Hickey noted in his memoirs, 'in person . . . unassuming, slim and delicate, his address mild and insinuating in an uncommon degree'; however, he was also possessed of a 'temper and behaviour at times ferocious beyond measure', as he had demonstrated in 1773.[101] It was manifest again two years later when an altercation with Thomas Walker, a cornet in Burgoyne's regiment of light dragoons, over a debt led him to assault Walker at Guilford. In the encounter that followed, Fitzgerald once again sought to minimise the risk to his person by covering his face and crouching. This was contrary to duelling etiquette, but perceiving that the best form of defence was attack,

Fitzgerald responded to Walker's decision to publish an account of the incident in which he charged his opponent with this and other improprieties with a tract of his own. In a text which vibrates with anger, he accused his opponent of wearing padding in their encounter, of reneging on his legal debts, and of cowardice for refusing to agree to meet him again.[102]

Having worn out his welcome in England, Fitzgerald returned to Ireland in time for the 1776 general election. His father was a candidate for County Mayo, where he made little impression against the powerful Browne and Cuffe interests. However, George Robert did not let the election campaign go by without a demonstration of his martial ardour; he met and killed Cornet Swords in a duel in Ballinrobe in May. He subsequently sought to carve out a political interest for himself, and following the death in 1780 of his wife, from whom he had been separated for a number of years, he married into the local gentry; Sidney, the daughter and heir of Matthew Vaughan of Carrowmore, County Mayo, became his wife in 1782.[103]

George Robert Fitzgerald's decision to return to reside in Ireland in the late 1770s and his marriage in 1782 were prompted by financial rather than by political imperatives. He was short of money, and his only source of cash was his father. His arrival was marked by an encounter in April 1779 with Alexander English in St Stephen's Green in which he was humiliated because one of his wounds, 'which he long exhibited in public by his uneasy gait', was to his buttocks.[104] Because of his financial needs, he determined to compel his father, to whom he had given £8,000 (presumably from Jane Conolly's fortune) on his marriage, to live up to his promise to allow him £1,000 a year from this money and from the family lands which were entailed unto him. This necessitated his continued presence in County Mayo, so he returned to Turlough, accompanied only by a bear, to claim what was his. It was not long before he had antagonised every man of consequence in Mayo and beyond. Besides his complete disregard for the sensibilities of others, his abominable treatment of his father and his accountrement of a set of local desperadoes as his personal Volunteer corps disturbed local gentlemen. His treatment of his father, whom he legally ousted from the family estate on the grounds of severe mismanagement and failure to pay monies owed, was such as no civilised gentleman could deem tolerable. Having expelled his father from the main estate house and allocated him a small residence and fifty acres, he failed to pay him his allowance, and when his father drew the matter to his attention, he first manacled him to his bear, then to a dray, and later imprisoned him in a 'cave'.[105]

His relations with his neighbours, meanwhile, degenerated to such an extent that his main contacts with them were violent altercations. He fought a duel with swords in Castlebar with Caesar French, who was receiver of the debts owed by the Fitzgeralds, after French had distrained some cattle. Both men were slightly wounded, though Fitzgerald had endeavoured to protect himself by wearing a padded waistcoat and by concluding the duel prematurely when it was clear he was being bested by 'throw[ing] himself on the ground'. He fought Hyacinth Martin with cudgels, also in Castlebar, over an unspecified cause. He quarrelled with the Rev. Mr Ellison,[106] a respected magistrate and agent to Lord Lucan, when Ellison took exception to his assertion that he would ride roughshod over the law.[107] Even the local law officers did not escape his violent attentions. When the high sheriff, Denis Browne, expressed unease with his behaviour, Fitzgerald promptly rode to Westport House and shot and killed Browne's favourite wolfhound on the pretence that it was a menace. This was a gratuitously offensive act, and it prompted Browne to issue a challenge. When the two antagonists met to choose weapons, which they determined would be the broadsword, Fitzgerald suddenly and without warning raised and fired his pistol at his opponent. He only barely missed. Taken aback by the sheer viciousness of Fitzgerald's action, Browne refused to proceed with the duel. He did, however, initiate legal proceedings, which Fitzgerald escaped on a technicality.[108]

If the high sheriff failed in his attempt to cause Fitzgerald to moderate his conduct, his brother Charles, who 'was always considered as the [family] favourite', felt compelled to take decisive action.[109] He had George Robert arrested and charged with the mistreatment of their father at Castlebar assizes in 1781. George Robert was fined £500 and sentenced to two years' imprisonment, but instead of accepting the sentence of the court, he broke custody and headed for Dublin, with his father in tow, to solicit a pardon. He was promptly arrested when he got to Dublin, retried and re-sentenced, but was set free after a number of months in confinement on condition of good behaviour.[110] Fitzgerald ignored the good fortune that had led to his early release, for he was not long free when he set about getting his revenge on 'Humanity Dick' Martin, another noted duellist,[111] who had heckled him during the trial at Castlebar in 1781 which led to his imprisonment. The two men encountered each other in the Smock Alley Theatre, where Fitzgerald assaulted Martin. This was cause enough for a duel; indeed, such was the level of animosity between the two men that they might have settled the matter there and then but for intervention of the high sheriff, who put them under arrest.[112] The interposition of the law usually resulted in quarrels being abandoned, but neither Martin nor Fitzgerald were prepared to let the matter rest. On 1 June 1783 Martin requested George William Lyster to convey a challenge to Fitzgerald in his Merrion Square house. Fitzgerald was enraged by this turn of events. He wanted the honour of sending the challenge, and he took out his fury on Lyster, whom he assaulted and wounded in a dangerous manner. This was too flagrant a breach of the law for the authorities to ignore; Martin, Lyster and Fitzgerald were all indicted at the Court of Kings Bench on 1 July.[113]

This effectively ensured there would be no early resolution of the affair, and it was not until 14 July 1784, when Martin was visiting Castlebar once again, that the two men were in a position to determine their differences once and for all. Unusually for Fitzgerald, he chose to fight with pistols. The two principals met in the barrack-yard at Castlebar and took up positions at about eight yards' distance. This was somewhat shorter than the norm, and on Fitzgerald's suggestion it was reduced further to five yards. This made a fatal outcome all the more likely, but, as things turned out, neither was seriously injured. Martin received a slight wound in the breast; Fitzgerald received a number of direct hits, but, as a medical examination subsequently revealed, he was uninjured. This puzzled everybody, Martin included, who suspected but declined at the time to state publicly that his opponent was wearing concealed armour. As far as he was concerned, this long-drawn-out saga was over, for though Fitzgerald continued for a time to demand that they should meet again, there was no further encounter between two of the country's most aggressive duellists.[114]

This in fact proved to be Fitzgerald's last affair of honour. He continued to behave in an erratic and utterly solipsistic manner until he was hanged in 1786 for his part in the assassination of Patrick Randle McDonnell (who was himself a duellist of some repute).[115] In his short life he had fought at least twelve duels. This is a long way short of the figure of twenty-six traditionally cited, but it is, by a substantial margin, many more than any other known Irish duellist fought in this or in any other period. Duelling, as Fitzgerald's life abundantly illustrates, was a hazardous business, and it is improbable that he would have lived to have fought so many had he not contrived, as the *Dublin Evening Post* observed delicately at the time of his trial for the murder of Patrick McDonnell, 'to have some advantage of his opponent'.[116] This was, of course, contrary to the code of honour, but then duelling was never simply a matter of honour for Fitzgerald. It was nothing less than a quasi-legal means of assassination or of exacting vengeance for perceived insult, and he was enabled to get away with this behaviour for so long because he was lucky and because he did not stray too far to the wrong side of the ill-defined line that separated duelling from murder. But, not even a duellist as ruthless and lucky as Fitzgerald could survive so many encounters unscathed, as this description of him shortly before he was hanged amply demonstrates:

> Every part of Fitzgerald's body was scarred with wounds, which he had received in the various rencontres and duels he had been engaged in. There was a large hole where a ball had lodged in one of his hips, another in the small of one of his legs; his head had been trepanned, and his right side was so perforated with pricks of a small sword that it had an appearance not easy to describe.[117]

The debate on duelling in the 1770s and 1780s

The activities of individuals like Beauchamp Bagenal, Alexander English and, most of all, George Robert Fitzgerald reinforced the already established reputation Ireland possessed internationally for duelling. Fitzgerald's confrontations with Henry Bate, John Scawen and Thomas Walker were widely publicised in Britain, and coming so soon after the Beauchamp–Townshend and Bagenal–Blaquiere rencontres, they served to confirm what many there already believed — that Irishmen were disposed to appeal to arms to resolve the slightest differences.[118] Sceptics of such stereotyping, and there were some, notably on the stage,[119] fought a losing battle to eradicate such perceptions as long as news reports from Ireland regularly included accounts of further duels. And their position was made more difficult by the involvement of Irishmen like Richard Brinsley Sheridan, Theophilus Swift and James Louis Rice, a Count of the Austrian Empire, in unseemly altercations in England in the 1770s. Sheridan, for example, twice fought Thomas Mathews, who was his rival for the hand of Elizabeth Linley, in a bad-tempered affair in April 1772 which he was lucky to survive. Swift's experience was less traumatic; he survived his encounter and went on to quarrel with Charles Lennox, later fourth Duke of Richmond, in 1789 and with others.[120] Rice, whom Horace Walpole unjustly derided as 'a sharper, not of the first order', was dangerously wounded in his encounter involving swords and pistols with Vicomte du Barre which arose out of a difference at gambling. Du Barre died of his wounds, but when the case came to trial at Taunton assizes in April 1779, Mr Justice Nares was sufficiently impressed by the evidence that Rice was the reluctant party to commend him to the jury, which returned a 'not guilty' verdict.[121]

One must not conclude from the condescension inherent in so much English commentary on the observation of the code of honour in Ireland that duelling was no longer practised in England. Quite the contrary; the occurrence in the last quarter of the eighteenth century of such celebrated encounters as Charles James Fox and William Adam (1779), the Earl of Shelburne and Colonel Fullerton (1780), Lord Macartney and General Stuart (1786), the Duke of York and Charles Lennox (1789), Lord Lauderdale and General Arnold (1792), the Earl of Lonsdale and Captain Cuthbert (1792), the Duke of Norfolk and Lord Malden (1796) and William Pitt and George Tierney (1798) indicates that the code of honour was still vibrant.[122] What happened in Britain in the last quarter of the eighteenth century was that the opposition to duelling was reinforced by the addition of new voices, and the emergence of a rational, as opposed to religion-based, current of opposition which, Donna Andrew has pointed out:

> criticised the very principles which underlay the code of honour. Its complaints were not desultory, but based on counter-principles and alternative values. It not only attempted to show the dangers of duelling but suggested some methods to supersede or outlaw the practice. Furthermore, it explained the genesis and historical function of the code of honour and strove to replace its view of society with a more rational and modern one. Its criticism therefore was constructive. What these reformers attempted to construct was a code of behaviour which would make the duel what it has in fact become: a mode of conduct belonging to past ages, vaguely romantic but definitely old-fashioned.[123]

Critics of the code of honour did not go unchallenged. There were also influential voices prepared to defend duelling, in the words of Lord Chesterfield, as a 'humane, sensible and equitable method of decision of right and wrong'.[124] Dr Johnson was representative. He maintained that if war was legitimate, then so too was duelling; it was a characteristic of a 'highly polished society' that 'an affront is held to be a serious injury', and he forcefully defended the right of an injured party to seek recompense by recourse to arms. Johnson readily conceded that his justification of duelling was not founded on rational grounds; and it troubled him, as it did many others, that the person in the right 'had not a better chance than he who was in the wrong', but he still sided with its advocates.[125] Ultimately, however, it was a matter of public attitude or, as Horace Walpole pungently and not wholly correctly put it, 'fashion' whether or not the code of honour flourished.[126] Duelling could not survive without public approval of the principles of the code of honour, and such criticism as was voiced in the 1770s, while an important pointer to the future, had, as Johnson's observations attest, most representative and influential voices still to persuade before it became the prevailing sentiment in society as a whole.

The perception of English commentators that duelling was more prevalent in Ireland than in England was given credence by the observations of travellers like Arthur Young and Thomas Campbell.[127] Both overlooked the existence of a current of opposition which survived despite the efflorescence in enthusiasm for duelling in the 1770s and 1780s. Irish critics were few in number and, on the whole, not very impactive, but in this respect they were not altogether different from their English contemporaries, Andrew's comments notwithstanding. The primary outlet for opposition to duelling in Ireland in the late eighteenth century was the press. In the main, criticism carried in Irish newspapers in the 1770s was anonymous,[128] and its philosophical origins religion rather than reason. 'The arbitrary decision of causes by the sword subverts the fundamental laws of the scripture; duels have neither precept nor precedent, command nor example in God's word,' one critic maintained in the

Hibernian Journal in 1772.[129] The same point was made more explicitly a year later by another commentator who reprobated duelling as nothing other than 'a spirit of revenge gilded over with the specious covering of a *principle of honour*'. The duel, he averred, could be likened to the act of self-destruction; as such it was an affront to the will of God because

> both the *suicide* and the *duellist* do boldly invade the divine providence, and presume to dispute with the Deity his unalienable claims.[130]

Such views were disputed by those who observed the code of honour. There was a general acknowledgment in these circles that to kill an opponent in a duel did not infringe the sixth commandment.[131] And as long as such beliefs were held, religious-based criticism of duelling had little impact. Indeed, some religious leaders even chose non-religious grounds for opposing duelling. Dean Richard Woodward, who as a young man had been wounded in an encounter in England, rested his opposition on the combination of his own experience and his conviction that it made little sense for people to continue 'abject slaves of a custom we detest'. Both reason and humanity, he contended, instructed otherwise.[132]

Guided by perceptions such as these, some critics of duelling and some figures in positions of power came to place greater faith in the law rather than in religion to produce the change in attitude that was necessary to curtail adherence to the code of honour.[133] They were encouraged to take this stance by the observable increase in duelling that took place in the 1770s, and by the realisation that it was not confined to the elite of society. Incidents such as that at Athlone on 21 April 1773 when an argument over a horseshoe prompted an encounter between a coachman and a blacksmith, or the attempt by two five-year-olds in Dublin in 1774 to duel, or the case reported in *Finn's Leinster Journal* involving a waiter and a porter who came to blows over a woman — all elicited calls for legislative intervention 'to put a stop to this growing evil'.[134] There were rumours in 1773 and 1774 that a bill to this effect was to be presented to parliament, but though bills making duelling illegal were introduced (but not approved) at Westminster, nothing was done in Ireland.[135] A majority of law officers and members of parliament (as the encounter between the high sheriff of County Tipperary, Wray Palliser, and Francis Mathew, M.P., in March 1774 bears witness) were manifestly unwilling to curb their freedom to defend their 'honour' by recourse to arms.[136]

In the army too the prevailing attitude remained indulgent, though there were signs that the authorities were no longer prepared to give duellists free rein. Lords Lieutenant continued to be granted the power to cashier 'the senders, receivers and deliverers' of challenges, though they opted not to avail of it.[137] As a consequence, the military's contribution to the overall level of duelling in Ireland in the 1770s and 1780s rose virtually proportionately to the general increase in duelling in society at large.[138] George III was less than content with this. The king's personal philosophy of life was at odds with the comparative libertinism of the age. He abhorred the laxity of morals and manners which tolerated practices such as duelling, and he did not hesitate, when circumstances permitted, to make his sentiments known. One such occasion occurred in 1774 when two soldiers, Lieutenant Colonel Pigott and Major Bruce of the 38th Regiment stationed at Kinsale, met with pistols following a quarrel. Bruce, who was the instigator of the disagreement, was so seriously injured by a ball to the ribs that his life was despaired of. He recovered, only to receive a warning from the king that 'if in his future deportment, there does not appear a very steady observance of discipline and decent behaviour, he must quit the service'.[139] This was an unusually explicit reprimand, and it seems to have galvanised the authorities to look at the problem anew, because less than a year later Lord Harcourt pronounced that the only way to control the enthusiasm for duelling in the military was to prohibit 'successions to take place in regiments where the vacancies have been occasioned by a duel'. This suggestion had been made to the Lord Lieutenant by the family of Lieutenant Franquefort of the 49th regiment following his death in a rencontre in a Dublin coffee-house in December 1774, and he believed it a potentially useful means of controlling the military's ardour for duelling because he recommended to the English Secretary of State, Lord Rochford, that officers in other corps should fill the vacancies created in the 49th and 17th Regiments as a consequence.[140] Further evidence that the authorities were no longer prepared to turn a blind eye to officers who sacrificed military discipline to the cause of 'honour' emerged three days later when Major Henry Eglinton Connor of the 16th Regiment was so abused by Captain Carew Smith on parade that he beat his tormentor with his cane. A duel seemed the most likely outcome until the army authorities intervened and arrested the two men. Determined that this incident should not serve as a precedent for further ill-behaviour on the parade ground, both men were ordered to be court-martialled. Because Connor was drunk at the time of the incident, the court held that he was an object of mercy, but it was insufficient to save his career. He was cashiered and allowed dispose of his company; Smith was simply reprimanded.[141]

If it appears from this that there was something of a clampdown by the authorities on duelling within the military in the 1770s, this was not in fact the case. Such efforts as were made to regulate duelling in the army were strictly limited. Their main purpose was to prevent a deterioration in military discipline when soldiers were on duty and, as far as possible, to discourage soldiers duelling with soldiers. No attempt was made to introduce a general prohibition because it was believed that it was both unenforceable and undesirable. Soldiers who were prepared to demonstrate their courage by risking their lives in defence of their honour were, it was widely believed, better fighting men.[142]

These manifestly modest efforts by the military to limit duelling within the ranks were not matched by similar initiatives by the civil authorities. However, public opinion was acutely aware of the increased disposition to duel, and there was sharp criticism of anything that was seen to encourage the duelling impulse. Thus Provost Hely-Hutchinson's efforts to introduce fencing into Trinity College and his celebrated altercation with William Doyle elicited a barrage of hostile comment from the opponents of duelling as well as from his own enemies for this very reason.[143] Sooner or later most critics appealed to the law for answers, but the law continued to mirror society in the ambivalence of its response.

Only one member of the judiciary — Judge Christopher Robinson of the Court of King's Bench — was prepared to speak out publicly against duelling. Robinson had the reputation of being a rigid upholder of the letter of the law, and at the commencement of the Dublin assizes in 1775 he condemned what he deemed the 'present polite but diabolical mode of revenging real or suppressed injuries' in defiance of 'the law of the land, the dictates of nature and the rights of society' and exhorted the grand jury 'to present and enquire of every such offence'. It was a timely observation. In contrast to the situation in England, where some judges were prepared to fine and imprison duellists for short periods, remarkably few men of honour were brought to trial in Ireland in the 1770s and early 1780s, owing to the disinclination of grand juries to present such cases for trial and to the readiness of judges to query their decision when they did so.[144] Robinson had few such qualms: he was quite prepared, as he demonstrated in 1777, to bind over M.P.s or anyone else brought before him in matters concerning an 'affair of honour'.[145] However, he was an isolated figure on the judicial bench. Most of his colleagues shared the opinion of Baron Eyre, the English judge, who observed in 1783 that it was inappropriate to apply 'the strict and rigid rule of law . . . to the subject of deliberate duelling' because it was 'in direct opposition to the feelings of mankind and the prevailing manners of the time'.[146] Some, indeed, were experienced duellists. Marcus Paterson, the Chief Justice of the Common Pleas (1770–87), John Scott, Lord Earlsfort, the Chief Justice of the King's Bench (1784–98), Peter Metge, Baron of the Court of Exchequer (1783–1801), John Toler, Lord Norbury, Chief Justice of the Common Pleas (1800–27) and Patrick Duigenan, a judge in the prerogative court, all fought one or more duels.[147] Some were prepared even to defend duelling. John Scott, who served a term as Attorney General between 1777 and 1782, was one such figure:

> There are cases where it may be, and when it is prudent for a man to fight a duel — cases in which the law does not afford him redress — cases of persevering malignity, cases of injured honour, cases of a wounded spirit; and a wounded spirit who can bear? In cases of this complexion the courts will never interfere with its discretionary authority against a man.

However, in cases where someone deliberately provoked a duel in order to get 'level with, or to humble his superior', and in cases where there was no provocation or sufficient grounds for combat, Scott claimed that the court would 'lend its discretionary arm and bear more or less heavily upon the party, according to the nature of the transgression'.[148] In practice, things did not operate so smoothly in the 1770s or early 1780s, when the proportion of duelling cases that ended up in court was at an all-time low (Table 3.8).

M.P.s meanwhile continued to decline to respond to the calls for legislative intervention to combat duelling, despite the shadow cast on the dignity of the Irish parliament abroad by the readiness of peers and commoners to yield to the temptation to appeal to arms to defend their honour.[149] It was reported in June 1777 that an unnamed M.P. was preparing a bill to outlaw duelling and to provide for the execution of defaulters, but no legislation along these lines was presented to the House of Commons.[150] Most M.P.s continued to believe that legislation was an inappropriate means to address this problem, and when Barry Barry, the M.P. for County Cavan, raised the subject in the Commons in December 1777, his intention was simply to tighten the rules of the house in order to prevent challenges being prosecuted as a result of differences arising from the hearing of petitions on controverted elections rather than to address the wider issue of societal duelling. Barry proposed three resolutions, the thrust of which was that if anybody offered a challenge as a consequence of matters presented in a petition to the legislature, they were deemed to be in 'high breach and violation of the privileges of parliament' and would be subject to proceedings of 'the utmost severity'. They met with a warm reception when they were debated on 28 January 1778. George Ogle, the outspoken M.P. for County Wexford, was their most vocal critic. He dismissed the thrust of the resolutions as 'absurd' on the grounds that 'a man's honour will be dearer to him than anything', but neither his opposition nor the presentation of a number of amendments deflected the house, and all three were approved *nem. con.*[151] The resolutions underwent their first test three weeks later when two Claremen, Macnamara and MacMahon, were charged with proffering a challenge to Dillon Massy arising out of comments he had made during the hearing of evidence on the contested County Clare election. M.P.s were disposed to punish them for their misconduct, but when the two transgressors showed 'penitance', the house accepted their apology and the accompanying promise that the matter would not be taken further.[152]

The willingness of the House of Commons to take action to protect its deliberations against disruption from external challenges and duels ought, one would have anticipated, to have paved the way for the ratification of a law or laws aimed at curbing duelling. In fact no further action was taken, and the continuing readiness of M.P.s to appeal to the code of honour in the years following demonstrates why. In November 1779 Barry Yelverton and John Scott, the Attorney General, almost came to blows, while in May 1780 John Toler found himself in trouble with one of the Hely-Hutchinson brothers for some slighting observations he had made about the Provost. In both cases a duel was only prevented by the intervention of the House of Commons. Three years later an unidentified M.P. was taken into custody for threatening an assault on a man who refused to take up a challenge.[153]

Although the failure of the House of Commons in the 1770s to take a legislative stand against duelling accurately reflects the reality of a situation in which the supporters of the code of honour were substantially more numerous and more powerful in the corridors of power than their critics, criticism of duelling became more vocal and better organised in the 1780s. The tone and approach of this opposition, which was rational rather than religious and suggestive rather than directive, was set by a curious pamphlet entitled *A Volunteer's queries*, published in Dublin in 1780. Modelled on Bishop Berkeley's *Querist*, the tract devoted twenty-four questions to the subject of duelling. Most were neutral in tone, but their overall thrust was to highlight the folly of a custom which demanded that an individual endanger his life to avenge an insult, and to persuade the reader that duelling was little more than a vice given respectability by custom.[154] A year later, a manual on swordsmanship arrived at similar conclusions from a different direction. Having discussed at length the virtues of swordsmanship, the author addressed his thoughts to the subject of duelling, which he dismissed as nothing other than 'an act of downright cowardice'. Duels, he asserted, were fought because people were afraid 'of the reproaches of mankind; it is this fear, this cowardice that stimulate men into actions they would otherwise reprobate and abhor'. If they allowed their finer rather than their baser emotions free rein, they would fulfil nobler purposes from which their relationship with God as well as with society at large would benefit.[155] The publication of these tracts did not herald a wave of anti-duelling activity. They did, however, signal the emergence of a more popular, rationally based critique of the code of honour, and it was not long before the popular press was relaying the argument that it required 'infinitely less courage to fight than not to fight a duel'.[156]

One sanctuary for the small band of anti-duellists in the country in the 1770s and 1780s was the Friendly Brothers of St Patrick, the number of knots of which rose impressively in the second half of the eighteenth century. They continued to recruit members from both the middle and upper classes, but their influence is difficult to assess. Based on the example of Sir Lucius O'Brien, who was a member, it is tempting to argue that there was a connection between membership of the brotherhood and individuals opposed to duelling, but this conclusion is invalidated by the fact that known duellists like George Ogle and Patrick Duigenan were also members. After the burst of publicity prompted by their reanimation in the 1750s, the organisation never reverted to the somnolent state which had characterised it in the early eighteenth century, but there is little evidence to indicate that it contributed in any way to the discouragement of duelling.[157] Indeed, the balance of evidence points the other way, as the Friendly Brothers were temporarily displaced as the main anti-duelling organisation in the kingdom in the 1780s by a new body which went by the name of the Knights of Tara.

According to Jonah Barrington, the founders of the Knights of Tara were 'southern fire-eaters', who grew so concerned with the number of unregulated and impromptu affairs of honour taking place that they formed the Knights in 1782 in an attempt to bring order to duelling. It is likely that the founders were influenced by publications like *A few mathematical and critical remarks on the sword* which deplored duelling but extolled swordsmanship on recreational grounds, for at an early meeting of the organisation in April 1783 they described themselves as 'a society instituted for the encouragement of the science of defence with the sword', ratified pietistic resolutions extolling the virtues of swordsmanship, and offered prizes to encourage fencing. According to Barrington, they also appointed a select committee to adjudicate all questions of honour referred to them. The full membership of this committee is not known, but the signatories of the resolutions agreed in April 1783 and the members of the steering committee of the organisation were predominantly from Counties Kilkenny and Dublin. These included the Hon. Thomas Butler, Colonel Butler, General Simon Luttrell and Major Wemys from County Kilkenny, Sir William Fortick of Belmont (chairman), Joseph Deane of Terenure and James Farrell of Blackpit from County Dublin, and Patrick Bellew from County Galway.[158]

As befitted an organisation which aspired to encourage recreational swordsmanship, the Knights did not take an explicitly anti-duelling stance.

Their main public activity was the organisation of public exhibitions in Capel Street Theatre.[159] These attracted large audiences for a time, but they had little impact on society at large and certainly not on the *aficionados* of duelling:

> The theatre of the Knights of Tara on these occasions was always overflowing. The combatants were dressed in close cambric jackets, garnished with ribbons, each wearing the favourite colour of his fair one; bunches of ribbons also dangled at their knees, and rose adorned their morocco slippers, which had buff soles to prevent noise in their lunges. No masks or visors were used as in these more timorous times; on the contrary, every feature was uncovered, and its inflections all visible. The ladies appeared in full morning dresses, each handing his foil to her champion for the day, and their presence animating the singular exhibition. From the stage-boxes the prizes likewise were handed to the conquerors by the fair ones, accompanied each with a wreath of laural, and a smile then more valued than a hundred victories! The tips of the foils were blackened, and, therefore, instantly betrayed the hits on the cambric jacket, and proclaimed without doubt the successful combatant. All was decorum, gallantry, spirit, and good temper.[160]

It was as organisers of such safe and sanitised events that the Knights of Tara flourished for number of years. However, it was not long before people tired of such spectacles and turned their attention elsewhere; the Knights had faded from the scene well before the end of the decade.

The Knights of Tara and the Friendly Brothers of St Patrick clearly failed to engender public momentum against duelling, but the intellectual armoury available to the anti-duelling lobby continued to be strengthened by the embrace of new arguments antipathetic to the code of honour. By the mid-1780s it had become commonplace to describe duelling as an anachronistic survival of a less civilised era. 'The practice is . . . inexcusable in the present times when the superstition on which it is grounded is almost universally exploded,' the *Volunteer Evening Post* proclaimed confidently in 1785:

> During the night of Gothic ignorance, our forefathers were seriously persuaded that in cases of direct and solemn appeal, the Deity would evidently and certainly interfere in favour of truth and justice and in vindication of injured innocence. Hence the burning plough-share for the determination of chastity; and an appeal to single combat on deficiency of evidence or to refute a charge of guilt. But in the present enlightened times, when the doctrine is exploded, the custom ought generally to have ceased with the reason. Every man will be sensible of the absurdity, if instead of the sword or the pistol, he should substitute the cast *of a die* to determine the propriety or folly of his conduct, annexing death, or a severe flagellation to him, whose *throw* might happen to be least successful.

But no matter what arguments were advanced by its opponents, the social elite of the country declined to stop duelling. Newspaper commentators continued to deplore 'the madness of this passion' which led gentlemen to reach for their pistols to expatiate 'every attack' up to and including the throwing of snowballs.[161] However, they had no ready solutions to offer and were frequently reduced to appealing to such hackneyed and inappropriate remedies as Gustav Adolph's threat to execute the survivors of fatal encounters.[162] There was simply no way that a solution as draconian as this would be approved, since even the most radical political activists of the day — the proponents of parliamentary reform — felt obligated to issue challenges to those who questioned their honour. In 1785 the Newry doctor William Drennan called out James Ogle because he accused him of issuing an 'untruth'.[163] The response accorded the critique of duelling advanced in the early and mid-1780s indicated that the fundamental reformation in attitude that was necessary to eradicate duelling had commenced, but that only a minority of the middle and upper classes from whom most duellists emanated yet concurred with opposition sentiment.

The regulation of duelling

Because of the incapacity of the authorities — civil and military — to regulate the code of honour, the onus lay with duellists to conduct themselves in a manner that reflected well on the code they observed. It is true that the authorities did intervene to stop nine known duelling parties settling their differences with pistols between 1771 and 1790 (Table 3.8). But, as the Trant–Colthurst rencontre highlights, they were powerless to prevent determined principals from meeting. The situation might have been different had recipients of challenges appealed to the law for protection, as the elderly Attorney General, Philip Tisdall, sought to do in 1777 when he took the Provost of Trinity College, John Hely-Hutchinson, to court for what he alleged was a deliberate attempt to provoke a duel.

Tisdall and Hutchinson had been on friendly terms until the latter sought and secured the provostship of Trinity College. Tisdall disapproved of the appointment, and he supported Patrick Duigenan and the anti-Hely-Hutchinson interest in the power struggle that took place in the college when Hely-Hutchinson took up office. Relations between the two men deteriorated to such an extent that it became a matter of deep concern for Lord Buckinghamshire, the Lord Lieutenant, who had hoped that they would co-operate in presenting government business in the House of Commons.[164] Instead he was forced to watch on helplessly as

Tisdall prosecuted Hely-Hutchinson for calling him an 'old scoundrel and a rascal' during a particularly heated exchange with Duigenan at the Four Courts. Tisdall contended that Hely-Hutchinson was too experienced a lawyer to utter such an expression by accident, and that it represented a deliberate attempt by the Provost to force him to risk his life in a duel or to discredit himself by declining to defend his honour. The Attorney General was too wily to fall for anything so transparent. More importantly, he was too old (he was seventy-five) and too prudent to succumb to the rampant enthusiasm for duelling currently evident in Ireland, and he neatly wrong-footed the Provost by instructing the Prime Serjeant, John Scott, to move in court for a motion to have an information taken against Hely-Hutchinson. This was unexpected. The fact that it involved two of the most prominent politicians in the land excited enormous interest, and details of the case were soon relayed by every newspaper in the county. Realising he had been outmanoeuvred, Hely-Hutchinson sought to negate the case against him by admitting that his words were 'too warm' but by denying that he wished to provoke a duel. The court did not accept his explanation. After a number of adjournments and a hearing that lasted several days the presiding judge reported in mid-May that Hely-Hutchinson had a case to answer and that the case should go to trial. Anxious above all that this should not happen, the Provost appealed, but he was unsuccessful. The anti-duelling interest was delighted. They anticipated that the case would do more for the anti-duelling cause than hundreds of admonitory columns and acres of print. However, they did not get a chance to test their thesis. Tisdall died before the case came to trial, and the case died with him.[165]

Hely-Hutchinson was very fortunate in the outcome. However, he could equally legitimately claim that he was unlucky, as it was unlikely that anybody other than Tisdall would have taken the case to court. Tisdall had lived most of his life in an era when the code of honour was less slavishly observed, and the instinctive reaction of at least part of the *corps d'élite* was to avoid unnecessary challenges. Few younger men, whatever their station, chose to conduct themselves in this manner in the 1770s.[166] Indeed, they were so devoted to the code of honour and convinced of the merits of duelling that they devoted more energy to ensuring that duels were fought within the rules than preventing them taking place. This necessitated regulations, and, in accordance with the self-regulating nature of the code of honour, duellists sought to provide them themselves.

The elaboration of a written code of behaviour for duellists in Ireland was a matter of some urgency by the 1770s because of the number of duels taking place and the suggestion that differing regions were developing different procedures around their preferred weapons. Galway duellists were reputed to favour the sword; Tipperary, Roscommon and Sligo the pistol; while Mayo duellists were supposedly equally at ease with both.[167] Too much weight should not be attached to these affirmations of regional specialisation. Of greater importance were the variations in the interpretation of the rules of duelling, and it was in order to eradicate these and to hasten the introduction of an agreed code that a number of *soi-disant* experts assembled at Clonmel in 1777 to determine a set of rules 'for general adoption throughout Ireland'. Though ultimately known as 'The Thirty-Six Commandments' from the number of 'rules' applied in County Galway, the fullest version extant contains only twenty-seven. These twenty-seven regulations are complete in themselves, and they provide a guide as to how the self-appointed duelling mentors believed the code of honour should operate.

The initial 'rules' appertained to the cause of duels. Verbal insults, as Rules 1–4 demonstrate, could be overcome with an apology; but in the event of no apology being offered, antagonists were obliged to fight 'till a severe hit be received by one party'. However, if the insult took the form of a physical blow (Rules 5 and 6), a 'verbal apology' would not suffice, and the matter could only be resolved by an exchange with weapons if the offender was not prepared to undergo the indignity of allowing himself to be hit with a cane and of begging the pardon of the person he had offended. Other causes afforded specific mention were allegations of cheating (Rule 9) and insulting a lady 'under a gentleman's care' (Rules 10 and 11), which was deemed a graver offence than to insult a gentleman.

Conduct on the duelling field was equally strictly defined. Once the principals in a duel 'had taken their ground', an apology could not be offered without an exchange of fire (Rule 7). Apologies could, of course, be proffered before the parties reached the 'ground' and after shots had been exchanged, but this did not extend to 'dumb shooting or firing in the air' (Rule 13). The challenger in a duel was deemed to be the aggressor, and for this reason he forfeited the choice of ground and of weapons. However, if 'the challenger gives his honour he is no swordsman', his opponent could not choose to fight with swords (Rules 16 and 17).

The active involvement of seconds was vital to the proper conduct of a duel, and the authors of the 'rules' acknowledged this by devoting much time to the elaboration and definition of their duties. Seconds were supposed to be of equal rank with the principals (Rule 14), and they were expected to follow carefully defined procedures. For example, in order to eradicate immediate duels, they were instructed not to deliver challenges at night (Rule 15). On the duelling field the second's duties included loading pistols, handing them to the principals and regulating firing (Rules 18, 19, 24). They were also obligated to attempt to reconcile the contending principals before the rencontre, and after shots had been fired or injuries inflicted (Rule 21). In the event of the seconds disagreeing and concluding that their difference could only be resolved with weapons, they were authorised to meet at the same time as the principals (Rule 25).

As well as these rules which appertained to how duels were conducted, there were 'rules' stipulating what should be done when a pistol misfired (it was the equivalent of a shot) (Rule 20), when one party was incapacitated (Rule 22), and when principals infringed the rules provided (Rule 23). The 'additional articles' added by the Galway committee appear to have been introduced with George Robert Fitzgerald in mind because they outlawed crouching, the protection of parts of the body by the hand, and movement towards one's opponent when the ground was measured. When the ground was not measured, movement was permissible.[168]

Taken together, these twenty-seven 'rules' represented the most coherent attempt to date to eradicate abuses in the way duels were conducted in Ireland. Even then, Irish duelling practice still had some way to go to catch up with Britain and continental Europe in that it was not yet usual, for example, for surgeons to accompany the principals onto the duelling field to provide prompt medical attention if injuries resulted.[169] None the less, by explicitly defining the rules by which participants should be guided, Irish duellists reflected the tendency in late eighteenth-century European society to ameliorate the hard edges of human behaviour.[170] The need to regularise, if not to sanitise, duelling, to which the 1777 'rules' are but the most obvious Irish testimony, was part of the price gentlemen had to pay to perpetuate their right to decide differences on points of honour by recourse to arms. Late eighteenth-century society operated according to more genteel principles than was the case in the seventeenth and early eighteenth centuries. Gentlemen were now expected to behave more decorously; it was no longer acceptable that duels should bear comparison, as was the case in early eighteenth-century Ireland, with legalised assassinations. This disposition to disencumber the code of honour of its more unsavoury features is emphasised by the increased disposition to praise the duellist who adopted a magnanimous attitude towards his opponent on the duelling field; he thereby demonstrated his humanity as well as his bravery.[171] Indeed, in some respects, such conduct was more necessary in Ireland than elsewhere because the visible increase in duelling that took place there in the last quarter of the eighteenth century bucked the general European trend.[172]

But the readiness of duellists to emphasise their commitment to self-regulation by ratifying the rules drafted at Clonmel in 1777, and the proposal at the same time to establish a committee, which would meet alternately at the quarter-sessions held at Clonmel and Galway, to oversee their enforcement,[173] was not prompted solely by duellists' anxiety to deflect criticism of the code of honour. Even the most enthusiastic *aficionados* of duelling were taken aback by the speed with which it spread its tentacles throughout society in the 1770s and 1780s. Reports like that in the *Freeman's Journal* in March 1787 that two boys attending school in Glasnevin were flogged because they had been discovered by an usher endeavouring to fight a duel[174] were too commonplace to be easily dismissed. Duelling was still a respectable, if controversial, social practice; its devotees appreciated that it would not take many incidents of this kind to turn the increasingly weighty force of public opinion against duelling. If that happened, the reluctant senators in College Green might not be able for long to withstand a demand for proscriptive legislation.

This prospect appeared remote in the 1770s and early 1780s, as Jonah Barrington's observation that the ability to conduct oneself in a duel was '*considered* a necessary part of a young man's education' attests.[175] Of course, not every young gentleman was schooled in the arts of the duel, but the widespread belief that it was a beneficial skill ensured that it was transmitted from one generation to the next. More significantly, because a duel was seen as 'a test of character', and the reward for those who performed creditably was the applause and approbation of their peers, young men were emboldened to demonstrate their courage by giving and receiving challenges.[176] *Per contra*, because to decline or to evade a challenge meant disgracing one's family as well as oneself, many duels were prompted by what even contemporaries regarded as trivialities.[177] Indeed, it is fair to say that some deemed it virtuous to be on the alert to perceive insult and to respond to every instance of the same with a challenge. This accounts for the formation of so-called duelling clubs, though most such bodies — which were few in number — devoted their energies to carousing rather than to fighting. The notorious Hellfire Club, which reputedly reserved its membership to those who had killed an opponent in a duel, has proved remarkably elusive in the duelling record.[178]

What sort of society was this which permitted members of the ruling elite to endanger their lives with such equanimity? In many ways, it was a society which was more concerned with image than with actuality. It was a consciously hierarchial society in which appearance and image were attentively and scrupulously attended to. It was also, of course, an intensely male society. Women were both legally and socially subservient to men, and were defined in law in terms of their relationship with men. Both sexes had clearly defined and distinct social roles, but it was the male's which carried status and power. Only men could vote and sit in parliament, to cite the most obvious. Women were expected to devote their energies to child rearing, household management and to making life easeful for their menfolk. Because of the occupational and attitudinal cleavages this gave rise to, men and women were separated mentally as well as physically for large stretches of their existence. Both sought congenial company; but in most instances they found it in their own rather than that of the opposite sex. Men hunted, caroused and conversed in the company of men; women embroidered, looked after children and conversed in the company of women. Each needed the other, but each had their own domains. On the whole, the lifestyle of many male members of the upper classes bears sustainable comparison with what today we call *machismo*. These men were prepared to duel over women, but they would never regard them as their equals. It was a duelling offence for a man to pass between a lady and buildings while walking the streets or to enter a theatre box in which there were ladies present in his surtout, boots or hat,[179] but the attitudes which encouraged this conduct operated to keep women confined rather than to afford them status. Fundamentally, duels over women were displays of territoriality by men *vis-à-vis* other males rather than chivalric gestures designed to protect what males deemed the 'weaker sex'.

Given eighteenth-century Irish gentlemen's preoccupation with honour and image, it is easy to find reasons to condemn their lifestyle and deportment. V. G. Kiernan has attributed their enthusiasm for duelling to the sheer 'inanity of a landowner's existence'. He interprets the aristocracy in Ireland as elsewhere as a vestigial remnant of a social class without a role because the state had expanded to take over their functions.[180] But this is too simplistic a view. In the first place, the state had clearly not expanded as much as Kiernan implies, or else duelling too would have been eradicated. More significantly, it does not acknowledge that the landed elite that dominated Ireland politically and economically throughout the eighteenth century did at least have one important function which it performed with some success — it preserved control of Ireland for and on behalf of itself and its sister elite in Britain. It is true that the Irish elite did not forge the same community of interests with their tenantry or play as decisive a role in the development of the kingdom's economy as did their British counterparts, but by no means were all Irish landowners feckless duelling enthusiasts. Moreover, duelling was more deeply entrenched in England than Kiernan allows. Although the contrary impression is often conveyed, only a minority of the Irish Protestant elite actually duelled; the rest got on with their existence as best they could. Most would have fought a duel if they had been put in a situation in which there seemed to be no alternative. But for every example of manifest 'inanity', such as that which took place in January 1777 when eight men who had been hunting decided to take pot shots at each other after consuming three bottles of whiskey as a result of which all were wounded, there were many more who conducted themselves decorously.[181] Those gentlemen who drank, hunted, gambled[182] and duelled to excess did so because they enjoyed that lifestyle. It may well have been inane, but it was an option Irish society offered them and the option they chose to exercise.

The conduct of duelling in the 1770s and 1780s

The decision of guardians of the code of honour at Clonmel in 1777 to lay down a code of practice for duellists mirrored the increased regularisation of the manner in which duels were fought in the last quarter of the eighteenth century. One of the most pertinent indices of this is provided by the presence of seconds. Only a fraction of the 225 duels that constitute our sample for the fifteen years 1776–90 provide detailed evidence on the way seconds conducted themselves, but the fact that less than 2 per cent of this sample were fought in their absence attests to the greater willingness to observe duelling etiquette. It is true also that seconds were more willing to intervene, as the 1777 rules instructed, to conciliate contending parties. Overall, seconds intervened in an attempt to conclude forty-five (or 20 per cent) of reported duels between 1776 and 1790. The relative rate of intervention did not change significantly over these fifteen years, and the success rate averaged about 36 per cent (Table 3.8).

There were, of course, plenty of opportunities for seconds to intervene, because of the sizeable number of duels taking place (Table 3.1). A survey of newspapers and primary sources similar to that which was undertaken for the early and mid-eighteenth century suggests a strikingly even quinquennial distribution in the number of duels taking place throughout this period. These figures do not represent an absolute measure of the total number of challenges that were issued or of the number of duels that were fought, but they do indicate strongly that the level of duelling was greater than at any other point in the century. Indeed, the level would have been greater if the averted duels for which there is a record had been fought. Averted duels amount to approximately 20 per cent of the total number of reported duels fought in the years 1771–90, but they are only statistically significant for the quinquennium 1781–5, when they amounted to 33 per cent of the total. In no other five-year period did they represent much more than 10 per cent of the sample of recorded duels (Table 3.1).

As in previous decades, most of those who duelled in the fifteen years 1776–90 were gentlemen (they provided one or both principals in 74 per cent of the duels sampled). Next to them were the military (22 per cent) and members of the middle classes (16 per cent), of which 7.6 per cent were lawyers and attornies. Four per cent were of lower-class origin (Table 3.1). These figures do not differ greatly from the figures calculated above for the early 1770s and the mid-eighteenth century, and they demonstrate that for all the increase in the rate of duelling, the profile of the participants had changed little.

Geographically, matters were less static. The most salient distributional change was the decline in the dominance of Leinster nationally. This province (inclusive of Dublin county and city which contributed 32 per cent of the national total) played host to nearly half the total number of locatable duels (45 per cent) in our sample for the years 1776–90. However, the gap between Leinster and Munster, the province with the second-highest total, was falling rapidly. Whereas the margin between the two provinces in the five years 1771–75 was a massive 47 per cent, it fell to 23 per cent between 1776 and 1790. Munster now contributed more than 22 per cent (a rise of 5 per cent) of the total number of reported duels. Connacht and Ulster also played host to more duels, but their increase was more modest. Connacht contributed 13 per cent and Ulster 8 per cent of the total (an increase of over 4 per cent on the situation in the early 1770s) (Table 3.2).[183]

Next to the emergence of Munster, the most significant changes in the distributional pattern of duelling between 1776 and 1790 was the continued decline of Dublin city as a popular duelling location in the 1770s and 1780s. Of seventy-two known duels that took place within the Dublin county boundary between 1776 and 1790, less than 24 per cent occurred in the city. A similar percentage took place in the county and suburbs, 7 per cent in Merrion Fields, 3 per cent in the North Lotts, and a massive 43 per cent in the Phoenix Park, which was now established as the country's premier duelling location (Table 3.3). The appeal of the Park lay in its size as well as its proximity to the city. It offered seclusion as well as convenience. Duellists and their seconds could go there with the knowledge that they had the leisure to duel according to the code of honour free from unwarranted interruption and within convenient access of the city should medical help prove necessary. No other location quite provided such facilities.

Its relative decline notwithstanding, no other county or city came close to displacing Dublin as the kingdom's premier duelling location in the 1770s and 1780s. Tipperary had the reputation of being an important duelling centre, but, if Table 3.4 is an accurate guide, it was not remarkable. County Tipperary was, it is true, one of the main duelling counties in Munster; together with County Cork it contributed no less than 78 per cent of the sample of reported duels collected from Munster between 1775 and 1790, and 64 per cent of the total between 1771 and 1800.

Ironically, though Cork did not have the duelling reputation of County Tipperary, it played host to twice the number of reported duels during these decades (Table 3.4).

The pistol, which was already established as the duellist's favourite weapon for some time before the tremendous increase in duelling that occurred in the early 1770s, consolidated its position during the following fifteen years (Tables 3.5 and 3.6). Pistols were the weapon of first choice of over 95 per cent of duellists during this period. The pistol was a dangerous weapon despite its popularity, for it was responsible for at least fifty-three deaths between 1776 and 1790. This meant that there was a 24 per cent chance that one of the principals would die every time a set of duelling pistols was fired in anger in these years.[184] And if we incorporate into this calculation the fifteen incidents in which a 'mortal' wound resulted, the percentage chances of one of the principals dying rise to 30 per cent. This is significantly higher than was the case in the early 1770s but, interestingly, the percentage of duels which concluded without any injuries was 3 per cent less. A total of 65, or 28.8 per cent, of the total of 225 reported duels in the fifteen years 1776–90 produced no injuries. Of course, duels did not just produce fatalities or no 'hits', and a truer understanding of the physical consequences of duelling on those who participated is provided by an analysis of total injuries. From the figures tabulated on Table 3.7, 69 per cent of sampled duels fought between 1776 and 1790 resulted in the death or injury of at least one of the participants. The odds on an individual duellist suffering death or injury were considerably less. Thirty-nine per cent of all duellists were killed or injured in this period (Table 3.7). These figures are considerably higher than the corresponding figures for the early 1770s, but still significantly lower than the high mortality and injury figures which were commonplace in the early eighteenth century.[185]

As well as the recourse to the pistol, the comparatively moderate levels of duelling deaths and injuries in the 1770s and 1780s can be attributed to the greater disposition to observe the rules of the code of honour. An excellent illustration of this is provided by the encounter which took place in March 1783 at the North Lotts between a Mr B—— and a Mr S——. Both fired a case of pistols without effect. This rankled with B——, and he demanded that his opponent reload. However, S——'s second deemed this 'contrary to rule' and led his principal away.[186] Such decisiveness was uncommon, perhaps because the breaches of duelling etiquette that continued to occur were strikingly less excessive than those of previous decades. Most centred on the persistent habit of engaging in indoor and immediate duelling. For example, two young men who quarrelled in a public house in March 1778 were so determined to settle their differences that they simply went outside and blazed; as a result, one of the two, 'the son of an eminent citizen', was killed.[187] Two years earlier, on Monday 24 June 1776, two gentlemen adjourned to a private room in Dublin for a similar purpose;[188] while in 1779 Hyacinth Kirwan and Robert D'Arcy faced each other in one of the rooms of the Mitre Inn in Tuam at about five yards and fired a case of pistols without effect.[189] In 1786 another such incident, involving a lawyer and a soldier who had quarrelled over the pronounciation of a Greek word, did not conclude until the former was shot dead 'across a table'; while in September 1787 a dispute between Lieutenant Lloyd and Surgeon Jobson of the 46th Regiment concluded in the back room of an inn in Coleraine, where Lloyd was shot dead.[190]

One cannot assume, of course, that the presence of seconds guaranteed that a duel would be conducted properly. It is true that in some 35 per cent of encounters between 1776 and 1790 the intervention of seconds reconciled disaffected antagonists,[191] but seconds could also make matters worse (Table 3.8). An excellent illustration of this is provided by the rencontre that took place in January 1778 when the seconds to two principals who exchanged shots without effect in the Phoenix Park so antagonised each other that they resolved to meet there and then. The main culprit was Captain Dalton, who was enraged by what he regarded as the unsatisfactory outcome to the meeting of the principals. His opponent, Counsellor Burleigh, was only slightly less hot-headed, but he was a better shot, for when the two men assumed their positions, his first ball hit Dalton square in the heart and killed him.[192] A better-documented example of seconds exacerbating matters occurred in County Kildare in December 1787 when William Barrington, Jonah's brother, met Lieutenant McKenzie following a disagreement at table. When the principals had fired their pistols without effect, a reconciliation was proposed, but McKenzie's second, Captain Gillespie, objected. 'Nothing but blood', he proclaimed, could compensate for Barrington's insult. It is not clear what happened next, but the outcome was that William Barrington was shot dead in an exchange of bullets with Gillespie rather than with McKenzie. This was most unusual, and the Barringtons were so enraged that Jonah instituted a prosecution for murder against Gillespie. However, when the case came to trial in Maryborough in March 1788 both Gillespie and McKenzie 'were most honourably acquitted'.[193]

Even allowing for bias in Jonah Barrington's account of the McKenzie–Barrington affair, there seems little doubt but that Captain Gillespie played a more proactive part than was provided for in the rules of duelling. Some seconds, of course, were simply incompetent. For example, when a journeyman barber and an apprentice tailor met in the Phoenix Park in 1789, the encounter went tragically wrong when the apprentice's pistol, which had been improperly charged, burst and shattered his hand so badly that lockjaw was anticipated.[194]

But however much blame or praise is directed at individual seconds, it was the principals alone who made the final decision and there were invariably some so incandescent with rage that no amount of intercession could persuade them to conclude a rencontre without bloodshed.[195] A good instance of this is provided by the meeting of Athenasius Nagle of Kilworth and Maurice Courtnay of Imokilly, County Cork, on Sunday 26 September 1779. The cause of this dispute is not known, but emotions clearly ran high, because, having discharged two cases of pistols each without effect and adjourned to shelter from a shower of rain, they loaded twice more. Sixteen shots were fired in all, and in both cases it was the last that did the damage. Courtnay was hit twice on the ribs, but because neither ball penetrated he left the field sore but otherwise little worse for his experience. Nagle, by contrast, was hit by his opponent's ball on the temple, and though he was still alive at the end of the encounter, he was deemed past recovery despite the prompt attention of a surgeon.[196] Two soldiers who are known only by their initials, Lieutenant T—— and Lieutenant H——, demonstrated similar resolve four years later when they exchanged eight shots before T—— was hit and killed. In Sligo in 1784 a soldier and a civilian also exchanged eight shots, but in this instance they ceased when the former was hit in the thigh. In 1782 two Connacht gentlemen were on their fifth shot when one, James D——n of Fairfield, County Galway, was hit in the chest and killed.[197] Similarly, in an encounter in Belfast between Still Wilson and Captain Fitzgerald, which arose out of Wilson's adulterous relationship with Fitzgerald's wife, Fitzgerald persisted with his attempt to kill his opponent even after he had disabled him by shooting off two of his fingers. In the normal course of events, it was customary in the late eighteenth century to conclude a duel once blood was drawn; but as the above incidents illustrate, angry men did not feel bound by these conventions.[198] Cases such as these were infrequent and invariably controversial, but they highlight the continuing disposition of some duellists to kill their opponent rather than to defend their honour.

The introduction of swords into an encounter was generally a good indicator that the combatants had more than honour alone in mind when they collided. When two gentlemen who met in Grangegorman Lane, Dublin, on Monday 25 May 1778 failed to achieve the desired result with pistols, they drew their swords and fought to a standstill; both were seriously injured, and one died as a result.[199] Death was not always the outcome of swordplay, but injuries were almost certain. Thus when two gentlemen met with swords in Castlebar in 1781 both were wounded — neither very seriously.[200] It was, of course, always possible to miscalculate, with humiliating consequences. When William Archer met Mr Kendellon on the green of Spring House, Clonmel, on 13 January 1779, he declined a request to remove his sword. However, since both principals possessed three pistols, it was calculated that it would not come into play, and the duel proceeded. The two men took their places at twenty yards' distance and fired alternately. After the first brace of shots, which missed their intended targets, Kendellon shortened the distance to twelve yards. Both men missed from this range as well. Archer fired his third pistol first and, having missed once again, drew his sword. This put Kendellon in something of a quandary, but he rose to the challenge by advancing towards his opponent with his pistol cocked. Realising his error, Archer 'retired in confusion (crying *murder, murder!*) till stopped by a morass about twenty yards behind him into which he plunged; whereupon Mr Kendellon came over him, telling him to beg his life which he scorned to take away'.[201] Others were not satisfied simply with upholding their honour. When John Wilson exchanged shots without effect with Henry Ivers at Sixmilebridge, County Clare, in March 1778, the two men were persuaded to conclude the encounter, honour intact, by some local gentlemen; but when the Ivers's party was leaving the scene, Henry was mortally wounded and his brother John shot dead by an assailant who fired from Henry Wilson's (John Wilson's brother's) house.[202] This was clearly a case for the authorities; for whatever the disinclination of the legal authorities to prosecute duellists, they could not ignore murder.

Despite the overwhelming evidence for an improvement in the way in which affairs of honour were conducted in the 1770s and 1780s, these incidents manifest that duels were by no means always neatly regulated, orderly affairs as described in duelling manuals.[203] That said, the overwhelmingly majority of duels were conducted according to rule and seldom elicited more than a three- to five-line news report as a result. Even that rarity, the double duel, could be conducted in a perfectly orderly manner if the rules of duelling were observed, as the examples fought in the Phoenix Park on 26 December 1785 and in September 1789 illustrate.[204] Most encounters involving the military,[205] attornies and other members of the middle and lower classes were likewise conducted according to rule.[206] In a number of instances, crowds of spectators assembled to watch what they evidently regarded as public entertainment, but on at least two of the occasions that this occurred the exchange bears closer comparison to a *jeu d'esprit* than a real rencontre, for the seconds loaded the pistols of the belligerents with gooseberries and eggs.[207] Audiences were simply not welcome when the principals were in earnest, and in such cases it was incumbent on all concerned to choose a secluded location. The importance of this was underlined in 1784 when two neighbouring gentlemen met near Dunnamon, County Roscommon. The tenants of both principals turned out to support their 'respective masters', but instead of dispersing quietly when the encounter was over (neither party was seriously injured), they turned on each other, and 'several persons [were] dangerously hurt' in the 'dreadful affray' that followed.[208]

The middle classes took their cue from their social betters, and this probably accounts for the unexceptional nature of most of the duels involving members of these interests. No social group ever behaves in a totally uniform manner, however, and there were a number of affairs of honour involving individuals from middle-class occupations which made the headlines. Perhaps the most notable arose out of a disputed election at Mercer's Hospital which so divided the staff that there were two duels involving four different surgeons; another surgeon only evaded a similar experience by swearing an information against two juniors who sought to challenge him.[209] This incident, as well as that at Ballinasloe in 1778 between a journeyman shoemaker (John Kelly) and a diaper weaver (Jonathan Lee), and another involving two journalists with the *Freeman's Journal* in Dublin in 1780 illustrate once more just how deeply duelling had permeated Irish society.[210] An even clearer illustration is provided by the encounter at Rathkeale races in July 1779 between the Rev. Mr D—— and Thomas Westropp junior of Ballysteen in which the latter was killed. This is the only known instance of an Irish clergyman killing his opponent in a duel, and it demonstrates conclusively that even clergy were prepared to fight if they deemed the provocation intolerable.[211]

The Volunteers too were unable to resist the temptations of the code of honour. Members managed successfully to refrain from duelling during the 1770s, when the threat of invasion was at its greatest. However, following the lessening of the invasion threat in the spring of 1780 duels began to occur with some frequency. In March 1780, Captain Maxwell and Mr McClane of Armagh could not be persuaded to conclude their bitter row until McClane was mortally injured.[212] Nine months later McDermott, the sheriff of County Roscommon, was arrested in London when he challenged Lieutenant Grant of the 61st Regiment for objecting to his disporting himself in a Volunteer uniform.[213] This was a comparatively harmless incident. A much more serious altercation took place in Cork in October 1781 when Lieutenant Robert Hickson, a soldier home on leave, was challenged by Mr Brereton of the Duhallow Rangers. Instead of following custom and waiting till the next day to fight, the two men commandeered a room in a coffee-house in Brown Street, drew their swords, and did not cease until Brereton was fatally wounded.[214] Duels involving Volunteers became more commonplace after this, as fractures began to appear within the organisation over the issues of legislative independence and parliamentary reform. There was a duelling incident in Dublin in 1782 involving two members of the Irish Brigade; in Killala in 1783 as a result of a disagreement over the election of Volunteer officers; and, with bayonets, in Monaghan in 1788 over a difference about manoeuvres.[215]

Incidents like these were only to be expected. Indeed, it would have been more surprising if the Volunteers had remained untouched by the duelling craze, given that students at Trinity College also demonstrated their fighting prowess in the 1780s, as if to confirm the worst prognostications of the opponents of Hely-Hutchinson's scheme to add fencing to the college curriculum.[216] Even families could not escape. In County Longford on 26 December 1782 Robert Moffat of Rynn was killed in a duel with his brother-in-law, Mr Furry, as a result of a difference arising out of Moffat's marriage three weeks earlier. A year later Andrew Irwin from County Fermanagh was killed by his first cousin, Mango Noble, in the Deerpark near Brookeborough.[217] The message of such incidents was that duelling was firmly rooted in Irish Protestant society, and that its extirpation, like its establishment, was likely to be prolonged.

Notes and References

1 Townshend to Macartney, 21 Oct. 1772 (P.R.O.N.I., Macartney Papers, D562/1/53).
2 In 1771 a potential duel between Henry Flood and Robert Waller, M.P. for Dundalk, was averted when the latter offered a 'submissive retraction' for 'some reflections' he had cast on Flood (*H.J.*, 6 Nov. 1771).
3 *H.J.*, 3 Nov. 1773; *F.L.J.*, 6 Nov. 1773.
4 *F.L.J.*, 6 Nov. 1773.
5 *H.J.*, 19 Nov. 1773; *F.L.J.*, 24 Nov., 1 Dec. 1773; Waller to Macartney, Dec. 1773, in Bartlett, ed., *Macartney in Ireland*, p. 183. For Allan see E. M. Johnston, 'The career and correspondence of Thomas Allan', *I.H.S.*, x (1957), pp. 298–324.
6 *F.L.J.*, 24 Nov. 1773.
7 Waller to Macartney, 19 Mar. 1774, in Bartlett, ed., *Macartney in Ireland*, p. 188. According to the standing orders of the House of Lords, a peer who believed he had received 'an affront or injury from any other member of the House' was obliged to bring the incident to the attention of 'the Lords in parliament' or else endure 'severe censure' (*Rules and orders to be observed in the upper House of Parliament of Ireland* (Dublin, 1784), p. 23).
8 *H.J.*, 5 Nov. 1774; *F.L.J.*, 8 Oct. 1774; Scott to Cuffe, [25 Oct. 1774] (P.R.O.N.I., Normanton Papers, T3719/C/8/6); Hamilton, *The only approved guide*, pp. 177–9; G. O. Sayles, 'The Irish parliament in 1782', *P.R.I.A.*, 56C (1954), pp. 259–60.
9 *F.L.J.*, 6 Nov. 1773.
10 Bartlett, ed., *Macartney in Ireland*, p. 183; James Kelly, 'The politics of "Protestant ascendancy": County Galway, 1650–1832' in Raymond Gillespie and Gerard Moran, eds, *Galway: politics and society* (forthcoming); *F.L.J.*, 19 Mar. 1774.
11 D.N.B.; T.C.D., Donoughmore Papers, C/1 and C/2.
12 Wood-Martin, *History of Sligo*, iii, 316; *Life of Grattan*, ii, 88–9; *H.J.*, 21 Nov. 1774.
13 Walsh, *Ireland sixty years ago*, pp. 24–5; *F.L.J.*, 26 Nov. 1774; *H.J.*, 21, 25, 28 Nov. 1774; *Life of Grattan*, i, 273–4.
14 Hely-Hutchinson to his wife, [13 Jan 1775] (T.C.D., Donoughmore Papers); S.E. Ó Cearbhaill, 'Seán Hely-Hutchinson', *Galvia*, ix (1962), p. 33.
15 *F.L.J.*, 18, 21 Jan. 1775; *H.J.*, 16 Jan. 1775; *Life of Grattan*, i, 273–4.
16 *H.J.*, 18, 23 Jan. 1775. Doyle also faced a third challenge from an individual named Walshe, but he was able to evade this (*Life of Grattan*, i, 275–6).
17 *F.L.J.*, 29 July, 5 Aug. 1775.
18 Townshend to Hely-Hutchinson, 25 Jan. 1775, in H.M.C., *Donoughmore*, p. 282. For Hely-Hutchinson and Townshend see their correspondence in Lewis Walpole Library, Townshend Papers.
19 Below, p. 140.

20 Beresford to Allan, 21 Mar. 1778, in William Beresford, ed., *Correspondence of . . . John Beresford* (2 vols, London, 1854), i, 22–4; *H.J.*, 10, 15, 27 Mar. 1778; *F.J.*, 25 Mar. 1778; *F.L.J.*, 25 Mar. 1778; A. S. Mag Shamhrain, *Sir Edward Newenham* (Belcamp College, Dublin, 1984), p. 11; E. A. Coyle, 'Sir Edward Newenham', *Dublin Historical Record*, xlvi (1993), p. 25.

21 Above, pp. 65–6.

22 R. J. Coughlan, *Napper Tandy* (Dublin, 1976), pp. 25–6.

23 Buckinghamshire to Hillsborough and enclosure, 21 Nov. 1780 (P.R.O., SP 63/471, ff 306–22); J. A. Froude, *The English in Ireland* (3 vols, London, 1881), ii, 292–4; Kiernan, *The duel*, pp. 124–5.

24 Peter Jupp, 'Earl Temple's viceroyalty and the question of renunciation, 1782–3', *I.H.S.*, xvii (1972), pp. 299–317; James Kelly, *Prelude to Union: Anglo-Irish politics in the 1780s* (Cork, 1992), pp. 50–53.

25 *The Parliamentary Register, or history of the proceedings and debates of the House of Commons of Ireland, 1781–97* (17 vols, Dublin, 1782–1801) (cited as *Parl. Reg. (Irl.)*), ii, 39–44; Warden Flood, *Memoirs of the life and correspondence of Henry Flood* (Dublin, 1838), 205–7. The version of the speech published in D.O. Madden, *The speeches of Henry Grattan* (Dublin, 1847), pp. 91–95 is tamer than that given in the *Parliamentary Register*.

26 *Parl. Reg. (Irl.)*, ii, 42–3.

27 Cooke to Eden, 29 Oct. 1783, in The Bishop of Bath and Wells, ed., *The journal and correspondence of William, Lord Auckland* (4 vols, London, 1861–2), i, 338–40; see also Northington to North, 29 Oct. 1783 (Beinecke Library, Osborn Collection, Northington Letterbook, ff 29–32); Burgoyne to Fox, 31 Oct. 1783 (B.L., Fox Papers, Add. MS 47568, ff 199–203).

28 *Parl. Reg. (Irl.)*, ii, 43–4; *Life of Flood*, pp. 208–9; Conolly to Leinster, 19 Oct. 1783, in Fitzgerald, ed., *Leinster Corresp.*, iii, 372–3.

29 Cooke to Eden, 29 Oct. 1783, in *Auckland corresp.*, i, 338–40; Annaly to Pery, 29 Oct. 1783, in H.M.C., *Emly*, ii, 181; *V.E.P.*, 16 Dec. 1783.

30 *D.E.P.*, 30 Oct. 1783; Lord Carlow to Lady Carlow, 31 Oct. 1783, in *Gleanings from an old portfolio*, i, 233–4; Ogilvie to Leinster, 30 Oct. 1783 (N.L.I., Fitzgerald Papers, MS 624, f. 119b).

31 Impartial observers were more critical of Grattan than of Flood. See the observations of Lord Carlow (*Gleanings from an old portfolio*, i, 233–4) and Alexander Knox (Lord Teignmouth, *Reminiscences of many years* (2 vols, Edinburgh, 1878), i, 187). Flood's speech of 1 November is in *Parl. Reg. (Irl.)*, ii, 61–70 and Warden Flood, *Life of Flood*, pp. 211–19.

32 Malcomson, *Foster*, p. 397; Flood to Chandos, 1 Nov. 1783 (Henry Huntington Library, Chandos Papers, STB, Box 10, no. 46).

33 Clogher to Buckinghamshire, 7 Nov. 1783, in H.M.C., *Lothian*, p. 423.

34 Above p. St George to Rutland, 15 June 1785, in H.M.C., *Rutland*, iii, 217; *Life of Grattan*, iii, 253.

35 Above, p. 130; below, p. 220.

36 *V.E.P.*, 3 July 1784. For Corry see A.P.W. Malcomson, *Isaac Corry: an adventurer in the field of politics* (Belfast, 1976). For his duel with Grattan see pp. 211–12.

37 *F.J.*, 14 June 1764; Burke, *Clonmel*, pp. 157–8.
38 Curran, *Life of Curran*, i, 130–35; see also *H.J.*, 4, 11, 13 Oct. 1780, for the Doneraile trial.
39 Woodfall to Eden, 16 Aug. 1785, in *Auckland corresp.*, i, 81; Cunninghame to Eden, [16 Aug. 1785] (P.R.O.N.I., Sneyd Papers, T3229/2/4); Curran, *Life of Curran*, i, 196–201; Marianne Elliott, *Wolfe Tone: prophet of Irish independence* (London, 1989), p. 69.
40 Curran, *Life of Curran*, pp. 253–80; O'Donovan, *Life by the Liffey*, p. 65; Gerard O'Brien, ed., 'Debate in the Irish parliament in 1787', *Analecta Hibernica*, no. 33 (1986), pp. 133–4; Emily Lorraine de Montluzin, *The Anti-Jacobins, 1798–1800* (London, 1988), pp. 90–92; *Annual Register*, xxxii (1790), p. 199.
41 A. P. W. Malcomson, 'Lord Shannon' in Esther Hewitt, ed., *Lord Shannon's letters to his son* (Belfast, 1982), p. xxxvi.
42 *H.J.*, 16 Oct. 1772.
43 James Kelly, 'Napper Tandy: radical and republican' in James Kelly and Uaitear Mac Gearailt, eds, *Dublin and Dubliners: essays in the history and literature of Dublin city* (Dublin, 1990), pp. 2–3.
44 *H.J.*, 3, 5 Jan. 1774.
45 *H.J.*, 28 Mar. 1774.
46 *H.J.*, 28 Mar. 1774.
47 *F.L.J.*, 5 Aug. 1775.
48 *F.L.J.*, 9 Aug. 1775; *H.J.*, 9 Aug. 1775; George O' Malley to Owen O'Malley, [July 1775] in *Analecta Hibernica*, no. 25 (1967), pp. 194–5; Kelly, 'The politics of Protestant ascendancy: County Galway, 1650–1832'.
49 Barrington, *Personal sketches*, ii, 29–30.
50 *F.L.J.*, 8 June 1776.
51 *F.L.J.*, 20 Apr. 1776; W. P. Burke, *History of Clonmel* (Waterford, 1907), pp. 154–5; *Dublin Weekly Journal*, 27 Apr. 1776. I would like to thank Mr Eugene Coyle for the latter reference.
52 *F.L.J.*, 5 June 1776.
53 O'Brien to Knox, 7 July 1776, in H.M.C., *Reports on various collections*, vi, *Knox MSS*, p. 232; L. F. MacNamara, ed., 'The diary of an eighteenth-century gentleman', *North Munster Antiquarian Journal*, xxiii (1981), p. 40; Kieran Sheedy, *The Clare Elections* (Dublin, 1993) pp. 77–80; Proceedings of the Select Grand Knot, 1751–78 (Friendly Brothers of St Patrick archive); Howard to Howard, 29 June 1773 (N.L.I., Wicklow Papers).
54 *H.J.*, 8 Sept. 1777.
55 Black, ed., 'Cavendish's parliamentary diary', ii, 100–1, 200–6.
56 Malcomson, 'Lord Shannon', in Hewitt, ed., *Lord Shannon's letters*, pp. lxii–lxiv.
57 *D.E.P.*, 9 Oct, 1783. It should be noted that, because of the indefinite nature of the reports, not all of the twenty-two duelling incidents reported in the press are incorporated into Tables 3.1–3.8.
58 *D.E.P.*, 24 May 1783.
59 For Egan see MacDougall, *Sketches of Irish political characters*, pp. 195–6.
60 *D.E.P.*, 23 Oct. 1783; Barrington, *Recollections*, ii, 4; D'Arcy to Dillon, 21 July 1783 (Dillon of Clonbrock Papers (P.R.O.N.I., T3366/30)).

61 Barrington, *Recollections*, pp. 296–9.
62 *D.E.P.*, 8 May 1787.
63 Dominick Trant, *Considerations on the present disturbances in the province of Munster and their causes, extent, probable consequences and remedies* (Dublin, 1787), pp. 48–50.
64 Dominick Trant's account of the duel with Sir John Colthurst, 20 Feb. 1787 (N.L.I., MS 1762); Edward to Vere Hunt, [17] Feb. [1787] (Limerick Archives Office, Vere Hunt Papers); *F.J.*, 15, 17 Feb. 1787; [ ] to Duchess of Leinster, 9 Mar. 1787 (N.L.I., Fitzgerald Papers, MS 618, f.75).
65 Dominick Trant's account . . . (N.L.I., MS 1762); *F.J.*, 17 Feb. 1787.
66 *D.C.*, 22 May 1790.
67 Shannon to Boyle, [9 June 1790] in Hewitt, ed., *Lord Shannon's letters*, pp. 6–7; *Clonmel Gazette*, 31 July 1790.
68 *D.C.*, 16 Dec. 1790.
69 *D.C.*, 8 May 1790; *Annual Register*, xxxii (1790), p. 204; Patrick Power, 'A Carrickman's diary, 1787–1809', *Journal of the Waterford and South-East of Ireland Archaeological Society*, xiv (1911), p. 102; xvi (1913), p. 179.
70 J. G. Simms, 'Connacht in the eighteenth century', *I.H.S.*, xi (1958), p. 128; *D.C.*, 11 May 1790.
71 *D.C.*, 11, 18, 20 , 27 May 1790. According to Mary McCarthy (*Fighting Fitzgerald and other papers* (London, 1930), p. 113n), Denis Browne fought a duel with one of the Binghams in 1783 which ensured his election.
72 E. B. Day, *Mr Justice Day of Kerry* (Exeter, 1938), pp. 6, 104–5; *D.E.P.*, 25 Oct. 1794.
73 *F.L.J.*, 5 Aug. 1775; also Corr, 'Reminiscences', passim.
74 Edward to Vere Hunt, [17] Feb. [1787] (Limerick Archives Office, Vere Hunt Papers, N.L.I., mic. p.5526).
75 His grandfather (who was wounded), his father, his brother (who was killed) and he himself all fought duels (Barrington, *Personal sketches*, ii, 34–7).
76 MacDougall, *Sketches of Irish political characters*, p. 223.
77 Barrington, *Personal sketches*, ii, 2–5.
78 McCarthy, *Fighting Fitzgerald*, p. 95; McNamara, *The story of an Irish sept*, p. 259.
79 Barrington, *Personal sketches*, ii, 3; W. J. Fitzpatrick, *Ireland before the Union* (Dublin, 1868), p.000 ; above, pp. 000–00.
80 Barrington, *Personal sketches*, ii, 5.
81 Barrington, *Personal sketches*, ii, 4; Bodkin, *Grattan's parliament*, pp. 142–4; above pp. 131–2, 144–5.
82 Walsh, *Ireland sixty years ago*, pp. 27–30; Barrington, *Personal sketches*, ii, 8–9.
83 Above, pp. 111–12.
84 *F.L.J*, 13 Mar. 1773; *H.J.*, 8 Mar. 1773.
85 Peter Somerville-Large, *Irish eccentrics* (London, 1975), p. 150.
86 *Hibernicus, or memoirs of an Irishman*, pp. 125–8; Barry, *An affair of honour*, pp. 10, 128–9; Bagenal, *Vicissitudes of an Anglo-Irish family*, pp. 148–55; *D.C.*, 31 July 1788; below, p. 196–7.
87 *H.J.*, 21, 25 Nov. 1774; Barrington, *Personal sketches*, ii, 8.

88 T. P. Power, *Land, politics and society in eighteenth-century Tipperary* (Oxford, 1993), passim.
89 *F.L.J.*, 14 Apr. 1774.
90 *F.L.J.*, 3 June 1775; P. C. Power, *History of south Tipperary* (Cork, 1989), p. 103; Burke, *Clonmel*, p. 156.
91 *H.J.*, 27, 30 Dec. 1776; Namier and Brooke, *House of Commons 1754–90*, i, 333; Paul Langford, *A Polite and Commercial People: England 1727–83* (Oxford, 1989), p. 589.
92 *F.L.J.*, 2 Jan. 1779.
93 *H.J.*, 28 Apr. 1779; Walsh, *Ireland sixty years ago*, pp. 26–7.
94 *The life and work of George Robert Fitzgerald containing every interesting circumstances which happened to that unfortunate man from his quitting school* . . . (London, 1786), pp. 5, 10.
95 *The life of . . . Fitzgerald*, pp. 41–3; *Memoirs of the late George Robert Fitzgerald . . . interspersed with anecdotes . . . by a gentleman of the County Mayo* (Dublin, 1786), pp. 7–16; *The life and times of George Robert Fitzgerald* (Dublin, 1852), pp. 19–21; McCarthy, *Fighting Fitzgerald*, p. 86; W. S. Childe-Pemberton, *The Earl Bishop: the life of Frederick, Bishop of Derry, Earl of Bristol* (2 vols, London, 1924), i, 310; Albert Spencer, ed., *Memoirs of William Hickey* (4 vols, New York, 1923), i, 287–8; *D.E.P.*, 17 June 1786.
96 *Authentic memoirs of George Robert Fitzgerald with a full account of of his trial and execution* (London, 1786), pp. 2–3; *The life of Fitzgerald*, pp. 7–8; *Memoirs of Fitzgerald*, p. 19; McCarthy, *Fighting Fitzgerald*, pp. 92–4; Fitzgerald, ed., *Leinster corresp.*, iii, 43, 50–51.
97 W. H. Drummond, ed., *The autobiography of Archibald Hamilton Rowan* (Dublin, 1840), pp. 59–67; *Life of Fitzgerald*, pp. 122–26; *Memoirs of Fitzgerald*, pp. 27–9.
98 *Autobiography of Rowan*, pp. 66–7.
99 Bate was a formidable individual. In 1777 he fought a duel with Captain Stoney in the Adelphi Tavern in London in which swords as well as pistols came into play. Having fired four shots without effect, the two antagonists drew their swords; both were wounded, but they were interrupted before they could inflict mortal injuries (*Annual Register*, xx (1777), p. 161).
100 Spencer, ed., *Memoirs of Hickey*, i, 287–96; *Authentic memoirs of Fitzgerald*, pp. 3–10, 16–19; *Life of Fitzgerald*, pp. 46–56, 62; P. C. Yorke, ed., *Diary of John Baker* (London, 1931), pp. 264–5; McCarthy, *Fighting Fitzgerald*, pp. 87–90; H.J., 15 Sept. 1773. Acording to the *Annual Register*, xvi (1773), p. 131, Fitzgerald's second shot went off by accident, and Scawen discharged his second pistol in the air.
101 Spencer, ed., *Memoirs of Hickey*, i, 287, 298.
102 *The reply to Thomas Walker esquire ci-devant cornet in Burgoyne's Light Dragoons, by George Robert Fitzgerald* (London, [1775]); *Life of Fitzgerald*, pp. 14–5, 22–3, 56–62; *Authentic memoirs of Fitzgerald*, pp. 10–16.
103 Above, pp. 000–00; *F.L.J.*, 5 June 1776; *Authentic memoirs of Fitzgerald*, pp. 26–8; *Life of Fitzgerald*, pp. 74–7.
104 Walsh, *Ireland sixty years ago*, pp. 26–7.

105 *Memoirs of Fitzgerald*, p. 34ff; *Authentic memoirs of Fitzgerald*, pp. 21–5; *Life of Fitzgerald*, pp. 40–52.
106 Most examples of clergy duelling involved members of the Church of England; see Lewis, ed., *Walpole corresp.*, ix, 153; B.L., Add. MS 36593, f. 164; Aylward, 'Duelling in the eighteenth century', p. 46; Hamilton, *The only approved guide*, pp. iii note; Humphrey Bullock, 'Duellist extraordinary', *Irish Monthly*, lxxxi (1953), pp. 277–81; *D.N.B.*, entry on Sir Henry Bate Dudley. For the best documented Irish example see below p. 179. See also, the remarks of Euseby Cleaver, Archbishop of Dublin, who maintained that there was need for sterner penalties for offending clergy (Cleaver to O'Hara, 25 June 1782 (N.L.I., O'Hara Papers, MS 16,943)). I wish to thank Peter MacDonagh for the latter reference.
107 Arthur Archdeacon, *Legends of Connaught* (Dublin, 1839), pp. 31–2, 37; *D.E.P.*, 15 June 1786; *Memoirs of Fitzgerald*, pp. 93–5. I would like to thank Desmond McCabe for the first reference.
108 *Memoirs of Fitzgerald*, pp. 38–47; *Authentic memoirs of Fitzgerald*, p. 29; *Life of Fitzgerald*, pp. 79–80; McCarthy, *Fighting Fitzgerald*, pp. 105–16; Shevawn Lynam, *Humanity Dick* (London, 1975), pp. 33–4.
109 *Life of Fitzgerald*, pp. 7, 80–86.
110 McCarthy, *Fighting Fitzgerald*, pp. 117–25; letters re disturbances in County Mayo, Oct. 1781 (P.R.O., SP 63/476, ff 258–62); Eden to Loughborough, 20 Oct. 1781, in *Auckland Corresp.*, i, 317; Lynam, *Humanity Dick*, pp. 34–6; *Life of Fitzgerald*, pp. 86–101; *Authentic memoirs of Fitzgerald*, pp. 32–46; N.A., Calendar of presentments 1698–1813, f. 219.
111 Martin had killed his cousin and friend, James Jordan, in a duel at Castlebar in March 1782 (*H.J.*, 1, 3, 5 Apr. 1782); Lynam, *Humanity Dick*, p. 62; *Life of Fitzgerald*, pp. 101–5.
112 McCarthy, *Fighting Fitzgerald*, pp. 118–19, 126–7; Lynam, *Humanity Dick*, pp. 35–6, 48–9; *D.E.P.*, 29 May 1783.
113 *D.E.P.*, 10 July 1783; *Authentic memoirs of Fitzgerald*, pp. 46–50.
114 McCarthy, *Fighting Fitzgerald*, pp. 128–30; Lynam, *Humanity Dick*, pp. 57–64; Martin to Temple, July 1784 in Duke of Buckingham and Chandos, ed., *Memoirs of the courts and cabinets of George III* (4 vols, London, 1853–5), i, 299–300; Hugh Staples, ed., *The Ireland of Sir Jonah Barrington* (London, 1968), pp. 224–33; *Galway Reader*, 4 (1953), pp. 123–4.
115 *Life of Fitzgerald*, pp. 25–40, 126; *Memoirs of Fitzgerald*, pp. 66ff; *The trials of George Robert Fitzgerald, Timothy Brecknock . . . and others* (Dublin, 1786).
116 *D.E.P.*, 15 June 1786.
117 *D.E.P.*, 17 June 1786.
118 M. M. Bevington, ed., *The Memoirs of James Stephen* (London, 1954), p. 307; Horace Walpole, *Last journals*, i, 269; Basil Cozens-Hardy, ed., *The diary of Silas Neville 1767–88* (Oxford, 1950), p. 240.
119 Leerssen, *Mere Irish and Fior-Ghael*, pp. 160–66; Kiernan, *The duel*, pp. 107–8.
120 Stanley Ayling, *A portrait of Sheridan* (London, 1985), pp. 33–6; Cecil Price, ed., *The letters of Richard Brinsley Sheridan* (3 vols, Oxford, 1966), i, 26–36; Aylward, 'Duelling in the eighteenth century', pp. 46–7; Countess of Minto,

ed., *Life and letters of Sir Gilbert Elliott, first Earl of Minto* (3 vols, London, 1874), i, 313–18; *Annual Register*, xxxi (1789), pp. 215–16; Mackay, *Extraordinary popular delusions*, pp. 685–6.

121 P. C. Yorke, ed., *Diary of John Baker*, p. 398; Walpole to Ossory, 20 Nov. 1778, in Lewis *et al.*, eds, *Walpole corresp.*; xxxiii, 71–2; *Annual Register*, xxi (1778), p. 211; xxii (1779), pp. 204–5; Mackay, *Extraordinary popular delusions*, pp. 684–5. For other illustrations of the same phenomonen see John Hamden, ed., *An eighteenth-century journal* (London, 1940), p. 88; *Dublin Gazette*, 8 Jan. 1765.

122 Croker to Follett, 12 Feb. 1841, in L. J. Jennings, ed., *The Croker Papers* (3 vols, London, 1884), ii, 407–8; *Annual Register*, xxii (1780), pp. 203–4, 235–6; xxxi (1789), pp. 208–10; xxxiv (1792), pp. 24, 29; xxxviii (1796), p. 14; xl (1798), pp. 227–8; Lord Colchester, ed., *The diary and correspondence of Charles Abbot, Lord Colchester* (3 vols, London, 1861), i, 154–5; James Hatton, ed., *Selection from the letters and correspondence of Sir James Bland Burges* (London, 1885), pp. 122–4; Lother to [ ], 9 June 1792, in H.M.C., *Le Fleming MSS*, p. 31.

123 Andrew, 'The code of honour and its critics', pp. 420–21; Langford, *A polite and commercial people*, pp. 587–8.

124 Bonamy Dobree, ed., *The letters of Philip Dormer Stanhope, fourth Earl of Chesterfield* (6 vols, London, 1932), v, 206.

125 G. B. Hill, ed., *Boswell's Life of Johnson* (6 vols, Oxford, 1934–64), ii, 179–8, 226–7; v, 24, 230; Boswell's *Tour of the Hebrides*, introduction. Dean Richard Woodward expressed the same concern in 1773 (*Report of the trial of Captain Macnamara for killing and slaying Colonel Robert Montgomery* (London, 1803), appendix, pp. 23–30).

126 Walpole to More, 2 July 1789 in Lewis *et al.*, eds, *Walpole Corresp*, xxxi, 305.

127 Arthur Young, *A tour in Ireland* (London, 1780), part 2, p. 78; Thomas Campbell, *A philosophical survey of the south of Ireland* (Dublin 1777); see also Burrowes diary, 10 June 1773 (P.R.O.N.I., T3551/1)

128 One known critic was Mathew Carey, who published anti-duelling sentiments in the *Hibernian Journal* in 1777 (E.L. Bradsher, *Mathew Carey* (New York, 1966), pp. 1, 4).

129 *H.J.*, 5 Feb. 1772.

130 *H.J.*, 24 Feb. 1773.

131 *H.J.*, 29 Mar. 1775.

132 *Report of the trial of . . . Captain Macnamara . . .*, appendix, pp. 23–40.

133 See *H.J.*, 24 Feb. 1773.

134 *F.L.J.*, 5 May 1773, 2, 26 Mar. 1774.

135 *F.L.J.*, 10 July 1773, 12 Jan. 1774; Billacois, *The duel*, p. 27.

136 *F.L.J.*, 19 Mar. 1774.

137 N.L.I., Joly MS 29, f. 64; King's Entrybook, P.R.O., HO 101/1, ff 2–6.

138 See Tables 2.1 and 3.1.

139 *F.L.J.*, 8, 15, 19 Jan. 1774; *Hibernian Gazette*, 17 Jan. 1774; Harcourt to Rochfort, 2 Apr. 1774, Rochford to Harcourt, 8 Apr. 1774, in *C.H.O.P.*, iv, pp. 200–1.

140 Harcourt to Rochford, 14 Jan. 1775 in *C.H.O.P.*, iv, p. 316.

141 Buckingham to Weymouth, and reply, 26 June, 22 July 1779 (P.R.O., SP 63/465, ff 185–6, 404).
142 See below, p. 236; Kiernan, *The duel*, p. 113.
143 Constantia Maxwell, *A history of Trinity College* (Dublin, 1946), pp. 124–7; Elliott, *Wolfe Tone*, p. 20; *H.J.*, 3 Feb. 1775 and passim. For a humorous parody on fencing see *F.L.J.*, 24 Feb. 1776.
144 *H.J.*, 25 Jan. 1775; Fitzpatrick, *Ireland before the Union*, pp. 39–40; *Annual Register*, xxiii (1780), p. 206; ibid., xxv (1782), pp. 213–14.
145 *H.J.*, 26 Nov. 1777.
146 Aylward, 'Duelling in the eighteenth century', p. 72.
147 Barrington, *Recollections*, pp. 278–80; *Hibernicus, or memoirs of an Irishman*, pp. 86–8.
148 MacDonagh, *Irish life and character*, pp. 33–4.
149 *F.L.J.*, 11 Feb. 1775; *H.J.*, 3 Feb. 1775; Lord Herbert, ed., *Pembroke Papers, 1780–94* (London, 1950), pp. 245–6.
150 *H.J.*, 30 June 1777.
151 Sir Henry Cavendish's parliamentary diary, v, ff 106–09, 124–7 (Library of Congress, Washington); E. and A. G. Porritt, *The unreformed House of Commons* (2 vols, Cambridge, 1903), ii, 414.
152 Cavendish's parliamentary diary, vi, 237–47.
153 Buckingham to Weymouth, 17 Nov. 1779 (P.R.O., SP 63/467, f. 117); R. V. Callan, 'The structure of Anglo-Irish politics during the American Revolution: Cavendish's diary of the Irish parliament, October 12 1779 to September 2 1780: edition of the partial text and a critical essay' (Ph.D. thesis, University of Notre Dame, 1973), ii, 213–14; *D.E.P.*, 20 Mar. 1783.
154 *A Volunteer's queries in spring 1780 humbly offered to the consideration of all description of men in Ireland* (Dublin, 1780), queries 127–40, pp. 38–44.
155 *A few mathematical and critical remarks on the sword* (Dublin, 1781), pp. 53–63.
156 *H.J.*, 1 Aug. 1781.
157 Portlock, *The . . . Friendly Brothers of St Patrick*, pp. 1–2; Proceedings of the Dublin Select Grand Knot, 1751–1778, ff 202–03, 310; Lena Boylan, 'The Friendly Brothers of St Patrick', *Dublin Historical Record*, xiv (1955–8), p. 37. Maurice Craig (*Dublin, 1660–1860*, pp. 210–11) claims that the lack of popularity of duelling among trading and commercial people can be attributed to the influence of the Friendly Brothers, but the claim remains to be substantiated.
158 *D.E.P.*, 5 Apr. 1783; N.L.I., Dudley Westropp Papers, Newscuttings, MS 24937. According to R. B. McDowell (*Land and learning: two Irish clubs* (Dublin, 1993), p. 12) Henry Flood and John Fitzgibbon were also members.
159 *D.E.P.*, 29 Apr. 1783; McDowell, *Land and learning*, p. 12.
160 Barrington, *Recollections*, pp. 283–5.
161 It was reported in late 1787 and again in 1789 that a gentleman reacted to being hit by a snowball by drawing his pistol and shooting his assailant dead (*D.C.*, 27 Dec. 1787; Maxwell, *Trinity College*, pp. 140–41).

162 *V.E.P.*, 24 June 1784; *D.C.*, 27 Nov. 1787.
163 Drennan to McTier, 15 Apr. [spring 1785], in D. A. Chart, ed., *The Drennan Letters* (Belfast, 1931), pp. 26–8.
164 Buckinghamshire's vindication (National Library of Scotland, Lothian Papers). There is a copy of this document in P.R.O.N.I., T3502/1.
165 *H.J.*, 23 Apr., 9, 12, 14, 16, 23 May, 18 June 1777; *Life of Grattan*, i, 278–9.
166 *H.J.*, 27 June 1777.
167 Walsh, *Ireland sixty years ago*, p. 25; Barrington, *Recollections*, pp. 281–2.
168 Barrington, *Recollections*, pp. 255–91.
169 Kiernan, *The duel*, p. 147. One of the first recorded examples of a surgeon attending a duel took place in 1787 when Lord Mountnorres met Francis Hely-Hutchinson (*D.E.P.*, 8 May 1787).
170 Kiernan, *The duel*, pp. 144–8; Michel Foucault, *Discipline and punish: the birth of the prison* (London, 1977).
171 Kiernan, *The duel*, pp. 66, 149–51.
172 Ibid., p. 185.
173 Barrington, *Recollections*, p. 290.
174 *F.J.*, 20 Mar. 1787; see also Hamilton, *The only approved guide*, p. xii n.
175 Barrington, *Recollections*, p. 281; Walsh, *Ireland sixty years ago*, pp. 21–2.
176 Hence Barrington's story that Lord Mountnorres came home from a duel in which he had been slightly injured pleased as punch at having manifested his courage; 'never did a man enjoy a wound more sincerely' (cited in Kiernan, *The duel*, p. 107).
177 MacDonagh, *Irish life and character*, p. 27; Clifford, ed., *Dr Campbell's diary of a visit to England*, p. 45.
178 Walsh, *Ireland sixty years ago*, p. 25; William Butler Odell, *Essay on duelling* (Cork, 1814), p. 19.
179 Barrington, *Personal sketches*, i, 129–30.
180 Kiernan, *The duel*, p. 117.
181 *H.J.*, 10 Jan. 1777.
182 *H.J.*, 25 July 1777; Kiernan, *The duel*, pp. 154–5.
183 Above, p. 113. Slightly less than 5 per cent of the recorded duels tabulated took place abroad; the remainder cannot be geographically fixed.
184 This figure is substantially greater than the 'small risk' of 'one in ten' identified by Brian Henry ('Crime in Dublin, 1780–96' (Ph.D. thesis, T.C.D., 1992), p. 44).
185 See above, pp. 113–14.
186 *D.E.P.*, 18 Mar. 1783. For another example see *H.J.*, 17 Sept. 1777.
187 *F.L.J.*, 18 Mar. 1778. For another example see *D.C.*, 22 Sept. 1789.
188 *F.L.J.*, 3 July 1776.
189 *F.L.J.*, 10 Apr. 1779.
190 *D.E.P.*, 4 Mar. 1786; *Dublin Chronicle*, 2 Oct. 1787.
191 For examples see *F.L.J*, 1, 11 May, 14 Dec. 1776; *H.J.*, 4 Apr., 17 Sept., 3 Dec. 1773; diary of Denys Scully, 11 Mar. 1788 (N.L.I., Scully Papers, MS 27571, ff 153–4).
192 *F.L.J.*, 7, 10 Jan. 1778.

193 Barrington, *Personal sketches*, i, 161–5; *Dublin Chronicle*, 13 Dec. 1787, 18 Mar. 1788.
194 *D.C.*, 27 June 1789.
195 For examples see *H.J.*, 17 Sept. 1777, 15 Mar. 1780; *D.C.*, 24 June 1788.
196 *F.L.J.*, 9 Oct. 1779.
197 *D.E.P.*, 23 Jan. 1783; *V.E.P.*, 3 July 1784; *H.J.*, 8 Apr. 1782. For further examples see *V.E.P.*, 15 Nov. 1785; *D.C.*, 6 Mar. 1788; *Belfast Newsletter*, 10 Apr. 1789; *Clonmel Gazette*, 13 Apr. 1789.
198 Pollock to Drennan, 22 Apr. 178[2] (P.R.O.N.I., Drennan Papers, D456/1).
199 *F.L.J.*, 30 May 1778.
200 *H.J.*, 11 June 1781.
201 *F.L.J.*, 20 Jan. 1779.
202 *F.L.J.*, 29 Mar. 1778.
203 These have not survived in the collections of the main libraries, but evidence of their existence is provided by Sir John Carr, who purchased a copy of *Advice to seconds* from a Nassau Street bookseller (*The stranger in Ireland* (London, 1806), p. 240).
204 *V.E.P.*, 29 Dec. 1785; *D.C.*, 17 Sept. 1789.
205 *H.J.*, 18 June 1777, 10 June 1790; *F.L.J.*, 12 Dec. 1778, 6 Feb. 21 Apr. 25 Aug. 1779, 11 July 1787; *V.J. (C.)*, 29 May 1786.
206 *V.J. (D.)*, 26 Aug., 9 Dec. 1785.
207 *F.L.J.*, 6 Apr., 7 Aug. 1776.
208 *V.E.P.*, 18 Nov. 1784.
209 *H.J.*, 25 June 1777.
210 *F.L.J.*, 28 Feb. 1778; *H.J.*, 20 Oct. 1780.
211 *F.L.J.*, 31 July 1779; Vere Hunt Diary, 1779 (typescript copy in possession of Mr John Hunt, Bailey, Howth, County Dublin); above, p. 156.
212 H.M.C., *Charlemont*, i, 371–2; *H.J.*, 31 Mar. 1780.
213 *H.J.*, 13, 18 Dec. 1780; Walsh, *Ireland sixty years ago*, pp. 25–6.
214 Courtney Moore, 'Fatal sword duel in Cork about the year 1786 [*sic*]', *J.C.H.A.S.*, 2nd series, ix (1903), pp. 24–6; J.C., 'Fatal sword duel in Cork a century ago', *J.C.H.A.S.*, 1st series, iii (1894), p. 200; *H.J.*, 10 Oct, 1781.
215 *H.J.*, 21 Oct. 1782; notes on the Volunteers, 9 June 1783 (P.R.O.N.I., T963); *D.C.*, 24 Dec. 1788.
216 Elliott, *Wolfe Tone*, pp. 23, 63; *D.C.*, 14 Apr. 1789; *H.J.*, 10 June 1790; above, p. 162.
217 *D.E.P.*, 4 Jan. 1783; *V.E.P.*, 14 Feb. 1784.

5

'A Shadow of Doubt': the late eighteenth century

The late 1780s and 1790s witnessed an identifiable intensification in societal opposition to the practice of duelling. The most tangible manifestation of this was a decline in the number of recorded encounters in the 1790s (Table 5.1). The scale of decline was strikingly less than the scale of increase that had taken place in the late 1760s and early 1770s, but it was real. Why this should happen is not immediately obvious, but a number of factors can be isolated. The most salient is the renewed willingness on the part of the courts in the late 1780s to intervene in duelling cases. The courts did not take a firm stand against the code of honour, but they were prepared to support those who had recourse to the law to resist unwarranted challenges and to act against those who blatantly abused the privilege of duelling. One of the reasons for this was the rejection of the comparatively relaxed moral and religious mood of the mid-eighteenth century. This coincides with the beginning of an evangelical revival, reaching its peak in the nineteenth century, which fostered a more censorious attitude towards such human tendencies as alcohol consumption, prostitution, suicide and duelling. Allied to this was a distinct change in the political mood of the country. The political atmosphere in the late 1780s and the 1790s was quite different to what it was in the 1770s and early 1780s because of the reinvigoration of that strand of conservative Protestantism which scorned the liberal aspirations of the Patriots and parliamentary reformers who had held the political initiative for much of the preceding decade.[1]

The limits of these phenomena must be noted. Irish society in the late eighteenth century was not transformed. The change that took place was

Thomas Russell (courtesy of the National Library of Ireland)

subtle and gradual. What one witnesses is the embrace and espousal by a growing number of the Protestant elite of a more religiously orthodox and ideologically conservative stand on social and political issues which fuelled resistance to the extension of civil rights to Catholics and fostered greater antipathy to practices like duelling. The events which prompted the reinvigoration of conservative Protestantism politically in the mid-1780s were the Rightboy disturbances. The events which prompted the authorities to take a firmer stand against duelling were a number of controversial, high-profile cases in 1786–8. Like the encounters involving Bellamont and Townshend and Blaquiere and Bagenal in the spring of 1773, they excited enormous public interest. The major difference was that they prompted resistance rather than acceptance of the practice of duelling.

The courts and duelling in the late 1780s

The courts were very indulgent towards duelling during the 1770s and early 1780s. In this, they reflected society at large. Based on news reports, it appears that only a small number of cases went to the coroner or to the law courts, and that when they did the usual verdict was manslaughter in self-defence, which was the equivalent of acquittal. In one instance in which a harsher verdict was returned, a pardon was forthcoming. The implication of such judicial indulgence was that there was, in effect, no legal sanction against duelling at this time. To be sure, sheriffs, magistrates and judges did intervene on occasions to prevent duels taking place,[1] but, as Table 3.8 attests, the recorded instances of this were few, and most duellists had no trouble evading the law or circumventing its provisions. A small number of judges (Christopher Robinson is the best known)[2] were sharply critical of the failure of the law to punish duellists, but once a jury accepted that the 'rules' of duelling were observed, judges had few sanctions available to them. This is highlighted by the case of Samuel Foster junior of North Earl Street, Dublin, who killed Mr Anderson of Bachelor's Walk in a duel on the North Circular Road on 16 April 1782. Foster was brought to trial at the Dublin Commission of Oyer and Terminer in October, when the jury returned a verdict of manslaughter in his own defence. In the normal course of events, Foster would have been set free immediately, but the judge, Arthur Wolfe, refused to order his release. This caused quite a stir. However, Wolfe was exceeding his powers. He found on reviewing the case law that he was acting illegally and that he had no choice but to release the defendant.[3]

Wolfe's inability to incarcerate Foster, though he clearly wished to do so, reflected the impotence of the law on the issue of duelling when there was no evidence of underhand goings on. The law had more teeth in cases where the code of honour was breached. It refused utterly to afford any indulgence to the survivors of fatal 'disputes' determined by fisticuffs, for example.[4] However, since most duellists were well informed legally and were inclined, in cases where there was any doubt, to absolve their opponents of blame, there was little the law could do in a large majority of cases. When a Mr McC—— was fatally wounded by his opponent, a Mr K——y, in consequence of a dispute which arose over billiards in County Tipperary in 1786, he found the energy 'with his last breath' to exculpate his antagonist.[5]

Matters did not continue thus, however, and the courts *began* the process of reasserting the authority of the law in a number of high-profile cases in the late 1780s. The first of these was the trial of George Robert Fitzgerald and Timothy Brecknock for the assassination of Patrick McDonnell in 1785. Strictly speaking, this had little to do with duelling, but since Fitzgerald's notoriety derived in the main from his reputation as a duellist, few people made the distinction. Certainly no case in living memory attracted such publicity. An unprecedented volume of space in the ever-growing national and local press relayed the proceedings of the trial in all its detail, while large amounts of space normally devoted to political issues were given over to homilies on the immorality of Fitzgerald's lifestyle. Pamphleteers were not slow to get in on the act, and a number of pamphlet accounts of the trial and of Fitzgerald's life were also produced in response to the public's craving for information.[6]

Though less well known, the sensational 'Sheemore duel', which involved the County Leitrim gentlemen Robert Keon and George Nugent Reynolds, was as impactive in its own way as the trial, conviction and execution of George Robert Fitzgerald. The origins of this quarrel are not entirely clear, but it derived its impetus from the fact that Reynolds advised his mother, who employed Keon, to discontinue his services. Keon took his dismissal very badly. Though an attorney by profession, the fees he earned from his work as an agent to Mrs Reynolds constituted an important part of his income, and he harboured deep resentment at their loss. Relations between the two men deteriorated to such an extent that Keon publicly whipped Reynolds at the County Leitrim assizes in 1786. According to the 'rules' of duelling authorised at Clonmel in 1777, an encounter had to follow, as Reynolds was well aware. He had been lucky to escape unhurt when he had exchanged shots with Colonel St George in March 1785 following a disagreement at the County Leitrim spring assizes.[7] Perhaps influenced by this, Reynolds was less than eager to meet his antagonist. Keon, for his part, showed no such disinclination. He was convinced that Reynolds's conduct was intolerable and that a duel was the only way to settle the matter. His brother Edward was less belligerent, and when James

Plunkett, who delivered Reynolds's challenge on Sunday 15 October, suggested to him that they should load both principals' guns with powder rather than bullets, to enable the two men to satisfy the demands of the code of honour without inflicting injury, Plunkett left the meeting convinced that both Edward and Robert Keon (the latter very reluctantly) had agreed. On the following morning Keon, attended by his brother Ambrose and two others, was the first to arrive at the appointed place at Drynaun. Reynolds appeared on horseback shortly afterwards and, on seeing Keon, alighted and walked towards him. Conceiving the whole affair to be simply a matter of form, Reynolds was not even carrying a pistol. He took off his hat as he approached Keon and was endeavouring to engage him in conversation when his opponent exclaimed 'Damn you, you scoundrel, why did you bring me here?', raised the loaded pistol he had in his hand, pointed it at Reynolds and shot him through the head. Reynolds died instantly.[8]

This was an extraordinary turn of events. The seconds had neither measured the ground, loaded the duelling pistols, nor requested the principals to take their positions when Keon took matters into his own hands. The rules of duelling had been so flagrantly violated that there was no avoiding a trial, and the press made this absolutely certain by affording the incident extensive coverage.[9] Keon was soon acutely aware that his impetuosity had got him into a most tricky situation, but he was hopeful that local opinion would come to his rescue. His trial was calendared initially for the County Leitrim spring assizes in 1787, but in the absence of a sufficiency of jurors (only sixteen prospective jurymen turned up), he and his brother Ambrose were remanded in custody. By this date the case had become such a *cause célèbre* that the Attorney General, John Fitzgibbon, who had ordered that the trial of George Robert Fitzgerald should be transferred from Mayo to Dublin to neutralise local sympathy for the accused, felt compelled to intervene. In May he applied for and received an *a certiorari* judgment transferring the trial and the County Leitrim jurors who were to determine the case to the Court of King's Bench in Dublin. There were good grounds for believing that the Keons would not be judged impartially in Leitrim because of what one observer termed the 'obstinacy and folly' of local jurors as their continued lack of co-operation caused the trial to be delayed further in June. By the time the court was again in session it was November, and the defendants had already been in custody for thirteen months. Despite this, Keon's lawyers applied for a further postponement on the grounds that the impartiality of the 242 prospective jurors who had made the journey from County Leitrim had been compromised by anti-Keon ballads. The Chief Justice of the Court of King's Bench, Lord Earlsfort, was not persuaded. Acutely conscious of the fact that the trial would have to proceed soon if it was to be held at all, Earlsfort directed counsel to begin.

Keon's defence rested on his contention that he had acted in self-defence; he had, his counsel pronounced, reacted to an assault by the enraged Reynolds. However, the evidence offered in support of his claim was too obviously fabricated to be credible. In his summing up, Earlsfort showed no sympathy for the defendant, and made it clear to the jury that they should return a verdict of murder if they accepted the crown's case that Keon had shot his opponent through the head illegally and without provocation. The jury did accept this, and to many people's surprise returned a guilty verdict. Keon made a number of last-ditch attempts to have the decision reversed, but without success. On 31 January 1788 Lord Earlsfort sentenced him to the traitor's death by hanging but not until dead and, while alive, to be disembowelled, decapitated and quartered. The sentence was carried out on 16 February.[10]

The imposition of the traitor's sentence on Robert Keon caused a sensation. It was not that people were unused to death sentences; they were commonplace. However, they were used to seeing defendants in duelling cases exonerated or acquitted no matter how badly they had behaved — not hanged, drawn and quartered. Keon evidently assumed the former outcome, if he gave his actions on the morning of 16 October any prior thought. For their part, the opponents of duelling were pleased with the result. The Keon–Reynolds encounter had provided them with a case around which they could coalesce, and it is no coincidence that anti-duelling sentiment was more visible than usual in 1786. The *Dublin Evening Post*, for example, responded to the Keon–Reynolds duel with a lengthy account of the encounter and a condemnation of 'the savage practice of duelling'.[11] It grieved the paper that neither appeals to reason nor to God carried weight with the adherents of the code of honour. In these circumstances, some commentators were tempted to endorse violent solutions. As well as Gustav Adolph of Sweden, Charles VI of France and Theodoric, the King of the Ostrogoths, were cited approvingly in support of the contention that the only certain way of eradicating duelling was by executing surviving duellists.[12] However, the anger manifested in the autumn of 1786 was of temporary duration, and by the time of Keon's execution the level of visible public opposition to duelling was little different to what it had been in the early 1780s.

But if the outcry of the press was ephemeral, the impact of Keon's ruthless behaviour on public sensibilities was more sustained. The late 1780s witnessed the emergence of a strand of thinking in Ireland which refused to accept that duelling was part of the natural order of things and which did not forbear from appealing to the law to safeguard their lives against the threat posed by unwelcome challenges. Ironically, this change in attitude was signalled by Beauchamp Bagenal, the notorious 'fire-eater' and M.P. for County Carlow, when he brought Weld, his neighbour, to court in July 1788 for sending a challenge and for making an assault on his life. The case came up for trial at the County Carlow summer assizes in 1788 before the newly appointed judge, Alexander Crookshank, who delivered 'an excellent charge' before sentencing Weld to one month's incarceration and a fine of £70.[13] This was unanticipated. It was also the first in a series of similar actions which suggests that a growing number of people in Ireland were not prepared to submit fatalistically to every challenge that came their way, and that they could anticipate the support of the courts if they appealed to them for help.

The courts further underlined their determination to take a stand against the abuse of the privilege of duelling in 1790 when W——m J——n was tried, found guilty and sentenced to death by Judge Hugh Carleton on the Connacht circuit in August 1790 for the murder of T—— B—— because he had 'discharged his pistol without waiting for the usual preliminaries'.[14] However, not all judges and juries were equally resolute, as Richard Hobart learned to his cost in 1788 when he was challenged by Thomas Baker following his intervention in a dispute. Unwilling to be pressurised into having a duel he deemed unwarranted, Hobart swore an information against his antagonist before the Recorder of Dublin and brought him to court. It proved an acutely disenchanting experience. He was put off by the legal formalities, taken aback by the expense (it cost him £80), and disturbed by the attitude of the jury which was determined to find in favour of Baker.[15]

The reluctance of the jury in the Hobart–Baker case to support the plaintiff highlights the sort of problems facing those who appealed to the law to evade unwanted challenges in the late 1780s. However, juries were to become more familiar with cases such as this, as others chose the same route. Thus, in December 1788 the Dublin alderman William Worthingon was indicted for an assault on John Binns, one of the common councillors of the corporation. At his trial Worthington offered an apology 'consistent with his character and station' in an attempt to bring proceedings to a favourable and early conclusion, but Binns (to the judge's surprise — he too desired to conclude the case) declined to accept the apology and insisted the trial went ahead. The outcome was a vindication of his decision. Worthington was found guilty of assault, fined £40, sentenced to five days' imprisonment and ordered to provide two sureties of £100 that he would keep the peace.[16] Binns's actions were not likely to endear him to men of honour, but he clearly demonstrated the legal sanctions available to gentlemen who wished to avoid challenges they deemed inappropriate and indicated that society was no longer as insistent as formerly that they took up their pistols to meet every challenge.

John Philpot Curran demonstrated the same point when he was challenged by a Captain Knightley in Cork in January 1789. During the course of Knightley's trial for attempted assassination, Curran, who was prosecuting, alleged he had acted like 'a ruffian'. Knightley took violent exception to this. Curran's words, he claimed, were 'such as no man of spirit, no man who honoured the King's commission could possibly submit to'. However, Curran was determined not to accept his invitation to resolve the affair with weapons. He instituted legal proceedings 'to prosecute the officer at common law for his challenge', and he was supported in his action by the gentlemen of the Cork bar, who contended 'that no lawyer's life could be safe for a moment if he was obliged to fight every culprit whom his exertions had brought to punishment'.[17] There is no record that the case did proceed to trial, which would suggest that Knightley swallowed his pride and did not pursue the quarrel. More significantly, the incident signalled that the distinction between man and office, which was essential if judges, lawyers, politicians and others active in public life were to perform their duties free from the fear of threats to their lives, was at last being taken on board in Ireland.

This distinction, however, was neither firmly held nor widely accepted, as Curran himself demonstrated some time later when he got into an unseemly altercation with one of the Binghams of County Mayo as 'a result of another matter being exaggerated'. Once again there is insufficient information to provide a full account of events, but Bingham was so irate he sought out Curran at the Four Courts and beat him severely with a whip in order to provoke him to issue a challenge. Curran was urged to pursue a legal remedy, but on this occasion he deemed the offence too personal to be settled in court, and he called on Bingham to make an 'open and public submission' or else meet him. This put Bingham in a spot, but realising that a prosecution was inevitable should he meet and kill Curran, he took the route of least resistance and offered a public apology.[18]

Curran's rejection of the legal option on this occasion provides an important caution against over-emphasising the disposition of gentlemen in the late eighteenth century to respond to insult by appealing to the courts rather than to their pistols. Despite this, the number of duelling cases that went to court increased perceptibly in the late 1780s, and this trend was not reversed. Thus, in October 1790 William Beere was fined £100 and sentenced to two months' imprisonment for challenging Arthur O'Connor during the 1790 Cork election,[19] while four years later, Vere Hunt was held in custody for ten days and had to provide sureties totalling £2,000 following an altercation in Cork.[20] These and other instances [21] demonstrate that the law had rediscovered its power to protect individuals who appealed for its protection against unwanted and unwarranted challenges. However, this remained an option chosen by no more than a minority. Duels continued to take place, though they now did so in an environment which was less indulgent than previously.

Sir Jonah Barrington was the first to allude to the commencement in the late 1780s of what he termed an 'extraordinary improvement . . . in point of decorum'.[22] The historian Constantia Maxwell made the same point. Based on her reading of the observations of contemporary visitors, she maintained there was 'a marked improvement in the manners of the Irish gentry' towards the end of the eighteenth century. Maxwell included a fall in the number of duels taking place alongside a reduction in alcohol consumption and gambling on her list of improvements, though some of those on whom she drew for testimony, Arthur Young included, are not to be relied upon on this issue.[23] Travellers who came to Ireland with preconceived, stereotypical notions concerning the supposed rudeness and lack of sophistication of the people of Ireland were prone to error when it came to analysing social behaviour. That said, Barrington and Maxwell are correct in identifying a shift in public attitudes in the mid- and late 1780s. This coincided with, and was a product of, two developments of enormous political and behavioural significance — the emergence of a powerful and politically significant middle class and an interventionist state which grew increasingly antipathetic to such aristocratic privileges as duelling.

The 1780s witnessed a new readiness on the part of the state in Ireland to increase its area of governmental and administrative responsibilities. Seen in the context of the establishment of a police force in Dublin in 1786, of the ratification of a magistracy act which provided for crown prosecutors in designated regions in 1787, of Thomas Orde's abortive plan for educational reform and Sir Jeremiah Fitzpatrick's efforts to humanise the prison system, the decreasing disposition of the courts and society to indulge duelling may appear insignificant, but it was part of the same phenomenon.[24] It reflected an increased concern with public morality and a greater preparedness by the state to use the vast reservoir of power at its disposal to determine public conduct.

These developments cannot be attributed simply to the eagerness of the state to extend its jurisdictional remit. They also reflected a demand in society at large that it did so. There was a growing disposition among elements of the Protestant middle class, politicised by their participation in the campaigns for commercial and constitutional reform in the 1770s and 1780s, for root-and-branch moral and religious regeneration. It was they who sponsored and, in the main, who paid for the upkeep of the dozens of Sunday schools that were founded in the late 1780s to cathecise the young and that represent the most visible testimony to the evangelical revival that was already under way. It was they also who provided a high percentage of the owners and readers of the newspapers which made space available for the reformative homilies and improving suggestions that became a staple feature of the Irish press in the second half of the 1780s. One of the papers most committed to this cause was the little-known *Dublin Chronicle*,[25] but it was ably supported by the respectably liberal and more mainstream *Dublin Evening Post*, which regularly allocated space to improving comment on subjects as diverse as alcohol abuse, crime, prostitution, sexual profligacy, duelling and other features of unregenerate behaviour.[26]

The main Irish outlets for evangelical and reformative sentiment in the 1780s and 1790s were newspapers and pamphlets. Ireland did not possess anti-duelling campaigners with the moral authority and literary skill of Granville Sharp or William Wilberforce.[27] Moreover, because the volume of space available in a newspaper was limited,[28] press commentary on the code of honour can appear fitful and apologetic even when the author was as skilled a wordsmith as Sylvester O'Halloran, who wrote an anti-duelling critique for the *Limerick Chronicle* in 1788.[29] Furthermore, because there was no obvious evidence that their opposition to duelling was having any effect, the tone of press comment was often pessimistic.[30] Irish critics of duelling were not unaware of the arguments in favour of a more rational approach to the resolution of differences than with weapons. The impact of the Enlightenment curtailed enthusiasm for duelling in France; it had a less visible impact in Ireland, but the very fact that there were calls for a more rational approach to the resolution of quarrels and, specifically, for the establishment of a court of honour to determine disputes indicates that it was not without effect.[31] In the eyes of its most zealous proponents, recourse to a court of honour should be compulsory for men in dispute; those who refused to co-operate would forfeit their life and property.

Duelling in the 1790s

Despite the evident invigoration of anti-duelling sentiment in the late 1780s, opposition to duelling among the social elite remained palpably weaker than the conviction that a man's honour could only be cleansed of the stain of insult by recourse to arms. This is clearly illustrated by the number of duels that took place. A survey of a range of primary manuscript and printed sources similar to that undertaken for the 1770s and 1780s would suggest that mounting public unease prompted a small decline in the number of duels fought in the 1790s (Table 5.1). Most of these duels were conducted according to the 'rules' laid down in the 1770s. Indeed, there is evidence of a further increase in the disposition of principals and seconds to conclude encounters without blood being spilled. For example, John Hely-Hutchinson, the second son of the Provost of Trinity College, and his opponent parted 'amicably' after exchanging one shot in the Phoenix Park in March 1789 following the intervention of their seconds.[32] In December of the same year seconds came to the rescue once more when Latin Fitzgerald of Ballanclona and Captain McDonnell of the 43rd Regiment clashed in County Meath. The cause of their altercation is not known, but both parties showed no inclination towards moderation. Quite the contrary; they were so determined to fight that they evaded the efforts of their friends to prevent the duel taking place; and they had to be persuaded by their seconds to line up at ten rather than six paces, and to sheath their swords when they failed to inflict a fatal injury with pistols.[33] Principals too contributed to the cultivation of a less aggressive atmosphere on the duelling field. When Lord Mountgarret met Counsellor Bu——ne on 6 June 1790 following a difference in court and incapacitated his antagonist with his first shot, he remained on the field to express his regret for the injury he had inflicted.[34]

Not every duellist behaved so well, of course. When Hyacinth Kirwan of Gardenfield, County Galway, disagreed with his nephew and heir, Patrick, over rents on a disputed parcel of property, long-simmering animosities bubbled to the surface, and Patrick died in the encounter that followed from 'a musket load in his stomach'. It was not within the rules of duelling to use a musket, but despite suspicions that Kirwan had infringed the code of honour, the coroner's court at Tuam returned a verdict of manslaughter at large and Hyacinth Kirwan escaped criminal prosecution.[35] He would probably have fared less well in Dublin, where the coroner and the courts were more scrupulous.[36]

Most contemporaries, visitors as well as natives, did not detect these developments. To their inexperienced eyes it simply appeared that duelling was rampant. C. T. Bowden, for example, maintained erroneously in his *Tour through Ireland* published in 1790 that scarely a week passed but two people were killed duelling.[37] The generally more observant Chevalier de Latocnaye gave a similar impression; his claim that there were 'ten or twelve duels' at Limerick races in 1797 receives some corroboration from Lady Mary Roche, but if so, it was unusual.[38] To be fair, the Irish press gave the impression that duelling was rampant, as its pages regularly featured reports of encounters in which serious injuries and fatalities occurred. Among the most eminent casualties in the early 1790s were Counsellor O'Callaghan, who was killed in Ennis in September 1791; Dennis O'Kelly, a noted hellraiser, who was shot dead in somewhat controversial circumstances by William Whaley in Dublin in July 1790; Hedges, a County Cork landowner, and Henry Vereker, a substantial landowner from County Clare, both of whom came to a premature end in

April 1792.[39] Vereker's death was precipitated by a 'ridiculous dispute about horses'. And it was the ostensible frivolousness of so many duels that most excited the ire of critics of the code of honour, who continued, albeit with less enthusiasm than they manifested in the late 1780s, to deplore the leniency of the courts and to condemn duelling as irrational, anti-religious, and a reckless waste of human talents.[40]

Ostensibly 'frivolous' quarrels that were prompted by the over-consumption of alcohol or gambling, rows over trivia, altercations at public venues like the theatre, and rencontres involving students attending Trinity College offered tempting targets for the critics of duelling.[41] In the latter instance, public criticism spurred the college authorities to take action. Trinity students had a long history of duelling, but a number of encounters in 1789 involving, among others, Otway and St Leger (which concluded without injuries) and Richard Rochfort and Richard Castles (in which the latter was killed) prompted the college board's intervention. Their instinctive reaction was to order Rochfort's expulsion when his case came before them in August, but they were prevented from taking such a stand by 'a doubt' about 'the competency of the Board to inflict this punishment'. However, following further reports of Trinity students' duelling, they refused to graduate two unnamed students and threatened to do the same to Otway and St Leger unless 'they acquit themselves to the satisfaction of the Board'. These were severe penalties, but they did not satisfy ten of the college's tutors (including Thomas Elrington, a future Provost); they lobbied the board to make duelling an offence meriting automatic expulsion.[42]

Public unease with reports of duels involving students was not replicated in the case of encounters involving the military. Soldiers on the Irish army establishment had long been devotees of the code of honour, and their readiness to demonstrate their duelling skills rose appreciably in the militarised environment of the early 1790s. Soldiers and civilians clashed repeatedly. Relations between the two interests reached their nadir in County Galway, where a total of six duels were fought within a week in September 1791.[43] There were no fatalities then, but three months later a Galway attorney named Harrison killed Lieutenant Grant of the 27th Regiment of Foot, who had previously wounded Caesar French in an encounter, with a shot to the heart. The two antagonists lined up at a mere seven yards, so it is no surprise that Harrison was also wounded in the rencontre or that he and his second were committed for trial.[44] Between this point and 1796 (when duelling *between* members of the military surpassed military–civilian rencontres in reported cases) encounters between military and civilians feature unusually prominently in the duelling record,[45] and neither the prosecution of offenders, the disapproval of superior officers, nor the threat to exclude officers from the same regiment from filling vacancies caused by death due to duelling had the desired dissuasory effect.[46]

If the increased disposition of army officers to duel in the 1790s was a by-product of the breakdown in law and order and the militarisation of Irish society, the polarisation of politics between radical and conservative, between those who aspired to emulate the French revolutionaries and those who loathed everything they stood for, also left its mark. This was to be expected. Political differences had provided the motive for many affairs of honour since the 1750s. Furthermore, few radicals felt sufficiently free of the aristocratic world they sought to subvert to resist offering or accepting challenges when the circumstances demanded. Some like Thomas Russell claimed to regard duelling as a 'shameful vice of the rich', but few were resolute enough to resist its power. Russell, for example, maintained it was his 'duty' to fight to defend his honour when he was involved in a rather ugly incident in Enniskillen with Lord Cole in November 1793.[47] This did not proceed to an exchange of shots. But a year earlier Hamilton Rowan (another prominent United Irishman with a duelling history) accompanied Mathew Dowling, the well-known radical attorney, to Holyhead for his encounter with Burrough — the Chief Secretary's private secretary. Dowling acquitted himself so well in this occasion that he was honoured with a dinner by his friends and colleagues on his return. Rowan was evidently regarded as an expert on the subject of the code of honour, because in 1793 he carried a challenge from Simon Butler to Robert Dundas, the Lord Advocate of Scotland, arising out of slighting remarks made by the latter during the trial of the Scottish radical, Thomas Muir.[48] Butler's challenge was declined, but his readiness to duel to defend his honour was shared by other members of the United Irishmen. It is noteworthy that Henry and John Sheares and Bagenal Harvey all accompanied Leonard McNally to the Phoenix Park for his rencontre with Jonah Barrington for speaking disparagingly of the United Irish organisation.[49]

The extent of the United Irishmen's adherence to the code of honour that was such an important symbol of aristocratic privilege, was most clearly demonstrated in 1792 when James Napper Tandy, the foremost radical of the day, clashed with John Toler, the Solicitor General. Toler was well known for his earthy oratory, and during a debate on a Catholic petition in the House of Commons on 20 February he took the opportunity to have some fun at Tandy's expense: 'I have seen', he pronounced, 'papers signed by Tobias M'Kenna with Simon Butler in the chair, and Napper Tandy lending his countenance. It is rather odd that they could not contrive to set a better face on the matter.' This offensive remark excited great mirth in the Commons because of Tandy's strikingly ugly physiognomy, but it posed the Dublin radical with a serious problem. He was honour-bound to avenge the insult if he desired to uphold his already precarious reputation as a gentleman, but it was a delicate matter to call out the Solicitor General. To add to his woes, Tandy utterly 'mismanaged' the affair. His first action was to request Toler to explain his remarks, but when the Solicitor General, who was experienced in affairs of honour and possessed of 'fearless determination', refused, but signalled his readiness to meet him in Merrion Fields, Tandy unwisely persisted with his request for an explanation rather than call him out. He subsequently claimed that he did this to force an explicit challenge from Toler in the belief that if *he* issued a challenge over something the Solicitor General had said in the House of Commons, he would be charged with breaching parliamentary privilege and, if he killed his opponent, with murder. These were both possibilities, but Tandy's plan backfired badly when Toler's second responded to his subsequent threat to 'appeal to the newspapers', on the grounds that the matter was a public rather than a private disagreement, by swearing a complaint for breach of parliamentary privilege. Tandy was ordered to be tried at the bar of the House of Commons, but rather than comply and accept whatever punishment was meted out he opted to evade being taken into custody by the serjeant-at-arms by scrambling through a window. It was an undignified and an unwise action. He was already being compared to Herod by his opponents for refusing to accept Toler's invitation to convey a challenge; his flight from the serjeant-at-arms gave them further ammunition with which to discredit him.

Tandy's United Irish colleagues regarded these developments with dismay. They had endeavoured to 'provoke Toler to fight' in the belief that it was the only sure way to safeguard Tandy's faltering reputation as a man of honour. His decision to go into hiding made the capital's foremost radical a figure of fun and the butt of tired jokes which severly hindered his friends efforts to clear his name. As each day passed and Tandy's stock dipped further, many United Irishmen concurred with William Drennan that Tandy was not just afraid to duel but of a spell in Newgate prison, where he almost certainly be sent for infringing parliamentary privilege. There was even talk of 'cast[ing] him off' because his manifest cowardice during the affair was '*injurious* to the [United Irish] *Society* and to the cause of *freedom*'. Finally, on the final day of the 1792 session, nearly two months after the affair had commenced, Tandy surrendered to the officers of parliament. He was brought before the bar of the house, where he refused to answer any questions put to him. He was sentenced to be incarcerated in Newgate prison until the Commons rose — but since this occurred less than an hour after he was sentenced, his stay was of minimum duration. He was accompanied to the prison by a large crowd of well-wishers, but neither this, the 'not guilty' verdict in his subsequent trial for sending a challenge, nor the decision of his Volunteer corps to reject the allegation of cowardice levelled at him for his behaviour during the affair could undo the damage done to his reputation in the public mind. William Drennan summed up the affair with characteristic incisiveness:

> Poor Tandy, after eighteen years' struggle against his own interest in the public cause, has nearly lost his reputation as a gentleman in a quarter of an hour.

Tandy sought to repair the damage by taking the Lord Lieutenant, the Chief Secretary, the Lord Chancellor, the Speaker of the House of Commons, the Attorney General and the law officers that had arrested him to court for abusing their power, but it was to no avail.[50] He was a casualty of the code of honour and of the perceptions that informed it.

Henry Sheares endeavoured to ensure that he did not suffer the same fate in 1793 when he publicly accused the Lord Chancellor, John Fitzgibbon (subsequently Earl of Clare), of perpetrating 'a gross and infamous calumny' when he linked the United Irishmen with 'sedition' in the House of Lords, but he received no satisfaction. Neither did Simon Butler, when he too took exception to remarks by Fitzgibbon.[51] As he had demonstrated in 1784 when he had declined to meet Tandy, Fitzgibbon did not deem middle-class political radicals worthy opponents. This did little for Butler and Sheares's reputations, but at least they avoided the ignominy heaped with such effect on Tandy for what was perceived, with justification, as his craven conduct in 1792.

If most people, radicals as well as conservatives, had possessed Fitzgibbon's resoluteness of mind, there would have been fewer duels in the 1790s. But this was not the case, and political differences precipitated a substantial number of affairs of honour throughout the decade. Few produced serious injuries, but the alacrity with which some men appealed to their weapons mirrored the tension in society. This is best attested to by the spate of duels provoked in mid-1794 by 'insinuations . . . thrown out against many respectable persons' following rumours that Dublin Castle had dispatched spies throughout the city.[52] One such incident involved John Devereux of Shelbeggan, County Wexford, who called out and wounded 'Citizen' Burke following the latter's allegation that he was a 'Castle spy'.[53] In May, Bagenal Harvey exchanged shots with Harding Giffard, the son of Sheriff John Giffard, following a disagreement over the administration's response to disturbances in County Cavan.[54] Giffard was injured in this encounter, but this did not persuade his father — the proprietor of *Faulkner's Dublin Journal*, one of Dublin Castle's main propaganda organs in the 1790s — to moderate his aggressive conservatism, for a year later he challenged James Potts, the proprietor of *Saunders' Newsletter*, for labelling him 'the dog in office' in the pages of his newspaper. Instead of accepting the challenge, Potts instituted legal proceedings which resulted in Giffard being sentenced to five months in jail for assault, to one month for sending a challenge, and to pay a fine of five marks. This outcome delighted Giffard's enemies, who were thoroughly fed up with his unprincipled behaviour, and they created such a stir when Giffard sought to ignore the sentence that he was compelled to surrender to the prison authorities. He was too well connected to serve the full sentence, and after a month the influential Under-Secretary, Edward Cooke, brokered a deal which resulted in his early release on condition that he made a £50 contribution to charity.[55]

Affairs of honour prompted by political differences in the 1790s spanned the range of the Protestant ruling elite from peers at one extreme to apothecaries at the other. The most sensational took place in the spring of 1795 and involved the Chief Commissioner of the Irish Revenue, John Beresford, and the former Lord Lieutenant, Earl Fitzwilliam. Following the eventful Fitzwilliam administration, during which the Lord Lieutenant dismissed Beresford from office only to be recalled himself for exceeding his authority on the subject of Catholic relief, the newly restored Chief Commissioner of the Revenue took such deep umbrage at what he perceived were slighting expressions contained in Earl Fitzwilliam's public defence of his actions — a pamphlet entitled *First letter to Lord Carlisle* — that he set proceedings in train to redeem his injured reputation in time-honoured fashion. Everything seemed set fair for an exchange of shots in Marylebone Fields in London until the intervention of the authorities, as the two principals readied themselves, terminated the affair.[56]

Two years later, in February 1797, in consequence of some pejorative remarks made by Lord Blayney about the emigrant French officers who commanded the Irish brigades, the Duc de Fitzjames, a *ci-devant* French nobleman, challenged Blaney to back up his words with deeds. As ex-soldiers both men were skilled in the handling of weapons, but both escaped this encounter with the slightest of wounds.[57] In the following year the country's most eminent commoner, Henry Grattan, challenged Patrick Duigenan, the pugnacious advocate of Protestant ascendancy, with whom he had a history of disagreement, over remarks he made in his tract *An answer to the address of Henry Grattan*. Despite his own penchant for extravagant expression, Grattan was so distressed by Duigenan's observations, and so fully convinced that 'a man's character is preferable to his life', that he requested Lord Tyrawly to offer Duigenan a challenge on his behalf.[58] No duel ensued as far as can be ascertained, but as this and the last two encounters considered attest, political tempers grew increasingly short in the confrontational atmosphere of the late 1790s. There was, for instance, a spate of non-fatal rencontres following the failure of the invading force commanded by General Hoche in December 1796. In January 1797 Edward Roche of Cork exchanged shots with his neighbour, Robert Uniacke Fitzgerald, because the latter impugned his loyalty, while in Dublin differences over the French's intentions prompted at least two duels involving peers and commoners.[59]

Despite the substantial number of affairs of honour that had their origins in the unique political circumstances of the period, most duels in the 1790s were prompted by personal rather than by political differences. Quarrels at the theatre or playhouse, for instance, continued to figure in the duelling record. The death of Edward Sweetman, the United Irishman and pro-Catholic agitator from County Wexford, in a bad-tempered encounter fought at six yards' distance at Cobham in England in January 1796 resulted from a challenge he received from Captain Watson for accidentally bumping the lady Watson was escorting at the opera.[60] Sweetman was unfortunate. He had a surgeon in attendance to prevent such a result. Indeed, it was increasingly common for duellists to be accompanied to the duelling field by a surgeon, and for the surgeon to work feverishly on the field to extract the ball if one of the principals was hit.[61] It was even alleged on a number of occasions that some seconds loaded their principals' pistols only with powder in order to ensure against fatalities,[62] but if this happened, it was infrequent, as the consequences of discovery were so serious.

Seventeen per cent of the encounters that constitute our sample of duels fought in the 1790s concluded in the death of one of the principals (the figure rises to 21 per cent when we add those described as 'mortally' wounded to the figure). This represents a small but significant decline on the situation in the 1770s and 1780s when the respective figures were 21 and 26.5 per cent (Table 3.7). However, when one adds in the number of duellists that were wounded in order to obtain a fuller impression of the casualty rate, the picture is less agreeable. A total of 57 per cent of the duels sampled concluded with the injury of one or both principals. This is nearly 8 per cent less than the respective figure for the 1770s and 1780s, and a long way below the 82 per cent registered by the sample of recorded duels for the 1750s and 1760s (Tables 2.5 and 5.5). One of the reasons for this further decline in the number of casualties was the complete displacement of the sword by the pistol as the duellist's weapon of choice. Swords are not recorded as having been used in any duel in the 1790s (Table 5.4). Moreover, the pistol was still a pretty unreliable weapon in unskilled hands; in an encounter in the Phoenix Park in 1799 one of the principals accidentally shot the horse that had brought one of the parties to the rendezvous.[63]

The most striking feature of Table 5.1, which tabulates the social origin of known duellists in the 1790s, is the large increase in the percentage of duels involving members of the military. Their participation rate doubled from its level in the 1770s and 1780s (Table 3.1). This was due in large part to the militarisation of the country.[64] It is surely significant that duelling virtually ceased during the 1798 rebellion, but resumed as soon as it was over and flourished in the following two years.[65]

Only a modest percentage of duellists were from the middle classes. Lawyers have been designated a category of their own in order to test the thesis that they were unusually disposed to duel; according to our sample, the number of duels in which one or both of the principals were lawyers rose from 7 per cent in the 1770s and 1780s to 12 per cent in the 1790s.[66] The identifiable involvement of individuals from such solid middle-class occupations as merchants, customs officials and woollen drapers also registered an increase from 7.5 per cent to over 14 per cent in the same period (Tables 3.1 and 5.1).[67] By contrast, individuals who were not regarded as gentlemen, even according to the elastic definition sometimes applied in Ireland, had recourse to pistols on only a small number of occasions. For example, in July 1796 a milliner and an attorney settled a dispute that arose while they were drinking, without bloodshed. Two years later two servants met in a field near Baggot Street, but were reconciled by their seconds after they had exchanged fire; whereas a planned encounter involving a Suffolk Street publican and a journeyman cutler never came off because the crowd of four or five hundred that gathered to watch attracted the attention of the authorities who arrested the principals.[68]

Those affairs of honour involving individuals from the lower classes were isolated events, and they elicited attention for this reason. Duels involving aristocrats and prominent political figures excited more sustained and deeper interest. Compared with the 1770s and 1780s, there were fewer encounters of this nature in the 1790s, but despite the evidence that anti-duelling sentiment was taking hold among sections of this elite, the code of honour remained sufficiently deeply entrenched to compel those aristocrats and politicians who perceived their honour to have been impugned to appeal to their pistols for redress. This is the implication of the real and averted duels involving John Beresford and Earl Fitzwilliam, Lord Blayney and the Duc de Fitzjames, and Henry Grattan and Patrick Duigenan. And there are others. When Counsellor Peter Burrowes was deemed to have insulted Lord Mountgarret at the Kilkenny assizes in 1794, Mountgarret's son, Somerset Butler, challenged Burrowes to a duel which concluded with an exchange of shots but no injuries.[69] In 1796, George Annesley, Viscount Valentia, fought a duel at Hamburg with John Bellenden Gawler who had been found guilty of criminal conversation with his (Valentia's) wife.[70] Four years later Walter Butler, the eighteenth Earl of Ormond, exchanged shots without injury with an army captain at Ringsend.[71]

Elections, of course, traditionally produced a large number of appeals to the code of honour, but the 1797 general election was comparatively uneventful in this respect. In Athlone two candidates, Sir Richard St George and William Handcock, were persuaded to settle their differences on the duelling field by their seconds, but in County Donegal, a bitter personal exchange between the M.P. Alexander Montgomery of Convoy and Sir Samuel Hayes of Drumboe Castle resulted in an exchange of shots. Sir Samuel, who was 'about 70', was hit in the thigh by the first ball of his opponent. Undaunted, he commanded a chair and fired his two shots from a sitting position. He was evidently a poorer marksman than his opponent, as he missed with both. Montgomery, by contrast, hit Hayes once again with his second shot, but he was not seriously injured. Indeed, he sought to pursue the disagreement, but he was dissuaded from doing so by his seconds, and the affair was brought to a close.[72]

The Montgomery–Hayes duel was unusually intense for a political encounter. Despite this, it attracted less attention than the fatal duel in County Wicklow in March 1797 between Robert Gore of Delgany and William Brabazon, Earl of Meath. The origins of their encounter lay in a dispute over recruitment for yeomanry corps both men sought to establish in north Wicklow. Meath claimed that Gore was poaching some of his tenants, and when he protested, the matter became a cause of acrimony. This need not have precipitated a duel, but Meath provided the *casus belli*, and he paid the ultimate price, as a result of accusing Gore of perpetrating 'a gross falsehood' in resolutions he had approving appertaining to the dispute. The death of a peer of the realm was major news, and the decision of the Meath family to employ one of the kingdom's most talented young barristers, William Saurin, to prosecute Gore for murder gave the case added piquancy. Saurin wisely chose to focus his prosecution on the disagreement over recruitment, but his case was undermined by the revelation of the defendant's counsel that Meath had accused Gore of uttering a 'falsehood' which was widely acknowledged as due cause for a duel. Furthermore, Saurin's argument that 'the law cannot admit that any members of that state should be the avenger of his own wrongs, be they imaginary or even real' was negated by the judge, Thomas Kelly, who justified recourse to pistols in matters of honour and who instructed the jury to acquit the accused if they entertained 'a shadow of doubt'. The jury did, for they returned a verdict of '*manslaughter* in his own defence', which they subsequently 'altered to a verdict of not guilty generally'.[73]

The readiness of Judge Kelly to defend the code of honour pleased the proponents of the duelling, who were acutely conscious of the slowly gathering opposition to the code of honour in society at large. It is noteworthy, for example, that none of the duels that comprise our sample for the 1790s took place within the Dublin city boundary, and that there was a greater willingness on the part of the part of principals to conduct their encounters at a further remove from the city than the Phoenix Park (Table 5.3) or at Holyhead, which played host to three duels involving Irishmen in the autumn of 1796.[74] This was an inevitable consequence of the increased propensity of sheriffs and magistrates to arrest and to bind over intending duellists, and of the courts to fine and imprison those who were prosecuted for sending challenges. In 1797 Peter Aylmer was sentenced to six months' confinement and a £50 fine for sending a challenge to the Mayor of Drogheda; while three years later the Court of King's Bench found both George Ledwell and Thomas Prior guilty of the same offence when the source of their ire, Colonel Cholmeley Deering of the Romney Fencibles, chose to prosecute rather than to accept the challenge presented to him.[75] However, for every sheriff prepared to take the necessary steps to bind an intending duellist to keep the peace, there were others like Thomas Judkin Fitzgerald, the high sheriff of County Tipperary in 1798, or Robert Sparrow, high sheriff of County Armagh in 1795, who felt no such obligation. They had not yet embraced the distinction drawn by Lord Macartney in 1786, John Philpot Curran in 1789 and the Advocate General of Scotland in 1793 between a man and the office he occupied, which was used by some office-holders to release them from the obligation of taking up challenges presented to them.[76]

The reluctance of so many Irish office-holders to embrace the distinction between the person and the office in matters of honour provides further evidence of the depth of the continuing commitment of Irishmen to the code of honour. At least nineteen duellists died and over forty were injured in the 1790s (Table 5.5), and some vicious acts of violence were perpetrated in the name of honour. One of the most infamous occurred at Kilworth, County Cork, in December 1797 when Lord Kingsborough killed Colonel Henry Fitzgerald.

Kingsborough had raised Fitzgerald, who was the natural son of his brother, but relations between the two men were not harmonious. For reasons that are not immediately identifiable, Fitzgerald was disinherited for marrying a foreigner. This relationship did not survive, and in 1797 Fitzgerald precipitated a major confrontation with the King family when he eloped to London with Lord Kingsborough's third daughter, Mary. A reward of one hundred guineas for information concerning Mary King's whereabouts enabled Robert King, Kingsborough's son, to trace Fitzgerald and to challenge him to justify his actions in a duel. As a result, Fitzgerald and he exchanged eight shots in Hyde Park on Sunday 1 October in a tense and ill-tempered encounter which the former was obliged to fight without a second and which only concluded because his powder and ball were exhausted. Nobody was hurt on this occasion, and the two men were only persuaded not to resume their quarrel at Tyburn on the following day by the intervention of the authorities, who bound both to keep the peace. Miss King, meanwhile, was taken back to Mitchelstown by her father, but instead of pursuing the prudent course of keeping out of the Kings' way, Fitzgerald was tempted (perhaps by Miss King) to return to Ireland and to take lodgings at Kilworth near to where she was staying. Informed of his presence, Kingsborough and his son sought Fitzgerald out, and when they discovered his whereabouts, Robert King demanded of him that he take up his pistol so that they could settle the matter once and for all like gentlemen. However, instead of embarking in an orderly manner on a duel the two men 'grappled with each other', whereupon Lord Kingsborough, who had accompanied or followed his son to Kilworth, drew his pistol and shot Fitzgerald dead. This was certainly not in accordance with the rules of duelling, but public opinion was on King's side. The press was sympathetic, and when Kingsborough demanded to be tried by the House of Lords in May 1798, no evidence was offered against him and he was acquitted. His son had previously been acquitted for want of prosecution at the Cork assizes.[77]

Strictly speaking, Kingsborough could have been prosecuted for murder, but there was no enthusiasm in the political or legal establishments for such a course. Indeed, the Irish House of Commons continued to produce its share of affairs of honour. During the Union debates in the spring of 1800 Isaac Corry, the erstwhile Patriot who was now Chancellor of the Exchequer, launched a series of bitter personal attacks on Henry Grattan for his opposition to the bill for a legislative union. Grattan, Corry alleged on 17 February, 'was a *tender* Irishman and a traitor . . . the cause of the late rebellion' who had had himself returned to parliament after an absence of three years 'to stir up another rebellion'. This was quite malevolent, and not to be outdone, Grattan in his reply described Corry as 'a half-bred lawyer, a half-bred statesman, a mock patriot, a swaggering bully and finished coxcomb, a coward, a liar and a rascal'. This was a more than adequate cause for a challenge, and having been bested in the verbal exchanges, Corry requested General Craddock, the M.P. for Thomastown, to act on his behalf. The two principals and their seconds met at Ballsbridge on the morning of 18 February. Both fired two shots, one of which drew blood but was not life-threatening, and the two parties departed the scene with honour satisfied.[78]

Both Grattan and Corry, it was widely agreed, conducted themselves impeccably on the duelling field. Having hit Corry with his first shot, Grattan fired his second into the air, and subsequently visited his opponent to inquire after his health.[79] Others were not so scrupulous, and the controversy over the Act of Union provided a number with opportunities to display their bravery. We can safely discount Barrington's claim that Lord Castlereagh, the Chief Secretary (who, some alleged, primed Corry to attack Grattan), oversaw the formation of a Castle duelling club at this time to take out the leading opposition spokesmen and thereby ensure the ratification of the Act of Union.[80] Eighteenth-century gentlemen did not need such encouragement to duel. In August 1799, for instance, Norman Steele of Moynalty travelled to Holyhead to meet Dacre Hamilton following a dispute over an anti-Union address which Steele sought to get up in County Monaghan.[81] As this and so many of the other encounters bear witness, too few of the Irish social elite were prepared to forgo a challenge to offer any comfort to the still small but growing section of the population who were convinced that duelling was socially as well as morally indefensible.

Table 5.1: Duelling, 1791–1810 – number of duels; social status of principals

Date	Number of duels sampled	Number of averted duels	Gentlemen	Military	Middle class	Lawyers	Lower class
1791–95	50	5	44	22	4	7	—
1796–1800	63	8	36	24	12	7	3
1801–05	42	8	34	20	4	3	1
1806–10	39	4	19	22	3	3	—

Table 5.2: The geography of duelling, 1791–1810

Date	Number of duels sampled	Dublin city and county	Rest of Leinster	Munster	Ulster	Connacht	Irishmen duelling abroad
1791–95	50	18	6	12	1	8	3
1796–1800	63	27	2	17	4	1	5
1801–05	42	18	3	13	—	4	3
1806–10	39	6	7	20	3	3	—

Table 5.3: Duelling in Dublin, 1791–1810

Date	Number of	Dublin	North	Phoenix	Merrion	Dublin
duels sampled	city from Dublin area	Lotts	Park	Fields	county and	suburbs
1791–95	18	—	2	10	—	6
1796–1800	27	—	—	11	3	13
1801–05	18	1	—	4	—	13
1806–10	6	—	—	1	—	5

Table 5.4: Duelling, 1791–1810 – weapons; shots fired

Date	Number of duels sampled	Weapons		Shots fired				
		Pertinent sample	Pistol	Size of sample	One shot	Two shots	Three shots	Four or more shots
1791–95	46	37	37	18	—	12	1	5
1795–800	63	54	54	33	2	14	1	16
1801–05	42	42	42	31	2	14	1	14
1806–10	39	38	38	29	1	19	—	9

Table 5.5: Duelling, 1791–1810 – mortality and injuries

Date	Number of duels sampled	Fatalities	Mortal wounds	One wounded	Two wounded	No injuries	Total injuries
1791–95	50	10	2	18	2	20	34
1796 1800	63	9	3	18	2	31	34
1801–05	42	7	—	14	4	17	29
1806–10	39	11	—	9	1	18	22

Table 5.6: Seconds; the law and duelling, 1791–1810

Date	Seconds			The law and duelling				
	No seconds	Seconds inter-vened	Reconciliation	Law inter-venes	Coroner's court hearing	Number of trials	Manslaughter	Murder
1791–95	—	7	3	3	—	2	1	1
1796–1800	—	16	15	5	1	2	2	—
1801–05	—	12	14	6	1	4	3	—
1806–10	1	17	16	3	3	5	3	2

Notes and References

1 James Kelly, 'The genesis of "Protestant ascendancy"' in Gerard O'Brien, ed., *Parliament, politics and people: essays in eighteenth-century Irish history* (Dublin, 1989), pp. 93–127; Jacqueline Hill, 'The meaning and significance of "Protestant ascendancy", 1787–1840' in *Ireland after the Union* (Oxford, 1989), pp. 1–22.
2 Above, p. 162.
3 *H.J.*, 19 Apr., 25, 28 Oct. 1782.
4 *D.C.*, 7 Aug. 1788.
5 *D.E.P.*, 19 Aug. 1786.
6 *Volunteer Evening Post, Dublin Evening Post* and *Freeman's Journal*, June–September 1786; *The trial of George Robert Fitzgerald and Timothy Brecknock . . .*, passim.
7 *V.E.P.*, 26 Mar. 1785. St George's ball pierced Reynolds's hat.
8 George Joseph Browne, *A report of the whole proceedings . . . on the trial of Robert Keon gent. for the murder of George Nugent Reynolds esq.* (Dublin, 1788), passim; Anon, 'George Nugent Reynolds: the Sheemore duel', *Ardagh and Clonmacnois Antiquarian Society Journal*, ii, no. 11 (1946), pp. 74–9; Liam Kelly, 'Defenderism in Leitrim during the 1790s', *Breifne*, vi (1986), p. 343 note 14.
9 *D.E.P.*, 19, 21, 24 Oct. 1786.
10 As note 9; *D.C.*, 8 Sept., 20 Oct., 20 Nov., 1 Dec. 1787, 2 Feb. 1788; *Clonmel Gazette*, 2, 18, 21 Feb. 1788.
11 *D.E.P.*, 24 Oct. 1786.
12 *D.E.P.*, 24, 26 Oct. 1786; *D.C.*, 22 Jan. 1786.
13 *D.C.*, 31 July 1788. There is a misleading account of the episode in Barry, *The code of honour*, pp. 128–9.
14 *Clonmel Gazette*, 25 Aug. 1790.
15 Diary of Richard Hobart, 1784–1803 (in possession of Dom Mark Tierney, Glenstall Abbey, County Limerick (N.L.I., microfilm p.7363)).
16 *D.C.*, 11, 13 Dec. 1788.
17 *Cork Remembrancer*, p. 200; *Belfast Newsletter*, 16 Jan. 1789.
18 *D.C.*, 21, 23 July; *Clonmel Gazette*, 23 July 1791.
19 *D.C.*, 23 Oct. 1790.
20 Vere Hunt Diary, 1794 (typescript copy in possession of Mr John Hunt, Bailey, Howth, County Dublin).
21 *D.C.*, 2 June 1791, 30 Apr. 1793.
22 Barrington, *Personal sketches*, ii, 199.
23 Maxwell, *Dublin under the Georges*, pp. 89, 170–71.
24 S. H. Palmer, 'The Irish police experiment: the beginnings of modern police in the British Isles, 1785–95', *Social Science Quarterly*, lvi (1975), pp. 410–24; James Kelly, 'The context and course of Thomas Orde's plan of education of 1787', *The Irish Journal of Education*, xx (1986), pp. 3–27; Oliver MacDonagh, *The Inspector General: Sir Jeremiah Fitzpatrick and social reform, 1783–1802* (London, 1981), pp. 42–148.

25 It is not mentioned in Brian Inglis, *Freedom of the press, 1784–1841* (London, 1954).
26 *D.C.*, May 1787–92; *D.E.P.*, 1786–90 passim.
27 Granville Sharp, *A tract on duelling, wherein the opinions of some of the most celebrated matters on crown law are examined and corrected* (London, 1779, 1790); Kiernan, *The duel*, pp. 192–3.
28 As well as anti-duelling comment appended to duel reports, the *Dublin Chronicle* published specific articles critical of duelling on 7 February 1789 and 6 May 1790.
29 J. B. Lyons, ed., 'The letters of Sylvester O'Halloran, part 2', *North Munster Antiquarian Journal*, ix (1962–3), pp. 49–50.
30 *D.C.*, 6 May 1790, 27 Oct. 1791.
31 G. A. Kelly, 'Duelling in eighteenth-century France . . . archaeology, rationale, implications', *The eighteenth century*, xxi (1981), pp. 239–45; Kiernan, *The duel*, pp. 167–8; *D.C.*, 6 May; *Clonmel Gazette*, 17 July 1790.
32 *D.C.*, 31 Mar. 1789.
33 *D.C.*, 7 Jan. 1790. For other examples see 18 Mar. 1792, 18 June, 30 July 1793; *F.J.*, 4 Aug. 1796.
34 *D.C.*, 8 June 1790; *Clonmel Gazette*, 12 Dec. 1789.
35 *D.C.*, 4, 6 Nov. 1788.
36 *D.C.*, 6, 15 July 1790.
37 C. T. Bowden, *Tour through Ireland* (Dublin, 1790). Compare this with the more realistic calculation that there were 33 duels in Britain and Ireland in 1790 – 14 of which resulted in fatalities (*Ennis Chronicle*, 17 Jan. 1791).
38 Chevalier de Latocnaye. *A Frenchman's walk through Ireland* (Belfast, 1917), pp. 120–21; Malcomson, ed., *Eighteenth-century Irish official papers*, ii, 201.
39 For these and other examples see *D.C.*, 19 May, 11 Aug., 10, 17 Sept., 17 Nov., 22 Dec. 1791, 19 Jan., 7, 12 Apr., 1 May 1792, 18 June, 30 July, 24 Sept., 20 Oct. 1793; *H.J.*, 16 July 1790; *Clonmel Gazette*, 17 July 1790, 2, 12 Nov. 1791, 28 Jan. 1792; Henry, 'Crime in Dublin', pp. 44–5.
40 *D.C.*, 9 Jan., 7, 12 Apr., 25 Aug. 1792.
41 *D.C.*, 13, 20, 22 Dec. 1791, 11 Apr., 24 Sept 1793; *Clonmel Gazette*, 17, 21 Dec. 1791; *F.J.*, 2 Nov. 1792, 21 Dec. 1793; Powell, ed., *Barnard Letters*, p. 39; Prim, 'Notes on Kilkenny inns and taverns', pp. 171–2.
42 Board minute, 22 Aug. 1789 (T.C.D., MUN/P/1/920); *F.J.*, 19 Feb. 1805; draft letter, [1789], and letter of tutors, 5 Dec. 1789 (MUN/P/1/921, 923).
43 *D.C.*, 24 Sept. 1791.
44 *D.C.*, 29 Sept., 24 Dec. 1791, 8 May 1792; *Cork Gazette*, 24 Dec. 1791; *Galway Reader*, iv (1953), p. 124.
45 *D.C.*, 3 Mar., 13 Dec. 1791, 1, 10 Mar., 23 Oct. 1792, 7 May, 7 Sept. 1793; *F.J.*, 25, 27 Jan., 15, 25 Feb. 1794, 12 May, 15 Aug. 1796, 9 Feb., 15 June 1797; *D.E.P.*, 9 Oct. 1794, 24 Oct. 1795; Wood-Martin, *Sligo*, iii, 317; Powell, ed., *Barnard Letters*, p. 39; Chart, ed., *Drennan Letters*, p. 161.
46 *D.C.*, 31 May, 23 Oct. 1792, 4 Apr. 1793; *D.E.P.*, 17 May 1796; *F.D.J.*, 25 Oct. 1792.

47 C. J. Woods, ed., *Journals and memoirs of Thomas Russell* (Dublin, 1991), pp. 83, 134–5; idem, 'The place of Thomas Russell in the United Irish movement' in Gough and Dickson, eds, *Ireland and the French Revolution*, pp. 88, 90; R. B. McDowell, *Ireland in the age of imperialism and revolution* (Oxford, 1979), pp. 48–9.

48 Above, p. 153; *D.C.*, 6 Dec. 1792; Chart, ed., *Drennan Letters*, p. 102; W. H. Drummond, ed., *Autobiography of Hamilton Rowan* (Shannon, 1972), pp. vii-viii, 164–7, 178.

49 R. R. Madden, *The United Irishmen* (Dublin, 1842), ii, 110–12; Barrington, *Recollections*, pp. 307–11.

50 Kelly, 'James Napper Tandy', pp. 12–13; *Proceedings of the trial of James Napper Tandy esqr. in the court of King's Bench . . . upon an indictment for sending a challenge to John Toler esq. . . .* (Dublin 1792); Frank MacDermott, *Theobald Wolfe Tone* (Dublin, 1939), pp. 88, 95–6; McDougall, *Sketches of Irish political characters*, p. 279; McDowell, *Ireland in the age of imperialism*, pp. 422–3; Chart, ed., *Drennan Letters*, pp. 82–9, 148–9; Teignmouth, *Reminiscences*, i, 171–2; *Autobiography of Hamilton Rowan*, pp. 162–4; R.B. McDowell, ed., 'Proceedings of the Dublin Society of United Irishmen', *Analecta Hibernica*, no.17 (1949), pp. 14–15, 18–20; *Life of Grattan*, iv, 65.

51 Madden, *United Irishmen*, ii, 26–31; Drummond, *Autobiography of Rowan*, pp. 167–70; privately printed account of Simon Butler's attempt to fight a duel with Fitzgibbon (S.P.O., Rebellion Papers, 620/20/28).

52 *D.E.P.*, 7 June 1794.

53 *The trial of John Devereux junior of Shelbeggan in the county of Wexford before a court martial held in the city of Cork on 27 November 1799* (Dublin, 1800), p. 47. I wish to thank Dr Kevin Whelan for bringing this reference to my attention.

54 *D.E.P.*, 20 May 1794.

55 Walsh, *Ireland sixty years ago*, p. 24; *D.E.P.*, 14, 16, 21 July, 1, 18, 20 Aug., 3 Oct. 1795; *H.J.*, 20 July 1795.

56 E. A. Smith, *Whig principles and party politics: Earl Fitzwilliam and the Whig party* (Manchester, 1975), pp. 210–12; *D.E.P.*, 4 July 1795; Milton to Fitzwilliam, 30 June 1795; Beresford to Fitzwilliam, 22 June 1795; Fitzwilliam to Beresford, 23 June 1795 (Sheffield City Libraries, Fitzwilliam papers, F 30a); *Life of Grattan*, iv, 204–5n.

57 *Annual Register*, xxxix (1797), p. 9; *Carey's General Evening Post*, 16 Feb. 1797.

58 Grattan to [Tyrawly], 8 July [1798] (manuscript letter in possession of Dr A. P. W. Malcomson); *Life of Grattan*, i, 119–20n; iv, 100, 402–4.

59 Esther Hewitt, ed., *Lord Shannon's letters to his son* (Belfast, 1982), pp. 45–6; *F.J.*, 17 Jan., 16 Feb. 1797.

60 *D.E.P.*, 26 Jan. 1796; *Walker's Hibernian Magazine*, 1796 p. 93; Elliott, *Tone*, p. 319; Kevin Whelan, 'Captain Edward Sweetman', *Irish Sword*, xvii (1989), pp. 219–20; Woods, ed., *Journals and memoirs of Russell*, p. 140 note 19.

61 Barrington, *Recollections*, pp. 307–11; *D.E.P.*, 7 June 1794; *F.J.*, 21 Oct. 1798.

62 It was claimed that the pistols used in the duel fought in 1798 involving Richard L[ongfield] were loaded with powder alone (*F.J.*, 8 May 1798). And

it will be recalled that in 1786 it was suggested that the Keon–Reynolds duel should be fought likewise (above, pp. 194–5).
63 *F.J.*, 8 May 1798.
64 McDowell, *Ireland in the age of imperialism*, pp. 519–93; P. C. Stoddhart, 'Counter-insurgency and defence in Ireland, 1790–1805' (D.Phil. thesis, Oxford University 1972)
65 Maurice Lenehan, *Limerick, its history and antiquities* (Cork, 1967), p. 407; *F.J.*, 21 Oct., 8 Nov. 1798, 2, 4 July 1799, 4 Feb., 27 Mar., 10 June, 31 July, 13 Dec. 1800; Patrick Power, 'A Carrickman's diary', *Journal of the Waterford and South-East of Ireland Society*, xv (1912), p. 128; Prim, 'Notes on Kilkenny inns and taverns', p. 171.
66 For examples see Wood-Martin, *Sligo*, iii, 317; *Clonmel Gazette*, 12 Dec. 1789, 15 June 1791; *Cork Gazette*, 6 July 1791; *F.J.*, 14 Jan. 1794, 16 Mar. 1797, 10 May, 14 June 1798, 22 Feb., 10 May, 2 July 1799.
67 For examples see *F.J.*, 14 Jan. 1794, 16 Mar. 1797, 16 Mar., 9 July 1799, 4 Feb., 15 May 1800.
68 *F.J.*, 7 July 1796, 22 Mar. 1798, 6 May 1800.
69 *D.E.P.*, 22 Apr. 1794; Barrington, *Recollections*, pp. 304–5.
70 *Annual Register*, xxxviii (1796), p. 24; G.E.C., *The complete peerage*, ix, 355–6, xii, 2.
71 *F.J.*, 10, 14 June 1800.
72 *F.J.*, 25 July, 8 Aug., 17 Oct. 1797; Young to Abercorn, 10 Oct. 1797; Knox to Abercorn, 20 Oct. 1797; Hayes to Abercorn 15 Nov. 1797 (P.R.O.N.I., Abercorn papers, T2541/1B3/6/29, 30, 33); J. H. Gebbie, ed., *An introduction to the Abercorn Papers* (Omagh, 1974), pp. 201–2.
73 *F.J.*, 28 Mar., 20 Apr., 28 May, 29 June 1797; William Ridgeway, *Report of the trial of Robert Gore esquire upon an endictment for the murder of . . . William, late Earl of Meath, at the Wicklow summer assizes 1797 before the Right Hon. Mr Justice Kelly* (Dublin, 1797); *Walker's Hibernian Magazine*, 1797, pp. 190, 281–6, 361–4. For another instance of a duel over recruitment see *Clonmel Gazette*, 29 May 1793.
74 *F.J.*, 20 Oct., 1796, 17 Jan. 1797.
75 *F.J.*, 31 Jan., 22 June 1797, 3, 13 May 1800; *A report of the trial of George Lidwell and Thomas Prior esqrs upon an information . . . for sending and delivering a challenge to Cholmeley Dering . . .* (Dublin, 1800).
76 *F.J.*, 6 Nov. 1798; Patrick Tohill, 'The Diamond fight of 1795', *Seanchas Ardmhacha*, iii (1958), pp. 26–7; *Annual Register*, xxviii (1786), pp. 203–4; *Autobiography of Rowan*, p. 178.
77 *F.J.*, 12, 28 Dec. 1797, 19 May 1798; Powell, ed., *Barnard Letters*, p. 85; Knox to Abercorn, 12 Dec. 1797 (P.R.O.N.I., Abercorn Papers, T2541/1B3/6/34); Daniel Owen Madden, *Revelations of Ireland in the past generations* (Dublin, 1877), pp. 45–57; *Walker's Hibernian Magazine*, 1797, p. 566.
78 Dillon to Lattin, 19 Feb. 1800 (N.L.I., Mansfield Papers, see Reports on Private Collections, no. 396, p. 2834); Malcomson, ed., *Eighteenth-century Irish official papers*, ii, 307; Cooke to Grenville, 18 Feb. 1800, in H.M.C.,

Fortescue, vi (1908), pp. 136–7; Bodkin, *Grattan's parliament*, pp. 252–7; A. Brooke Tyrrell, 'Homage to Grattan, 1746–1820', *Dublin Historical Record*, xxxvii (1983), pp. 42–3; *Cornwallis corresp.*, iii, 196; *Life of Grattan*, v, 100–4, 107–9.

79 *F.J.*, 22 Feb. 1800; Bodkin, *Grattan's parliament*, p. 257.

80 Bodkin, *Grattan's parliament*, pp. 235–6; Fitzpatrick, *Ireland before . . . the Union*, p. 165n; *Life of Grattan*, v, 71, 73–4.

81 Steele to Shirley, 31 Mar. 1799 (P.R.O.N.I., Shirley Papers, D3531/A/5, pp. 110–11, 113).

PART III

DUELLING IN DECLINE

In the nineteenth century adherence in Ireland to the code of honour, which sustained the practice of duelling, withered and declined. This process took several decades, but it was virtually complete by 1850. Duelling survived in the public domain for a number of decades thereafter as a motif in popular novels, improving middle-class journals and religious tracts, but it no longer possessed the catchment of devotees that had sustained it for nearly three centuries, and within a generation it was regarded as little more than a historical curiosity.

Although duelling had passed its zenith by the beginning of the nineteenth century, affairs of honour remained commonplace during the first thirty years of the new century. For as long as hostilities with France continued, the swollen wartime armies ensured that military duelling remained at an above-average level. Per contra, *few aristocrats were tempted to risk their lives over matters of honour, though political and electoral disagreements compelled some of the most prominent and influential figures in the land to continue to enter the duelling lists. As this implies, there was a perceptible decline in the social status of duellists in the early nineteenth century. This was a by-product, first and foremost, of the changing values and outlook of the Protestant landed and political* corps d'élite *that comprised Ireland's traditional duelling constituency, which prompted members of that elite to look with ever-increasing disdain on the precepts that fuelled the code of honour. It was also a product of the embrace by Catholic gentlemen, particularly in Munster and Connacht, of these precepts. Leading Catholics like Daniel O'Connell were involved in some of the most publicised encounters of the early nineteenth century. O'Connell's subsequent disavowal of the code of honour presaged a similar response from many of his co-religionists, but duelling proved more resistant to eradication than its increasingly numerous and vehement critics found comfortable. That said, the dramatic decline in the number of duels fought in Dublin (though the code of honour remained popular in Connacht and Munster for longer) and the foundation in 1830 of an Irish association committed to the suppression of duelling hastened its demise. It lost its central place in the value system of both the Protestant governing elite and the emerging Catholic leadership in the 1830s and 1840s, and it had all but given way to the middle-class values that became normative in Victorian Britain and Ireland by mid-century.*

6

The Turning of the Tide: the early nineteenth century

The Act of Union (1800) was a significant moment in the history of duelling in Ireland. By effecting the abolition of the Irish parliament, the scene of events which had provided the source of so many affairs of honour in the second half of the eighteenth century, it deprived the code of honour of one of its most important public stages. Furthermore, the abandonment of an annual parliamentary session reduced the appeal of the city of Dublin to the landed elite of the kingdom, who became increasingly disinclined in the early nineteenth century to reside in the city for other than short periods. As a result, Dublin was transformed gradually into a middle-class city in which essentially aristocratic norms such as the code of honour had diminishing meaning and relevance.

Parallel with and indivisible from this, fundamental attitudinal changes dimmed the social compulsion to duel. In the first instance, the intensifying evangelical revival in the early decades of the century prompted Protestant leaders to give a higher priority to issues of public as well as private morality, and the increased appeal of their arguments in favour of greater personal and religious discipline fostered the emergence of a more censorious attitude towards extravagant behaviour like duelling and drinking. Secondly, the feelings of unease and vulnerability laid bare by the 1798 rebellion, the emergence of Catholic emancipation as the dominant political issue of the day and the increasingly democratic ideology underpinning political discourse heightened the sense of communal solidarity that bound the Irish Protestant elite. In the short term, this provided the cause for many duels; in the longer term, it hastened the

Edward Hay (courtesy of the National Library of Ireland)

displacement of the intrinsically aristocratic ethos that had shaped public consciousness in the eighteenth century by an increasingly democratic one in the nineteenth, which represented less fertile soil for the values encapsulated by the code of honour. Thirdly, as the nineteenth-century state became more interventionist, it became more willing to intervene to regulate human behaviour, and manifestly less inclined to indulge the extra-legal behaviour permitted to ruling elites throughout Europe in the seventeenth and eighteenth centuries. The speed at which these developments took place must not be overestimated. Fundamental long-term shifts in public attitude were necessary before duelling went into terminal decline, and this took nearly half a century.

Duelling in the early nineteenth century

Irish society in the first decade of the nineteenth century was haunted by the memory of the 1798 rebellion. This is reflected in the duelling record as in so many other aspects of life, and the residual passions and tensions of the 1790s provided the occasion for a number of well-publicised encounters. Perhaps the most emblematic involved William Todd Jones, the Presbyterian radical, who had been a prominent advocate of Catholic relief in the 1790s,[1] and Sir Richard Musgrave, the hardline Protestant M.P. and controversialist. Musgrave's *magnum opus*, *Memoirs of the different rebellions in Ireland*, was first published in 1801, and among its many controversial affirmations it claimed that Todd Jones was induced to support Catholic relief by 'sordid and sinister motives'.[2] Jones was so deeply offended by this allegation that he penned a rebuttal, which he had printed and distributed in Liverpool (Musgrave's current place of residence) as well as Ireland. It was an intemperate production, as even his friends acknowledged, and Musgrave was incensed. He described it as 'a furious tirade' couched in 'Billingsgate vocabulary' more appropriate 'to the scurrilous railings of a drunken fishwoman'. However, he did not believe it was worth endangering his life over it, because he declined Jones's request for a duel and signalled his willingness by letter to offer him a private apology for the offence he had caused. This did not appease Jones, who sought deliberately 'to wound' Musgrave's 'feelings' by showing an amended version of his offer of an apology about town and by posting it in a public room in Eustace Street. Musgrave was so furious at what he deemed a breach of faith that he responded by demanding an apology for Jones's 'unwarrantable printed letter' of the previous year. Jones refused, and Musgrave issued a challenge. The two men met at Rathfarnham towards the end of May 1802 and concluded their complex affair with an exchange of shots, one of which hit and wounded Musgrave.[3]

Another chronicler of the 1798 rebellion who felt compelled to appeal to arms to defend his reputation was Edward Hay. In 1802, before his controversial *History of the insurrection of the county of Wexford* was published, he exchanged shots at Passage, County Waterford, with Joseph Smith of Tipperary. Nobody was injured, which may have encouraged Hay to pursue his dispute with Musgrave over 'slander[ous]' references to him in the former's *Memoirs of the different rebellions*. No duel ensued in this instance because Musgrave, who was still recuperating from the injury he had received at the hands of Todd Jones, was determined not to fight.[4] Hay did not possess equal self-discipline. In 1807 he was wounded in an encounter with Major John Devereux that arose out of 'disputes' occasioned by the acrimonious election for the constituency of County Wexford.[5]

As this indicates, political disagreements continued to prove a fruitful source of affairs of honour between political opposites in the early nineteenth century. During the 'rowdy' election for Dublin city in 1802 George Ogle, the inveterate proponent of 'Protestant ascendancy' who had the support of anti-Catholic elements in the city, was challenged by Bernard Coyle, a Catholic activist, following a remark which Coyle interpreted as a slight on Catholic loyalty. Coyle and Ogle disliked each other personally as well as politically, as they amply demonstrated by rebuffing all efforts to effect a reconciliation and by firing two brace of pistols each. No injury ensued.[6] By contrast, when two Cork-born members of the Irish Legion in France, Captains Thomas Corbet and John Swiney, disagreed in May 1804 following Corbet's accusation that Swiney had not raised his hand in assent during a ceremony in which the members of the Legion publicly professed their allegiance to Napoleon, they embarked on an encounter of exceptional intensity. Both men were arrested and imprisoned before they could resolve their difference with pistols, but their anger was not diminished by their detention, for when they were released a number of months later they immediately set proceedings in train to conclude their disagreement with a duel. Moreover, because neither was prepared to give quarter, their encounter became a fight to the death. In all, nine or ten shots were exchanged, initially at ten paces but later at six. Corbett, who was the more aggressive of the two principals, was hit three times and died of his wounds. Swiney was more fortunate: he received a wound to the leg from which he recovered.[7]

This was an unusually murderous encounter, and the commanding officer of the Legion was replaced for allowing it to take place. However, there were so many regiments of soldiers and militia arrayed throughout western Europe at this time that it was impossible to police the armed forces against duelling. In this respect Ireland was no different to France. In the first decade of the nineteenth century the military contributed a higher proportion of duellists than they had at any time since the late seventeenth century. As Table 5.1 reveals, the increase in the percentage of recorded duels involving members of the armed services identifiable in the 1790s was intensified in the first decade of the new century. The military provided one or both antagonists in 22.4 per cent of those duels sampled from the 1780s (Table 3.1), in 41 per cent of those sampled for the 1790s, and 52 per cent of those sampled for the first decade of the nineteenth century (Table 5.1). Some of these duels were the direct result of the military build-up occasioned by the Napoleonic wars in Europe, for a number of the most publicised duels in County Cork during these years involved naval officers who were not stationed in Ireland and who only disembarked to fight. In February 1803, for example, Lieutenant Turner of H.M.S. *Le Determiné* exchanged six shots with Stephen French. Four years later Lieutenants Hills and Burney of H.M.S. *Dryad* were both wounded in an encounter in which four shots were fired; while in December 1807 when Lieutenants Phillimore and Medlicott of H.M.S. *Polyphemus* disembarked at Haulbowline to settle a difference, Phillimore died from the wounds he received in the duel that followed.[8]

These were exceptional cases. Most military duellists were stationed in Ireland. A substantial percentage were civilians serving in the militia and yeomanry, but a clear majority were regular army officers.[9] There was little love lost between the militia, yeomanry and army, if the frequency with which members of the different forces engaged each other in duelling is an accurate guide. The number of such incidents is too small to permit meaningful statistical scrutiny, but what evidence there is suggests that encounters between members of the regular army were less likely to result in death or serious injury than those involving military and civilians.[10] Part of the reason for this was the further increase in the reconciliation of principals by seconds (Table 5.6);[11] while reports that military duellists were prepared to shoot into the air rather than at their opponent and that officers favoured the dismissal or ostracism of colleagues who duelled indicate diminishing enthusiasm among the soldiery for the sanguinary implications of the code of honour.[12] Duels between military and civilians, by contrast, showed less disposition towards moderation. 'Severe wounds' were commonplace, particularly in encounters in which the principals let their desire for victory or vengeance dull their sensibilities. Duels in which four or more shots were fired (Table 5.4) were more likely to conclude with a death or serious injury than those with less. This was not invariable,[13] but individuals like James Moore O'Donel, the former M.P. for County Mayo who was killed by Major Denis Bingham at Galway in 1801, and Francis Enright, the Limerick attorney who was shot dead by Lieutenant Delmage of the Rathkeale yeomanry, would have lived longer if the disposition towards reconciliation was still stronger.[14]

The military did not have it all their own way in duels with civilians. In May 1807 Henry George Bailer shot his naval antagonist through the heart in an encounter near Limerick city, while Captain J. Otway was severely injured by A. W. Bellew at Granard, County Longford, in December of the same year. Otway was hit by his opponent's second shot after the seconds had failed to reconcile the principals following their initial exchange. Inevitably, injuries were more likely to ensue when principals were determined to repulse all attempts at mediation.[15] This point emerges clearly from the 1802 encounter between Captain Laurence Hearn of Ballyduff, County Kilkenny, and John Davis of Summerhill in the same country. Following the issuing of the challenge, the two men were bound over by magistrates in County Kilkenny to keep the peace, but, unwilling to let the matter rest, they left the jurisdiction for a venue in County Carlow, where Hearn was fatally wounded in the exchange of shots that followed.[16]

As the law was interpreted, there was little sheriffs or magistrates could do to prevent determined duellists from putting their lives on the line in the name of honour. There is no evidence, for instance, that John Davis was ever prosecuted for his part in the death of Captain Hearn, while juries continued to look benignly on those members of the military accused of killing an opponent in a duel, particularly if there was no evidence of foul play. Thus when Joseph Kelly, the paymaster of the 32nd Regiment of Foot, was tried in 1806 for the murder of Captain William Harrison in an encounter on the Cork road that arose out of a violent disagreement over the punishment appropriate for Harrison's servant, he was acquitted by the jury because his opponent had refused his apology on the morning of the duel — even though he (Kelly) was clearly the aggressor in the incident that precipitated the challenge.[17] In 1807, following the death of Lieutenant Phillimore, his killer, Lieutenant Medlicott, was released by the local authorities in County Cork after the coroner's inquest concluded that the duel had been fought in accordance with the code of honour.[18]

If the high percentage of encounters involving members of the military is the most visible feature of early nineteenth-century duelling trends, the increased disinclination of gentlemen to endanger their lives was more important in the longer term. Direct evidence for this is provided by the fact that the percentage of instances in which the seconds intervened and effected a reconciliation after the principals had fired just one shot each increased markedly in the early nineteenth century (Table 5.6).[19] The exchange of one shot aimed by each principal at his antagonist was seen in some quarters as the minimum necessary to fulfil the terms of the code of honour, but this was not so. On occasions in the eighteenth century individuals pressed to fight a duel against their better judgment signalled their disapproval on the duelling field by firing into the air or into the ground. They were few in number, but it is not a coincidence that this practice grew in popularity in the early nineteenth century parallel with rising disenchantment with the code of honour, because it permitted individuals opposed to duelling to demonstrate that they were not activated to take this stand by cowardice.[20] The most publicised encounter of this type took place in June 1806 when the Marquis of Ely responded to the fire of Mr L—— by discharging his pistol into the air.[21] Behaviour such as this partly accounts for the high percentage of recorded duels (43 per cent of our sample) in the first decade of the nineteenth century that concluded without injury to either of the principals (Table 5.5). This was exceptionally high. The only other decade to come close to this was the 1790s, when a similar percentage of sampled duels concluded without injury. The figure for the 1770s and 1780s was 32 per cent (Table 3.7); it was 24 per cent during the 1750s and 1760s (Table 2.5).

To be sure, all duels were not fought in this spirit. At least eighteen people died in eighty-one encounters known to have taken place between 1801 and 1810. This would imply that there was at least a 22 per cent chance that each duel would end in the death of one of the principals (Table 5.5), which compares unfavourably with a death rate of 7 per cent in those duels that took place in Britain in 1807.[22] Moreover, when we include all injuries to gain a fuller picture of the overall casualty rate, the contrast is even more striking. In all fifty-one duellists were killed or injured in eighty-one reported duels fought in Ireland in the ten years 1801–10, compared with a 12 per cent casualty rate registered in Britain from a smaller sample taken in 1807. This means that 57 per cent of the sampled duels fought in the first decade of the nineteenth century in Ireland resulted in the death or injury of one or both principals, and that 32 per cent of all duellists in this period were killed or injured on the duelling field (Table 5.5). This is an increase on the casualty rate calculated from a similar sample of duels that took place in the 1790s,[23] and can be attributed to the intensity of the duels between military and civilian principals. As this implies, duels between civilians, like duels between military, tended to be less sanguinary, though there are numerous exceptions. For example, when William B——s of County Londonderry met Mr B——e of Bordeaux 'in consequence of a dispute at the theatre' at Sandymount in Dublin in 1802, the two principals, having exchanged the regulation four shots and disregarded the appeals of their seconds to desist, continued firing until both were hit. Neither was seriously hurt, and while this was true of many injuries inflicted in similar circumstances,[24] not everyone was so lucky. Many suffered severe life-impairing wounds to the groin, chest, thigh and arms, some of which resulted in fatalities and more of which would have done so but for the increased presence of surgeons on the duelling field.[25]

Few of those who pursued affairs of honour in the early nineteenth century were from the nobility. Excepting the Marquis of Ely, who fired in the air rather than at his opponent, and Lord Massereene, who challenged Joseph Macartney in June 1804 but who was prevented from fighting by the intervention of magistrates, no peers and remarkably few distinguished commoners had recourse to weapons to avenge insult in the first decade of the new century. George Nixon of Nixonhall, D'Arcy Mahon of Cloon, John Spotswood of Valentia, John Hayes of Kenna, County Kerry, George Peacocke Comyn of Clare, Jeffrey Brownrigg of County Limerick and Robert Wrixon of Mallow were among the most eminent; all owned some land, but few possessed large estates, and none were of the status or stature of, say, Henry Grattan or John Hely-Hutchinson.[26]

The growing disinclination of gentlemen to duel was replicated by other social groups. Despite their reputation, lawyers were involved in few duels; so too were students and members of the middle class (Table 5.1).[27] There were occasional incidents like that reported in 1803 involving two 'shop boys belonging to woollen drapers' who exchanged shots in the Phoenix Park. One of the participants was injured in this instance. Three years later, when Rogers and Long, two clerks in a Dublin office, met at Blackrock, one died and one was seriously wounded.[28] However, these were exceptional. It was more commonplace for differences among individuals from this and lower social groups to be resolved by fisticuffs.[29]

The law and duelling in the early nineteenth century

The continued disposition of individuals from so many walks of life to endanger their lives by duelling distressed the steadily appreciating number of critics of the code of honour in early nineteenth-century Ireland. Occasionally the Dublin press appended observations critical of the code of honour to duelling reports, but neither this, specific commentaries urging sterner action (execution, immolation, exclusion from public office) against duellists, nor proposals for the compulsary arbitration of disputes by means of a court of honour elicited a response from those in power.[30]

As we have established in the instance of members of the military, judges and juries were generally well-inclined towards the defendant in duelling cases, but there was growing support for the view that the law allowed young men an undesirable measure of latitude,[31] and the early nineteenth century witnessed a palpable hardening in the resolve of the legal authorities towards duelling. This change in attitude was clearly signalled when Judge Robert Day, whom Daniel O'Connell deemed '*a mass of corruption*', followed the English legal practice of jailing those prosecuted for offering challenges by sentencing Nicholas Connolly Hussey of Dingle, in 1804, to six months in prison and a £100 fine for 'posting' Patrick Moriarty of Killarney, a medical doctor with whom he was in dispute over a payment. Daniel O'Connell, who knew Hussey, thought the sentence unjust,[32] but similar judgments had been handed down in a number of recent cases. In March 1802 Mansergh, an ill-mannered and none too brave 'half-mounted' gentlemen from County Tipperary,[33] was sentenced to a fortnight's imprisonment and a five-mark fine by the Dublin recorder's court for attempting to provoke Michael Dunlop to duel. In May of the same year a Mr Harman received a prison sentence of six months for sending a challenge to a Mr Russborough,[34] while on the same day that he sentenced Connolly Hussey, Judge Day condemned Robert Potter to three months imprisonment and to pay a fine of one mark for endeavouring to provoke Thomas Judkin Fitzgerald to challenge him because of his anger at Fitzgerald's impugning his loyalty in 1798.[35] Moreover, judges like Day showed less and less hesitation in letting it be known that they took a dim view of duelling and those who practised it. In his charge to the grand jury in the Connolly Hussey case, Day was harshly critical of the defendant, whom he likened to 'an unprincipled half-gentleman, [a] profligate brawler, who for want of worthier means resolves to *fight* himself into notice'. As far as he was concerned, 'a greater nuisance was never inflicted on society than a duellist, and . . . he best deserves the name and char[acte]r of a gentleman who is not prone to take offence and never means to give it'.[36] Day's forthright condemnation attests to the wish of some judges to commit the legal system into taking a more active stand against duelling, However, the absence of reports of further cases of this kind would indicate that only a small proportion of those who received challenges were prepared to have recourse to the law rather than to their pistols. This effectively transferred the onus for combating duellists to local sheriffs and magistrates.

By the beginning of the nineteenth century it was established practice for the authorities to intervene when possible to prevent duels taking place. This tendency was strengthened appreciably in 1802 when, following a number of incidents in which the intervention of the authorities prevented challenges developing into duels, the county sheriff of Dublin was fined £100 at the spring assizes for releasing an individual who had confessed to an 'alleged murder in a duel'.[37] Galvanised by this, magistrates, sheriffs and justices of the peace in Dublin county and city redoubled their efforts to prevent threatened duels proceeding to term.[38] Magistrates elsewhere were also more active, and this seems to have given confidence to some individuals disinclined to accept challenges, as there was a rise in the number of instances towards the end of the first decade of the nineteenth century in which gentlemen negated the bellicose intentions of their opponents by lodging an 'information' with the courts which generally resulted in the challenger being bound to keep the peace.[39] The greater readiness of gentlemen as well as magistrates, sheriffs and justices of the peace to use such means to prevent duels provides further evidence of the rise in the level of oppositon to the code of honour. As ever, the key was the judiciary, and the courts offered conflicting signals.

The powers available to the law to combat duelling were displayed to the public particularly vividly in 1808 by two highly publicised court cases involving Judge Edward Mayne of the Court of Common Pleas. The first concerned William Hammond, 'a gentleman of respectability and fortune in County Clare', who fired the shot in the duel at Sixmilebridge on 23 January 1808 in which William Foley of Shepperton was fatally wounded. The duel was conducted in a fair and honourable manner, and the jury had no hesitation in returning a verdict of 'guilty of manslaughter in his own defence' when the case came for trial at the County Clare assizes. In the normal course of events, this would have resulted in the defendant being set at liberty, but Judge Mayne was not prepared to allow this. He sent the jury back 'with a recommendation to find a verdict of manslaughter generally or to alter the word manslaughter to homicide'. The jury refused to heed his advice. Despite this, Judge Mayne sentenced Hammond to twelve months' imprisonment and to be burnt in the hand. Hammond was appalled by this prospect, but when he appealed the case to the Court of King's Bench, it declined to reverse Mayne's sentence. Hammond did secure an early release, but he died shortly afterwards in another duel.[40]

Edward Mayne was the most inveterately anti-duelling member of the Irish judicial bench in the early nineteenth century. His hostility to the code of honour derived from his strong religious belief. He was, J. E. Walsh observed, 'a serious solemn man and a rigid moralist',[41] and he displayed this side of his personality once again a few months later when Major Alexander Campbell was brought for trial for the murder in a duel on 23 June 1807 of Captain Alexander Boyd of the 21st Regiment of Foot. The *casus belli* in this instance was Captain Boyd's observation at dinner that while on parade Campbell had issued an instruction incorrectly 'according to the king's order'. Campbell had been reprimanded by General Kerr for the same reason earlier in the day, and he interpreted Boyd's comment as a grievous insult. He was so angered that he left the company for his apartment where he had left his pistols. On his return to the garrison mess, he challenged Boyd to a duel and insisted they settle the matter there and then. Boyd initially refused, but Campbell was so persistent that he reluctantly accompanied him to an inner mess room where they exchanged shots in the absence of seconds or other witnesses at a distance of no more than seven yards. Boyd was mortally wounded, but on his death-bed agreed with the importunate Campbell, who came to him in search of exculpation, that the duel was 'fair'. However, his exoneration was not unconditional; he also pronounced: 'Campbell, you are a bad man —— you hurried me.' Boyd died shortly afterwards, and, after a number of months in hiding, Campbell surrendered himself for trial at the County Armagh summer assizes before Judge Mayne.

The case against Campbell was strong but not overwhelming. Boyd, the prosecution contended, was the victim of an act of aggression: he was 'forced to accept a challenge . . . on a most frivolous disagreement; he [wa]s refused the intervention of friends, and hurried to the field of slaughter. The killing [wa]s perpetrated without witnesses', and the dying man had 'denie[d] that all was fair'. If Campbell was acquitted on the grounds that what he did was within the code of honour, the prosecution concluded, it 'must produce daily and hourly murder'. This was not a compelling argument given the pattern in previous cases of this nature, but the defence had nothing to counter the stream of witnesses who affirmed the prosecution's interpretation of events. Instead Campbell's counsel concentrated its efforts on demonstrating that he was a man of honour and good character. This did not impress Judge Mayne, who pointedly left it to the jury to decide by declining to defend the code of honour or to appeal for the jurors' sympathies, as many of his colleagues did in similar circumstances when they wanted the defendant acquitted. The jury evidently shared his outlook, because they returned a guilty verdict with a recommendation of 'mercy on the score of character only'. Judge Mayne was unimpressed; he pronounced the death sentence and ordered that Campbell should be hanged.[42]

This was an unexpected outcome, but it was widely anticipated that a pardon would be forthcoming. Indeed, the grand jury of County Armagh petitioned the Lord Lieutenant, the Duke of Richmond, to commute Campbell's sentence; but Judge Mayne undermined their appeals by refusing to recommend Campbell as a fit subject for mercy. The execution of the sentence was delayed to allow the defendant to petition the king; but despite an appeal from Mrs Campbell and a personal plea to the Prince of Wales from Lord Moira, the sentence stood, and Campbell was executed on 24 August 1808 before a 'vast crowd'.[43]

The refusal of Judge Mayne to support the pleas for clemency in the case of Alexander Campbell is but the most dramatic indication of the increasing hostility of elements of the judicial bench towards duelling and duellists in the early nineteenth century. It was manifested also in the tendency of lawyers and judges to go to greater lengths than hitherto to spell out explicitly the distinctions between homicide, manslaughter and murder in court in an attempt to persuade juries that in cases of 'provocation' and 'passion', manslaughter verdicts were not appropriate. 'The law is made under the contemplation of human infirmity and not for the shelter of demoniac fury,' the prosecution argued pertinently during the trial of Alexander Campbell in 1808. The defenders of duelling, by contrast, emphasised the imperatives of the code of honour. 'Its rigid maintenance is of much importance,' Campbell's counsel maintained; 'any violation of it, if passively suffered, [is] attended with . . . serious evils, . . . the loss of reputation and the consequent exclusion from the society of honourable men.'[44]

The traditional defence of the code of honour articulated by Major Campbell's counsel in 1808 carried visibly less weight with judges and juries in the early nineteenth century than it had done formerly. This was further demonstrated in 1810 when two attornies, Cornelius O'Brien and Cornelius McDonagh, his second, were tried for the murder of Francis Drew, another attorney, at the Trim assizes in August. As was made clear in court, Drew was the aggressor. He first accused O'Brien of improper conduct and, when O'Brien responded in kind, provided the *casus belli* by describing his antagonist as a liar. The two men were bound over when they undertook to resolve the matter with pistols at Bray in County Wicklow, but undaunted they travelled to County Meath and embarked on another encounter which, Drew's second acknowledged, was conducted impeccably. The judge and jury were impressed by this, but when the jury returned a verdict of guilty of manslaughter, Judge William Cusack Smith of the Court of Exchequer declined to encourage them, as sympathetic judges frequently did, to return a 'not guilty' verdict or to release O'Brien. Instead he discoursed at some length on the evils of duelling and duellists, whom he termed 'a tribe of pests', and sentenced the defendant to six months in prison because this was not his first duel. In its own way, this was almost as significant a penalty as the sentence of death imposed on Alexander Campbell until Judge Cusack Smith undermined its impact by commuting the sentence to one week in response to an emotional plea for clemency by O'Brien.[45]

The verdict in this case, and in that of Alexander Campbell, influenced public behaviour. Contemporaries observed a diminution in adherence to the code of honour and a contraction in the level of duelling in the early years of the nineteenth century. When Lord Teignmouth was a guest of Charles Grant, the Irish Chief Secretary, in the winter of 1818–19, he observed that the 'Fifteen Acres' in the Phoenix Park was no longer used for duelling.[46] This was a recent development. The Park played host to at least eleven encounters in the second half of 1790s, but it had declined rapidly as a favoured duelling spot in the new century. Duelling within the environs of the city of Dublin also declined in absolute terms during this period as duellists opted for less predictable locations in Sandymount, Blackrock and Drumcondra to minimise the likelihood of the authorities interrupting or apprehending them (Table 5.3).

The gradual physical marginalisation of duelling to which these changes in location bear witness provides a further perspective on the impact of anti-duelling sentiment in early nineteenth-century Dublin. The situation was different elsewhere. Opinion in Munster, for example, was less influenced by anti-duelling argument, and this partly accounts for the emergence of this province as the main regional bastion of the code of honour in the kingdom at this time (Table 5.2).

The emergence of Munster as the main duelling region in the country in the early nineteenth century was not lost on the judiciary, and they did not mask their disapproval as the case of Rowan Cashell, a lawyer connected with the Ventry family who got involved in an altercation over a bet with eighteen-year-old Henry Arthur O'Connor of Causeway, County Kerry, attests. Cashell's conduct was provocative, and that of his antagonist little better; but when they finally met on the duelling field at Ballyseedy, Cashell dispatched his opponent with his first shot. There were allegations of 'unfairness' from O'Connor's family, but they were not well founded and the jury was not persuaded, for it returned a 'not guilty' verdict. This was too commonplace a result to deserve special attention, but the case was well publicised and Judge Robert Day availed of the opportunity of his charge to the jury to deprecate the custom of duelling in its new heartland, and his address to the defendant to advise him to avoid 'all such places and societies' as lent themselves to quarrels.[47]

As well as their own unease, the preparedness of judges to penalise those involved in duels and to impose sentences of up to eighteen months and orders demanding substantial sureties from individuals who issued challenges[48] was a response to the closer public scrutiny of their actions in cases of this nature in the early nineteenth century.[49] This was a new development, and it partly derived from public dissatisfaction with the judgments handed down in a number of celebrated cases in which the law was seen to countenance if not to encourage duelling. The most notorious involved two soldiers, James MacNamara, a captain in the Royal Navy who had earned a reputation as a brave sailor and an intrepid duellist when he was stationed at Cork, and Lieutenant-Colonel Robert Montgomery of the 9th Regiment of Foot, who was the son of the Irish baronet Sir Robert Montgomery. The cause of the duel was a trivial dispute that arose when their dogs quarrelled in Hyde Park on 6 April 1803. Neither man was prepared to give quarter, and they resolved, as a consequence, to settle their difference with pistols on nearby Primrose Hill. The duel was fought fairly, but in the exchange of shots Montgomery was killed and MacNamara wounded. This was not especially unusual, but when the cause of the encounter became public knowledge, the press gave it extensive coverage, most of it critical. This excited enormous public interest in MacNamara's trial, which followed on 22 April. The proponents as well as the opponents of duelling were fully aware of the importance of the outcome, as the number and eminence of the naval officers (Lords Hood, Nelson, Hotham and Minto, Sir Hyde Parker and Sir Thomas Trowbridge among many others) that provided character testimonies on MacNamara's behalf indicates. MacNamara too rose to the occasion, and his address to the jury was as powerful a defence of the code of honour as was heard in an English or Irish courtroom in the early nineteenth century. Addressing the jury from a litter because he had not fully recovered from his injuries, MacNamara eloquently defended his actions as the only option open to a soldier:

> I am a captain in the British Navy . . . To maintain my character in that station, I must be respected. When called upon to lead others into honourable dangers, I must not be supposed to be a man who had sought safety by submitting to what custom has taught others to consider a disgrace.

This was reason enough for the jurors. Their martial sensibilities heightened by the ongoing war with France, they were so eager to acquit the defendant that they returned a 'not guilty' verdict, though this was procedurally incorrect because MacNamara had admitted to manslaughter.[50]

The Montgomery–MacNamara encounter and a host of other well-known and not so well-known early nineteenth-century foreign and domestic duels (Hamilton–Burr, Burdett–Paulett, Falkland–Powells, Paget–Cadogan, Castlereagh–Canning, and so on) were extensively reported in the Irish press, which seemed to possess an insatiable appetite for such events.[51] Ireland also produced its share of celebrated cases during these years. In a well-publicised trial in 1805 Richard Rochford was found not guilty of the murder of Richard Castles in a duel in August 1789 when he was a student at Trinity College, though he had not taken his place at the distance measured by the seconds.[52] However, interest in this trial was modest compared with that of William Congreve Alcock for the murder of John Colclough at Wexford assizes in 1808, which attracted onlookers from all parts of the country. More importantly, it indicated that, recent judgments notwithstanding, the courts could not yet be relied upon to take a consistent anti-duelling stance.[53]

As already noted, political and electoral rivalries continued to serve as one of the most common cause of challenges in the late eighteenth century. The total number of duels attributable to political differences fell in absolute terms as a result of the changed configuration of Irish politics following the abolition of the Irish parliament, but intense electoral rivalries continued to prompt recourse to arms (Table 3.9). The most hotly contested constituency in the early nineteenth century was County Wexford, which provided the cause for duels between John Tottenham and John Colclough in 1801 and between the Marquis of Ely and Mr L—— in 1806.[54] Nobody was killed in either of these encounters, but in 1807 when the electorate of County Wexford was called upon to choose new representatives for the fifth time in seven years, there were three more duels. The most infamous involved the Tory candidate, William Congreve Alcock of Wilton, County Wexford, who was M.P. for Waterford city between 1801 and 1803, and his opponent John Colclough of Tintern Abbey, who had been returned unopposed for County Wexford in the 1806 general election but who had shown signs of weakness in the face of 'personal and insulting' criticism in a by-election earlier that year.[55]

The contest in 1807 pitched Colclough and his running mate, Richard Brinsley Sheridan, who had the support of 'the Catholics and liberal Protestants', against William Alcock and his running mate, Abel Ram, who were backed 'by the ascendancy party', which was determined to regain control of a constituency they had lost the previous year. The intensity of their rivalry led to much ill-feeling, and it spilled over when Alcock accused Colclough of 'interfering' with the freeholders on the estate of Mrs Cholmondeley, whom he (Alcock) believed had been promised to him. This was not an issue on which compromise was possible, as Alcock needed the votes of freeholders on estates like that of Mrs Cholmondeley if he was to reverse the outcome of 1806, and this is why he and his supporters pursued the campaign 'with a zeal bordering on fury'.

During the trial that followed the encounter that ensued from the above dispute, in which Colclough was killed by Alcock's first shot, the Colclough family's counsel (Jonah Barrington) accused the Alcock camp of orchestrating a premeditated 'personal attack' in order to ensure victory for the ascendancy interest over the growing liberal interest whose natural constituency was the large number of Catholic freeholders in the county.[56] There was some substance to this charge in so far as Mrs Cholmondeley's tenants' preference was to vote for Colclough. Moreover, Alcock's behaviour was not above question. He did not present his challenge until his opponent refused 'to hand over the votes', and when he did present it, he did so in a quite gratuitously aggressive manner. In addition, the duel was not fought strictly within the rules. The principals did not wait the recommended time between the issuing of the challenge and the fighting of the duel; Alcock wore spectacles; and his seconds declined all suggestions of mediation. Strictly speaking, it was not within the rules of duelling to wear spectacles or any other aid during an encounter, and Barrington contrived to ensure that his witnesses made much of this fact during the trial. However, their testimony and the failure of Alcock's second to accede to mediation were negated by Colclough's failure to show any inclination to delay the encounter when the challenge was issued because of the imputation of cowardice arising out of his conduct during the 1806 by-election.[57]

Because of its political implications, the attitude of the trial judge, Sir William Cusack Smith, was vital to the outcome of the trial, and Cusack Smith, a confirmed Tory, was determined that the verdict would favour Alcock. In what Judge Robert Day, who was present, deemed 'a most ingenious and elegant charge', Cusack Smith placed little emphasis on the prosecution's allegation of premeditation and the inappropriateness of the defendant's wearing spectacles. Instead he accused the Colclough interest of attempting to make the law 'an engine of private resentment or political revenge' by pursuing the issue to trial, and discoursed at length on the tension between the law and the code of honour. He was in no doubt but that the latter deserved precedence on this occasion. And in one of the most remarkable charges delivered by an Irish judge in a duelling case, he employed the defence successfully used by Alexander MacNamara five years previously to make it clear to the jury that an acquittal was the only appropriate verdict:

> If an officer at the head of his regiment be called a coward, and a scoundrel, and instead of cutting the offender down, challenge[s] and kill[s] him in a duel, he is a murderer by law; and if you are bound to find the prisoner Alcock guilty you will be equally obliged to return a verdict of conviction against a gallant officer under the circumstances which I have described. Yet on the other hand, the military punishment and intolerable disgrace which must inevitably follow from his submitting to the affront, it cannot be necessary for me to dwell upon. If an aged, an infirm and beloved and respectable parent be insulted and reviled, or even struck and beaten in the presence of a son, and this latter happen to kill the assailant in a duel, the transaction will be murder; and if you cannot acquit the prisoner, you could not acquit the child. If a husband find his wife in the embraces of another and kill him unarmed and unresisting this is manslaughter of the lowest and most venial kind. But if, giving the adulterer further time for preparation and a fairer chance for life, he put arms in his hands, and meets and kills him in a duel, the offence altering its character, becomes at once murder, and if you are bound to convict the prisoner here, you would be also bound to a conviction in the case which I have supposed. Not because in morals the criminality is equal, but because both offences are murder in the eye of the law. But let me ask of your consciences and your hearts as men, could you convict the officer, the husband or the son?

The partisan jury assembled to try Alcock had no difficulty in accepting this interpretation of events. They arrived at the verdict Judge Cusack Smith desired 'in one moment', and William Alcock was set at liberty.[58]

Judge Robert Day commented approvingly in his diary on the way Baron Cusack Smith manipulated the jury, because he too believed acquittal was the most appropriate verdict in this case. 'No judge in the Un[ited] K[ingdo]m', he observed, 'probably could have conducted the charge w[i]th such address as the Baron who without compromising the law yet flung out such grounds by insinuations as quieted their consciences touching the pious perjury w[hi]ch they were predetermined to commit.' However, Day, who had led the way in punishing those who offered challenges in the early years of the century and was to do so again in 1809, was disturbed by the ease with which Irish judges 'enter into the chivalrous temper of their country' and 'consider the cause of a duellist as an exception in the law of murder'.[59] Day had cause to be concerned. The judgment in the Alcock case all but negated the judgment in the Boyd–Campbell case. It also reflected poorly on the judicial bench because it revealed that it was as ambivalent as society at large on the issue of duelling. There were, it is true, a number of judges prepared to take a firm anti-duelling stance, but there were others (perhaps a majority) for whom 'the law of opinion' took precedence.[60] And as long as the legal establishment remained ambivalent, it was inevitable that there would be judges less skilled and knowledgeable than he in matters of law who would follow the example of Judge Cusack Smith. Thus when Thomas and John Fenton were tried in March 1816 for the murder of John Hillas, a Sligo magistrate, in a duel, Judge William Fletcher of the Court of Common Pleas ensured a 'not guilty' verdict by maintaining in his charge to the jury that though 'the law says the killing of a man in a duel is murder . . . I tell you at the same time, a fairer duel than this I never heard of in the course of my life'.[61]

The changing nature of duelling in the early nineteenth century

The ambivalence of the public as well as of the judiciary towards duelling in Ireland in the early nineteenth century reflected a society in transition. At one level, old patterns of deference were breaking down, as the changing nature of the relationship between landlord and tenant highlighted by two duelling cases attests. In 1797 when Robert Gore was tried for the murder of the Earl of Meath, counsel for the Meath family, William Saurin, maintained that a tenant owed it to his landlord to submit to his wishes: 'The tenant that does not reserve to himself power to serve the landlord under who he derives the whole of his property, is in my mind ungrateful and unprincipled, and he who solicits him to resign that essential reservation is, I think, extremely INDELICATE.'[62] A decade later, when William Congreve Alcock called out John Colclough for canvassing tenantry he believed were committed by their landlord to him but who wished to vote for his opponents, Jonah Barrington described his actions as based upon 'a principle founded upon tyranny . . . an open declaration of war against law and constitution, a violation of the first rights of freeman'.[63] Such conflicting visions of the landlord–tenant relationship could coexist side by side, but in early nineteenth-century Ireland the influence of the egalitarian ideas advanced by the French Revolution and the re-emergence of the demographically dominant Catholic population as a political force ensured that the pressure for change in society came from those whose vision of the future was democratic rather than aristocratic.[64] This had enormous implications for the landed elite which had long dominated Irish society and for the code of honour they desired to uphold and make respectable.

In the short term, the impact on duelling of the embarkation by Irish society on the journey that saw it abandon *ancien régime* for increasingly egalitarian democratic values was ambiguous. On the one hand, it led to a reduction in the number of duels fought, owing to the dilution in the intensity with which people observed the values of the code of honour; on the other, it provided lots of opportunity for duels between those in power and those seeking access to the political system, as the acrimonious nature of electoral politics in County Wexford amply attests.[65] Travellers' testimonies do not always provide a reliable guide to the pattern and nature of duelling in Irish history, but it is noteworthy that early nineteenth-century visitors as diverse as Sir John Carr and Lord Teignmouth concluded that duelling was in decline.[66] Moreover, they did so in spite of the fact that Irishmen abroad, such as Thomas Moore, helped to sustain the image of Ireland as a hotbed of duelling by their involvement in well-publicised encounters, which provided ammunition for satirists like Edward du Bois to perpetuate the stereotype of Irish gentlemen as incorrigible duellists.[67] Domestically, the most divisive issue in early nineteenth-century Irish politics was the struggle of the Catholic masses for empowerment in the face of resistance from the bulk of the ruling Protestant elite. It was this that provided the impetus for many duels, and which also helped to ensure that observance of the code of honour became less socially and religiously exclusive in this period.

There was tangible change in the social and religious profile of those who duelled in the early nineteenth century, as its constituency came to centre in the lesser gentry and professions. The various arms of the legal profession, for example, demonstrated a continued enthusiasm for the code of honour, as the duelling activities of sheriffs, magistrates, clerks and justices of the peace bear ample witness.[68] Lawyers were even better inclined, as is emphasised by John Philpot Curran's wry comment that they should be sure to carry 'Wogden's case' with them at election time (Wogden was a celebrated pistol-maker).[69] Part of the reason for this was the emergence of attornies and barristers as a more visible and conscious interest in the early nineteenth century as the aristocracy and gentry gradually withdrew from public life, and advocacy became more professionalised following the introduction of assistant barristers in 1796 and crown prosecutors in 1801. This also produced more confrontations in court which led, irrevocably, to more challenges, though by no means as many as Barrington implies. Occasionally fatalities ensued. In February 1814, for example, Counsellor Hatchell died as a result of an encounter on Sandymount Strand with Marlay, an attorney from Molesworth Street.[70]

Of the major professions, the army remained the firmest bastion of the code of honour. There was a diminution in the number of recorded duels involving members of the armed forces in the 1810s,[71] but the authorities remained unwilling to resort to stern sanction to eradicate it completely. The army's greatest general, the Duke of Wellington, disapproved of the practice, but he was not prepared to take action against those who duelled if he perceived that the honour and character of Britain and its army would be diminished. The Duke of Richmond took a sterner view when he was Lord Lieutenant of Ireland between 1807 and 1813; his refusal to commute the death sentence imposed on Alexander Campbell in 1808 was widely interpreted as an important signal, but he did little else to combat duelling.[72]

Ultimately the army authorities were to hasten the eradication of duelling from the armed forces by providing for the court martial of duellists in the ranks.[73] But that did not take place until it was firmly established that the social status of those who appealed to arms in the name of the code of honour had declined irrevocably. This was in train, but it had still some way to go, as the greatest in the land were still prepared to appeal to their weapons to defend their honour, as Lord Castlereagh and George Canning demonstrated in 1809, and as Lord Dunraven almost did in the 1810s. Aspirant and incumbent M.P.s did so with greater regularity, particularly at election times, as the experiences of Alcock and Colclough (Wexford, 1807), Richard Martin and Denis Bowes Daly (Galway, 1815), Christopher Hely-Hutchinson and Patrick W. Callaghan (Cork, 1820) all manifest.[74] Sometimes a difference of opinion in the House of Commons threatened to spark off an encounter, as happened in April 1813 when

William Fitzgerald, M.P. for Ennis, and General Montague Mathew, M.P. for County Tipperary, were obliged by Speaker Abbot to promise that they would not have recourse to arms following a disagreement on the Irish estimates,[75] but these were the exceptions. Most duellists in the early nineteenth century were 'young gentlemen' of short tempers and small fortunes. Daniel O'Connell's cousin Alexander McCarthy of Kilgarvan, County Kerry, who was killed in a duel by John Raymond of Tralee in 1817, fits this definition, as do the two ill-circumstanced young hotheads named Lalor and Dumes who were fined £1,000 for ignoring Baron Cusack Smith's instruction not to prosecute their quarrel a short time later.[76]

Part of the explanation for the decline in the social status of duellists is provided by the enthusiastic embrace of the code of honour by the Catholic gentry. Duelling was contrary to the law of the Catholic Church, and some ecclesiastics, like Archbishop Bray of Cashel, did incorporate a condemnation of the practice into their diocesan statutes, but the search for status and the desire to emulate Protestants proved more compelling to many Catholics.[77] The repeal of the penal laws, specifically the restriction on the carrying of arms in 1793, once again opened the code of honour to the Catholic gentry. They had manifested no moral or religious antipathy to the practice when abroad during the eighteenth century, and, freed of restrictions, they embraced it eagerly.[78] The palpable improvement in their economic fortunes in the second half of the eighteenth century facilitated this, and before the century was over some Catholics were demonstrating as much enthusiasm for duelling as their more experienced Protestant neighbours.[79] Their political emergence in the early nineteenth century provided a further stimulus and the occasion for a series of celebrated duels in which members of the Catholic leadership, most notably Daniel O'Connell, were called upon repeatedly to prove their bravery under fire.

Daniel O'Connell was involved in a substantial number of duelling incidents during his lifetime. His first recorded appeal to the code of honour took place in 1794 when he was studying law in England, and he challenged Douglas Thompson, the son of a brewer, to a duel over a young woman.[80] No encounter ensued, but O'Connell was not persuaded by this good fortune to keep out of trouble. He invited a challenge in 1800 or 1801 when he struck his cousin John Sigerson with a cane in court. Once again he escaped having to exchange shots. A few years later he found himself arbitrating a quarrel between Walter Prendergast of Tralee and Edward Orpen of Clontogh in which several shots were fired without any injuries resulting. O'Connell believed Orpen was the aggressor in this encounter, and it disturbed him that 'so valuable a fellow' as Prendergast could be obliged to endanger his life by a social convention.[81] This later became a constant refrain in his thinking on duelling.

Meanwhile his own relentless manoeuvring within Catholic and legal circles made him plenty of enemies which almost culminated in confrontations on a number of occasions. In 1808 Charles O'Conor had to be dissuaded from presenting a challenge when O'Connell outmanoeuvred him at a Catholic Committee meeting, and he almost came to blows with H. D. Grady in Limerick in 1812.[82]

O'Connell was not the only Catholic leader to find that his heightened public and political profile made him vulnerable to disputes on matters of honour. In 1810 the urbane Denys Scully felt compelled to challenge Luke Plunkett of Portmarnock over a slighting reference that appeared in the *Evening Herald*, while his brother, Edmund Scully, emerged with 'much credit' as a consequence of his 'intrepidity and coolness' under fire when he exchanged shots with Nicholas Sadleir, one of candidate John Bagwell's agents, during the County Tipperary election some months later. Daniel O'Connell's brother John was less fortunate. He exchanged shots without effect with Maurice O'Connor, the provost of Tralee, in 1812, but a year later he was seriously wounded in an encounter with Richard Blennerhassett that flowed from a dispute over Catholic emancipation.[83]

Of course, not all duels involving Catholics were of political origin. One of O'Connell's correspondents, Peter McSwiney of Adrigole, County Cork, who was an experienced duellist, was obliged to go on the run in 1812 for killing a tithe proctor. And O'Connell himself was only prevented in 1813 from exchanging shots with a fellow Catholic lawyer, Counsellor Maurice Magrath of Cork, whom he challenged following a misunderstanding at Limerick courthouse, by the mediation of Nicholas Leader.[84] O'Connell's failure on this, as on previous occasions when his reputation was at stake, to fire his pistols in anger was not lost on his opponents, and questions were raised in hostile circles about his courage and, by extension, his honour. O'Connell ignored these taunts, but they left a mark, and his subsequent baiting of the Attorney General, William Saurin, during the Magee trial is probably not unconnected. His more aggressive handling of his confrontation with John D'Esterre in January 1815 was certainly influenced by the criticism of him that flowed from the Magrath incident.[85]

The ostensible cause of O'Connell's encounter with D'Esterre was his description of Dublin Corporation as 'beggarly' in the course of a speech in which he condemned that body for opposing Catholic emancipation. However, John D'Esterre, a provisions merchant and naval contractor on the brink of bankruptcy who was a member of the corporation, interpreted the remark as personal, and he challenged O'Connell on 26 January to justify his assertion. He may have anticipated that because of O'Connell's failure up to this to fire his pistols in anger in any of the affairs of honour in which he had been implicated, O'Connell would back down rather than fight, and that he would thereby acquire kudos in Protestant circles for exposing the Catholic champion as a coward. If so, he had seriously misjudged, for O'Connell not only accepted the challenge, but managed to make D'Esterre look bad in the public eye by publicly expressing his bemusement at his tardiness in naming the place where they should meet.

O'Connell's attempt to deflect criticism from himself by making it known that D'Esterre was responsible for the delay only achieved part of its purpose. Questions continued to be posed about his courage which he, 'the best abused man in the country', realised he had to answer if he and the cause he represented were not to suffer. Consequently, having evaded a clumsy attempt by D'Esterre and his ultra-Protestant allies to humiliate him by horse-whipping him at the Four Courts, he repulsed all last-minute efforts to effect a reconciliation. A mutually acceptable location was finally determined, and when the two principals raised their pistols in a field in County Kildare in the late afternoon on 1 February, O'Connell's ball was the only one that found its target; D'Esterre fell mortally wounded and died soon afterwards. This gave O'Connell victory in an encounter that was widely perceived as symbolic of the larger Catholic–Protestant dispute over emancipation as well as a genuine test of O'Connell's courage. Although he had disabused those who had queried his courage and, in the process, 'laid low' an opponent whom his brother-in-law deemed 'the champion of intolerance and the beggarly Corporation of Dublin', O'Connell was ill at ease with the congratulations and applause that rained in on him. Even the Catholic Archbishop of Dublin, Daniel Murray, felt compelled to express his happiness at the outcome, though officially duelling was designated a reserved sin by his church.[86] O'Connell had yet to realise that his emergence as the leader of the Catholic population (and his triumph over D'Esterre was an important milestone on that road) involved him assuming the mantle of Catholic champion; his followers wanted him to lead them to triumph over their Protestant opponents on the duelling field as well as on the hustings and whatever other venue or location that arose.[87]

Having overcome the threat posed to his reputation and, by extension, to his standing as the leading Catholic spokesman by John D'Esterre, O'Connell was immediately presented with another by the Chief Secretary, Robert Peel. O'Connell and Peel actively disliked each other. O'Connell was wont to belittle the Chief Secretary as 'Orange Peel', and if this was both imprecise and unfair, it accurately reflected Catholic perceptions of Peel's stance on the key question of Catholic emancipation. Indeed, it was a debate on this very subject in the House of Commons on 30 May 1815, during which Peel offered some ostensibly innocent criticism of O'Connell's stance on emancipation, that plunged these champions of the Catholic and Protestant interests into a complex affair that threatened to bring ruin or death to one or both.

The affair can be said to have commenced when O'Connell, interpreting Peel's remarks as a personal affront, maintained at Catholic Board meetings in July and August that Peel was too prudent to reiterate the remarks he made in parliament publicly and to his face. In the sensitive world of the code of honour, this was virtually equivalent to a challenge, and Peel, who could not tolerate any 'reflection on his courage or integrity', was unable to ignore it. He directed Sir Charles Saxton, a former Irish Under-Secretary, to seek out O'Connell and to inform him of his readiness to avow publicly what he had said in parliament. Despite this, an amicable settlement was still possible, as neither O'Connell nor Peel was eager to push matters to an exchange of shots, but Saxton and other ultra-Protestants at Dublin Castle were confident that they could manipulate the incident to heap humiliation on O'Connell's head and thereby to rid themselves of their most remorseless and outspoken critic. Their aim was to replicate the Magrath incident of 1813, but O'Connell had learned this lesson well and he was too wily to fall for such an obvious ploy. Thus when Saxton published a select version of events in an attempt to expose O'Connell as a coward, he countered with a release of his own in which he alleged that Peel was afraid to settle the dispute like a gentleman (i.e. with pistols).

By now matters had proceeded too far for either side to agree to mediation. Everything seemed set fair for confrontation till Mary O'Connell, terrified by the prospect of losing her beloved husband, intervened and informed the sheriff of Dublin, who responded by placing O'Connell under house arrest. Peel was able to avoid the same fate by going into hiding. More importantly, from the point of view of the macho world of male honour which determined public attitude on such matters, he had seized the initiative in the affair, and he pressed home his advantage by signalling his readiness to travel to Ostend to settle the matter outside British and Irish legal jurisdiction. O'Connell had little choice but to agree. The intervention of his wife had made him look foolish in the public eye, and he was the subject of a series of hostile pasquinades which imputed that he was sheltering behind his wife's skirts. In order to free himself to travel to Ostend, he was forced to engage in an elaborate and time-consuming charade which involved him bringing his wife and family to Kerry. The delay reflected badly on O'Connell. No less importantly, it gave the Home Office time to take counter-measures. Officials were determined that there should not be a duel, and they deployed formidable resources to preventing O'Connell reaching Belgium. They intercepted him *en route* to Calais and effectively ensured that there would be no encounter by making it clear that he would be prosecuted with the full rigour of the law if he proceeded with the affair and executed if found guilty of killing Peel. O'Connell accepted that this represented the end of the affair that had caused him so much grief. The penalty if he pressed on outweighed all possible advantage, and he made no attempt to prosecute the matter further.[88]

Daniel O'Connell emerged from this complex affair with honour intact and, more importantly from the point of view of his wife and followers, alive. However, he had not emerged unscathed. The whole affair was very trying personally as well as politically. He was acutely conscious that he could not be seen to show weakness if he aspired to be a political heavyweight. Henry Grattan junior, who was well schooled by his father in the importance of correct public image to a popular politician, pinpointed its significance when he observed *à propos* of Francis Burdett's failure to respond appropriately when his honour was impugned in the House of Commons in 1811 that it had 'cast a doubt on his courage, which in a leader of the people is fatal'.[89] Indeed, O'Connell was subject to strong criticism from within as well as from without his own ranks for his poor management of the affair with Peel. His decision to write to the press was deemed unwise, while the 'unfortunate' intervention of his wife was presented in a particularly negative light.[90] Peel, by contrast, had an easy time and his public image suffered little as a consequence. That said, O'Connell chose the better option by declining to prosecute the duel when the Home Office intervened. Had he and Peel met and Peel triumphed, it would have been interpreted as a victory for the Protestant opponents of Catholic emancipation which would have set back his political career (had he survived), and the cause of Catholic relief. On the other hand, had O'Connell won and killed his opponent in the process, his political prospects would also have been damaged because he would almost certainly have been prosecuted and, possibly, convicted as the English law authorities had promised. This was not a matter of little consequence. Just two years previously two Irish army officers, Lieutenants Edward McGuire and Daniel O'Brien, were sentenced to death at Hampshire assizes for ignoring an order to keep the peace by engaging in a duel with Lieutenant Blundell on the Isle of Wight. Both sentences were eventually commuted, but the increasingly hostile attitude of the courts to duelling was underlined in 1814 when W. H. Souper was sentenced to death at Winchester assizes for the murder of John Duterich in a duel.[91] O'Connell was able to avoid a possible similar date with destiny by his decision to observe discretion and caution following the intervention of the authorities; he emerged from the affair, as he had entered it, as the Champion of Irish Catholics and the *bête noir* of Protestants on both islands.

There was one positive result for O'Connell from his aborted affair with Peel. Because he was bound over to keep the peace in Britain as well as Ireland in 1815, O'Connell was effectively precluded from duelling for some time thereafter. He endeavoured, but failed, to have the recognisances imposed on him lifted in 1817, and this worked to his advantage in December of the same year when some characteristically scathing criticism of John Leslie Foster, the Tory Advocate General, prompted Foster to demand that he disavow the expressions or acknowledge they applied to him only as a public official. O'Connell initially declined to reply, but when Foster issued a challenge, he was placed in an awkward position. His decision to embrace Foster's distinction between the private and public roles concluded the affair and effectively signalled that O'Connell had freed himself of the constraints of the code of honour.[92] He was certainly less disposed to duel and less bound by the code of honour thereafter.[93] In this he reflected society at large.

Notes and References

1 Patrick Rogers, 'A Protestant pioneer of Catholic emancipation', *Down and Connor Diocesan Magazine*, vi (1934), pp. 14–22.

2 Sir Richard Musgrave, *Memoirs of the different rebellions in Ireland* (Dublin, 1801), p. 96; *F.J.*, 12 Nov. 1802.

3 *Authentic detail of an affair of honour between William Todd Jones Esq and Sir Richard Musgrave* (Dublin, 1802); Brian McDermott, ed., *The Catholic question in Ireland and England, 1798–1822: the papers of Denys Scully* (Dublin, 1988), pp. 52–3; *F.J.*, 1, 3 June 1802; *Annual Register*, xliv (1802), p. 411.

4 *F.J.*, 11 Sept. 1802; Edward Hay, *History of the insurrection of the County of Waterford*, A.D. *1798* (Dublin, 1803), appendix; idem, *Strictures: authentic detail of the extravagant and inconsistent conduct of Sir Richard Musgrave, baronet; with a full refutation of his slander against Edward Hay* [Dublin, 1803].

5 *F.J.*, 4 June 1807.

6 *F.J.*, 19 Jan., 1 July 1802; Hamilton, *The only approved guide*, pp. 197–8; Walsh, *Ireland sixty years ago*, p. 24; Patrick Tohill, 'The Diamond fight of 1795 and the resultant expulsions', *Seanchas Ardmhacha*, iii (1958), p. 25.

7 B. A. Kennedy, 'Light on a revolting duel fought in 1804', *Irish Sword*, iv (1959), pp. 136–8; Seán Ó Coindealbháin, 'The United Irishmen in County Cork, vii', *J.C.H.A.S*, 2nd series , lvii (1952), pp. 97–8; idem., 'John Swiney, the Cork United Irishman: his duel with Thomas Corbett', *J.C.H.A.S*, 2nd series, lx (1955), pp. 22–7; *F.J.*, 21 Feb. 1805.

8 *F.J.*, 15 Feb. 1803, 12 Oct., 30 Dec. 1807; Niall Brunciardi, *Haulbowline, Spike and Rocky Islands* (Fermoy, 1982), p. 18.

9 For examples see *F.J.*, 2, 23 July, 29 Sept. 1801, 13 May, 29, 31 July 1802, 14 June 1803, 22 Sept. 1804, 12 June, 17, 25 Sept. 1806, 7 Apr., 12 May, 7, 21 Aug., 30 Dec. 1807, 12 Apr. 1809, 13 Feb., 15 June 1810.

10 For examples see *F.J.*, 1 Aug. 1805, 17 Aug. 1806, 15 June 1810.

11 *F.J.*, 2 July 1801, 31 July, 23 Dec. 1802, 14 June 1803, 12 Sept. 1804, 12 June 1806, 31 July, 21 Aug. 1807, 12 Apr. 1809.

12 *F.J.*, 23 Dec. 1802, 22 Sept. 1804, 12 Mar. 1810; Carr, *The stranger in Ireland*, p. 241.

13 See *F.J.*, 23, 30 July, 29 Sept. 1801, 4 Sept. 1802, 14 June 1803, 2 Feb. 1804, 25 Sept. 1806.

14 *F.J.*, 2, 4 July 1801, 10 Nov. 1803; G. C. Bolton, *The passing of the Irish Act of Union* (Oxford, 1966), p. 111.

15 *F.J.*, 12 May, 30 Dec. 1807.

16 *D.E.P.*, 11 May 1802; *F.J.*, 13 May 1802.

17 *A report of the trial of Mr Joseph Kelly paymaster of the 32nd Regiment of Foot for the murder of Captain William Harrison of the same regiment before the Hon. Justice Mayne at the spring assizes for the county of Cork, Saturday 5 April 1806* (n.p., 1806).

18 Brunciardi, *Haulbowline* . . ., p. 18.

19 For examples see *F.J.*, 12 Apr., 19 Oct. 1802, 4 Aug. 1804, 17, 30 July, 13 Aug. 1808, 9 Oct. 1809, 24 Apr. 1810.

20 For examples see F.J., 31 Dec. 1805, 7 Apr. 1807.
21 *F.J.*, 19, 20 June 1806.
22 *F.J.*, 14 Jan. 1808.
23 Above, pp. 207–08.
24 For examples see *F.J.*, 7 June, 11, 17 Dec. 1802, 8 Feb., 7 June, 22 Oct. 1803, 23 Feb. 1810.
25 *F.J.*, 11 Dec. 1802.
26 Macartney to Macartney, 7 June 1804 (P.R.O.N.I., Macartney Papers, D562/18/66); *F.J.*, 19 Oct., 17 Dec. 1802, 7 June 1803, 7 Apr., 17 July 1807.
27 *F.J.*, 10 Mar., 19 May 1801, 15 July 1802.
28 *F.J.*, 5 Feb. 1803, 6 May 1806.
29 For examples see *F.J.*, 5 May 1803, 14 Jan 1810 .
30 Sir Thomas Bond, *Hints tending to increase the wealth and promote the peace and welfare of the Irish nation* (Dublin, 1803), pp. 18–9 (I wish to thank Dr Kevin Whelan for drawing this pamphlet to my attention); *F.J.*, 1 Jan., 7 Nov. 1805, 7 May 1806, 8 Mar. 1810.
31 McDermott, ed., *Scully Papers*, p. 61.
32 R.I.A., Sir Robert Day's charges delivered to the grand juries, ii, ff 241–5; Maurice O'Connell, ed., *The correspondence of Daniel O'Connell* (8 vols, Dublin and Belfast, 1973–80), i, 75–6, 126; *F.J.*, 16 Aug. 1804. For English practice see *Annual Register*, xliv (1805), p. 400; liv (1812), pp. 146–7.
33 In an encounter with Andy Ryan, Mansergh fled after he had fired two shots at Cashel in 1802 (N.L.I., Scully Papers, MS 27571, ff 313–14).
34 *F.J.*, 10 Mar., 14 May 1801.
35 R.I.A., Sir Robert Day's charges delivered to the grand juries, ii, 237–40.
36 Ibid., ff 241–5.
37 *F.J.*, 17, 22 April 1802.
38 *F.J.*, 7 June 1802, 17 Jan. 1804, 11, 12 Dec. 1810.
39 *F.J.*, 25 July 1809, 8, 16 Nov. 1810.
40 *F.J.*, 19 Jan., 24 May 1808; Guinness and Ryan, *Irish houses and castles*, p. 58.
41 Walsh, *Ireland sixty years ago*, pp. 30–31.
42 Ibid.; *The trial of Major Campbell for the murder of Captain Boyd in a duel on 23 June 1807 with the evidence in full, the charge of the judge and details of Major Campbell's last moments, execution, etc* (London, 1808), pp. 1–58; 'A correct and impartial report of the trial of Major Alexander Campbell, late of the 21st Regiment of Foot for shooting Captain Boyd . . . in a duel in Newry on 22 June 1807' (B.L., Add. MS 29736, ff 1–6); Mackay, *Extraordinary popular delusions*, pp. 686–8;'The condemned soldier', *Dublin University Magazine*, ii (1833), pp. 398–401; *Annual Register*, l (1808), pp. 80–82.
43 *The trial of Major Campbell*, pp. 58–62; Arthur Aspinall, ed., *The correspondence of George, Prince of Wales,1770–1812* (7 vols, London, 1964–70), vi, 300, vii, 46; Kiernan, *The duel*, pp. 123–4; *Dublin University Magazine*, ii (1833), p. 400; *Annual Register*, l (1808), pp. 88–90; Beckett to Campbell, Aug. 18108 (P.R.O., HO 100/48, f .143).
44 *The trial of Major Campbell*, pp. 7–8, 19–20.

45 *A full and accurate report of the tryal of Cornelius O'Brien and Cornelius McDonagh for the murder of Francis Drew Esq. at the late assizes of Trim held before the Hon. Sir William Cusack Smith Bart. . . . containing the very eloquent appeal made by Mr O'Brien to the court on his receiving sentence* (Dublin, 1810); *F.J.*, 23 Feb., 10 July, 30 Aug. 1810.

46 *F.J.*, 25 Aug. 1806; Teignmouth, *Reminiscences*, i, 168.

47 J. F. Fuller, ed., 'Trial of Rowan Cashell, gentleman, attorney for the wilful murder of Henry Arthur O'Connor late of Tralee . . .', *J.C.H.A.S.*, vii (1901), pp. 149–66; *Trial of Rowan Cashell . . . who stood indicted for the wilful murder of Henry Arthur O'Connor . . . in a duel on 7 August 1815, at the assizes held at Tralee on 26 March 1816 before the Hon. Mr Justice Day* (Cork, 1816); Gaughan, The Knights of Glin, pp. 80–81.

48 Hamilton, *The only approved guide*, p. 200.

49 See the 'Observations on the charge to the jury' in *Trial of Rowan Cashell*, pp. 20–28, and the remarks of Chief Baron Smith in which he defends the actions of judges in duelling cases (*F.J.*, 11 July 1810).

50 W. M. Medland and Charles Weobly, *A collection of remarkable and interesting trials* (2 vols, London, 1808), i, 52–64; *Report of the trial of an inquisition upon a verdict of manslaughter against Captain MacNamara for killing and slaying Colonel Robert Montgomery* (London, 1803); N. C. Macnamara, *The story of an Irish sept* (London, 1896), pp. 296–302; Greig, ed., *Farington diary*, ii, 200; Rayner and Cooke, *The complete Newgate calendar*, iv, 270–75; *F.J.*, 25 Aug. 1803; Mackay, *Extraordinary popular devulsions*, pp. 689–90.

51 *F.J.*, 3 Nov. 1803, 21, 23 Aug. 1804, 15 Jan. 1805, 27 Sept. 1806, 6, 11 May 1807, 6, 10 Mar., 8 June, 26 Sept., 4 Oct. 1809, 18 Oct., 9, 21 Nov. 1816; Vere Hunt Diary, 21 Sept. 1809; Theophilus Swift, *The challenge, in which a late conduct of Dr Dobbin's family is considered* (Dublin, 1811).

52 *F.J.*, 19 Feb. 1805; *A report of the trial of Richard Rochfort upon an indictment for the murder of Richard Castles in a duel* (Dublin, 1805).

53 Robert Day's diary, 1807–15, p. 5 (Beinecke Library, Osborn Collection).

54 *F.J.*, 20 Jan. 1801, 20 June 1806.

55 The others involved Edward Hay and Major John Devereux and Standish Loquay and Thomas McCord. In the latter, Loquay was wounded in the groin (*F.J.*, 2, 4 June 1807; Annual Register, xlix (1807), p. 448).

56 Kevin Whelan, 'Politicisation in County Wexford and the origins of the 1798 rebellion' in Hugh Gough and David Dickson, eds, *Ireland and the French Revolution* (Dublin, 1990), pp. 156–178; Ronald Thorne, ed., *The history of parliament: the House of Commons, 1790–1820* (5 vols, London, 1986), ii, 698–700; iii, 54–5, 481–2; Barrington, *Personal sketches*, pp. 310–06; *F.J.*, 2 June 1807.

57 William Ridgeway, *A report of the trial of William Congreve Alcock and Henry Derenzy on an indictment for the murder of John Colclough at Wexford assizes on 26 March 1808 before the Hon. Baron Smith* (Dublin, 1808), pp. 1–64; Barrington, *Personal Sketches*, i, 300–6; Thomas Cloney, *A personal narrative of . . . transactions in the County Wexford . . . during . . . 1798* (Dublin, 1832), pp. 170–76 (I wish to thank Dr Kevin Whelan for the latter reference); Kiernan, *The duel*, p. 209.

58 Ridgeway, *A report of the trial of William Congreve Alcock*, pp. 65–84; idem, *A correct report of the charge delivered at Wexford, March 28 1808, by the Honourable Baron Smith at the trial of William Congreve Alcock* . . . (Dublin, 1808), pp. 17, 19–20; *Dublin University Magazine*, 76(1850), pp. 40–41.
59 Robert Day's diary, 1807–15, pp. 5–6 (Beinecke Library, Osborn Collection); R.I.A., Sir Robert Day's charges delivered to grand juries, iii, 42–5.
60 *Dublin University Magazine*, xxvi (1850), p. 41ff.
61 McDonagh, *Irish life and character*, p. 34; *Annual Register*, lviii (1816), pp. 318–22.
62 *Report of the trial of Robert Gore*, p. 12.
63 Ridgeway, *A report of the trial of William Alcock*, p. 10.
64 See the essays of Dunne and Curtin in Gough and Dickson, eds, *Ireland and the French Revolution*, pp. 68–82, 139–55; P. J. Jupp, 'Irish parliamentary elections and the influence of the Catholic vote, 1801–1820', *Historical Journal*, x (1967), pp. 163–96; Vere Hunt Diary, 26 May 1813.
65 Vere Hunt Diary, 26 May 1813; above, pp. 237–9.
66 Carr, *The stranger in Ireland*, p. 231; Teignmouth, *Reminiscences*, i, 158.
67 Lord John Russell, ed., *Memoirs, journal and correspondence of Thomas Moore* (8 vols, London, 1853–6), i, 199f; Kiernan, *The duel*, p. 210; R. R. Madden, *Memoirs, chiefly autobiographical* (London, 1891), pp. 10–11; Greig, ed., *Farington diary*, v, 104–5; Edward du Bois, *My pocket book, or hints for a righte merrie and conceitede tour* (London, 1808), pp. 81–2; *F.J.*, 26 Aug. 1810.
68 Guinness and Ryan, *Irish houses and castles*, p. 58; Lady Gregory, ed., *Sir William Gregory, an autobiography* (London, 1894), pp. 13–14; Corr, 'Reminiscences', pp. 306, 308.
69 Hamilton, *The only approved guide*, pp. 222–3; Barrington, *Recollections*, p. 281.
70 G. A. Kelly, 'Duelling in eighteenth-century France', pp. 239–40; *F.J.*, 24 Apr., 20 May 1817; Wood-Martin, *Sligo*, iii, 320; *Annual Register*, lvi (1814), p. 13.
71 Kiernan, *The duel*, p. 191; Wood-Martin, *Sligo*, iii, 317–18; *F.J.*, 14 Aug. 1816, 19 Mar., 20 May, 16 Aug. 1817.
72 Anthony Powell, ed., *Barnard Letters, 1778–1824* (London, 1928), pp. 266–71; Hamilton, *The British code of the duel*, appendix, pp. vi–viii; Aspinall, ed., *Correspondence of George, Prince of Wales*, vi, 301.
73 Kiernan, *The duel*, pp. 186–7, 191.
74 Peter Dixon, *Canning* (London, 1976), pp. 135–7; Wendy Hinde, *George Canning* (London, 1973), pp. 226–8; *Annual Register*, li (1809), pp. 239, 504–8; A. P. W. Malcomson, *In pursuit of the heiress: aristocratic marriage in Ireland, 1760–1820* (Belfast, 1982), p. 35; Thorne, ed., *History of parliament*, iv, 565; C. J. F. MacCarthy, 'An antiquary's notebook', *J.C.H.A.S*, xcii (1987), p. 122. R. D. Browne, M.P. for County Mayo, was also involved in a duel (Corr, 'Reminiscences', p. 308).
75 *Diary and corresp. of Lord Colchester*, ii, 443.
76 *O'Connell corresp*, i, 237; *F.J.*, 15 Aug. 1817; *Annual Register*, lix (1817), pp. 68–9.
77 Burke, *Clonmel*, p. 157n.

78 Kiernan, *The duel*, pp. 210; above, pp. 46–7.
79 L. M. Cullen, 'Catholic social classes under the penal laws' in Whelan and Power, eds, *Endurance and emergence*, p. 70.
80 Oliver MacDonagh, *Daniel O'Connell: the hereditary bondsman* (London, 1988), pp. 36–8.
81 *O'Connell corresp.*, i, 123–5; MacDonagh, *The hereditary bondsman*, p. 83.
82 *O'Connell corresp.*, i, 288; ii, 256–7; Gerard O'Brien, 'Beginning of the veto controversy', *Journal of Ecclesiastical History*, xxxviii (1987), p. 85; McDermott, ed., *Scully Papers*, p. 339.
83 McDermott, ed., *Scully Papers*, pp. 234–8, 384, 401; *O'Connell corresp.*,i, 318–19; Gaughan, *The Knights of Glin*, p. 80.
84 *O'Connell corresp.*, i, 281, 337–9; MacDonagh, *The hereditary bondsman*, pp. 133–4.
85 *O'Connell corresp.*, i, 349–50; MacDonagh, *The hereditary bondsman*, pp. 133–4.
86 MacDonagh, *The hereditary bondsman*, pp. 133–8; MacDonagh, *Irish life and character*, pp. 37–8; *O'Connell corresp.*, ii, 3–11; viii, 186–7; *Annual Register*, lvi (1815), pp. 11–13.
87 See the comments of Prince Pückler-Muskau in Flora Brennan, ed., *Pückler's progress: the adventures of Prince Pückler-Muskau in England, Wales and Ireland, 1826–9* (London, 1987), p. 219.
88 Norman Gash, *Mr Secretary Peel* (London, 1961), pp. 162–7; idem, *Sir Robert Peel* (London, 1972), p. 187; MacDonagh, *The hereditary bondsman*, pp. 138–41; *O'Connell's corresp.*, ii, 61–71; McDermott, ed., *Scully Papers*, pp. 561–4.
89 Grattan to Grattan, 4 June 1811 (N.L.I., Grattan Papers, MS 2111). Henry senior possessed similar views (Grattan to McCan, [*c.* 1810] (P.R.O.N.I., Fitzwilliam (Langdale) Papers, Mic 71/1)).
90 MacDermott, ed., *Scully Papers*, pp. 561–2.
91 *Annual Register*, lv (1813), pp. 310–13; *Irish Farmer's Jn.*, 2 (1813–14), p. 395. I owe the latter reference to John McHugh.
92 *O'Connell corresp.*, ii, 145, 154–5, 168–9; MacDonagh, *The hereditary bondsman*, p. 163.
93 *O'Connell corresp.*, ii, 256.

7

'A Social Monster': the mid-nineteenth century

The readiness of Robert Peel and Daniel O'Connell — two of the most able politicians of their generation — to risk their lives over a few disputed remarks uttered in the heat of debate emphasises just how entrenched the code of honour remained in the value system of the ruling elite in Britain and Ireland in the early nineteenth century. The emergence from the 1780s of a progressively more weighty body of political, religious and legal opinion which opposed duelling indicated that the tide of public opinion was shifting, but it was not until the second quarter of the nineteenth century that the critics gained the initiative and public opinion came to accept that the eradication of duelling was in the best interest of society at large.

The rising tide of opposition

Although the courts continued to use their powers in the 1820s to prevent challenges being issued and duels being fought,[1] there was no sustained official campaign against the code of honour. As in so many other areas of opinion, Ireland was influenced by what happened in England, and the increased disposition of the Irish courts to use the law must be seen in the context of the emergence of a strong, sustained and coherent critique of the code of honour in Britain which extolled the rule of law and deemed duelling, in the words of W. E. Gladstone, as 'barbarous, inhuman and unchristian'.[2] Critics of the code of honour posited a quite different vision

The O'Gorman Mahon, by Daniel Maclise
(courtesy of the National Gallery of Ireland)

of society to that advanced by its defenders, as Rowland Ingram, one of the more percipient contributors to the debate on the subject, explained:

> The main purpose of civil government, as far as regards the intercourse of subjects, one with another, is the prevention of mutual wrong; and this it can only accomplish by forbidding the commission of such wrong, upon peril of certain pains and penalties, which it is *exclusively* authorised to inflict . . . Society itself could have no other existence than the Chimera, or the Minotaur, if the laws by which it is regulated, did not provide against . . . violation. Here, if anywhere, their control must be absolute, and their voice preemptory.[3]

Duelling represented precisely such a 'violation', because it derived its moral impetus from the presumption that gentlemen were entitled to put themselves above the law in disputes relating to honour. The only way to deprive them of this privilege was to enforce the existing laws against duelling or, if they were deemed inadequate, to introduce new ones.[4]

Circumstances were conducive to the embrace in Ireland in the early nineteenth century of the argument that it was in the public's interest to eradicate duelling. In the first place, the changed economic environment in the aftermath of the Napoleonic wars severely squeezed the smaller landlords and middlemen who provided the code of honour with one of its most enthusiastic constituencies in the late eighteenth century, and hastened the disappearance of the latter. Secondly, the tide of religious fervour that fuelled the campaign for moral reform in the early nineteenth century continued to grow, as Lord Teignmouth noted on a visit in 1821 when he commented on the 'great moral change' that was taking place. The 'old breed of gentlemen, buckeens and middlemen' that had provided the most committed duellists was nearing extinction, and their place was being taken by better-educated, less custom-bound individuals, who had less and less time for a code they regarded as anachronistic. The decline in reliance on the horsewhip, recourse to which prompted many duels; the attempt by some schools to discourage military games; the preparedness of an increased number of gentlemen (who were not in the public eye and who had less to lose) to refuse challenges; and the willingness of an individual of Daniel O'Connell's stature (who was very much in the public eye) to condemn 'in strong and sarcastic terms the vice of duelling' — all lend credence to Teignmouth's observation.[5]

The current of opposition to duelling in Ireland in the early nineteenth century took the expected two forms — the religious and the secular. Envigorated by the moral fervour that propelled the concurrent evangelical revival,[6] journalists and divines produced increasingly vehement condemnations of duelling. The *Freeman's Journal*, for example, carried lengthy critiques of the code of honour in the early years of the new century,[7] but it was not until the second decade, when Protestant clergymen joined in, that opposition began in earnest. Their arguments were not exclusively religious. They routinely condemned duelling as contrary to the law of God, but they appealed also to the secular authorities to use the rule of law to create an environment in which duelling could not flourish.

The first Irish clergyman to offer a sustained critique of the code of honour was William Butler Odell, who produced his *Essay on duelling, in which the subject is morally and historically considered* in 1814. Odell maintained that history proved that duelling was 'a vice' which mirrored 'the dark malevolence of the human passion'. From its origins among the 'barbarous nations who swarmed from the northern hive on the Roman Empire' with whom it was 'the favourite occupation', it had spread forth like a canker. But civilisation, he averred, had now reached a point when it could cleanse itself of such practices. Odell was attracted by the forceful manner with which Louis XIV of France, Gustav Adolph of Sweden and Joseph II of Austria had responded to duelling in their territories. He acknowledged that it was not possible simply to legislate it out of existence, but he argued that if it was not prohibited, it would continue to flourish, and he deplored the courts' passivity for this reason. He placed his firmest hopes for progress on men overcoming the base emotions — passion, revenge, pride and shame — on which duelling thrived, and he appealed to them to ignore 'the petulance of every ignorant and unmannered character' who sought to duel, and instead to embrace the 'courage' to defy and to despise duellists.[8]

Odell's *Essay on duelling* reflected the main currents in contemporary anti-duelling sentiment. Charles Bardin, by contrast, took a more traditional religion-centred stand. Bardin, a curate in the Church of Ireland parish of St Mary's in Dublin, in 1822 published a sermon in which he condemned duelling as a 'violation of the laws of God and man' and urged his readers to heed the word of God to 'love your enemies'. Vengeance, he pronounced, was God's exclusive prerogative; if people were 'uniformly religious', duelling would be no more.[9]

The Dublin-based evangelical 'minister of the gospel', J. B. M'Crea concurred. Taking as his text 'Cursed be their anger, for it was fierce', he contended that it was not possible to be a Christian and to adhere to the code of honour: 'Where there is anger, wrath, malice, strife, blood, there is not Christ. A DUELLIST CANNOT BE A CHRISTIAN,' he pronounced defiantly.[10] His religious convictions notwithstanding, M'Crea was not loath to appeal to secular insight in support of his cause. Duelling existed, he affirmed, because public opinion 'sanctioned' it, though it was outside the control of 'civil institutions [and] the maxims of inspirations'. Duelling was as much 'an infraction of the law of humanity' and 'a rebellion against the civil government' as 'an invasion of the prerogatives and statutes of the Almighty' who commanded 'thou shalt not kill'. For this reason, it could only be eradicated by a fundamental reformation of manners. It was not coincidental, he pronounced, that duelling

> only exists among irreligious men; and that it prevails most with those who are men of voluptuous and intemperate habits. Infidels, gamesters, drunkards, theatricians and intriquants — persons of licentious manners, violent passions and morbid consciences are the common heroes in these combats which outrage heaven and earth.[11]

However, if the young were eductated 'in the Bible' and parents

> exercise the discipline of restraint upon the passions and desires of their children . . . the lists of pleasure, ambition and false taste may not lead to erroneous ideas of virtue, honour and good breeding. The ballroom with its meritricious attractions, the playhouse with its lascivious exhibitions, the billiard-table, backgammon and the turf with their seductive recreations must be peremptorily forbidden, and thus be limited the temptation to envy, jealousy, covetousness and rage. Then shall we see a speedy terminator to the reign of terror which the Moloch of 'honour' has too long maintained.

In order to hasten such an eventuality, M'Crea urged that duellists should be ostracised by polite society, as 'drunkenness has been', and that the law should be made 'more efficient'.[12]

M'Crea's combative tract demonstrates unambiguously that duelling was perceived by the evangelicals and social reformers who aspired to remodel Irish society along more godly lines as but one of the social ills it was essential to eradicate in order to effect the moral reformation they desired. This was an aspiration with which Joseph Michael J. G. Hamilton, the most prolific early nineteenth-century anti-duelling activist, empathised. Hamilton's biographical details are obscure, but he was definitely not on the evangelical wing of Irish Protestantism. He resided with his wife, Emelia, on Phillipsburg Avenue in Dublin's northern suburbs, where he researched and wrote a range of tracts in support of what he termed 'Christian Patriotism'. A committed supporter of Daniel O'Connell's Catholic Association, he edited the *Waterford Chronicle* during the election campaign in that county in 1826 and made his mobile printing-press available to O'Connell when he stood against Vesey Fitzgerald in County Clare in 1828.[13]

Hamilton's commitment to the anti-duelling cause dates from 1818.[14] His first anti-duelling tract, *Some short and useful reflections upon duelling*, was published anonymously in Dublin in 1823. Like most writers on the subject, Hamilton borrowed heavily from others (including William Butler Odell) and quoted a wide range of testimony in support of his contention that duelling was contrary to 'law, morality and religion'. The law of various European states — Germany, Austria, Sweden and Poland — against duelling was cited approvingly, and he went to great lengths to refute the argument that the merit of the duel lay in the fact that it was a conflict of equals. He adduced some statistics to support his contention on this point, but these do not withstand scrutiny. He was on surer ground when he discussed the pain and despair duelling brought to families; his introduction of this theme reflects the growing consciousness of the family unit and the ideological conviction that a code of honour which demanded that men should be always ready to risk their lives in defence of their honour was incompatible with family and spousal responsibilities.[15]

In an attempt to hasten the eradication of duelling, Hamilton devoted an extensive section of his work to the provision of 'advice to seconds' in which he alerted them to the manifold ways they could prevent disputes proceeding to an exchange of shots.[16] However, his most concrete suggestion was for the foundation of an Irish anti-duelling association, such as currently existed in New York, and he called on the royal family, nobility and Catholic and Protestant clergy to join in order to persuade the public by example of the merits of taking a more active anti-duelling stand. Hamilton believed that a society of this nature should set itself three objectives. It should endeavour 'to promote a more general opinion that the practice of duelling originated in a false idea of true honour'; it should 'promote the establishment of one or more courts for redress of injured feeling'; and it should seek 'to obtain the enactment of new legislative measures' aimed at legislating duelling out of existence. In respect of the last point, Hamilton recommended that seconds present at and 'accessory to the fighting of a duel' should be fined £1,000 and be compelled to surrender half their personal property for distribution to the poor and 'be declared for ever incapable of holding any honourable, confidential or lucrative situation in the public service, or of following any of the learned professions, of receiving, or of appearing at any public entertainment or amusement'.[17] Given past events, this draconian proposal was unlikely to find favour with the gentlemen of the House of Commons or the peers of the House of Lords, even though it was mild compared with his ghoulish recommendation for the treatment of principals who died in a duel:

> In the case of the death of either party [in a duel], let the body of the deceased be soldered up in a leaden coffin to prevent an offensive smell; let it be drawn on every anniversary of the death for one hour upon a sledge though the most public parts of the town or city next to the scene of action, accompanied by the survivor, or in the case of his flight from public justice, let him be represented by the common executioner, with the word Cain upon his forehead, and the name of the survivor upon his back.[18]

There was not the slightest prospect of a proposal as bizarre as this being sanctioned. Prospects for an anti-duelling association were only slightly less promising; a similar organisation established in Britain in 1810 made little headway.[19]

Undaunted by the difficulties, Hamilton pressed on and in 1825 resumed his anti-duelling campaign with a tract entitled *The royal code of honour*. In essence a code of conduct for duellists, it comprised sixty articles appertaining to all aspects of duelling. As might be expected, more than half were devoted to the prevention of affairs of honour proceeding to violence; while many of the remainder aimed at reducing the chances of serious injury resulting by stipulating that every encounter should follow clearly defined procedures.[20] In many respects, Hamilton's code was a logical extension of British and European duelling manuals and the rules for duelling approved in Ireland in the 1770s which sought to bring order to duelling and to ensure against the occurrence of the disorderly and bloody encounters that were commonplace in the early eighteenth century. There was need for such guides because, notwithstanding the marked improvement in the conduct of duellists since then, there were still instances in which duels were fought at six or seven yards' distance.[21]

The anonymous author of the most impressive contemporary guide to duelling, *The British code of duel* which was published in London in 1824, shared with Hamilton a wish that duels should be conducted in a disciplined and orderly fashion. Somewhat unexpectedly, he made no attempt to provide a coherent philosophical defence of the code of honour. Symptomatic of the defensive position into which duellists had been manoeuvred by the early nineteenth century, he devoted the core of his work to an inchoate outline and justification of the practice of duelling. He was able, by this means, to provide a lengthy guide to the proper behaviour of principals and seconds in order, he propounded, 'to preserve to *gentlemen* in their purity, the rights which have so long remained to them under the recognized laws of honour to preclude the absurd encroachments which have for some years obtained.'[22]

It is unlikely that Joseph Michael Hamilton and the author of *The British code of duel* appreciated the similarities in their approaches to the regulation of duelling. Hamilton remained the most prolific opponent of the code of honour, and in 1829 he reissued his *Short and useful reflections* and his *Royal code of honour* in an omnibus edition with 'the outlines of a court for the adjournment of disputes' and a host of anecdotes and accounts of Irish duels which served to present the code of honour in a most unfavourable light.[23] It is not immediately clear why Hamilton chose to republish his anti-duelling tracts after a four-year interval during which he did not publish on the subject, but it is probable that it was in response to the increase in anti-duelling activity at this time.

Galvanised by the controversial death of Standish O'Grady in Dublin in March 1830,[24] most of the small network of protestant anti-duelling activists in the country gathered together at Morrison's Hotel in Dawson Street in April. Chaired jointly by Rear-Admiral Oliver and Lieutenant-General Sir Augustine Fitzgerald, the meeting was prompted by a number of speeches sharply critical of the code of honour to approve a series of resolutions condemning duelling 'as directly opposed to the letter and to the spirit of the word of God' and authorising the establishment of a provisional committee. This committee was instructed to draft rules for the establishment of an 'Association for the Suppression of . . . Duelling' and to secure the support and participation of influential persons. It reported two months later, on 10 June, at a meeting convened to launch the association formally. This meeting was mostly taken up with financial and organisational matters, and it was decided to delegate responsibility for running the association to a committee of twenty-one, headed by Fitzgerald and Oliver, which was charged with overseeing the dissemination of the anti-duelling message of the organisation and the establishment of auxiliary associations.

Theologically as well as politically, the outlook and composition of the Association for the Suppression of Duelling was protestant. Among the members of the committee of twenty-one were four clergymen (J. B. M'Crea, B. W. Mathias, Caesar Otway, Robert Stevelly) of evangelical leanings. The organisation aspired to broaden its support base by agreeing that 'all clergymen' who joined the organisation should be made 'honorary members of the committee', but this did not have the desired effect. The nexus of ex-army officers, clergymen, medical doctors and minor gentlemen who constituted the active membership of the organisation was unable to tap into on the growing hostility to duelling among the population at large. Although the rules of the association stipulated that there should be an annual general meeting in 1832, there is no record of a second annual report, and the society seems to have fallen quickly into desuetude.[25]

One reason for the demise of the Association for the Suppression of Duelling was its failure to attract the support of anti-duelling activists whose religious and political outlook differed from that of its members. They appear not to have acquired the services of Joseph Hamilton, for instance. He was not a member of the committee of twenty-one, though John Schoales, who favoured the Hamiltonian idea of excluding all duellists from holding public office, was. Hamilton had outlined his thinking on this issue in 1829 at a 'general meeting to consider the best means of preventing the breach of courtesy and waste of life' that was a feature of duelling. His conviction was that a court of honour should be established to arbitrate disputes and, like the members of the Association, he held that if enough peers, M.P.s, knights, barristers, military officers, surgeons and others could be persuaded to support the idea of such a court, differences could be resolved before principals felt compelled to appeal to their weapons.[26] This was possible, but Hamilton did not possess the necessary contacts or influence to permit the establishment of such an organisation. It was not that he did not try. Parallel with the foundation of the Association for the Suppression of Duelling, he increased his own activities. In October 1830 he addressed a petition to King William IV drawing attention to the dozens of fatalities that had resulted from duels in the preceding seventy-five years and urging the king to direct parliament to establish a court of honour to arbitrate disputes. Those who refused to be bound by its decisions must, he explained, be ostracised socially, excluded from holding public office (including the army and the navy) and barred from voting or from receiving any legacy, premium or insurance.[27]

Hamilton's schemes, like those of the Association for the Suppression of Duelling, came to nothing. Nevertheless, the Association was a milestone in the development of anti-duelling sentiment in Ireland. For over a decade Joseph Hamilton and a number of evangelical clergymen had laboured in isolation. The founding of an Association for the Suppression of Duelling offered tangible evidence that their efforts were not without impact and that there was mounting public antipathy to the practice. The Association may not have made a decisive impression, but it ensured that anti-duelling sentiment was kept in the public eye, along with temperance, sabbath-breaking, suicide, gambling and swearing, which were other issues about which Hamilton and the Protestant moralists who were in the vanguard of the anti-duelling cause held equally censorious opinions.[28]

Daniel O'Connell and duelling in the 1820s and 1830s

The establishment of the Association for the Suppression of Duelling was the most visible indicator in the early nineteenth century of the mounting confidence of the critics of the code of honour in Ireland. Duels continued to take place, but the fact that the Irish county constabulary was authorised to combat duelling from its foundation in 1822, that Church of Ireland clergymen were less passive, and that a number of experienced duellists actually came out publicly in support of Joseph Hamilton's suggestions indictates that public opinion was increasingly disinclined to countenance appeals to the code of honour to settle differences.[29] Duelling was in irrevocable decline, though it still had its champions — even in the police.

According to one 'constabulary officer', who personally regarded duelling as an efficient way of settling disputes, the Irish police force was prepared in its early days to allow duels to proceed if it was clear that they would be conducted fairly.[30]

The reluctance of the state to embrace the anti-duelling cause meant that the onus for its control and eradication lay with its practitioners, and Daniel O'Connell pointed the way forward. Having demonstrated his bravery under fire in the 1810s and been bound to keep the peace, O'Connell became increasingly hostile to duelling in the 1820s and 1830s. In 1828, for example, when the County Clare landlord Edward Hickman threatened to call him out if he canvassed his tenants, O'Connell cleverly turned the tables by making Hickman's assertion of his authority over his tenants an election issue.[31] He demonstrated the courage of his new-found anti-duelling convictions once again a year later when Donogh O'Brien of Dromoland accused him of being motivated by 'selfish purposes' when he lambasted Lucius O'Brien for doing 'nothing for the county of Clare'. O'Connell was determined that this should not precipitate a duel, and he resolutely refused to personalise the dispute for this reason. There was 'blood — human blood — on my hand', he explained to Pierce O'Mahony, 'and nothing can tempt me to commit that crime again'.[32] O'Connell's resolve was to be tested repeatedly in the sharply confrontational atmosphere of Irish politics in the 1830s. In the summer of 1830, for instance, he and Major William Macnamara had a sharp disagreement when O'Connell sought to extricate himself from a promise he had made to Macnamara that he would support him electorally in County Clare. It was a classic duelling situation, but neither man wished to settle it with weapons. Morgan O'Connell, Daniel's son, did send Macnamara a challenge at one point, but it was declined, and the affair was subsequently resolved.[33] Three months later O'Connell was put to the test once again when, following his description of the Chief Secretary, Sir Henry Hardinge, as a 'contemptible English soldier', Hardinge called on him 'either to avow or to disavow' the charge as a prelude to his issuing a challenge. O'Connell refused, and in his public response averred that he 'spoke of . . . Hardinge in his public capacity as an instrument of despotism. He did not say one word of him in his private capacity.'[34]

O'Connell's public avowal of the distinction, already several generations old, between a politician's 'public' and 'private' roles was another important moment in the history of the decline of duelling in Ireland, because it paved the way for other Irish politicians to do the same with a clear conscience and hastened the exclusion of duelling from the political arena. Of course, not all politicians accepted this distinction, as O'Connell was well aware. He was personally unpersuaded by the argument that 'those who deem a duel the proof of valour' believed 'that he who refuses to fight a duel must be timid', and his high standing encouraged others to follow his example. It is noteworthy, for instance, that his son Maurice declined to accept a challenge from William Richard Mahon in 1831.[35] However, O'Connell's denunciation of duelling 'as a practice inconsistent with common sense, [and] above all, as a violation, plain and palpable, of the divine law' was regarded in some quarters as hypocritical and cowardly. It galled many of those who suffered the lash of his lacerating tongue that they could not redeem their injured reputations in time-honoured fashion by means of a duel. Indeed, Lord Alvanley, the Tory peer, whom O'Connell termed a 'bloated buffoon' in 1835, was so angered by O'Connell's refusal to meet him that he attempted to have him expelled from Brooks's Club. He failed, but shortly afterwards Morgan O'Connell, who possessed little of his father's political acumen or personal resolve, challenged and exchanged a harmless series of shots with Alvanley on the grounds that he had insulted his father by seeking his expulsion from Brooks's.[36]

O'Connell's extravagant rhetoric and controversial political views ensured that he received an above-average number of challenges. Had he accepted them all, it is improbable that he would have lived to reach old age. His standing as the Catholic champion, his utter lack of sensitivity to the feelings of his political opponents, and his visceral hostility to the proponents of 'Protestant ascendancy' would almost certainly have pitched him against somebody who would have outshot him. What his career and that of a number of his colleagues demonstrate conclusively is that adherence to the code of honour in the early nineteenth century was not determined along religious lines. It also demonstrates that the politically fractious atmosphere of the 1820s and 1830s was conducive to the survival rather than to the demise of duelling and that the critics of the code of honour still had much to do if they aspired to its early eradication.

Duelling in decline

Despite the convincing evidence for the intensification of anti-duelling sentiment in the 1820s and 1830s, adherence to the precepts of the code of honour remained strong in some circles. This is most clearly indicated by the duels that took place, and by the reverence afforded to so-called duelling enthusiasts like The O'Gorman Mahon and 'Fireball' Macnamara, who had acted as Daniel O'Connell's second in his encounter with John D'Esterre.[37] But as the Rhinecrew duel of 1826 demonstrates, duels and duellists in the 1820s, as at any other time, were as likely to be sordid and petty as heroic and edifying. This encounter was prompted by the anger of Joseph Daunt of Kilcashin, County Cork, at a court judgment that went against him, and was pressed by one of the seconds until Daunt was shot dead, though the honour of both principals (Daniel O'Connor of Manch House, a local magistrate, was the other) had been satisfied by the initial exchange of shots.[38]

If Daunt's death could have been avoided, the same is true of most political duels in this period. O'Connell demonstrated this by simply refusing to fight another duel after his eventful contretemps with Peel in 1815. Henry Grattan junior too won praise for declining a challenge from Major T. N. Edgeworth over remarks he made about the Dublin Paving Board; but most, Grattan included, refused to take the firmly anti-duelling stance favoured by O'Connell. In June 1820, for instance, Grattan met the second Lord Clare in Hyde Park as a consequence of some slighting observation he made about the peer's father.[39] Just over a decade later, in August 1831, he was almost involved in another encounter when he took exception to some uncomplimentary remarks by George Robert Dawson, the M.P. for County Londonderry, about the 'hotheadedness' of Irishmen, but their disagreement was mediated and resolved without firearms.[40]

Inevitably, elections continued to provide the occasion for appeals to the code of honour. Both the general election of 1826 and the County Clare by-election in 1828 prompted duels. At Waterford in 1826 the owner of the *Waterford Chronicle*, Philip Barron, was called to account by Richard Sarjeant, the son of Alderman Sarjeant, for slandering his father, and was obliged to travel to County Kilkenny to fight because Barron was bound to keep the peace in County Waterford. During the election itself two attornies on opposite sides exchanged fire without perpetrating any injury.[41] In the same year at Glasnevin, County Dublin, John Bric, a young Kerry barrister who was an ardent supporter of O'Connell, died as a result of an encounter with Major William Hayes, a Cork conservative, as a consequence of a dispute over the impending election in Cork.[42] Two years later another *intime* of O'Connell, Tom Steele, exchanged shots with William Smith O'Brien, who was also a member of the Catholic Association, as a consequence of Smith O'Brien's opposition to O'Connell's decision to stand against Vesey Fitzgerald in County Clare.[43] Other prominent figures involved in Catholic politics displayed an equal readiness to defend their reputations with arms. Nicholas Purcell O'Gorman, who was secretary to the Catholic Association for a time, fought with Counsellor Wallace; in 1834 Richard Lalor Sheil had to be taken into custody by the serjeant-at-arms in the House of Commons to prevent a meeting with Lord Althorp following a rancorous personal exchange; while the ebullient O'Gorman Mahon continued to pursue the idiosyncratic path that precipitated him into many affairs of honour.[44]

Of course, not all duels had a political *fons et origo*. And the 1820s played host to a respectable but declining number of encounters arising from a wide variety of others factors. Some, as Joseph Hamilton amply chronicles, were prompted by ostensibly trivial differences over handkerchiefs, games of leapfrog, the throwing of nuts and the weight a horse should carry in a race; others were prompted by such well-established causes as disputes over women (though this was less significant in nineteenth- century Ireland than it was in seventeenth-century France), gambling, differences at cards or over property, and unspecified insults, assaults and disputes (Table 3.9).[45] Despite these, the number of duels diminished as adherence to the code of honour slowly weakened.

In one respect duelling grew in popularity. The early nineteenth century witnessed an increased tendency for duels to become public spectacles. This was contrary to duelling etiquette, which laid down that duels should be fought privately in isolated locations where there was little likelihood of interruption or of the presence of unwelcome onlookers. The populace saw things quite differently. For them, as well as for many of a more elevated station, as Bishop Thomas Barnard observed in April 1798, duelling was a 'sport' comparable to fox- or stag-hunting, rather than a private trial by combat between members of the social elite. The crowds that attended duels (and they did so in only a minority of cases) in the eighteenth century were generally passive; they were attracted by the spectacle of witnessing their social superiors engage in a trial by arms, as their presence at the Flood–Agar encounter attests.[46] On such occasions the peasantry present generally supported their own landlord if he was attentive to their needs. A kind landlord, Barrington observed, 'reigned despotic in the ardent affections of the tenantry, their pride and pleasure being to support him'. Indeed, it was not unknown for a landlord to duel on behalf of his tenantry.[47] However, as old patterns of deference broke down under the weight of population growth, economic change and popular politicisation, the peasantry's involvement in duels became more active and partisan. For instance, when John Colclough and William Congreve Alcock met in 1807, they were watched by 'a great concourse' which was so anxious that Colclough should triumph that when he was hit, Alcock and his party deemed it politic to beat an expeditious retreat.[48] This was a sensible precaution because some late eighteenth-century[49] and more early nineteenth-century crowds were not prepared to stand by passively when their champion was defeated, as is indicated by a number of encounters. For instance, when 'two fellows who had some previous animosity' at Ballinagerah, County Kerry, determined to settle their difference in 1810 by 'single combat' after 'divine service', the encounter escalated into a general 'faction fight' in which 300–400 people exchanged blows and a person other than one of the principals was mortally injured.[50] In County Sligo, when Philip C. Perceval shot Hyacinth O'Rourke in the presence of 'an immense crowd of country people' in 1782, he had to ride for his life from the enraged mob, whose sympathies were enlisted on the side of O'Rourke.[51] William McDonagh, a 'squireen' from Portumna, County Galway, had a comparable experience. He was the second in an encounter that took place in Queen's County in February 1829 between John Doolan of Cloghjordan Park and William Sadleir of Scalaheen, County Tipperary. 'An immense crowd', estimated at two thousand, watched the encounter, and when it produced no injuries, a section, led by one David Davis, behaved so offensively as to provoke McDonagh into a duel. Davis's impetuosity cost him his life; but because one of McDonagh's bullets, which missed its intended target, killed a spectator,[52] he only escaped from the enraged crowd by mounting his horse and fording the nearby River Shannon.[53] A similar incident took place at Castle Hyde, County Cork, three years later when Dr James O'Brien of Mitchelstown challenged Counsellor Thomas O'Mahony of Loughananna for interrupting mass in a dispute over tithes. 'Hundreds of people' turned up for the encounter, and when O'Mahony was hit they 'made an ugly rush' for O'Brien, but he and his second were able to effect their escape.[54] Although these examples would suggest otherwise, crowd interference was not prompted solely by displeasure with the outcome. In County Sligo in 1826 a local crowd intervened after two shots were fired to prevent the principals persisting with a combat, while a similar occurrence in County Roscommon obliged two County Longford gentlemen to make up.[55]

These incidents were unusual. In most encounters the crowd was content to observe passively.[56] Indeed, the most important trend revealed by the increased involvement of the crowd and the lowly gentry status of so many of the principals and seconds in such encounters is the breakdown in adherence to the rules of honour. Rural 'half-mounted gentlemen' appreciated the symbolic importance of being able to determine disputes by recourse to arms, but they possessed little of the sophistication of their aristocratic contemporaries (few of whom now duelled)[57] or predecessors in Britain and Ireland who had sought in the eighteenth century to cultivate a mystique about duelling.

One should not conclude from this that duelling was now the exclusive preserve of down-at-heel gentry. The Dukes of Bedford and Buckingham (1822), Sir Alexander Boswell and Charles Stuart (1822), the Duke of Wellington and Lord Winchelsea (1829), Charles William Stuart, the M.P. for County Tipperary, Lord George Bentinck and Captain Ker, Lord George Bentinck and George Osbaldesten (1831), Lord Alvanley and Morgan O'Connell (1835) and Lord Cadogen (1840) all bear witness to the fact that the compulsion to avenge insult still survived among the elite.[58] That said, the protests of outrage that greeted certain duels indicated that its days were numbered. This is best attested to by the stir caused in Dublin in 1830 by the encounter between Standish Stamer O'Grady of County Limerick and the Waterford-born army officer, Captain John Rowland Smyth. The cause of this was quite straightforward. O'Grady was riding his horse along Nassau Street on St Patrick's Day 1830 when he was forced against the railings of Trinity College to avoid a cabriolet that approached him at speed. Angered by this, O'Grady struck out instinctively with his whip. This was an entirely predictable response, and the incident might have been overlooked, but for the fact that a question had already been posed over Captain Smyth's valour as a result of a previous incident and that the 'horsewhipping' of another army officer a few days earlier had caused the officer's corps to determine that they would 'have to leave Dublin' if they let further insults pass unavenged. Attempts at mediation proved abortive, and when the two men met near the Grand Canal at Dolphin's Barn, Smyth mortally wounded O'Grady with his first shot. This was not unusual, but the fact that O'Grady was the son of the Chief Baron of the Irish Court of Exchequer, that he had been duped into taking up a disadvantageous position on the duelling field, and that Smyth, who was the aggressor in the encounter, was found guilty of manslaughter and sentenced to a term variously recorded as between one and two years in prison when the case went to trial in August, kept it high in the public mind. Opinion in Dublin, in particular, was 'aroused' to anger by the whole sorry episode, and it served as a stimulus for the foundation of the Association for the Suppression of Duelling.[59]

The perceptible intensification of public hostility to duelling prompted by the Smyth–O'Grady encounter had a substantially greater impact than the law in hastening the decline in adherence to the code of honour in the 1830s. Fatal encounters continued to take place, but they were significantly fewer in number. In 1833 Captain Smith, an uncle of John Rowland Smyth, was shot and killed by Colonel MacDonald at Fermoy following an 'angry discussion' over the relative merits of various regiments. Some months later in Devon, Dr Peter Hennis of Youghal was fatally wounded in a well-publicised encounter with Sir John Jeffcott as a result of a disagreement over a woman.[60] However, most duels now concluded without serious injury. Thus Patrick Lavelle and Norton, his antagonist, who owned two of Dublin's 'leading newspapers' exchanged shots without effect in the 1830s; so also did Lord Londonderry and Henry Grattan junior in 1839 following remarks made by Londonderry in the House of Lords; while the Lord Mayor of Dublin, Arthur Perrin, also emerged unscathed from a four-shot exchange with Edward Southwell Ruthven, a parliamentary candidate in the city in 1835.[61]

One can establish a clearer perspective on the way in which the code of honour was observed in Ireland at this time by examining it from a regional perspective. By the second quarter of the nineteenth century the code of honour was more warmly observed in the provinces of Munster and Connacht than elsewhere in the country, though 'the last notable Tipperary gentleman' to duel was Richard Butler, Earl of Glengall, in 1826.[62] The following paragraphs seek to provide a flavour of duelling in Connacht in an attempt to define the main features of duelling in its rural context during its decades of decline.

By the early nineteenth century Connacht gentlemen possessed a reputation for being inveterate duellists. The province had, it is true, produced a number of notorious 'fire-eaters', but the life histories of Robert and Richard Martin, George Robert Fitzgerald and Hyacinth O'Rourke and the deceptiveness of memory offered a distorting impression, as Connacht was, after Ulster, probably the least duel-prone province in the kingdom in the eighteenth century. An examination of the duelling incidents that took place in the early years of the new century bear witness to the fact that though the code of honour was strongly entrenched, it was by no means a duellist's paradise.[63] For instance, when it was suggested in 1805 that the assizes should no longer be held in Ballinrobe, it was forecast that James Cuffe would defend 'his rights' with pistols against local critics who supported the suggestion as the town was 'settled on him'; but no duels ensued. As this suggests, dynastic rivalries were a feature of life in Connacht that facilitated duelling. In 1801 the political animus of the Brownes of Westport and Binghams of Castlebar, which was a well-established feature of County Mayo politics, pitted Major Denis Bingham and James Moore O'Donel against each other. O'Donel, who had previously been injured in a political riot involving supporters of the two families in 1790, was killed on this occasion.[64]

The intensification of political animosities in Connacht in the 1810s and 1820s provided more opportunity for quarrels, but though there is evidence to suggest that more duels were fought, relatively few produced casualties. Indeed, most of those that concluded with fatalities did not have a political genesis. This is true of the O'Joynt–McKim encounter at Ballina in 1812 (during which McKim was killed by a ball in the head); the Dillon–Kane encounter at Merlin Park in Galway in 1816, in which the former died; and the Nolan–Browne encounter over land in County Roscommon, in which the latter was injured.[65] By contrast, when Richard Martin and Denis Bowes Daly clashed during the electoral contest for Galway county in 1815, they did not proceed to an exchange of shots. Over a decade later, when James Browne and Lord Bingham had a political disagreement, a duel was avoided because Judge Beaton bound them to keep the peace and warned them that they would forfeit their sureties of £10,000 apiece if they travelled to France to evade his jurisdiction.[66]

Others were less amenable. In 1828 Richard O'Donel of Mayo and J. Steward exchanged shots without injury as a consequence of a difference that arose out of O'Donel's enthusiastic celebration of Daniel O'Connell's victory in the County Clare by-election. Two years later O'Donel forced William Westby to apologise or agree to meet him following an altercation.[67] O'Donel was one of the last of a dying breed of devotees of the code of honour. Most Connacht gentlemen were less eager to fight than commentators averred. Major O'Malley, for instance, put a precipitate end to insulting behaviour by Andrew Glendinning in 1827 by applying to the Court of King's Bench for a criminal information against him for offering a challenge,[68] which suggests that the disposition of gentlemen to have recourse to the law to rescue them from unwelcome challenges was not an exclusively urban phenemonon.[69] In another instance Owen Kelly from County Mayo was sentenced to six months in jail for 'using language to provoke a duel' with a Captain Stewart.[70] Of course, the threat of incarceration or ruin did not deter all. George Bingham (later Lord Lucan) sacrificed his military command when he took up the challenge presented by Major Charles Fitzgerald over a supposed broken promise, and others continued to risk their lives and their liberties over relative trivia.[71]

But despite the continuing enthusiasm of some gentlemen for the code of honour, the heightened reluctance of most individuals, the increasingly interventionist stance of magistrates, justices of the peace and the constabulary hastened a fall-off in the number of duels taking place.[72] Determined duellists had long been able to evade local efforts to bind them over by travelling to a neighbouring jurisdiction, but in the mid-nineteenth century this was no longer the case. In July 1838, for example, when Blake Bermingham and Francis Crean, two magistrates resident in Claremorris, County Mayo, quarrelled, the head constable, George Abbott, engaged in a frantic eighty-mile chase in a horse trap to bind one of the principals on £1,000 bail to keep the peace. In County Sligo in the previous year the constabulary twice interrupted Counsellors Baker and Casserly when they endeavoured to meet at Five-mile-bourn.[73] On most occasions this was sufficient to prevent an encounter taking place, since only the most determined or reckless duellists chose openly to defy the law.

By the mid-1840s most duels were concluded before any injuries could be inflicted by the intervention of the police and judiciary.[74] The activities of the police made it progressively more difficult for intending duellists, but the constabulary could not completely eradicate duelling so long as gentlemen believed that it reflected aversely on them if they were not prepared to defend their honour against insult with their lives. This explains why individuals like Lord George Loftus (who met Lord Harley at Boulogne in December 1839), Captain Beresford (a former M.P. for Athlone), Augustus Moore of Moore Hall, Henry Grattan junior, Lord James Browne and George Ourley Higgins all got caught up in affairs of honour during the 1840s.[75] Increasingly, however, individuals either simply went through the motions, ensuring that there were no injuries by firing in the air, or they appealed to the law to avoid endangering their lives, as John O'Connell did when John O'Shea challenged him in 1846.[76]

By this date the campaign against duelling was nearing a successful conclusion, as adherence to the code of honour was in terminal decline.[77] Tradition and memory kept the ethos alive for a number of years, but it was in plain retreat. A few decades earlier the opponents of duelling had engaged in a heated debate with the supporters of the code of honour, but though there were still individuals prepared to affirm the merits of a system whereby gentlemen operated a self-policing code of honour, they were increasingly isolated. This fact was underlined within a few years of Queen Victoria's accession to the throne when an English association for the discouragement of duelling was founded (1842) and the government was put under pressure by elements *within* the army, who had the support of Prince Albert, to amend military regulations to make duelling or the presentation of a challenge a cashiering offence. Eventually, in 1844, the Articles of War were revised 'to allow army officers to tender or accept apologies in case of insult or injury without reflection on their honour'.[78] By now also the Catholic and the Protestant press in Ireland were united in the view that duelling was 'a social monster, like . . . [the] fabled Frankenstein' and that it was essential that the rule of law was applied to eradicate it. No emotional or moral arguments could be advanced, it was asserted, which justified giving individuals the authority to set right their own wrongs.[79] The perception of duelling as a 'relic of barbarism' that no longer had a place in the new economic and moral world of Victorian Britain and Ireland was especially powerful. *The Kerry Magazine* illustrated the change in attitude very well when it advised its male readers in 1854 that a real gentleman

> never offer[s] offence to the feelings and habits of those with whom he mixes from a principle of love to the comfort and happiness of those all around him.[80]

This was very different advice to that given to young men in the seventeenth and eighteenth centuries, when it was contended that a gentleman proved his manliness by deeds of physical and martial bravery rather than by kindliness.

The fact that journals like the *Irish Catholic Magazine* and the *Kerry Magazine* felt it necessary to issue such advice in the 1850s attests to the persistence in some quarters of belief in the code of honour. Sir William Gregory demonstrated this in 1851 when he challenged and fought George Vaughan of the English Turf Club as a result of a difference over a horse. Nobody was injured, but Gregory's account of the affair leaves little doubt that his actions were disapproved of and that he did not feel good about his own conduct.[81] This is understandable when it is appreciated that this was one of the last recorded duels in England. Gentlemen were now expected to have recourse to methods other than weaponry to deal with insulting behaviour.[82] Some years later when William Smith O'Brien challenged an M.P. for disparaging the 1848 rebellion, and Captain O'Shea directed The O'Gorman Mahon in 1881 to convey a challenge to Charles Stewart Parnell over his liaison with Mrs O'Shea, no duel ensued on either occasion. By then, as the experience of the Sligo harbour commissioner who was dismissed from his post in 1869 for issuing a challenge demonstrates, duelling was simply no longer socially or legally acceptable.[83]

Notes and References

1 *O'Connell corresp.*, ii, 308–9, 335, iii, 30.
2 Andrew, 'The code of honour', pp. 420–21, 426–8; W. Gilpin, 'On duelling', *Annual Register*, l (1808), pp. 178–90; 'An enquiry into the nature of true courage', 1826 (B.L., Gladstone Papers, Add. MS 44718, ff 78–82). For British anti-duelling sentiment see Peter Chalmers, *Two discourses on the sin [and] danger of duelling* . . . (Edinburgh, 1822); J. C. Bluett, *Duelling and the laws of honour examined and condemned upon principles of commonsense and revealed truth* (London, 1836); Barker-Benfield, *The culture of sensibility*, p. 81.
3 Cited in Andrew, 'The code of honour', pp. 421–2.
4 Ibid., pp. 423–4.
5 Teignmouth, *Reminiscences*, i, 285; Ballitore Register, vol. 1 no. 1, (Beinecke Library, Osborn Collection, Ballitore Papers, Miscellaneous journals and essay file); Hamilton, *The only approved guide*, pp. 236–7; *O'Connell corresp.*, ii, 449–51; iii, 87.
6 Joseph Liechty, 'Irish evangelicalism, Trinity College, Dublin, and the mission of the Church of Ireland at the end of the eighteenth century' (Ph.D. thesis, St Patrick's College, Maynooth, 1987); D. H. Akenson, *The Church of Ireland: ecclesiastical reform and revolution, 1800–85* (Yale, 1971), pp. 132–42; Desmond Bowen, *The Protestant crusade in Ireland, 1800–70* (Dublin, 1978).
7 *F.J.*, 1 Jan., 7 Nov. 1805.
8 William Butler Odell, *Essay on duelling, in which the subject is morally and historically considered and the practice deduced from the earliest time* (Cork, 1814), passim.
9 Charles Bardin, *A sermon preached in St Mary's Church, Dublin, on 20 and 27 of January 1822* (Dublin, 1822), passim.
10 J. B. M'Crea, *Duelling being the enlargement of a discourse on a late fatal event preached in D'Olier Street Chapel, Dublin Street* (Dublin, 1830), p. 5.
11 Ibid., pp. 8–9, 18.
12 Ibid., p. 19.
13 *O'Connell corresp.*, iii, 85, 385.
14 Joseph Hamilton, *Extracts from various works of Joseph Hamilton* (Dublin, [1831]).
15 A Christian Patriot [Joseph Hamilton], *Some short and useful reflections upon duelling which should be in the hands of every person who is liable to receive a challenge or an offence* (Dublin, 1823), pp. 11–36.
16 Ibid., pp. 41–68.
17 Ibid., pp. 40, 102–6.
18 Ibid., p. 106.
19 Andrew, 'The code of honour', p. 431.
20 Joseph Hamilton, *The royal code of honour for the regulation of duelling as it was respectfully submitted to the European sovereign* (Dublin, 1825), passim.

21 Hamilton, *The only approved guide*, pp. 241–2; Corr, 'Reminiscences', pp. 308, 310–11.
22 *The British code of duel: a reference to the laws of honour and the character of gentlemen* (London, 1824), p. 74 and passim.
23 Joseph Hamilton, *The only approved guide through all stages of a quarrel, containing the royal code of honour, reflections upon duelling, and the outline of a court for the adjustment of disputes with anecdotes, documents and cases interesting to Christain moralists who decline the combat, to experienced duellists and to benevolent legislators* (London and Dublin, 1829), pp. 1–172.
24 Below, p. 267.
25 *First report of the Association for the Suppression of the Anti-Christian Practice of Duelling presented at the public meeting held in Dublin June 10 1830* (Dublin, 1830), pp. 1–4.
26 Hamilton, *Extracts from various works*; idem, *The only approved guide*, pp. 49–56.
27 *First report of the Association for the Suppression of . . . Duelling*, pp. 10–14; *Belfast Newsletter*, 29 Oct. 1830. I wish to thank John McHugh for drawing the latter source to my attention.
28 Hamilton, *Extracts from various works*, passim; J. B. Lyons, *Scholar and sceptic: the career of James Henry, 1798–1876* (Dublin, 1985), p. 38.
29 S. H. Palmer, *Police and protest in England and Ireland, 1780–1850* (Cambridge, 1988); Wood-Martin, *Sligo*, iii, 318–19; Hamilton, *The only approved guide*, pp. xv–xvi.
30 A retired constabulary officer, 'Leaves from my notebook', *Dublin University Magazine*, lxxxviii (1876), pp. 453, 455–6.
31 MacDonagh, *The hereditary bondsman*, p. 252.
32 *O'Connell corresp.*, iv, 83, 89–91.
33 Oliver MacDonagh, *The emancipist: Daniel O'Connell, 1830–47* (London, 1989), pp. 36–7; *O'Connell corresp.*, iv, 176–8, 183–5; Paul Johnson, *The birth of the modern world society 1815–30* (London, 1992), p. 469. Both Maurice and Morgan O'Connell had previously sought to defend their father's honour against slight in 1823 (Denis Gwynn, *The O'Gorman Mahon: duellist, adventurer and politician* (London, 1934), pp. 38–9).
34 *O'Connell corresp.*, iv, 220; viii, 232–4; MacDonagh, *The emancipist*, pp. 50–51.
35 *O'Connell corresp.*, iv, 262–3, 322–5, 326, 327–8.
36 MacDonagh, *The emancipist*, pp. 125–6; *O'Connell corresp.*, v, 295–6, 299–300; Kiernan, *The duel*, pp. 211–12; Earl of Malmesbury, *Memoirs of an ex-minister: an autobiography* (2 vols, London, 1884), i, 64–5. O'Connell's rhetorical excesses also prompted Benjamin Disraeli to present a challenge, but Morgan O'Connell declined this (Malmesbury, *op. cit.*, i, 65–6).
37 McDonagh, *Irish life and character*, p. 47; Macnamara, *Story of an Irish sept*, pp. 290–91; Gwynn, *The O'Gorman Mahon*, passim.
38 Courtney Moore, 'The Rhinecrew duel, A.D. 1826', *J.C.H.A.S.*, ix (1903), pp. 171–4; idem, 'The Rhinecrew duel in 1826', *J.C.H.A.S.*, xii (1906), pp. 177–81; W. J. O'Neill Daunt, *A life spent for Ireland* (repr., Shannon, 1972), p. 10n.
39 *Annual Register*, lxii (1820), pp. 208–09.

40 George Peel, ed., *The private letters of Sir Robert Peel* (London, 1920), p. 137.
41 *O'Connell corresp.*, iii, 255; Hamilton, *The only approved guide*, pp. 150–63.
42 *Annual Register*, lxviii (1826), pp. 195–6; Ian d'Alton, *Protestant society and politics in Cork, 1812–44* (Cork, 1980), p. 137; Corr, 'Reminiscences', p. 308; Bernard Neary, *Dublin 7: a local history* (Dublin, 1992), p. 106.
43 Gwynn, *The O'Gorman Mahon*, pp. 85–94; Richard Davis, *The Young Ireland movement* (Dublin, 1987), p. 49; idem, *William Smith O'Brien: Ireland, 1848* (Dublin, 1989), p. 6.
44 *O'Connell corresp.*, vi, 95; Gwynn, *The O'Gorman Mahon*, pp. 102–9, 150–54; Sheedy, *The Clare elections*, p. 167.
45 Hamilton, *The only approved guide*, pp. 95–6, 119, 186, 206, 245; G. N. Nuttall-Smith, *The chronicles of a Puritan family in Ireland* (Oxford, 1923), pp. 62–6; Corr, 'Reminiscences', pp. 306, 310–11.
46 A retired constabulary officer, 'Leaves from my notebook', p. 452; Kiernan, *The duel*, pp. 65–6; Hamilton, *The only approved guide*, p. 227; Powell, ed., *Barnard Letters*, p. 84; above, pp. 102–03.
47 Barrington, *Personal sketches*, i, 5–6; ii, 149; *D.E.P.*, 16 Nov. 1786; Teignmouth, *Reminiscences*, i, 257–8; Gregory, ed., *William Gregory's autobiography*, pp. 16–18.
48 Ridgeway, *A report of the trial of William Alcock*, p. 48.
49 Following the Prendergast–Gahan encounter in 1761, Gahan had to ride 'boldly across the river' to escape the wrath of the 'infuriated crowd' because he had killed Prendergast (Burke, *Clonmel*, p. 154).
50 *F.J.*, 25 June 1810.
51 Wood-Martin, *Sligo*, iii, 316–17; Betty MacDermott, *O'Ruairc of Breifne* (Manorhamilton, 1990), pp. 182–3.
52 The duel between Redmond Byrne and Thomas O'Connor in County Cork in 1820 also resulted in the wounding of 'a poor man' walking nearby (*Annual Register*, lxxii (1820), p. 257).
53 Nuttall-Smith, *The chronicles of a Puritan family*, pp. 62–7; Hamilton, *The only approved guide*, pp. 77–8; Gregory, ed., *Sir William Gregory*, pp. 15–16. For a different version of this encounter see Corr, 'Reminiscences', p. 311.
54 Courtenay Moore, 'Some account of the duel between Dr O'Brien and Councillor O'Mahony at Castlehyde . . .', *J.C.H.A.S.*, v (1890), pp. 262–3.
55 Wood-Martin, *Sligo*, iii, 320–21; Hamilton, *The only approved guide*, p. 84.
56 *Annual Register*, liv (1812), p. 31.
57 *Dublin University Magazine*, ii (1833), p. 398.
58 B.L., MacVey–Napier Papers, Add. MS 34613, ff 36–67; *Annual Register*, lxiv (1822), pp. 62, 82, 1829, pp. 58–63; Neville Thompson, *Wellington after Waterloo* (London, 1986), pp. 91–2; Gwynn, *The O'Gorman Mahon*, pp. 76–82; Norman Gash, *Pillars of government and other essays* (London, 1986), pp. 128–9, 173–4; *O'Connell corresp.*, iv, 33–4; Johnson, *Birth of the Modern World*, pp. 489–90; Kiernan, *The duel*, pp. 212, 214; *F.D.J.*, June 1831. I wish to thank Mr Eugene Coyle for the last reference.
59 *Annual Register*, lxxii (1830), pp. 137–8; *Dublin University Magazine*, lxxxviii (1876), pp. 454–5; 'The tragic tale of Stanmer O'Grady and Captain

Smyth of Ballinatrae', *New Ireland Review*, x (1898–9), pp. 30–37; Corr, 'Reminiscences', p. 313.

60 *Dublin University Magazine*, lxxxviii (1876), pp. 455–6; Robert Day, 'Duel between Sir John Jeffcott and Doctor Hennis', *J.C.H.A.S.*, viii (1902), pp. 258–9; *Annual Register*, lxxv (1833), pp. 105–10. In another duel Richard Harley of Ella, County Mayo, seriously wounded J. W. Williams in England (*Ballina Impartial*, 5 July 1824).

61 Corr, 'Reminiscences', pp. 309–10; *Annual Register*, lxxxi (1839), pp. 80–81; *O'Connell corresp.*, iv, 257–8.

62 Burke, *Clonmel*, p. 154n.

63 Above, pp. 55–6; 151–7; Mr and Mrs S. C. Hall, *Ireland* (London, 1853), p. 134; 'The duelling field: Merlin Park', *Galway Reader*, iii (1950–51), p. 115; J. G. Simms, 'Connacht in the eighteenth century', *I.H.S.*, xi (1958), p. 129.

64 Ormsby to Gore, 26 Apr. 1805 (T.C.D., Arran Papers, MS 7589/21); Simms, 'Connacht in the eighteenth century', p. 128. I wish to thank Dr Desmond McCabe for this and other references to duelling in County Mayo.

65 *Annual Register*, liv (1812), p. 31; lviii (1816), 32; Corr, 'Reminiscences', p. 310.

66 Thorne, ed., *History of parliament*, iii, 656; *Connaught Journal*, 6 Apr. 1826; Hamilton, *The only approved guide*, pp. 204–5.

67 *Mayo Constitutio*n, 14 July 1828, 4 Mar. 1830.

68 Browne to [ ], 10 Feb. 1827 (T.C.D., Sligo Papers, MS 6403).

69 *Mayo Constitution*, 8 Mar., 1 July 1830; *Ballina Impartial*, 14 Mar. 1831.

70 *Mayo Constitution*, 1 July 1830.

71 *Mayo Constitution*, 16 Sept. 1830; Cecil Woodham-Smith, *The reason why* (London, 1953), pp. 29–30; Kiernan, *The duel*, pp. 138–9; Wood-Martin, *Sligo*, iii, 319–20; *Connaught Telegraph*, 3 Apr. 1839.

72 *Dublin University Magazine*, lxxxviii (1876), p. 452; Wood-Martin, *Sligo*, iii, 320–21.

73 N.A., Outrage Papers, 1838, 21/92; Wood-Martin, *Sligo*, iii, 321; Desmond McCabe, 'Law, conflict and social order: County Mayo, 1820–1845' (Ph.D. thesis, U.C.D., 1991), p. 449.

74 N.A., Outrage Papers, 1840, 21/19471; *Ballina Advertizer*, 14 Oct. 1842; *Mayo Constitution*, 29 July 1845.

75 *Annual Register*, lxxxi (1839), p. 265; lxxxv (1843), p. 65; *Ballina Advertizer*, 7 Oct. 1842; *F.L.J.*, 1 Apr. 1840.

76 *O'Connell corresp.*, viii, 119–20, 123.

77 The situation was similar in England (Gash, *Sir Robert Peel*, pp. 187–8).

78 Kiernan, *The duel*, pp. 215–17; Gash, *Sir Robert Peel*, p. 187. For an interesting insight into the unwillingness of ministers to prohibit duelling outright see B.L., Peel Papers, Add. MS 40538, ff 388–98.

79 'A propos of duelling', *Duffy's Irish Catholic Magazine*, i (1848), pp. 93–4.

80 *The Kerry Magazine*, i (1854), pp. 23–4.

81 Gregory, ed., *Sir William Gregory*, pp. 149–53.

82 According to Barker-Benfield (*Culture of sensibility*, p. 81), the last duel took place in England in 1852. The last known duel to take place in Ireland

occurred at Passage, County Cork, in 1862 and involved two Italians (N.L.I., Larcom Papers, MS 7620). For an account of how one Irish gentleman in the late nineteenth century responded to insulting behaviour see McDowell, *Land and learning*, p. 55.

83 Davis, *Young Ireland*, p. 163; Wood-Martin, *Sligo*, iii, 322; Gwynn, *The O'Gorman Mahon*, pp. 259–60.

Conclusion

The demise of duelling as a social phenomonen in the mid-nineteenth century in Ireland was a triumph for the rule of law over that of traditional privilege, and for the emerging middle class over traditional aristocratic mores. These contrary tendencies had been engaged in a visible struggle for pre-eminence since at least the 1780s when there was a perceptible increase in public commitment to law and morality. The code of honour flourished for a number of decades thereafter, but it never again attained the degree of popularity it had achieved when it was at its height in the 1770s and 1780s. The warm embrace by Catholic gentlemen in the early nineteenth century of the social values of their Protestant counterparts (who had provided the overwhelming bulk of duellists in the eighteenth century) helped bolster it. However, duelling was unable to secure a new lease on life, as the essentially aristocratic value system on which it depended was already under pressure from that of the emerging middle class who placed greater emphasis on 'proper' behaviour and demanded that the state appropriate the responsibility of arbitrating between individuals in dispute. From one perspective, this was an inevitable result of the emergence in industrialising Britain of a propertied middle class increasingly determined to enforce its social priorities and ideological concerns.[1] A similar viewpoint was fostered in Ireland by evangelical Protestantism and by the emergence in the 1820s of a powerful Catholic middle-class interest led by Daniel O'Connell, which repudiated the code of honour once it became a political force in its own right, and it no longer felt any need to prove its credibility by imitating the manners of its more aristocratic Protestant opponents. In this respect, the decision of Daniel O'Connell to decline challenges, and the support provided to the Catholic Association by such inveterate anti-duellists as Joseph Hamilton, were not serendipitous developments but an affirmation of the behavioural as well as political implications of the emergence of the Catholic middle class as a force in Irish life. This was a social development of enormous significance. In the mid-1810s Daniel O'Connell had felt compelled to put his life on the line on a number of occasions in the knowledge that if he had not done so, it would have set back the political cause and the legal career he was so anxious to advance. Less than a decade later he felt sufficiently confident to reject such quintessential aristocratic mores as duelling and to identify explicitly with the more egalitarian and disciplined way of life espoused by the middle class. It is for this, as well as for the better-known political reasons,[2] that the 1820s are such an important moment in Irish history. Thereafter not alone were Irish Protestants precipitated into a desperate rearguard action to preserve the traditional bases of their political ascendancy, but the Irish aristocracy was faced with the decision of embarking on an ill-omened struggle if it desired to hang on to one of the most symbolically important privileges it had espoused since it came into being in the seventeenth century. It did not do so, because the code of honour no longer enhanced its position in society or gave it a coherent identity. The change in consciousness this reflected is highlighted by the palpably different attitudes towards duelling of the United Irishmen and the Young Irelanders. Quite a number of the former, as we have seen, practised duelling because they did not, as Thomas Russell put it so well, possess 'spirit enough to renounce duel[l]ing'; of the latter, only the aristocratic William Smith O'Brien appears to have demonstrated any enthusiasm for the code of honour.[3]

There were, of course, many early nineteenth-century adherents of the code of honour who resolutely defended it as a valuable tradition, but they became increasingly isolated. Joseph Hamilton cited one individual who acknowledged that duelling was 'barbarous', but who continued to defend it as 'the means of civilization; . . . [it] acts as a kind of safety valve to the ebullition of passion'.[4] Such views were no longer tenable in a world in which a steadily growing percentage of the population perceived duelling as 'barbarous'. This included most of the upper classes. Throughout the eighteenth and early nineteenth centuries the number of peers who duelled was relatively small. 'A man of tact and discretion could generally steer clear of insult or annoyance,' a constabulary officer observed pertinently, but he could not legislate for the behaviour of others, and there were enough tactless and indiscreet individuals, particularly among the gentry, to ensure that even the most cultivated and urbane gentleman might feel compelled to respond to a personally offensive gesture or action with a challenge. Moreover, the nature of the code of honour is such that the onus is on the injured party to offer the challenge. Increasingly, however, most of the social elite came to share the views of the opponents of duelling. At the outset they declined to accept challenges for all but the most serious insults; with time they forbore duelling altogether. Squeezed from below by the hostility of the middle classes, from above by the mounting apathy of the aristocracy, and from without by the opposition of law and religion, the practice of duelling attenuated and withered until it was finally abandoned in the mid-nineteenth century.

It did not die completely, however. Indeed, it bloomed for a time in the imaginary sphere. Just as the harsh reality of duelling — bad temper, injustice, bloodshed, disabling injuries and painful deaths — disappeared from real life, it was taken up the story-writers and novelists who were attracted by its dramatic and romantic possibilities. Mid-nineteenth-century novelists like Samuel Lover, Charles Lever and William Makepeace Thackeray created a fictional world replete with bluff squires and bellicose attornies who were ever ready to appeal to their pistols to remedy some wrong.[5] Little of what they wrote reflected the brutal reality of duelling; but the combined impact of their work sharpened the already established image Ireland possessed as a duellist's Olympus. It may have been unsubstantiatable in reality, but it remained potent in popular consciousness.

The focus of writing on the subject of duelling shifted perceptibly under the mounting weight of Victorian respectability and the moral sway of the Catholic Church. It is striking just how less exuberant and less accepting in tone the magazines and journals that published articles and stories on the subject became in the late nineteenth century. Journals like the *New Ireland Review* routinely carried duelling stories and anecdotes, but they were invariably moral tales, published to edify the reader and to expose duelling as a debased brutal practice which was contrary to the law of God as well as that of man.[6] Most of the readers of journals and reviews of this type needed little convincing of this fact, but the repeated affirmations of the negative merit of duelling served to detach the last vestige of heroism from the practice.

To the proponents of the code of honour, duelling was meant to be pure, clinical and non-controversial. Like its gentlemen practitioners, it was idealised as being above the grime and gore of ordinary life. In practice, of course, it was impossible to divest duelling of its intrinsic messiness, since it is not possible to orchestrate the killing or wounding of another human being with swords or pistols without blood and pain. Indeed, even ostensibly innocent hits frequently resulted in serious injury or death because of the primitiveness of the medical service on offer. Thus when Patterson, a widower with five children, was shot in the knee by Dr Caldwell at Magherafelt in November 1787, his leg had to be amputated because the doctor searching for the ball cut an artery instead of a vein.[7] Furthermore, many duels arose not because the 'insult' that prompted the challenge merited such a response but because the antagonists were either badly behaved or intoxicated or both. For instance, when four young men 'possessed of genteel farms' in the environs of Dunlavin, County Wicklow, fell out after an evening's drinking in February 1782, they determined that their differences could only be resolved by trial of arms. They had only one pistol between them but, undaunted, they agreed to proceed on the basis that they would each receive fire. This was not within the rules of duelling, but having determined on this course of action, they proceeded to put it into practice and did not conclude until one of their party, Joseph Higinbotham, was shot dead.[8] Even by the relaxed standards of eighteenth-century Ireland, this was an unusual case, but it was hardly unparalleled. The number of duels for which a record has been discovered (nearly 650 for the period 1716–1810) indicates that this was a violent society populated, at the upper level at least, by wilful men who put their individual reputations above their lives, their families, their religion and the law. They felt compelled to do this because displays of the 'white feather' would expose them 'to insufferable insults, not only form the challenger, but from every other impertinent coxcomb, who would fain establish his own reputation of courage on the known timidity of a man branded with the infamous name of coward'.[9] It may appear difficult, at this remove, to appreciate fully the pressure men felt under to safeguard their reputation against being 'tainted with the slightest brand of dishonour', but it was so compelling that few were sufficiently secure or sufficiently disinterested to ignore it.[10] And it was thus from the beginning.

After a disorderly period in the seventeenth and early eighteenth centuries during which an exceptionally high percentage of duels fought in Ireland breached the 'rules' that were deemed to apply on such occasions, there was a tangible improvement in adherence to duelling etiquette as the ruling elite that dominated the country became outwardly more refined. However, for every Lord Orrery or Lord Charlemont who devoted his life to aesthetic pursuits or who behaved impeccably, there were several others who preferred to give alcohol, horses and the code of honour greater priority. And it was they and their descendants, not the denizens of the salons of Dublin and London, who drafted the 'rules for duelling' introduced in the 1770s and who provided a majority of the so-called 'fire-eaters' described so engagingly by Barrington. Moreover, they did not occupy different worlds. Charlemont and Orrery did not, as far as I can discover, take up pistols in defence of their honour, but several of their closest friends and acquaintances like Henry Flood, Henry Grattan, John Hely-Hutchinson, the Earl of Bellamont and George Ogle did. In other words, the cultured and the rude existed side by side and were, in their own way, equally part of the social milieu of the elite that dominated Irish politics and society in the eighteenth and early nineteenth centuries.

Although it was, in many respects, an 'open elite' in that it was possible (religion permitting) to gain access through political service, legal excellence and land purchase, the Irish ruling elite in the early modern era was also highly status-conscious because everybody aspired 'to move in the sphere of gentlemen'.[11] This status consciousness is vividly encapsulated in the refusal of Lieutenant Johnston at Youghal to meet Thomas Barry after he had insulted him because he was the son of an apothecary, and by John Beresford's unhappiness with being obliged to meet Sir Edward Newenham.[12] It was the view of some middle-class critics that the Irish showed a 'ridiculous fondness' for status, but few were able to withstand its lure, as is illustrated by the readiness of the radicals of the 1790s to duel. Facts such as this, combined with the sheer intimacy of the demographically small Irish ruling elite encouraged visitors to arrive at the mistaken conclusion that 'there was scarcely a gentleman . . . who had not been out'.[13] This was not true, though the reckless lifestyle of some families and the political activities of others produced many examples of cases in which several generations of the same family displayed their prowess on the duelling field on more than one occasion.

In attempting to explain why Ireland was such fertile soil for the code of honour, one is hampered by the absence of comparable studies for other European countries. In their absence, one is obliged to look at Irish society in isolation. What this reveals is that duelling emerged as a feature of Irish society, as a direct consequence of the coming into being of a landed elite as a result of conquest and colonisation in the sixteenth and seventeenth centuries. The elite that came into being in Ireland was broadly similar to that already in place throughout most of the rest of western Europe in so far as it was privileged, landed and very conscious of its position *vis-à-vis* monarchy, which aspired with varying degrees of success in Britain as elsewhere to exercise absolute power. It was also extremely well armed as a consequence of the increase in the production and circulation of weapons in the seventeenth century and extremely well versed in their use as a consequence of its martial tradition and the enthusiasm of early modern society for warfare.

Because of these factors, and the inability of all but the most powerful monarchs (Louis XIV is perhaps the best example) to aggrandise and exercise sufficient power to make everybody within their domains submit to their commands, landowning aristocracies and ruling elites throughout western Europe were able to compel their rulers to yield them the privileges which they deemed peculiar to their caste. One of the most talismanic was exemption from full obedience to the law. This was not a novel claim, but it was particularly symbolic at this time because of the dependence of absolutist rulers on the law to impose their will. Few monarchs, of course, were prepared to allow their nobility this right *a priori*, but most acknowledged it *in practice*, either because they were unable or unwilling to discipline those who infringed anti-duelling decrees, or because it was the price they were prepared to pay to retain the good-will of the most powerful interest group in their domains.

Given that this was the situation, *mutatis mutandis*, in sixteenth- and seventeenth-century Britain, it is hardly surprising that the landed elite that came to control the bulk of the land of Ireland aspired to imitate the example of the British landed elite from which it was largely derived and with which it was so intimately connected. Neither the Tudor nor Stuart monarchs possessed the resolution or authority to eradicate duelling, while the constitutional monarchy inaugurated by the Glorious Revolution simply did not have the power. As a consequence, the landed elite that was the overwhelmingly dominant social and political force in Irish society by the early eighteenth century faced little opposition when it espoused the code of honour and sought to pursue the aristocratic remedy of determining personal grievances with weapons.

The surviving record indicates that the number of duels that took place in sixteenth- and early seventeenth-century Ireland was small. Duelling did not commence in earnest until after the Restoration, and while it was firmly in place by the 1680s, it was not until the threat posed to the 'Protestant interest' by Jacobitism was firmly dispatched that duelling assumed its familiar character. The pistol, for example, gradually displaced the sword, and the causes of duels came to reflect an elite that was more at ease with its itself and its ascendant position. For all that, the rule of law remained quite weak, the violent and unregulated character of so many of the duels in early eighteenth-century Ireland typify a society still in transition from a martial to a civil state.

Duelling only became a quotidian feature of Irish society in the mid-eighteenth century when the Protestant elite that dominated that society was at its most secure and comfortable. It was also at this time that political differences within this elite between the Patriots and the more committed supporters of the interests of the British government assumed greater importance, and it is no coincidence that the dramatic increase in duelling that took place in the 1760s and afterwards can be connected with the intensification of political activity in these years. Then, as in the seventeenth and early eighteenth centuries, duelling reflected existing tensions; gentlemen were always more inclined to give the lie, thereby eliciting challenges, to those with whom they were already at loggerheads. To fight a duel did not facilitate political advancement, as it did in seventeenth-century France;[15] but to decline to fight in a situation where it was believed appropriate could have serious negative consequences, as James Napper Tandy learned to his cost.

This negative incentive was powerful enough to persuade hundreds of individuals to risk their lives in rencontres and for the law against murder to become virtually moribund in affairs of honour. However, matters did not remain thus forever. Before the end of the eighteenth century there were unmistakable signs of the emergence of a point of view which rejected the argument that the law had no role in affairs of honour. The pattern of growth of the criminal law in eighteenth-century Ireland remains unstudied, but the readiness of the Irish parliament to sanction the appointment of barristers in the 1780s and to inaugurate a limited crown prosecution service in the 1790s reflects the acceptance of the need for a more interventionist legal system. At the same time, the gradual emergence of a powerful and influential middle class, which had little sympathy with traditional aristocratic values, created an environment in the early nineteenth century in which it was increasingly less acceptable to duel. Invigorated economically by decades of growth, politically by the popularisation of the principles of democratic politics, and morally by evangelical religion and resurgent Catholicism, they were not inclined to tolerate the desires of gentlemen and *soi-disant* gentlemen to kill each other in defiance of the law, just as they were not prepared any longer to acquiesce in their monopolising political power.

These developments encouraged the state to take a more interventionist stance with respect to the observance of the law, as it had already begun to do in respect to such aspects of human endeavour as education and policing. Because of the presence of a large number of devotees of the code of honour in the highest circles of power, specific anti-duelling laws were not forthcoming, but as the public's mood grew increasingly less tolerant, so the number of duels that were fought went into irrevocable decline. It was not possible in the nineteenth century to reconcile the aristocratic penchant for privilege with the increasingly democratic and intrusive nature of government. As a result, by the end of the nineteenth-century duelling in Britain as well as Ireland was a curiosity of a bygone age.

Notes and References

1 See Paul Langford, *Public life and the propertied Englishmen, 1689–1798* (Oxford, 1991).
2 Fergus O'Ferrall, *Catholic emancipation: Daniel O'Connell and the birth of Irish democracy, 1820–30* (Dublin, 1985).
3 Above, pp. 198–200, 257, 264; Woods, ed., *Russell journals*, p. 135.
4 Hamilton, *The only approved guide*, p. xiv.
5 Samuel Lover, *Handy Andy: a tale of Irish life* (London, 1898); *The novels of Charles Lever*, edited by his daughter (London, 1897–8); William Thackeray, *The memoirs of Barry Lyndon* (London, 1879); *Bob Norbery: or sketches from the notebook of an Irish reporter* (Dublin, 1844).
6 *New Ireland Review*, x (1898–9), pp. 224–8; xii (1900), 284–90.
7 Journal of a tour through part of Ireland by Rev. D A. Beaufort, 1787–8 (T.C.D., MS 1019, pt iii, p. 38).
8 *Hibernian Journal*, 4, 8 Mar. 1782.
9 *Memoirs of George Robert Fitzgerald*, p. 67; Corr, 'Reminiscences', pp. 306, 312–13.
10 Woods, ed., *Russell journals*, p. 135; Corr, 'Reminiscences', p. 306.
11 *D.E.P.*, 8 Aug. 1786.
12 Hamilton, *The only approved guide*, pp. 242–3; above, pp. 128–9.
13 Hall, *Ireland*, p. 134.
14 Billacois, *The duel*, p. 77–8.
15 Ibid., pp. 77–8.

Bibliography

Primary Sources

1. Manuscripts

British Library
Althorp Papers
Fox Papers (Add. MS 47568)
Gladstone Papers (Add. MS 44718)
Heraldic precedents (Add. MS 6297)
Lansdowne MSS 160, 846
MacVey–Napier Papers (Add. MS 34613)
Miscellaneous MSS (Add. MS 29736)
Nicholas Papers (Egerton MS 2542)
Peel Papers (Add. MSS 40247–8, 40538)
Royal MS 10B 1X
Ware Manuscripts (Add. MS 4784)
Whitefoord Papers (Add. MS 36593)

Keele University Library
Sneyd Papers (P.R.O.N.I., T3229)

East Sussex Record Office
Additional Sheffield Papers (P.R.O.N.I., T3465)

Friendly Brothers of St Patrick, St Stephen's Green, Dublin
Minute book of the County Kildare Knot, 1777–91
Minute book of the General Grand Knot, 1763–78
Minutes of the proceedings of the Select Grand Knot of Dublin, 1751–94

Hampshire Record Office
Normanton Papers (P.R.O.N.I., T3719)

Henry Huntington Library, San Marino, California
Chandos Papers (STB, Box 10)

Library of Congress, Washington
Sir Henry Cavendish's parliamentary diary, 1776–89

Limerick Archives Office
Vere Hunt Papers (N.L.I., microfilm, p.5526)

National Archives, Dublin
Calendar of miscellaneous letters and papers prior to 1760
Calendar of presentments, affidavits and examinations, 1698–1813
Outrage Papers, 1838, 1840
Prim Collection (MS 37)
Proclamations, 1701–1800
Rebellion Papers (620/20/28)
Townshend Papers (MSS 724–31)

National Library of Ireland
Bowen-Miller of Milford Papers (microfilm p.3793)
Dillon of Clonbrock Papers
Fingall Papers (MS 8021)
Fitzgerald Papers (MSS 618, 623–4, 13022)
Grattan Papers (MS 2111)
Joly MS 39
Larcom Papers (MS 7620)
Mansfield Papers
O'Hara Papers (MSS 16943, 20391)
O'Malley Papers (MS 5619)
Ormonde Papers (MSS 2307, 2444, 2456)
Scully Papers (MS 27571)
Dominic Trant's account of the duel with Sir John Colthurst, 1787 (MS 1762)
Dudley Westropp Papers (MS 24937)
Wicklow Papers

National Library of Scotland
Lothian Papers

Northumberland Record Office
Potter Papers (MS 650)

Public Record Office
Chatham Papers (30/8/83)
Home Office Papers (HO 100 vol 148)

King's Bench Papers (KB 7/7, 7/8)
King's Entrybook (HO 101/1)
Privy Council Papers (PC 1/7)
St George Papers (C110, Box 56)
State Papers, Ireland (SP 63/ vols 419, 465, 467, 471, 476)
State Papers (SP 67 vol 2)

Public Record Office of Northern Ireland
Abercorn Papers (T2541)
Burrowes Diary (T3551/1)
Chatsworth Papers (T3518)
Drennan Papers (D456)
Fitzwilliam (Langdale) Papers (Mic 71)
Macartney Papers (D562)
Shannon Papers (D2707)
Shirley Papers (D3531)
Villiers Stuart Papers (T3131)
Willes Papers (T2855)
Wilmot Papers (T3019)
Notes on the Volunteers (T963)

Royal Irish Academy, Dublin
Sir Robert Day's charges delivered to the Grand Juries (4 vols)

Sheffield City Libraries
Wentworth Woodhouse Muniments
Burke Papers (P.1)
Fitzwilliam Papers (F.30)

Trinity College, Dublin
Arran Papers (MS 7589)
Daniel Beaufort's Journal, 1787–8 (MS 1019)
Donoughmore Papers
Trinity College Muniments (P/1)

Yale University
Beinecke Library: Osborn Collection
Ballitore Papers
Blathwayt Papers
Robert Day's Diary, 1807–15
Lifford Files
Northington Letterbook
Smith Letters
Townshend Papers
Waite–Macartney Letters

Sterling Library
Burnet Papers

Lewis Walpole Library, Farmington, Connecticut
Townshend Papers

Warwickshire Record Office
Willes Papers

Private Collections
Malone Papers (in possession of Mrs A. O'Neill, Rathganny, Multyfarnham, County Westmeath (N.L.I., microfilm p.1561))
Vere Hunt Diary (typescript copy in possession of Mr John Hunt, Bailey, Howth, County Dublin)
Diary of Richard Hobart, 1784–1803 (in possession of Dom Mark Tierney, Glenstall Abbey, County Limerick (N.L.I., microfilm p.7363))
Grattan letter, 1798 (in possession of Dr A. P. W. Malcomson, Ulsterville Avenue, Belfast)

2. Printed Primary Material: Documents, Memoirs and Correspondence

Abercorn: *An introduction to the Abercorn letters*, ed. J. H. Gebbie (Omagh, 1972)
Abstract of the by-laws, rules and orders made by the governors of the Royal Hospital of King Charles the Second (Dublin, 1828)
Anon., 'A letter on a fatal duel', *Journal of the Royal Historical and Archaeological Society*, 4th series, ii (1870–71), pp. 13–4
Anon., 'Flood's bail bond, 1 Sept. 1769', *Journal of the Kilkenny and South-East of Ireland Archaeological Society*, iii (1854–5), pp. 316–7
Annesley: *The Annesley Case*, ed. Andrew Lang (London, 1912)
Auckland: *The journal and correspondence of William, Lord Auckland*, ed. Bishop of Bath and Wells (4 vols, London, 1861–2)
Baker: *Diary of John Baker*, ed. P. C. Yorke (London, 1931)
Barnard: *Barnard Letters, 1778–1824*, ed. Anthony Powell (London, 1928)
Barrington: *Recollections of Sir Jonah Barrington* (Dublin, n.d.)
——: *The Ireland of Sir Jonah Barrington*, ed. Hugh Staples (London, 1968)
Bellingham: *Diary of Thomas Bellingham, an officer under William III*, ed. Anthony Hewitson (Preston, 1908)
Beresford: *The correspondence of John Beresford*, ed. William Beresford (2 vols, London, 1854)
Berry, H. F., ed., *The registers of the Church of St Michan's, Dublin, 1636–85* (Dublin, 1907)
Bland Burgess: *Selection from the letters and correspondence of Sir James Bland Burgess*, ed. Sir James Hatton (London, 1885)
Boulter: *Letters written by His Excellency Hugh Boulter, D.D. . . . to several ministers of state in England and some others* . . . (2 vols, Dublin, 1770)
Boswell: *Boswell: the applause of the jury, 1782–85*, ed. I. S. Lustig and F. A. Pottle (London, 1981)

Bradstreet: *The life and uncommon adventures of Captain Dudley Bradstreet* (London, [1929])

Buckingham: *Memoirs of the courts and cabinets of George III*, ed. Duke of Buckingham and Chandos (4 vols, London, 1853–5).

Burke: *The early life, correspondence and writings of Edmund Burke*, by A. P. I. Samuels (Cambridge, 1923)

Campbell: *Dr Campbell's diary of a visit to England in 1775*, ed. J. L. Clifford (Cambridge, 1947)

Chesterfield: *The letters of Philip Dormer Stanhope, fourth Earl of Chesterfield*, ed. Bonamy Dobrée (6 vols, London, 1932)

Church Papers: 'Calendar of Church miscellaneous papers, 1652–1795' in *Public Record Office of Ireland: 58th Report of the Deputy Keeper* (Dublin 1951)

Colchester: *The diary and correspondence of Charles Abbot, Lord Colchester*, ed. Lord Colchester (3 vols, London, 1861)

Cornwallis: *Correspondence of Charles, first Marquis Cornwallis*, ed. Charles Ross (3 vols, London, 1859)

Croker: *The Croker Papers*, ed. L. J. Jennings (3 vols, London, 1884)

Cumberland: *Memoirs written by himself* by Richard Cumberland (2 vols, London, 1807)

Daunt: *A life spent for Ireland*, by W. J. O'Neill Daunt (repr. Shannon, 1972)

Day: *Mr Justice Day of Kerry*, by Ella B. Day (Exeter, 1938)

Delany: *Autobiography and correspondence of Mary Granville, Mrs Delany*, ed. Lady Llanover (6 vols, London, 1861–2)

Diary: 'A Carrickman's diary, 1787–1809', ed. Patrick Power, *Journal of the Waterford and South-East of Ireland Archaeological Society*, xiv (1911), pp. 97–102, 145–50; xv (1912), pp. 30–37, 62–70, 124–37; xvi (1913), pp. 18–27, 74–85, 176–82; xvii (1914), pp. 4–16, 120–27

Diary: 'The diary of an eighteenth-century gentleman', ed. L. F. Macnamara, *North Munster Antiquarian Journal*, xxiii (1981), pp. 25–65

Drake: *Amiable renegade: the memoirs of Captain Peter Drake, 1671–1753*, ed. Sidney Burrell (Stanford, 1960)

Drennan: *The Drennan Letters*, ed. D. A. Chart (Belfast, 1931)

Dublin: *Dublin: a traveller's companion*, ed. T. and V. Pakenham (London, 1988)

Essex: *Essex Papers, 1675–77*, ed. C. E. Pike, Camden Society, 3rd series, vol. xxiv (London, 1913)

Farington: *The Farington diary*, ed. John Greig (3 vols, London, 1922–24)

Flood: *Original letters to Henry Flood*, ed. T[homas] R[odd] (London, 1820)

Flood: *Memoirs of the life and correspondence of Henry Flood*, by Warden Flood (Dublin, 1838)

Flood: 'Documents re Flood duel', ed. James Prim, *Journal of the Historical and Archaeological Society of Ireland*, 3rd series, x (1868), pp. 234–41

Fontaine: *Memoirs of the Reverend Jaques Fontaine, 1658–1728*, ed. D. W. Ressinger (London, 1992)

George: *The correspondence of George, Prince of Wales, 1770–1812*, ed. Arthur Aspinall (7 vols, London, 1964–70)

Grattan: *Memoirs of the life and times of Henry Grattan*, by Henry Grattan Jr (5 vols, London, 1839–46)
Grattan: *The speeches of Henry Grattan*, ed. D. O. Madden (Dublin, 1847)
Gregory: *Sir William Gregory: an autobiography*, ed. Lady Gregory, (London, 1894)
Hickey: *Memoirs of William Hickey*, ed. Albert Spencer (4 vols, New York, 1923)
Harcourt: *Harcourt Papers*, ed. W. E. Harcourt (10 vols, privately printed, 1888–1905)
Inchiquin: *Inchiquin Manuscripts*, ed. John Ainsworth (Dublin, 1943)
Irish papers: *Eighteenth century Irish official papers*, vol. ii, ed. A. P. W. Malcomson (Belfast, 1990)
Irish parliament: 'The Irish parliament in 1773', ed. M. Bodkin, *Royal Irish Academy Proceedings*, 48C (1942), pp. 145–232
Irish parliament: *The Irish parliament in 1775*, ed. William Hunt (Dublin, 1907)
Irish parliament: 'The Irish parliament in 1782', ed. G. O. Sayles, *Royal Irish Academy Proceedings*, 56C (1954), pp. 227–86
Johnson: *Boswell's Life of Johnson*, ed. G. B. Hill (6 vols, Oxford, 1934–64)
Leinster: *Correspondence of Emily, Duchess of Leinster*, ed. Brian Fitzgerald (3 vols, Dublin, 1945–57)
Macartney: *Macartney in Ireland, 1768–1772*, ed. Thomas Bartlett (Belfast, 1978)
Malmesbury: *Memoirs of an ex-minister: an autobiography by the Earl of Malmesbury* (2 vols, London, 1884)
Minto: *Life and letters of Sir Gilbert Elliott, first Earl of Minto*, ed. Countess of Minto (3 vols, London, 1874)
Moore: *Memoirs, journal and correspondence of Thomas Moore*, ed. Lord John Russell (8 vols, London, 1853–6)
Moran: *Spirilegium Ossoriense*, ed. P.F. Moran (3 vols, Dublin, 1874–84)
Neville: *The diary of Silas Neville, 1767–88*, ed. Basil Cozens-Hardy (Oxford, 1950)
O'Connell: *The correspondence of Daniel O'Connell*, ed. Maurice O'Connell (8 vols, Dublin and Belfast, 1973–80)
O'Halloran: 'The letters of Sylvester O'Halloran, part 2', ed. J. B. Lyons, *North Munster Antiquarian Journal*, ix (1962–3)
O'Malley: 'Reports on private collections', ed. John Ainsworth, *Analecta Hibernica*, xxv (1967), pp. 187–202
Orrery: *The Orrery Papers*, ed. Countess of Cork and Orrery (2 vols, London, 1903)
Pembroke: *Pembroke Papers*, 1780–94, ed. Lord Herbert (London, 1950)
Pepys: *The diary of Samuel Pepys*, ed. Robert Latham (11 vols, London, 1970–83)
Peel: *The private letters of Sir Robert Peel*, ed. George Peel (London, 1920)
Portarlington: *Gleanings from an old portfolio containing some correspondence between Lady Louisa Stewart and . . . Countess of Portarlington*, ed. Mrs Godfrey Clark (3 vols, privately printed, Edinburgh, 1895)
Proclamations: *Stuart Royal Proclamations*, ed. J. F. Larkin and P. L. Hughes (2 vols, Oxford, 1973–83).
Rowan: *The autobiography of Archibald Hamilton Rowan*, ed. W. H. Drummond (Dublin, 1840)
Russell: *Journals and memoirs of Thomas Russell, 1791–95*, ed. C. J. Woods (Dublin, 1991)

Scully: *The Catholic question in Ireland and England, 1798–1822: the papers of Denys Scully*, ed. Brian McDermott (Dublin, 1988)
Sheridan: *The letters of Richard Brinsley Sheridan*, ed. Cecil Price (3 vols, Oxford, 1966)
Spectator: *The Spectator*, ed. D. F. Bond (5 vols, Oxford, 1965)
Sunden: *Memoirs of Viscountess Sunden*, ed. Mrs Thompson (2 vols, London, 1847)
Steele: *Steele: selections from the Tatler, Spectator and Guardian*, ed. Austin Dodson (Oxford, 1896)
Stephen: *The memoirs of James Stephen*, ed. M. M. Bevington (London, 1954)
Swift: *The correspondence of Jonathan Swift*, ed. Harold Williams (5 vols, Oxford, 1963–5)
Taylor: *The works of Jeremy Taylor* (3 vols, London, 1835)
Teignmouth: *Reminiscences of many years*, by Lord Teignmouth (2 vols, Edinburgh, 1878)
Trail: 'James Trail: his journal', ed. M. A. K. Garner, *Proceedings of the Belfast Natural History and Philosophical Society*, 2nd series, ix (1970–77)
Ulster: *Records of the General Synod of Ulster* (3 vols, Belfast, 1890–98)
United Irishmen: 'Proceedings of the Dublin Society of United Irishmen', ed. R. B. McDowell, *Analecta Hibernica*, no. 17 (1949), pp. 1–143
Walpole: *The correspondence of Horace Walpole*, ed W. S. Lewis *et al.* (42 vols, New Haven, 1937–80)
Walpole: *The last journals of Horace Walpole*, ed. A. Francis Stewart (2 vols, London, 1910)
Watts: *The life, times and correspondence of Isaac Watts*, ed. Thomas Milner (London, 1834)
Wentworth: *The Wentworth Papers, 1705–39*, ed. J. J. Cartwright (London, 1883)
Willes: *The letters of Lord Chief Baron Edward Willes to the Earl of Warwick, 1757–62*, ed. James Kelly (Aberystwyth, 1990)
Wray: *The Wrays of Donegal*, by C. V. Wray (London, 1945)

3. Record Publications

Calendar of ancient records of Dublin, eds Sir John and Lady Gilbert (19 vols, Dublin, 1889–1944)
Calendar of the Carew Manuscripts preserved . . . at Lambeth (6 vols, London, 1868)
Calendar of Home Office Papers, 1760–75 (4 vols, London, 1878–99)
Calendar of the Justiciary Rolls or proceedings in the Court of Justiciar of Ireland (2 vols, London, 1905–14)
Calendar of the State Papers, domestic series, 1603–1704, Elizabeth, James I, Charles I, Commonwealth, Charles II, James II, William and Mary, Anne (84 vols, London, 1857–1972)
Calendar of State Papers relating to Ireland in reigns of James I, Charles I, Commonwealth, Charles II, James II, William and Mary (22 vols, London, 1860–1910)

4. *Publications of the Historical Manuscripts Commission*

Bath MSS, vol. ii
Beaufort MSS (12th Report, appendix ix)
Carlisle MSS (15th Report, appendix vi)
Charlemont MSS (12th Report, appendix 10; 13th Report, appendix vii)
De L'Isle and Dudley MSS, vol. vi
Dillon MSS (2nd Report, appendix)
Downshire MSS, vols ii and iii
Donoughmore MSS (12th Report, appendix ix)
Eyre Matcham MSS (Reports on various collections, vi)
Emly MSS (14th Report, appendix 9)
Fortescue MSS, vol vi
Graham MSS (7th Report, appendix)
Hastings MSS, vol ii
J. M. Heathcote MSS
Kenyon MSS (14th Report, appendix iv)
Knox MSS (Report on various collections, vi)
House of Lords MSS (3rd Report, appendix; 8th Report, appendix i)
Le Fleming MSS (12th Report, appendix vii)
Lothian MSS
Earl of Mar and Kellie MSS
Ormonde MSS, vols ii, new series v, vi, vii
Pine Coffin MSS (5th Report, appendix)
Polwarth MSS, vol v
Portland MSS (15th Report, appendix iv)
T. H. G.Puleston MSS
Rutland MSS, vols ii and iii
Stopford–Sackville MSS (2 vols)
Sutherland MSS (5th Report, appendix)
Spencer MSS (2nd Report, appendix)
Weston Underwood MSS (10th Report, appendix i)

5. *Parliamentary Proceedings, Journals, etc.*

Journals of the House of Commons of the kingdom of Ireland, 1613–1800 (19 vols, Dublin, 1796–1800)

The parliamentary register, or history of the proceedings and debates of the House of Commons of Ireland (17 vols, Dublin, 1782–1801)

A. R. Black, ed., *An edition of the Cavendish Irish parliamentary diary, 1776–78* (3 vols, Delavan and Westport, 1985)

Callan, R. V., 'The structure of Anglo-Irish politics during the American Revolution: Cavendish's diary of the Irish parliament, October 12 1779 to September 2 1780: edition of the partial text and a critical essay' (Ph.D. thesis, University of Notre Dame, 1973)

O'Brien, Gerard, ed., 'Debate in the Irish parliament in 1787', *Analecta Hibernica*, no. 33 (1986), pp. 129–97

Rules and orders to be observed in the upper house of parliament of Ireland (Dublin, 1784)
The statutes at large passed in the parliaments held in Ireland, 1310–1800 (20 vols, Dublin, 1789–1800)

6. *Pamphlets and other Contemporary Publications*

An account of a battle fought between Mr Smith, an attorney in Smithfield, and Mr Lee, son to Captain Lee in the County of Westmeath (Dublin, 1719)
An account of a barbarous and bloody murder committed on . . . Mr Huddleston, innkeeper in Ballagh . . ., Friday 3 September 1725 by one Byrn, a solicitor (Dublin, 1725)
An account of a duel, fought at Talla-Green, in the county of Catherlow between Lieutenant Barkley, a lieutenant of horse, and Mr Edw. Culling, steward to the late Lord Chief Justice Doyn's eldest son (Dublin, 1719)
Ancient Irish histories: the chronicles of Ireland (2 vols, Dublin, 1809)
Attendoli, Dario, *Discorso intorno all' honore* (Vinegia, 1552)
——, *Il duello* (Vinegia, 1552)
Authentic detail of an affair of honour between William Todd Jones and Sir Richard Musgrave (Dublin, 1802)
Authentic memoirs of George Robert Fitzgerald with a full account of his trial and execution (London, 1786)
Bardin, Charles, *A sermon preached in St Mary's Church, Dublin, on 20 and 27 of January 1822* (Dublin, 1822)
Barrington, Jonah, *Personal sketches of his own times* (3 vols, London, 1827–32)
Biographical, literary and political anecdotes of several of the most eminent persons of the present era (3 vols, London, 1797)
Blackstone, Sir William, *Commentaries on the laws of England* (4 vols, Oxford, 1765–9)
Bluett, J. C., *Duelling and the laws of honour examined and condemned upon principles of commonsense and revealed truth* (London, 1836)
Bond, Sir Thomas, *Hints tending to increase the wealth and promote the peace and welfare of the Irish nation* (Dublin, 1803)
Bowden, C. T., *Tour through Ireland* (Dublin, 1790)
The British code of duel: a reference to the laws of honour and the character of gentlemen (London, 1824)
Browne, G. J., *A report of the whole proceedings . . . on the trial of Robert Keon gent. for the murder of George Nugent Reynolds esq.* (Dublin, 1788)
Bryskett, Lodowick, *Literary works*, ed. J. H. P. Pafford (London, 1972)
Campbell, Thomas, *A philosophical survey of the south of Ireland* (Dublin, 1777)
Carr, Sir John, *The stranger in Ireland* (London, 1806)
Cloney, Thomas, *A personal narrative of . . . transactions in the County Wexford . . . during . . . 1798* (Dublin, 1832)
Cockburn, John, *The history and examination of duels, showing their heinous nature and the necessity of suppressing them* (London, 1720)
Comber, Thomas, *A discourse of duels, shewing the sinful nature and mischievous effects of them . . .* (London, 1687)

Cosby, Pole, 'Autobiography of Pole Cosby of Stradbally, Queen's County, 1703–37', *Journal of the Kildare Archaeological Society*, v (1906–8), pp. 79–99, 165–84, 253–73, 311–24, 423–36

du Bois, Edward, *My pocket book, or hints for a righte merrie and conceitede tour* (London, 1808)

A few mathematical and critical remarks on the sword (Dublin, 1781)

First report of the Association for the Suppression of the Anti-Christian Practice of Duelling (Dublin, 1830)

A full and accurate report of the tryal of Cornelius O'Brien and Cornelius McDonagh for the murder of Francis Drew esq. at the late assizes of Trim held before the Hon. Sir William Cusack Smith Bart . . . containing the very eloquent appeal made by Mr O'Brien to the court on his receiving sentence (Dublin, 1810)

A full and true account of a bloody duel fought between Henry Haze and —— Peper, esqrs at Drogheda on Saturday 22 February 1729 . . . (Dublin, 1729)

A full and true account of a duel . . . between Lieutenant James Smith and [Pat] Kelly, the brewer's son of Proper Lane . . . (Dublin, [1726])

The fundamental laws, statutes and constitutions of the ancient and most benevolent order of the Friendly Brothers of St Patrick (various editions, Dublin, 1751–1847)

Hales, John, *Golden remains of the ever memorable Mr John Hales* (London, 1673)

[Hamilton, Joseph] A Christian Patriot, *Some short and useful reflections upon duelling which should be in the hands of every person who is liable to receive a challenge or an offence* (Dublin, 1823)

Hamilton, Joseph, *The royal code of honour for the regulation of duelling as it was respectfully submitted to the European sovereigns* (Dublin, 1825)

——, *The only approved guide through all stages of a quarrel, containing the royal code of honour, reflections on duelling, and the outline of a court for the adjustment of disputes with anecdotes, documents and cases interesting to Christian moralists who decline to combat to experienced duellists and to benevolent legislators* (Dublin and London, 1829)

——, *Extracts from various works of Joseph Hamilton* (Dublin, *c.* 1831)

Hay, Edward, *History of the insurrection of the County of Wexford,* A.D. *1798* (Dublin, 1803)

[Hay, Edward], *Strictures: authentic detail of the extravagant and inconsistent conduct of Sir Richard Musgrave, baronet; with a full refutation of the slander against Edward Hay* (Dublin, 1803)

Hibernicus, or memoirs of an Irishman now in America (Pittsburgh, 1828)

The history of Sir John Perrot, Knight of Bath and Lord Lieutenant of Ireland (London, 1728)

James I, *A publication of his maties edict and severe censure against private combats and combatants* (London, 1611)

The laws of honour: or an account of the suppression of duels in France (London, 1685)

The life of George Robert Fitzgerald, containing every interesting circumstance which happened to that unfortunate man from his quitting school (London, 1786)

Latocnaye, Chevalier de, *A Frenchman's walk through Ireland* (Belfast, 1917)

Madden, Samuel, *Reflections and resolutions proper for the gentlemen of Ireland* (Dublin, 1816)

M'Crea, J. B., *Duelling: being the enlargement of a discourse on a late fatal event, preached in D'Olier Street Chapel, Dublin* (Dublin, 1830)
MacDougall, Henry, *Sketches of Irish political characters* (Dublin, 1799)
Massa, Antonio, *Contra l'uso del duello* (Venetia, 1557)
Medland, W. M., and Weobly, Charles, *A collection of remarkable and interesting trials* (London, 1808)
Memoirs of George Robert Fitzgerald and Patrick Randall McDonnell esqrs interspersed with anecdotes tending to illustrate the remarkable occurrences of their lives, particularly the late transaction of the county of Mayo (Dublin, 1786)
Musgrave, Sir Richard, *Memoirs of the different rebellions in Ireland* (Dublin, 1803)
Odell, William Butler, *Essay on duelling, in which the subject is morally and historically considered and the practice deduced from the earliest time* (Cork, 1814)
O'Flaherty, Roderic, *A chorographical description of West or h-Iar Connaught* (Dublin, 1846)
Possevini, Giovanni, *Dialogo dell' honore* (Vinegia, 1553)
Proceedings of the trial of James Napper Tandy esqr. in the Court of King's Bench . . . upon an endictment for sending a challenge to John Toler esq. (Dublin, 1792)
Receuil des édits, declarations des arrets de la cour de parlement contre les duels, publiez depuis l'année 1599 jusques à present (Paris, 1660)
The reply to Thomas Walker esquire, ci-devant cornet in Burgoyne's Light Dragoons, by George Robert Fitzgerald (London, [1775])
A report of the trial of Mr Joseph Kelly, paymaster of the 32nd Regiment of Foot, for the murder of Captain William Harrison of the same regiment before the Hon. Justice Mayne at the spring assizes for the county of Cork, Saturday 5 April 1806 (n.p., 1806)
A report of the trial of George Lidwell and Thomas Prior esqrs upon an information for sending and delivering a challenge to Cholmeley Dering (Dublin, 1800)
Report of the trial of Captain Macnamara for killing and slaying Colonel Robert Montgomery (London, 1803)
Report of the trial of an inquisition upon a verdict of manslaughter against Captain Macnamara for killing and slaying Colonel Robert Montgomery (London, 1803)
A report of the trial of Richard Rochfort, esquire, upon an indictment for the murder of Richard Castles in a duel (Dublin 1805)
Ridgeway, William, *Report of the trial of Robert Gore esquire upon an endictment for the murder of . . . William, late Earl of Meath, at the Wicklow summer assizes 1797 before the Right Hon. Mr Justice Kelly* (Dublin, 1797)
——, *A report of the trial of William Congreve Alcock and Henry Derenzy on an indictment for the murder of John Colclough at Wexford asssizes on 26 March 1808 before the Hon. Baron Smith* (Dublin, 1808)
——, *A correct report of the charge delivered at Wexford, March 28 1808, by the Honourable Baron Smith at the trial of William Congreve Alcock . . .* (Dublin, 1808)
Savaron, Jean, *Traité contre les duels* (Paris, 1610)
Sharp, Granville, *A tract on duelling, wherein the opinions of some of the most celebrated matters on crown law are examined and corrected* (London, 1779, 1790)
Swift, Theophilus, *The challenge, in which the late conduct of Dr Dobbin's family is considered* (Dublin, 1811)

Sym, John, *Lifes preservative against self-killing*, ed. Michael MacDonald (London, 1988)

Trant, Dominick, *Considerations on the present disturbances in the province of Munster and their causes, extent, probable consequences and remedies* (Dublin 1787)

Trelon, Odé, *Advis sur la presentation de l'édit de sa majesté contre la damnable coustume des duels* (Paris, 1604)

The trial in ejectment . . . between Campbell Craig, lessee of James Annesley . . . and Richard Earl of Anglesey before the barons of His Majesty's Court of Exchequer in Ireland . . . (London, 1744)

Trial of Rowan Cashell . . . who stood indicted for the wilful murder of Henry Arthur O'Connor . . . in a duel on 7 August 1815, at the assizes held at Tralee on 26 March 1816 before the Hon. Mr Justice Day (Cork, 1816)

The trial of William, Lord Byron . . . for the murder of William Chaworth esq. before the Right Honourable the House of Peers in Westminster Hall (Dublin, 1765)

The trial of Major Campbell for the murder of Captain Boyd in a duel on 23 June 1807 with the evidence in full, the charge of the judge and details of Major Campbell's last moments, execution, etc. (London, 1808)

The trial of Captain Edward Clark, commander of His Majesty's Ship the Canterbury, for the murder of Captain Thomas Innes of His Majesty's Ship the Warwick in a duel in Hyde Park, March 12 1749 (Dublin, 1750)

The trial of John Devereux junior of Shelbeggan in the county of Wexford before a court martial held in the city of Cork on 27 November 1799 (Dublin, 1800)

The trials of George Robert Fitzgerald, Timothy Brecknock . . . and others . . . (Dublin, 1786)

The tryal and examination of Captain Jones, who was try'd this 24 November 1725 . . . for the murder of Nicholas Nugent at Lucas's coffee house . . . (Dublin, 1725)

Tryal and examination of William Todd, attorney, for the murder of Pierce Rice, 20 February last at the Golden Bottle (Dublin, 1730)

Tuckey, F. H., *The county and city of Cork remembrancer* (Cork, 1837)

A Volunteer's queries in the spring of 1780, humbly offered to the consideration of all description of men in Ireland (Dublin, 1780)

Wetenhall, Edward, *Hexapta Jacobae: a specimen of loyalty . . .* (Dublin, 1686)

The whole tryal and examination of Mr Robert Martin who was try'd at the King's Bench on Friday 2 May 1735 for the murder of Lieutenant Henry Jolly (Dublin, 1735)

Wildair, J., *Three letters to the young gentlemen of the present age* (Dublin, 1748)

Young, Arthur, *A tour in Ireland* (London, 1780)

7. Newspapers and Periodicals

Annual Register, 1758–1840
Ballina Advertizer, 1842
Ballina Impartial, 1824–31
Belfast Newsletter, 1789, 1830
Carey's General Evening Post, 1797
Connaught Journal, 1826

Connaught Telegraph, 1839
Corke Gazette, 1790–91
Corke Journal, 1756
Clonmel Gazette, 1787–93
Dublin Chronicle, 1787–93
Dublin Courant, 1724, 1747–9
Dublin Gazette, 1712, 1725–32, 1740
Dublin Evening Post, 1783–7, 1794
Dublin Intelligence, 1702, 1712, 1726–30
Dublin Mercury, 1755
Dublin Weekly Journal, 1725–30, 1776, 1840
Duffy's Irish Catholic Magazine, 1848
Ennis Chronicle, 1791
Faulkner's Dublin Journal, 1744–5, 1749, 1758–9, 1831
Finn's Leinster Journal, 1767–79, 1787, 1840
Flying Post, 1702
Freeman's Journal, 1763–8, 1771–2, 1778, 1787, 1797–1810, 1816–17
The Galway Reader, 1950–51
Gentleman's Magazine, 1745–6
Hibernian Journal, 1771–82
The Hibernian Gazette or Universal Advertizer (Clonmel), 1774
Hume's Dublin Courant, 1724
Irish Farmer's Journal, 1813–14
Mayo Constitution, 1828, 1830, 1845
Needham's Postman, 1724
New Ireland Review, 1898–1900
Public Gazetteer, 1761–3
Pue's Occurrences, 1717–19, 1732–42, 1751–68
Universal Advertizer, 1759–61
Volunteer Evening Post, 1784–5
Volunteer Journal (Cork), 1786
Volunteer Journal (Dublin), 1784–5
Walker's Hibernian Magazine, 1796–7.
The Weekly Journal or Saturday Post (London), 1721

Secondary Sources

1. Published Works

Andrew, D. T., 'The code of honour and its critics: the oppositon to duelling in England, 1700–1850', *Social History*, v (1980), pp. 415–434
Akenson, D. H., *The Church of Ireland: ecclesiastical reform and revolution, 1800–85* (New Haven, 1971)
Anglo, Sydney, 'How to kill a man at your ease: fencing books and the duelling ethic' in idem, ed., *Chivalry in the Renaissance* (Woodbridge, 1990), pp. 1–12

Anon., 'An affair of honour a hundred years ago', *Dublin University Magazine*, lxxviii (1871), pp. 376–7
Anon., 'The condemned soldier', *Dublin University Magazine*, ii (1833)
Anon., *The life and times of George Robert Fitzgerald* (Dublin, 1852)
Anon., 'George Nugent Reynolds: the Sheemore duel', *Ardagh and Clonmacnois Antiquarian Society Journal*, ii, no. 11 (1946), pp. 74–9
Anon., 'The tragic tale of Stanmer O'Grady and Captain Smyth of Ballinatrae', *New Ireland Review*, x (1898–9), pp. 30–37
A retired constabulary officer, 'Leaves from my notebook', *Dublin University Magazine*, lxxxviii (1876), pp. 453–65
Archdeacon, Arthur, *Legends of Connaught* (Dublin 1939)
Ayling, Stanley, *A portrait of Sheridan* (London, 1985)
Bagenal, P. H., *Vicissitudes of an Anglo-Irish family, 1530–1800* (London, 1925)
Bagwell, Richard, *Ireland under the Tudors* (3 vols, London, 1885)
Barber, Richard, *The knight and chivalry* (Ipswich, 1974)
Barker, J. R. V., *The tournament in England, 1100–1400* (Woodbridge, 1986)
Barker-Benfield, G. J., *The culture of sensibility: sex and society in eighteenth-century Britain* (Chicago, 1992)
Barnard, T. C., *Cromwellian Ireland* (Oxford, 1975)
——, 'Crises of identity among Irish Protestants 1641–85', *Past and Present*, no. 127 (1990), pp. 38–83.
Barry, Michael, *An affair of honour: Irish duels and duelists* [*sic*] (Fermoy, 1981)
Bartlett, Thomas, 'The Townshend viceroyalty' in Thomas Bartlett and D. W.Hayton, eds, *Penal era and golden age* (Belfast, 1979), pp. 88–112
Beresford, John, *Mr Du Quesne and other essays* (Oxford, 1932)
Billacois, François, *The duel: its rise and fall in early modern France* (New Haven, 1990)
——, *Le duel dans la societé Française* (Paris, 1986)
Bodkin, M. MacDonnell, *Grattan's parliament: before and after* (London, 1912)
Bolton, G. C., *The passing of the Irish Act of Union* (Oxford, 1966)
Bottigheimer, K. S., *English money and Irish land* (Oxford, 1971)
——, 'The Restoration land settlement in Ireland: a structural view', *Irish Historical Studies*, xviii (1972), pp. 1–21
Bowen, Desmond, *The Protestant crusade in Ireland, 1800–70* (Dublin, 1978)
Bradsher, E. L., *Mathew Carey* (New York, 1966)
Bradshaw, Brendan, *The Irish constitutional revolution of the sixteenth century* (Cambridge, 1979)
Brady, Ciaran, 'Court, castle and country: the framework of government' in Ciaran Brady and Raymond Gillespie, eds, *Natives and newcomers* (Dublin, 1986), pp. 22–49
Brennan, Flora, ed., *Pückler's progress: the adventures of Prince Pückler-Muskau in England, Wales and Ireland, 1826–29* (London, 1987)
Brunciardi, Niall, *Haulbowline, Spike and Rocky Islands* (Fermoy, 1982)
Bullock, Humphrey, 'Duellist extraordinary', *Irish Monthly*, lxxxi (1953), pp. 277–81.
Burns, R. E., *Irish parliamentary politics in the eighteenth century* (2 vols, Washington, 1989–90)

Burke, Peter, *The historical anthropology of early modern Italy* (Cambridge, 1981)
Burke, W. P., *History of Clonmel* (Waterford, 1907)
Burtchaell, G. D., *Genealogical memoirs of the members of parliament for the county and city of Kilkenny* (Dublin, 1888)
Bush, M. L., *Noble privilege* (Manchester, 1983)
——, *Rich noble, poor noble* (Manchester, 1988)
C.J., 'Fatal sword duel in Cork a century ago', *Journal of the Cork Historical and Archaeological Society*, 1st series, iii (1894), p. 200
Campbell, J.K., *Honour, family and patronage* (Oxford, 1964)
Casway, J. I., *Owen Roe O'Neill and the struggle for Catholic Ireland* (Philadelphia, 1984)
Childe-Pemberton, W. S., *The Earl-Bishop: the life of Frederick, Bishop of Derry, Earl of Bristol* (2 vols, London, 1924)
Clark, W. S., *The Irish stage in the country towns* (Oxford, 1965)
Cole, R. C., *Irish booksellers and English writers, 1740–1800* (London, 1986)
Connolly, Sean, 'Violence and order in the eighteenth century' in Patrick O'Flanagan *et al.*, eds, *Rural Ireland: modernisation and change, 1600–1900* (Cork, 1987), pp. 42–61
——, *Religion, law, and power: the making of Protestant Ireland, 1660–1760* (Oxford, 1992)
Corr, M., 'Reminiscences of duelling in Ireland', *Macmillan's Magazine*, xxix (1873–4), pp. 304–14
Coughlan, Rupert, *Napper Tandy* (Dublin, 1976)
Coyle, Eugene, 'Sir Edward Newenham: the eighteenth-century Dublin radical', *Dublin Historical Record*, xlvi (1993), pp. 15–30
Craig, M. J., *The Volunteer earl* (London, 1948)
Craig, Maurice, *Dublin, 1660–1860* (Dublin, 1969)
Crawford, J. G., *Anglicizing the government of Ireland: the Irish Priry Council and the expansion of Tudor rule 1556–1578* (Dublin, 1993)
Crummey, R. O., *Aristocrats and servitors: the boyar elite in Russia, 1613–89* (Princeton, 1983)
Cullen, L. M., *An economic history of Ireland since 1660* (London, 1972)
——, 'Economic development, 1691–1750' and 'Economic development, 1750–1800' in T. W. Moody and W. E. Vaughan, eds, *A New History of Ireland*, iv (Oxford, 1986), pp. 146–95
——, 'Catholic social classes under the penal laws' in T. P. Power and Kevin Whelan, eds, *Endurance and emergence: Catholics in Ireland in the eighteenth century* (Dublin, 1990), pp. 57–84
Cummins, S. A., 'Extra-parliamentary agitation in Dublin in the 1760s' in R. V. Comerford *et al.*, eds, R*eligion, conflict and coexistence in Ireland* (Dublin, 1990), pp. 118–34
Curran, William Henry, *The life of John Philpot Curran* (2 vols, Edinburgh, 1822)
Day, Robert, 'Duel between Sir John Jeffcott and Doctor Hennis', *Journal of the Cork Historical and Archaeological Society*, 2nd series, viii (1902), pp. 258–9
de Montluzin, E. L., *The Anti-Jacobins, 1798–1800* (London, 1988)
Dickson, David, 'Middlemen' in Thomas Bartlett and D. W. Hayton, eds, *Penal era and golden age* (Belfast, 1979), pp. 162–85

——, 'Henry Flood and the eighteenth-century Irish Patriots' in Ciaran Brady, ed., *Worsted in the game: losers in Irish history* (Dublin, 1989), pp. 97–108
——, 'Catholics and trade in eighteenth-century Ireland: an old debate revisited' in T. P. Power and Kevin Whelan, eds, *Endurance and emergence: Catholics in Ireland in the eighteenth century* (Dublin, 1990), pp. 85–100
D'Alton, Ian, *Protestant society and politics in Cork, 1812–44* (Cork, 1980)
Davis, Richard, *The Young Ireland movement* (Dublin, 1987)
——, *William Smith O'Brien: Ireland 1848* (Dublin, 1989)
Dixon, Peter, *Canning: politician and statesman* (London, 1976)
Elliott, Marianne, *Wolfe Tone: prophet of Irish independence* (Yale, 1989)
Ellis, S.G., *Tudor Ireland: crown, commmunity and the conflict of cultures* (London, 1985)
Ferguson, A. R., *The Indian summer of English chivalry* (Durham, 1960)
Fitzgerald, Brian, *Lady Louisa Conolly: an Anglo-Irish biography* (London, 1950)
Fitzgerald, Lord Walter, 'The duel between two of the O'Connors of Offaly in Dublin Castle on 12 September 1583', *Journal of the Royal Society of Antiquaries of Ireland*, xl (1910), pp. 1–5
Fitzpatrick, W. J., *Ireland before the Union* (Dublin, 1868)
Foucault, Michel, *Discipline and punish: the birth of the prison* (London, 1977)
Fothergill, Brian, *The Strawberry Hill set: Horace Walpole and his circle* (London, 1983)
Fraser, A. M., 'The Friendly Brothers of St Patrick', *Dublin Historical Record*, xiv (1955–8), pp. 34–40
Froude, J. A., *The English in Ireland* (3 vols, London, 1881)
Fuller, J. F., 'Trial of Rowan Cashell, gentleman, attorney for the wilful murder of Henry Arthur O'Connor late of Tralee . . .', *Journal of the Cork Historical and Archaeological Society*, 2nd series, vii (1901), pp. 149–66
——, 'Amyas Griffith: a chequered career', *Kerry Archaeological Magazine*, iii (1914–16), pp. 162–75
Gantz, Ida, *Signpost to Eyrecourt* (Bath, 1975)
Gash, Norman, *Mr Secretary Peel* (London, 1961)
——, *Sir Robert Peel* (London, 1972)
——, *Pillars of government and other essays* (London, 1986)
Gaughan, J. A., *The Knights of Glin* (Listowel, 1978)
Gentles, Ian, *The New Model Army in England, Ireland and Scotland, 1645–53)* (Oxford, 1991)
Gilbert, John, *A history of the city of Dublin* (3 vols, Dublin, 1859–61)
Gillespie, Raymond, *Colonial Ulster: the settlement of east Ulster, 1600–41* (Cork, 1985)
——, 'Landed society and the interregnum in Ireland and Scotland' in Rosalind Mitchison and Peter Roebuck, eds, *Economy and society in Scotland and Ireland, 1500–1939* (Edinburgh, 1988), pp. 38–47
——, 'The trials of Bishop Spottiswood, 1620–40', *Clogher Record*, xii (1987), pp. 320–33
Gough, Hugh, and Dickson, David, eds, *Ireland and the French Revolution* (Dublin, 1990)

Guinness, Desmond, and Ryan, William, *Irish houses and castles* (London, 1971)

Gwynn, Denis, *The O'Gorman Mahon: duellist, adventurer and politician* (London, 1934)

Hamden, John, *An eighteenth-century journal* (London, 1940)

Hayton, D. W. 'Anglo-Irish attitudes: changing perceptions of national identity among the Protestant ascendancy in Ireland, *ca* 1690–1750', *Studies in the Eighteenth Century*, xvii (1987), pp. 145–57

——, 'From barbarian to burlesque: English images of the Irish, *c.* 1660–1750' in *Irish Economic and Social History*, xv (1988), pp. 5–31

Hill, Jacqueline, 'The meaning and significance of "Protestant ascendancy", 1787–1840' in *Ireland after the Union* (Oxford, 1989), pp. 1–22

Hinde, Wendy, *George Canning* (London, 1973)

Hutton, Ronald, *Charles II: King of England, Scotland and Ireland* (Oxford, 1989)

Inglis, Brian, *Freedom of the press, 1784–1841* (London, 1954)

James, Mervyn, *Family, lineage and civil society: a study of politics and mentality in the Durham region, 1500–1640* (Oxford, 1974)

——, *Society politics and culture: studies in early modern England* (Cambridge, 1988)

Johnson, Paul, *The birth of the modern world society 1815–30* (London, 1992)

Johnston, E. M., 'The career and correspondence of Thomas Allan', *Irish Historical Studies*, x (1957), pp. 298–324

——, *Great Britain and Ireland, 1760–1800* (Edinburgh, 1963)

Jupp, P. J., 'Earl Temple's viceroyalty and the question of renunciation', *Irish Historical Studies*, xvii (1972), pp. 299–317

——, 'Irish parliamentary elections and the influence of the Catholic vote, 1801–1820', *Historical Journal*, x (1967), pp. 163–96

Keen, Maurice, *Chivalry* (New Haven, 1974)

Kelly, G. A., 'Duelling in eighteenth-century France: archaeology, rationale, implications', *The Eighteenth Century*, xxi (1981), pp. 236–54

Kelly, James, 'The context and course of Thomas Orde's plan of education of 1787', *Irish Journal of Education*, xx (1986), pp. 3–27

——, 'The origins of the Act of Union: an examination of Unionist opinion in Britain and Ireland, 1650–1800', *Irish Historical Studies*, xxv (1987), pp. 236–63

——, 'Interdenominational relations and religious toleration in late eighteenth-century Ireland', *Eighteenth-Century Ireland*, iii (1988), pp. 39–67

——, 'The genesis of "Protestant ascendancy"' in Gerard O'Brien, ed., *Parliament, politics and people: essays in eighteenth-century Irish history* (Dublin, 1989), pp. 93–127

——, 'Napper Tandy: radical and republican' in James Kelly and Uaitear Mac Gearailt, eds, *Dublin and Dubliners: essays in the history and literature of Dublin city* (Dublin, 1990), pp. 1–21

——, *Prelude to Union: Anglo-Irish politics in the 1780s* (Cork, 1992)

——, 'Parliamentary reform in Irish politics, 1760–90' in David Dickson, Daire Keogh and Kevin Whelan, eds, *The United Irishmen* (Dublin, 1993), pp. 74–87

——, 'The politics of Protestant ascendancy: County Galway 1650–1832' in Raymond Gillespie and Gerard Moran, eds, *Galway: politics and society* (forthcoming)

Kelly, Liam, 'Defenderism in Leitrim during the 1790s', *Breifne*, vi (1986), pp. 341–54
Kennedy, B. A., 'Light on a revolting duel fought in 1804', *Irish Sword*, iv (1959), pp. 136–8
Kennedy, Joe, 'Callan: a corporate town, 1700–1800' in William Nolan and Kevin Whelan, eds, *Kilkenny: history and society* (Dublin, 1990), pp. 289–304
Kiernan, V. G., *The duel in European history* (Oxford, 1988)
Langford, Paul, *Public life and the propertied Englishman, 1689–1798* (Oxford, 1991)
——, *A polite and commercial people: England 1727–1783* (Oxford, 1989)
Leerssen, Joep, *Mere Irish and Fíor-Ghael* (Amsterdam, 1986)
Lenehan, Maurice, *Limerick: its history and antiquities* (Cork, 1967)
Lynam, Shevawn, *Humanity Dick: a biography of Richard Martin, M.P., 1754–1834* (London, 1975)
Lyons, J. B., *Scholar and sceptic: the career of James Henry, 1798–1876* (Dublin, 1985)
MacCarthy, C. J. F., 'An antiquary's notebook', *Journal of the Cork Historical and Archaeological Society*, xcii (1987), p. 122
McCarthy, Mary, *Fighting Fitzgerald and other papers* (London, 1930)
MacCarthy-Morrogh, Michael, *The Munster plantation: English migration to southern Ireland, 1583–1641* (Oxford, 1986)
McClelland, Aiken, 'Amyas Griffith', *Irish Booklore*, ii (1972–6), pp. 7–21
McCracken, J. L., *The Irish parliament in the eighteenth century* (Dundalk, 1971)
——, 'The social structure and social life, 1714–60' in T. W. Moody and W. E. Vaughan, eds, *A New History of Ireland*, iv (Oxford, 1986), pp. 31–56
McDermott, Betty, *O'Ruairc of Breifne* (Manorhamilton, 1990)
McDermott, Frank, *Theobald Wolfe Tone* (Dublin, 1939)
MacDonagh, Michael, *Irish life and character* (London, 1905)
MacDonagh, Oliver, *The Inspector General: Sir Jeremiah Fitzpatrick and social reform, 1783–1802* (London, 1981)
——, *Daniel O'Connell: the hereditary bondsman* (London, 1988)
——, *Daniel O'Connell: the emancipist* (London, 1989)
McDowell, R. B., *Ireland in the age of imperialism and revolution* (Oxford, 1979)
——, *Land and learning: two Irish clubs* (Dublin, 1993)
Mackay, Charles, *Extraordinary popular delusions and the madness of crowds* (repr., New York, 1932)
MacLysaght, Edward, *Irish life in the seventeenth century after Cromwell* (London, 1939)
Macnamara, N. C., *The story of an Irish sept* (London, 1896)
Madden, Daniel Owen, *Revelations of Ireland in the past generation* (Dublin, 1877)
Madden, R. R., *The United Irishmen* (2 vols, Dublin, 1842)
——, *Memoirs, chiefly autobiographical* (London, 1891)
Mag Shamhrain, A. S., *Sir Edward Newenham* (Belcamp College, Dublin, 1984)
Makesy, Piers, *The coward of Minden: the affair of Lord George Sackville* (London, 1979)
Malcomson, A. P. W., *Isaac Corry: an adventurer in the field of politics* (Belfast, 1976)
——, *John Foster: the politics of the Anglo-Irish ascendancy* (Oxford, 1978)
——, 'Lord Shannon' in Esther Hewitt, ed., *Lord Shannon's letters to his son* (Belfast, 1982), pp. xxiii–lxxix

——, *In pursuit of the heiress: aristocratic marriage in Ireland, 1760–1820* (Belfast, 1982)
Maxwell, Constantia, *Country and town in Ireland under the Georges* (London, 1940)
——, *Dublin under the Georges, 1714–1830* (London, 1936)
——, *A history of Trinity College, Dublin, 1592–1892* (Dublin, 1946)
Miller, John, *James II: a study in kingship* (London, 1989)
Molloy, J. Fitzgerald, *The romance of the Irish stage* (2 vols, London, 1897)
Mooney, Tighernan, and White, Fiona, 'Dublin winter season' in David Dickson, ed., *The gorgeous mask: Dublin, 1700–1850* (Dublin, 1987), pp. 1–16
Moore, Courtenay, 'Some accounts of a fatal duel fought at Brigtown, Mitchelstown in 1695', *J.C.H.A.S.*, 2nd series, ix (1903), pp. 83–5
——, 'Fatal sword duel in Cork about the year 1786 [*sic*]', *J.C.H.A.S.*, 2nd series, ix (1903), pp. 24–6
——, 'Some account of the duel between Dr O'Brien and Councillor O'Mahony at Castlehyde . . .', *J.C.H.A.S.*, 2nd series, v (1899), pp. 262–3
——, 'The Rhinecrew duel, A.D. 1826', *J.C.H.A.S.*, 2nd series, ix (1903), pp. 171–4
——, 'The Rhinecrew duel in 1826', *J.C.H.A.S.*, 2nd series, xii (1906), pp. 177–81
Munter, Robert, *The history of the Irish newspaper, 1685–1760* (Cambridge, 1967)
Neary, Bernard, *Dublin 7: a local history* (Dublin, 1992)
Nuttall-Smith, G. N., *The chronicles of a Puritan family in Ireland* (Oxford, 1923)
O'Brien, Gerard, 'The beginning of the veto controversy in Ireland', *Journal of Ecclesiastical History*, xxxviii (1987), pp. 80–94
Ó Cearbhaill, S. E., 'Seán Hely-Hutchinson (1724–1794)', *Galvia*, ix (1962), pp. 25–35
Ó Coindealbháin, Seán, 'The United Irishmen in County Cork, vii', *Journal of the Cork Historical and Archaeological society*, 2nd series, lvii, (1952), pp. 87–98
——, 'John Swiney, the Cork United Irishman: his duel with Thomas Corbett', *J.C.H.A.S.*, lx (1955), pp. 22–7
O'Connell, Philip, 'The plot against Fr Nicholas Sheehy', *Proceedings of the Irish Catholic Historical Committee, 1965–7* (Dublin, 1968), pp. 49–61
O'Donovan, John, *Life by the Liffey* (Dublin, 1986)
O'Ferrall, Fergus, *Catholic emancipation: Daniel O'Connell and the birth of Irish democracy, 1820–30* (Dublin, 1985)
Palmer, S. H., 'The Irish police experiment: the beginnings of modern police in the British Isles, 1785–95', *Social Science Quarterly*, lvi (1975), pp. 410–24
——, *Police and protest in England and Ireland, 1780–1850* (Cambridge, 1988)
Palmer, William, 'That "insolent liberty": honor, rites of power and persuasion in sixteenth-century Ireland', *Renaissance Quarterly*, xlvi (1993), pp. 308–27
Parker, Geoffrey, *The military revolution: military innovation and the rise of the west, 1500–1800* (Cambridge, 1988)
Pitt-Rivers, Julian, 'Honor' in *International encyclopaedia of the social sciences* (12 vols, New York, 1968), vi, 503–11
——, *The fate of Shechem or the politics of sex: essays in the anthropology of the Mediterranean* (Cambridge, 1977)

Porritt, E. and A. G., *The unreformed House of Commons* (2 vols, Cambridge, 1903)
Portlock, R. F., *The ancient and benevolent order of the Friendly Brothers of St Patrick: history of the London knots 1775–1973* (privately printed, London, 1973)
Power, P. C., *History of south Tipperary* (Cork, 1989)
Prim, James, 'Notes on Kilkenny inns and taverns', *Journal of the Kilkenny and South-East of Ireland Archaeological Society*, n.s., iv (1862–3), pp. 152–80
Reyner, J. C., and Cook, G. T., eds, *The complete Newgate Calendar* (5 vols, London, 1926)
Robinson, Philip, *The plantation of Ulster: British settlement in an Irish landscape, 1600–1670* (Dublin, 1984)
Roberts, Michael, *Gustavus Adolphus: a history of Sweden, 1611–32* (2 vols, London, 1953–58)
Roebuck, Peter, ed., *Macartney of Lisanoure* (Belfast, 1983)
Rogers, Patrick, 'A Protestant pioneer of Catholic emancipation' in *Down and Connor Diocesan Magazine* (1934), pp. 14–22
S., G., 'Court martial held two centuries ago at Portaferry, County Down', *Ulster Journal of Archaeology*, 1st series, viii (1860), pp. 62–9
Sergeant, P. W., *Little Jennings and fighting Dick Talbot* (2 vols, London, 1913)
Sheedy, Kieran, *The Clare elections* (Dublin, 1993)
Sheldon, E. K., *Thomas Sheridan of Smock Alley* (Princeton, 1967)
Simms, J. G., 'Connacht in the eighteenth century', *Irish Historical Studies*, xi (1958), pp. 116–33
Simms, Katharine, *From kings to warlords* (Suffolk, 1987)
Smith, E. A., *Whig principles and party politics: Earl Fitzwilliam and the Whig party* (Manchester, 1975)
Somerville-Large, Peter, *Irish eccentrics* (London, 1975)
Stevenson, John, *Life in County Down over two centuries* (Belfast, 1917)
Stewart, A. T. Q., *A deeper silence: the hidden origins of the United Irishmen* (London, 1993)
Stone, Lawrence, *The crisis of the aristocracy in England, 1558–1641* (Oxford, 1965)
——, *The family, sex and marriage in England, 1500–1800* (Oxford, 1977)
Swift, John, *History of the Dublin bakers and others* (Dublin, [1948])
Thompson, Neville, *Wellington after Waterloo* (London, 1986)
Thorne, Ronald, ed., *The history of parliament: the House of Commons, 1790–1820* (5 vols, London, 1986)
Tohill, Patrick, 'The Diamond fight of 1795 and the resultant expulsions', *Seanchas Ardmhacha*, iii (1958), pp. 17–50
Tyrrell, A. Brooke, 'Homage to Grattan, 1746–1820', *Dublin Historical Record*, xxxvii (1983), pp. 31–43
[Walsh, J. E.], *Sketches of Ireland sixty years ago* (Dublin, 1847)
——, *Ireland ninety years ago* (Dublin, 1885)
——, *Ireland one hundred and twenty years ago* (Dublin, 1911)
——, *Rakes and ruffians: the underworld of Georgian Dublin* (Dublin, 1979)
Wauchope, Piers, *Patrick Sarsfield and the Williamite wars in Ireland* (Dublin, 1992)
Whelan, Kevin, 'Captain Edward Sweetman', *Irish Sword*, xvii (1989), pp. 219–20
——, 'Politicisation in County Wexford and the origins of the 1798 rebellion' in

Hugh Gough and David Dickson, eds, *Ireland and the French Revolution* (Dublin, 1990), pp. 156–78

——,'Catholic mobilization, 1750–1850' in L. M. Cullen and Louis Bergeron, eds, *Cultures et pratiques politiques en France et en Irlande* (Paris, 1991), pp. 235–58

Winton, Calhoun, *The early career of Richard Steele* (Baltimore, 1964)

Wood-Martin, W. G., *History of Sligo county and town from the close of the revolution of 1688 to the present time* (3 vols, Dublin, 1892)

Woods, C. J., 'The place of Thomas Russell in the United Irish movement' in Hugh Gough and David Dickson, eds, *Ireland and the French Revolution* (Dublin, 1990), pp. 83–100

2. Unpublished Theses

Bartlett, Thomas, 'The Townshend viceroyalty, 1767–72' (Ph.D., Q.U.B., 1976)

Corboy, J. J., 'The Jesuit mission in Ireland, 1595–1626' (M.A., U.C.D., 1941)

Cummins, S. A., 'Opposition and the Irish parliament, 1759–71' (M.A., St Patrick's College, Maynooth, 1978)

Henry, Brian, 'Crime in Dublin, 1780–96' (Ph.D., T.C.D., 1992)

Hughes, Raymond, 'Galway town, 1692–1750: a study in local administration and society' (M.A., U.C.G., 1985)

Liechty, Joseph, 'Irish evangelicalism, Trinity College, Dublin, and the mission of the Church of Ireland at the end of the eighteenth century' (Ph.D., St Patrick's College, Maynooth, 1987)

McCabe, Desmond, 'Law, conflict and social order: County Mayo, 1820–45' (Ph.D., U.C.D., 1991)

Morris, P. A., 'Ormonde's army: the Irish standing army, 1640–1669, with special reference to personnel and administration after the Restoration' (Ph.D., Vanderbilt, 1980)

Stoddhart, P. C. 'Counter-insurgency and defence in Ireland 1790–1805' (D.Phil., Oxford University, 1972)

3. Works of Reference

Burke's *Peerage, baronetage and knightage* (London, 1959)

G. E. C[ocayne], *The complete peerage*, ed. Vicary Gibbs, *et al.*, (13 vols, London, 1910–40)

Dictionary of National Biography (22 vols, London, 1908–9)

Lodge, John, *The peerage of Ireland* (7 vols, Dublin, 1789)

Moody, T. W., *et al.*, eds, *A New History of Ireland*, ix (Oxford, 1984)

Walker, Brian, ed., *Parliamentary election results in Ireland, 1801–1922* (Dublin, 1978)

Index